Requiem
of the
Rose King

14

AYA KANNO

Based on *Henry VI* and *Richard III*
by William Shakespeare

Story Thus Far

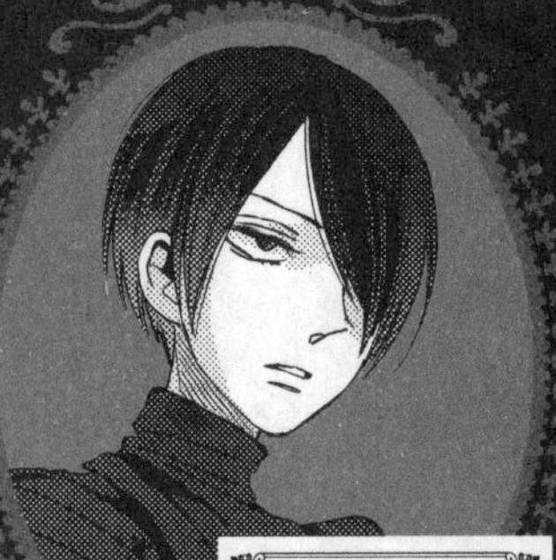

RICHARD

The third son of York. Born a hermaphrodite, he has been shunned by his mother since childhood.

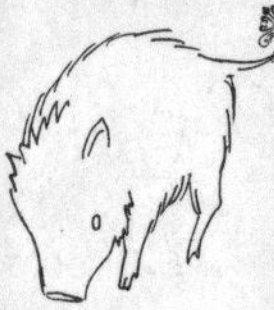

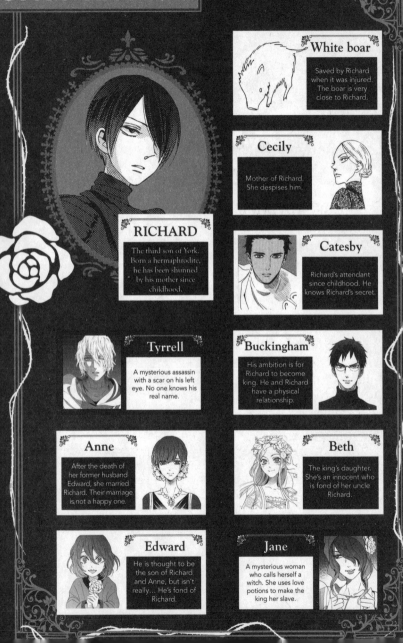

White boar

Saved by Richard when it was injured. The boar is very close to Richard.

Cecily

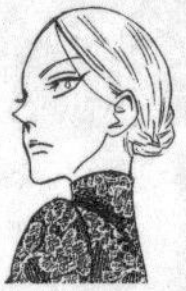

Mother of Richard. She despises him.

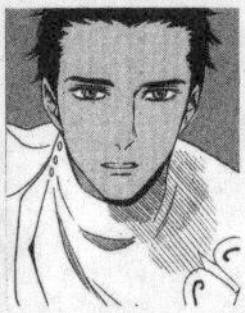

Catesby

Richard's attendant since childhood. He knows Richard's secret.

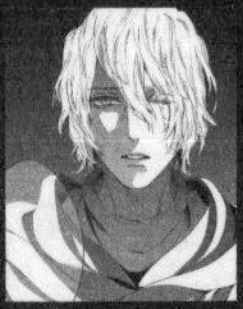

Tyrrell

A mysterious assassin with a scar on his left eye. No one knows his real name.

Buckingham

His ambition is for Richard to become king. He and Richard have a physical relationship.

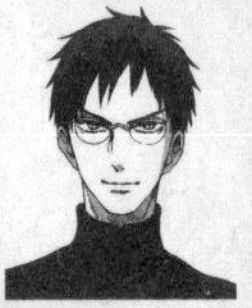

Anne

After the death of her former husband Edward, she married Richard. Their marriage is not a happy one.

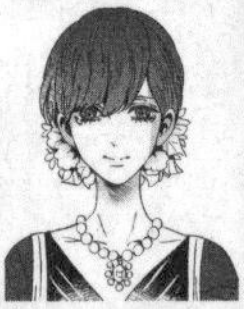

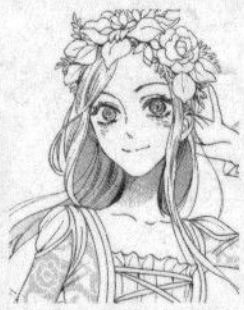

Beth

The king's daughter. She's an innocent who is fond of her uncle Richard.

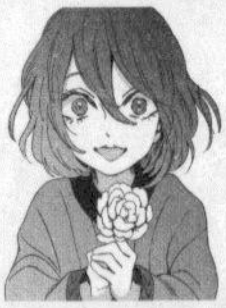

Edward

He is thought to be the son of Richard and Anne, but isn't really... He's fond of Richard.

Jane

A mysterious woman who calls herself a witch. She uses love potions to make the king her slave.

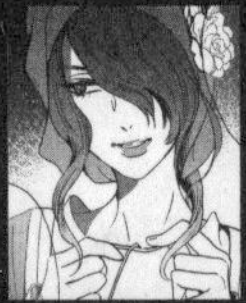

Characters &

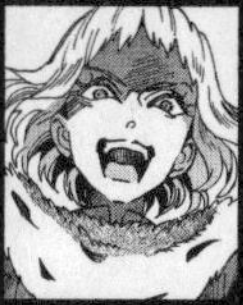

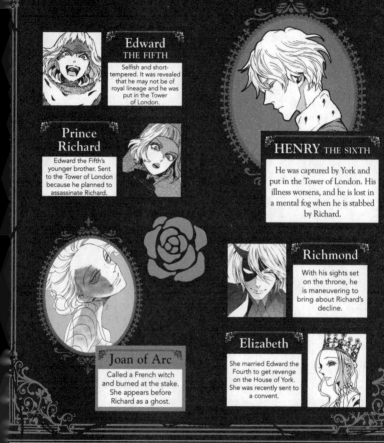

Edward THE FIFTH

Selfish and short-tempered. It was revealed that he may not be of royal lineage and he was put in the Tower of London.

Prince Richard

Edward the Fifth's younger brother. Sent to the Tower of London because he planned to assassinate Richard.

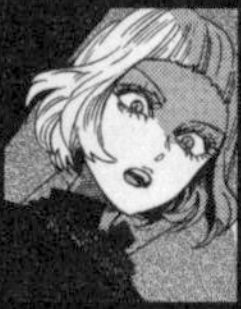

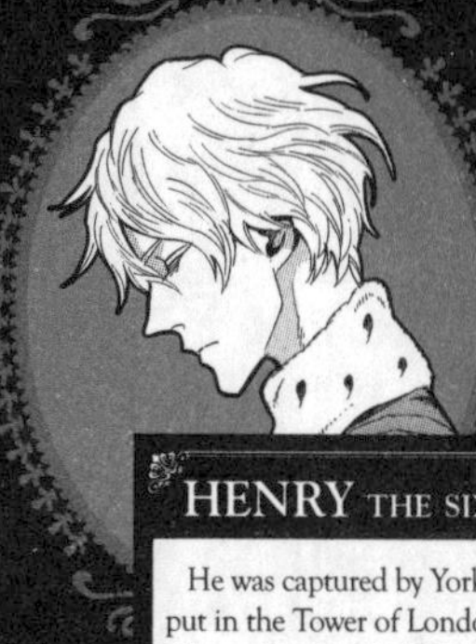

HENRY THE SIXTH

He was captured by York and put in the Tower of London. His illness worsens, and he is lost in a mental fog when he is stabbed by Richard.

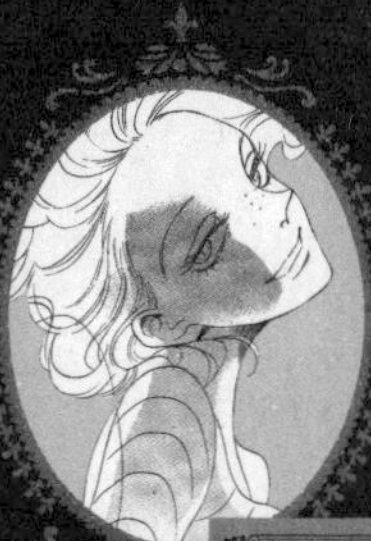

Joan of Arc

Called a French witch and burned at the stake. She appears before Richard as a ghost.

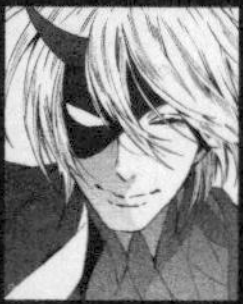

Richmond

With his sights set on the throne, he is maneuvering to bring about Richard's decline.

Elizabeth

She married Edward the Fourth to get revenge on the House of York. She was recently sent to a convent.

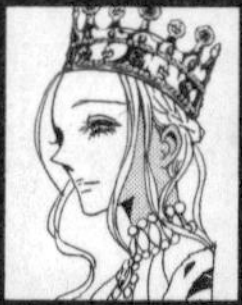

Story thus far...

England, the Middle Ages.

Elizabeth's scheme to ensure her son takes the throne ends in failure, and Edward the Fifth and his younger brother Richard are taken to the Tower of London. Thanks to Buckingham's expert oratory and Richard's realistic performance, Richard gains the support of the people and at last ascends to his long-desired throne.

At a celebratory banquet, the masked Richmond puts on a play that causes an immediate uproar with its allusions to the king. Although Richard is suspicious, he invites the other man to a costume ball he calls "the devil's paradise." There he corners Richmond, a member of the Lancaster faction who also has his sights set on the throne.

The banquet is in full swing when Richard dresses as a woman at Anne's suggestion. Incognito, he hears Buckingham express his true feelings. The pair slip out of the ball and make love from the heart for the first time. Buckingham asks that Richard call him by his real name, Henry. Hearing this, Richard's heart is upended. Meanwhile, Tyrrell has come chasing after the lovers...!

Requiem
— of the —
Rose
King

Contents

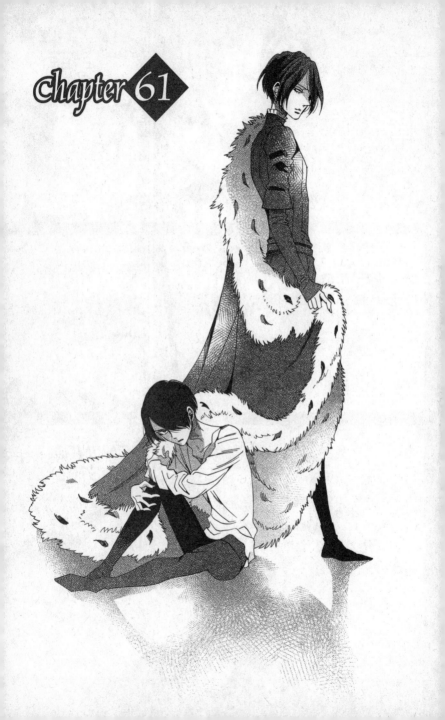

Chapter 61

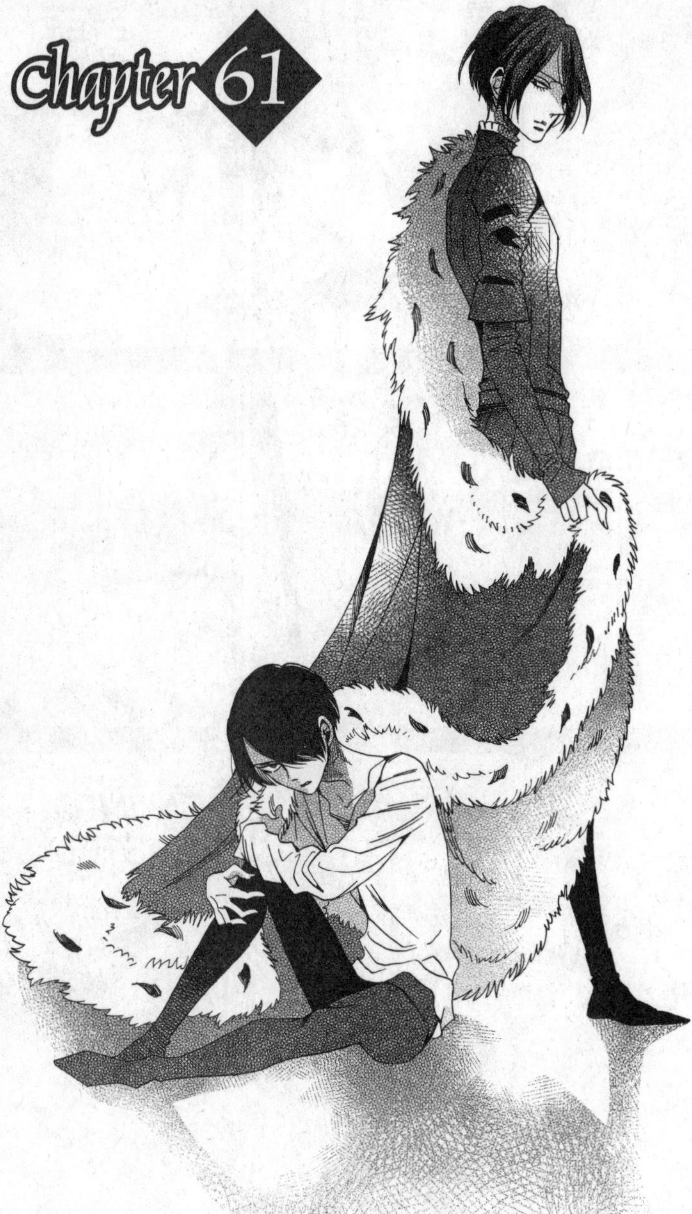

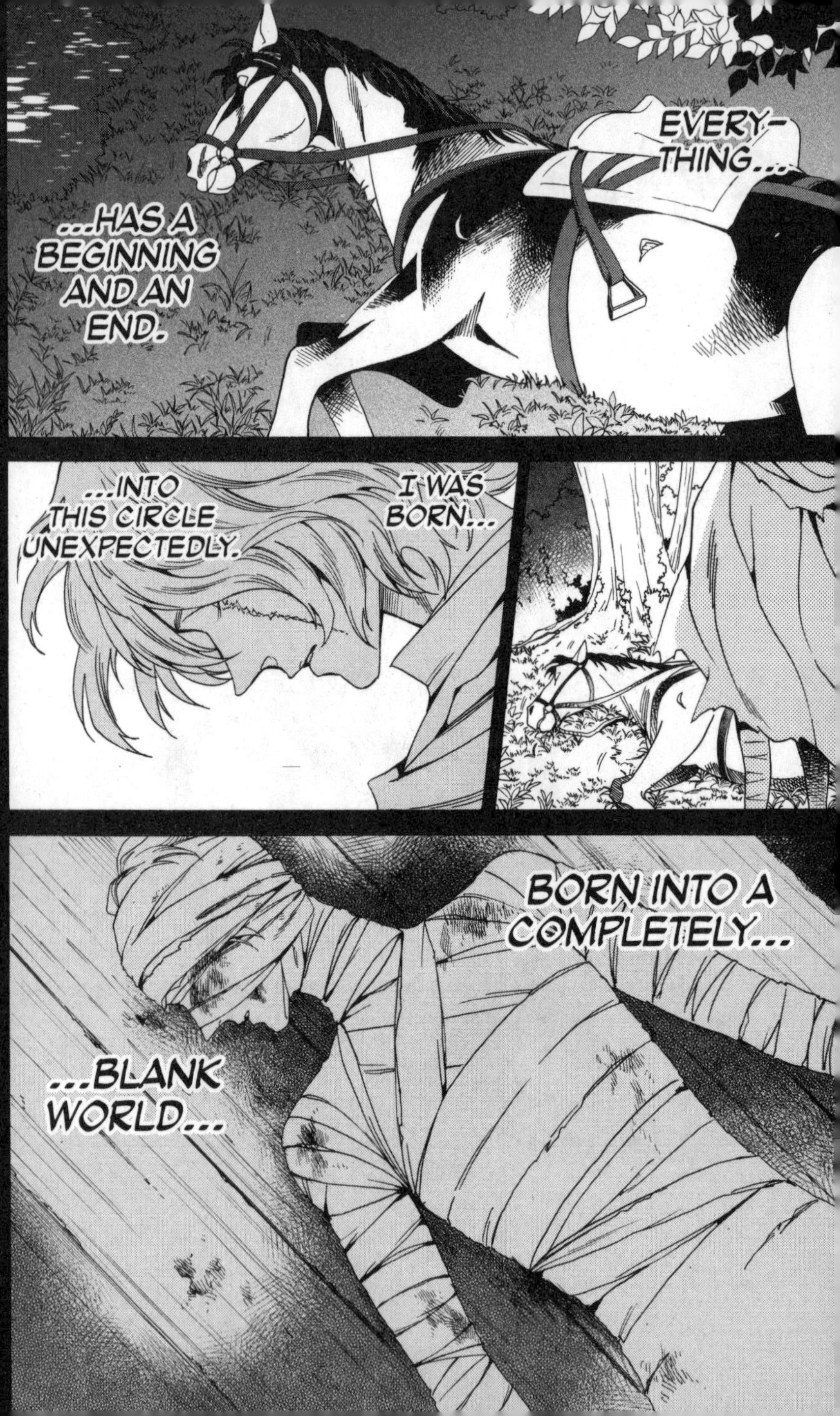
EVERY-THING...
...HAS A BEGINNING AND AN END.
I WAS BORN...
...INTO THIS CIRCLE UNEXPECTEDLY.
BORN INTO A COMPLETELY...
...BLANK WORLD...

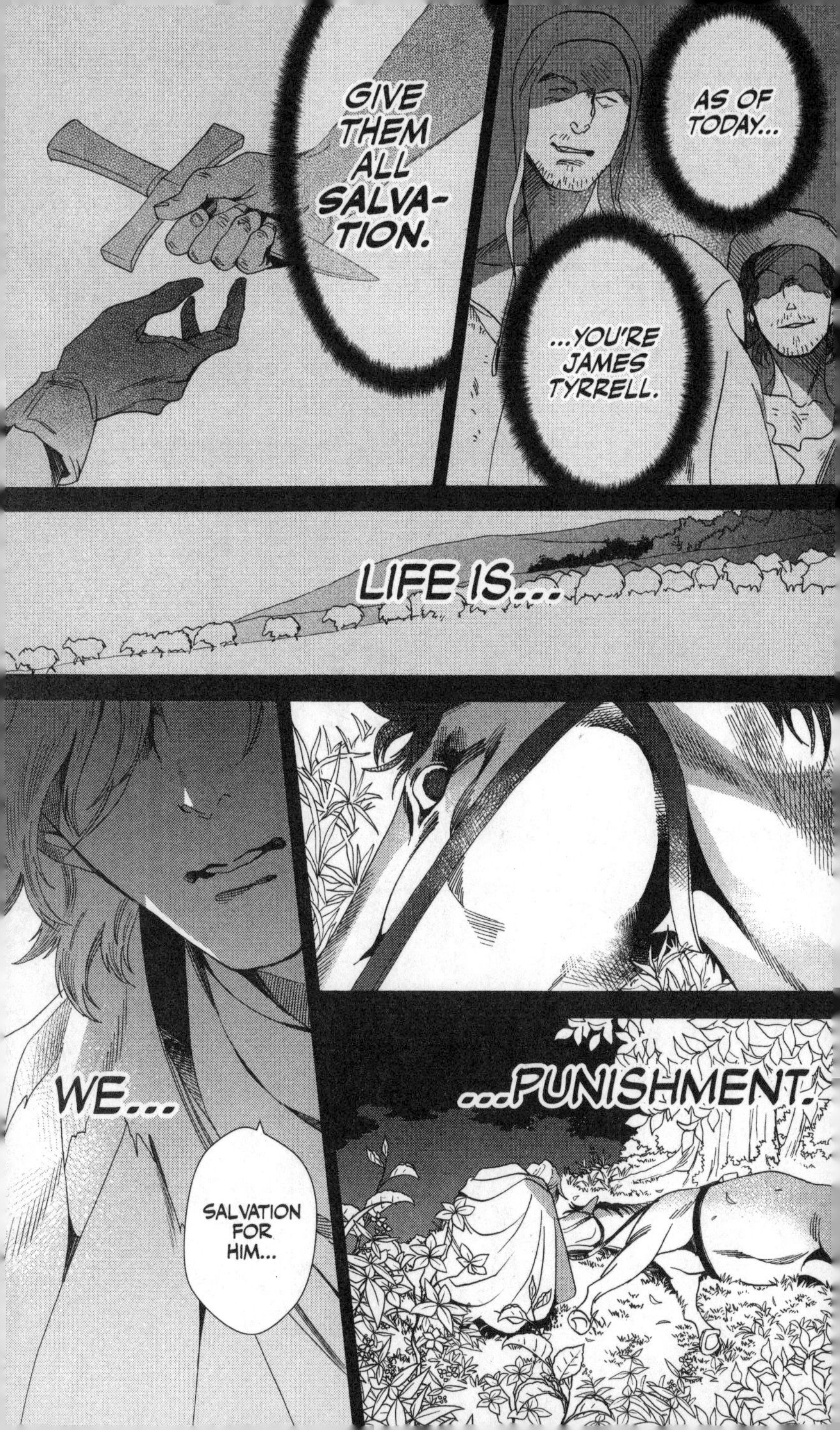
AS OF TODAY...
...YOU'RE JAMES TYRRELL.
GIVE THEM ALL SALVATION.
LIFE IS...
...PUNISHMENT.
WE...
SALVATION FOR HIM...

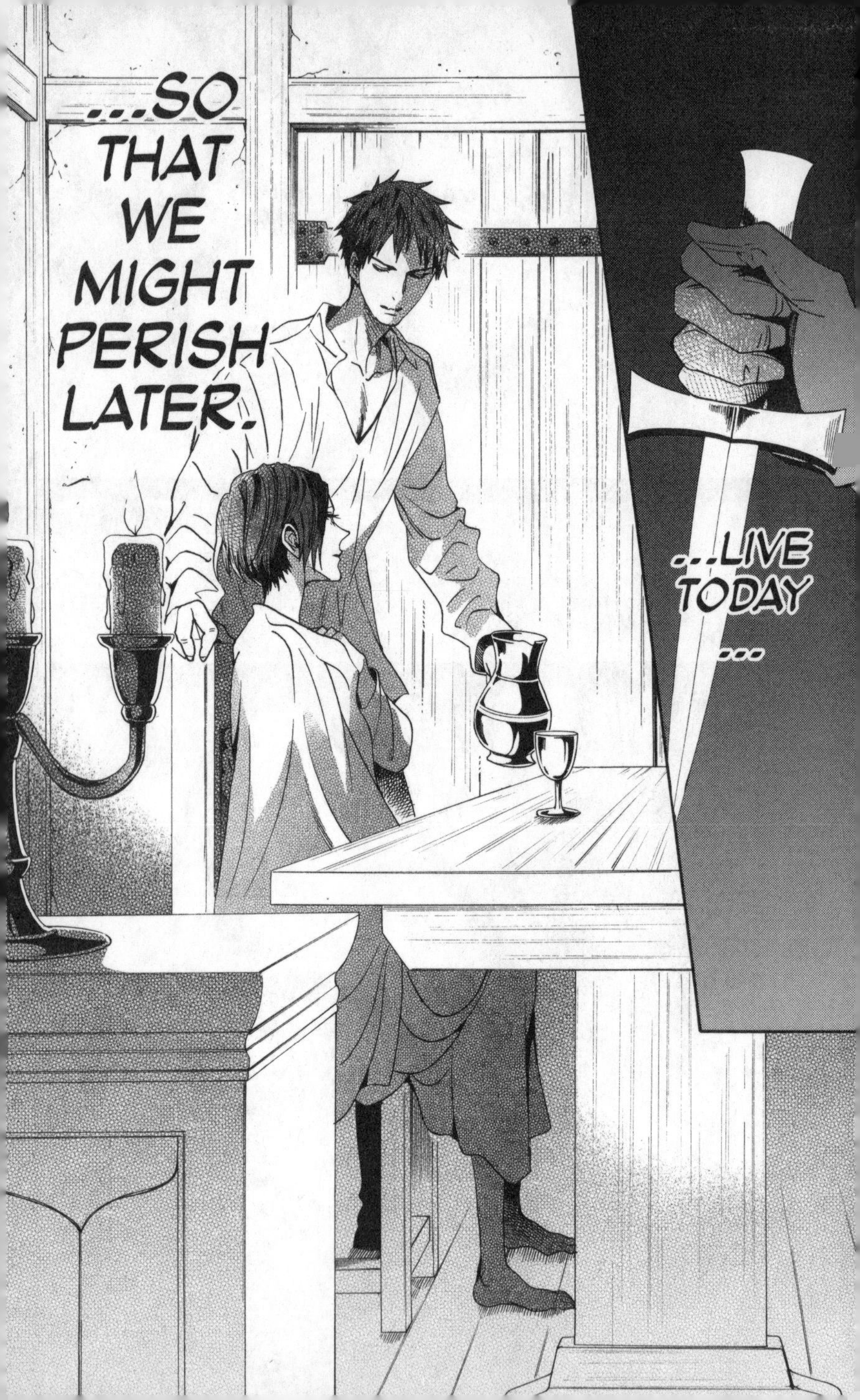
...LIVE TODAY...
...SO THAT WE MIGHT PERISH LATER.

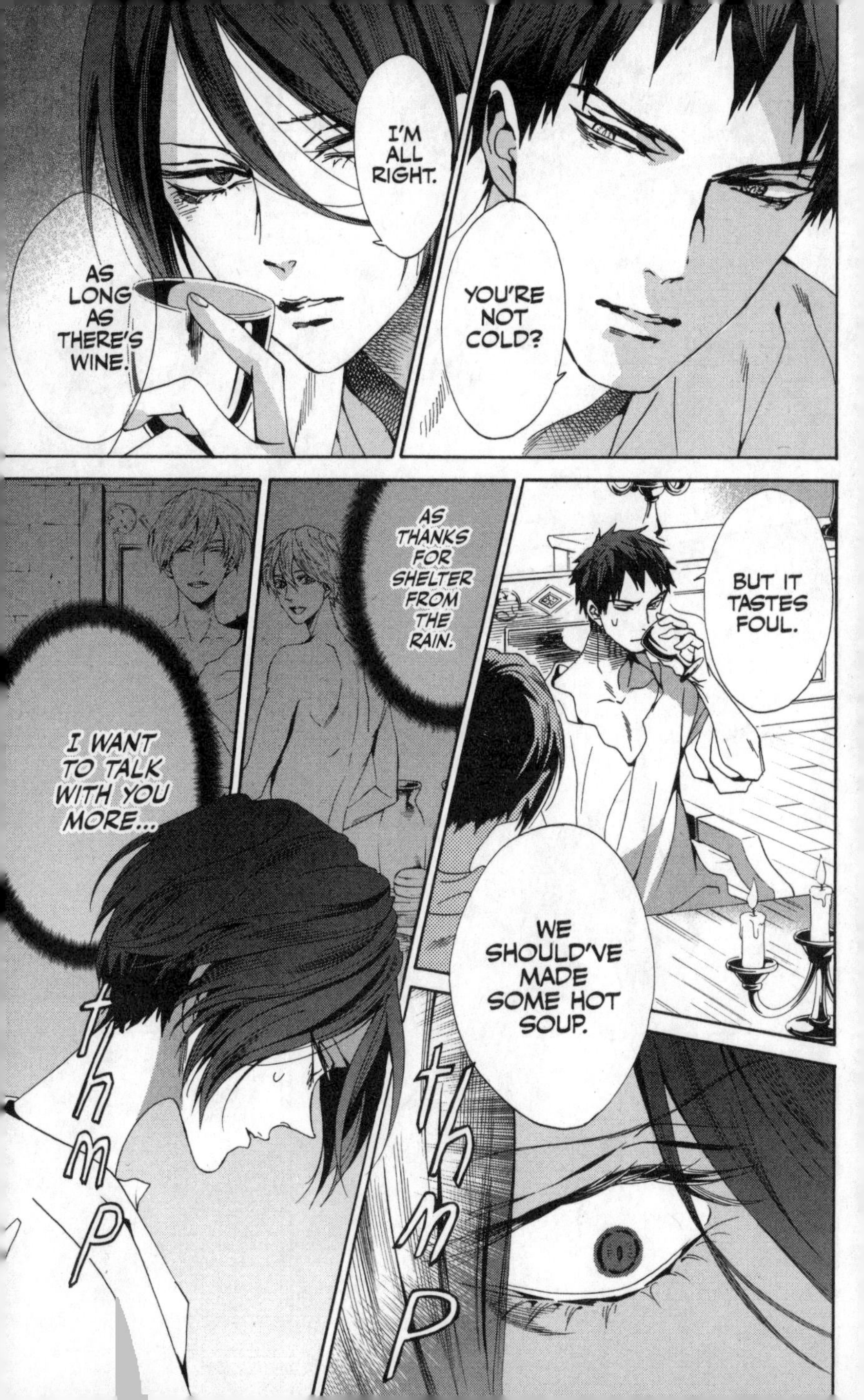
YOU'RE NOT COLD?
I'M ALL RIGHT.
AS LONG AS THERE'S WINE.
BUT IT TASTES FOUL.
WE SHOULD'VE MADE SOME HOT SOUP.
AS THANKS FOR SHELTER FROM THE RAIN.
I WANT TO TALK WITH YOU MORE...
thmp
thmp

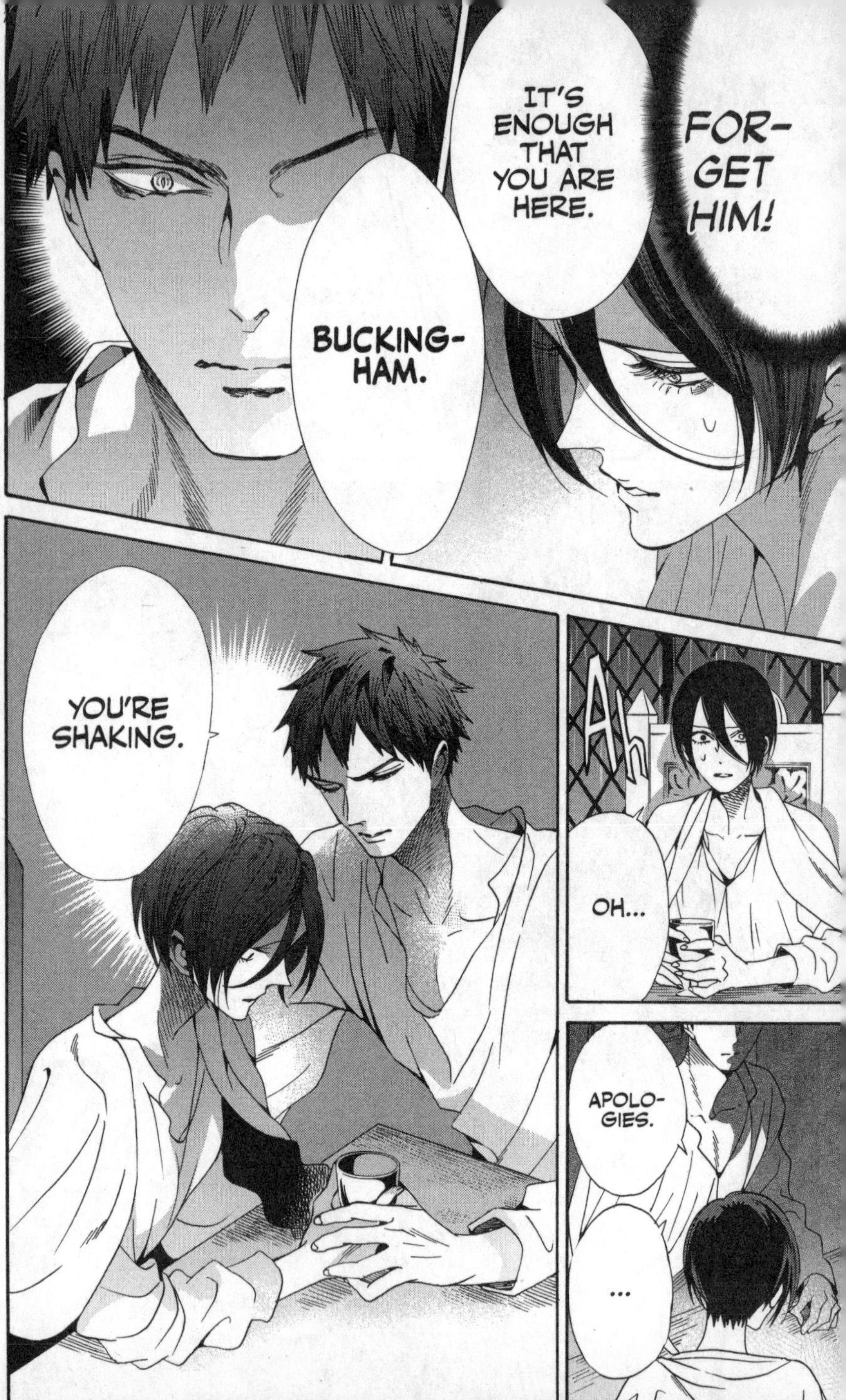
FOR-GET HIM!
IT'S ENOUGH THAT YOU ARE HERE.
BUCKING-HAM.
Ah
OH...
APOLO-GIES.
...
YOU'RE SHAKING.

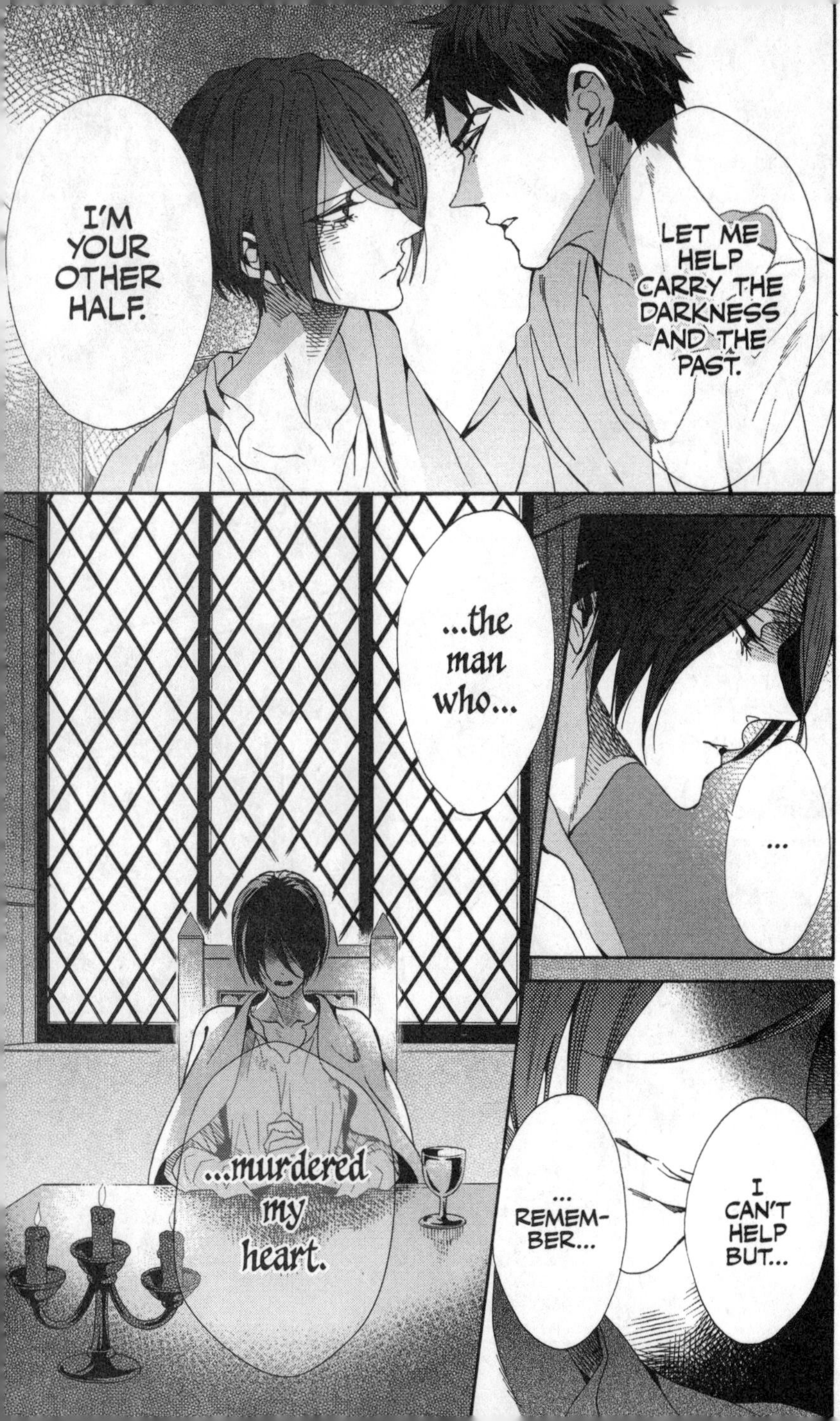
LET ME HELP CARRY THE DARKNESS AND THE PAST.
I'M YOUR OTHER HALF.
...
I CAN'T HELP BUT...
...REMEMBER...
...the man who...
...murdered my heart.

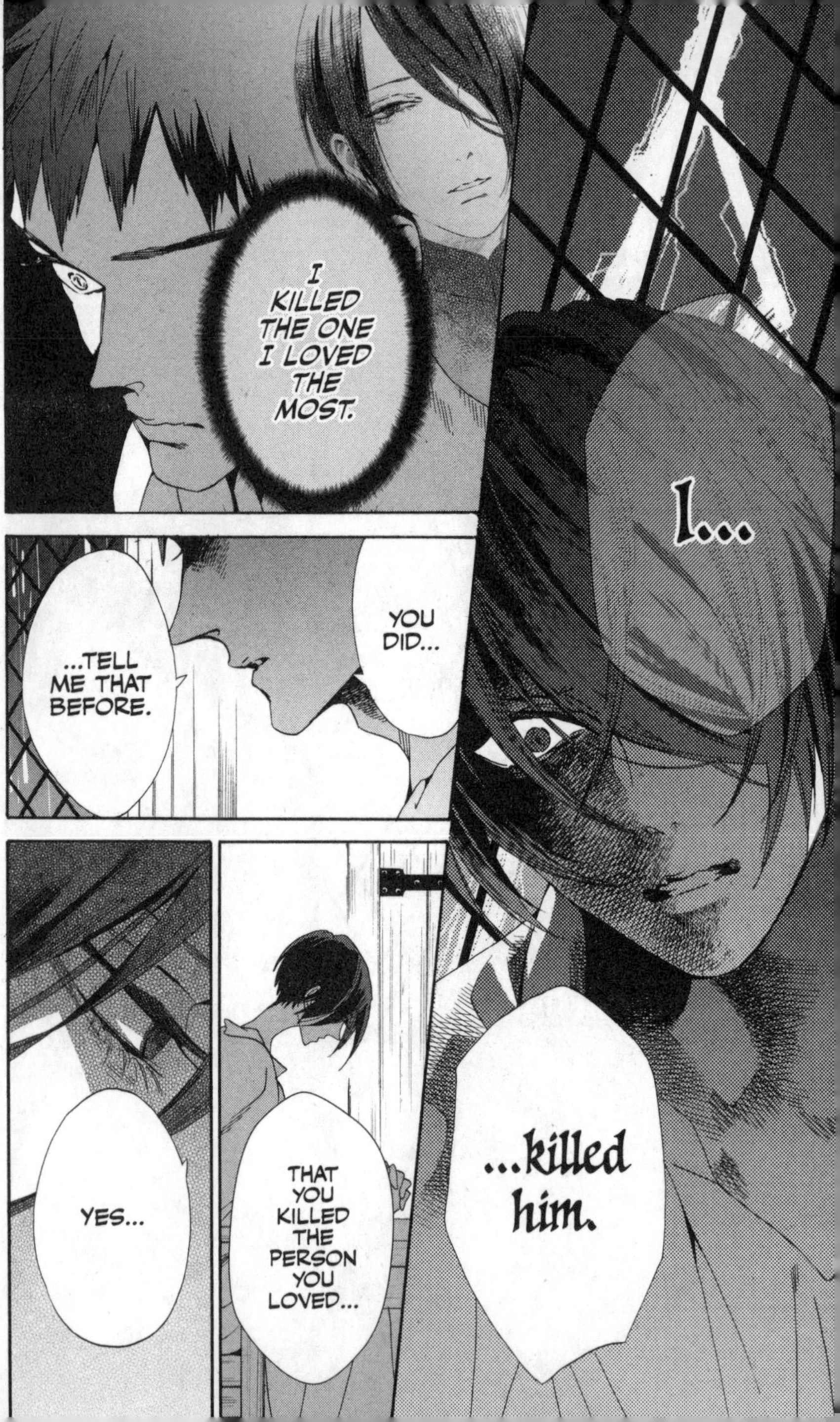
I...
...killed him.
I KILLED THE ONE I LOVED THE MOST.
YOU DID...
...TELL ME THAT BEFORE.
THAT YOU KILLED THE PERSON YOU LOVED...
YES...

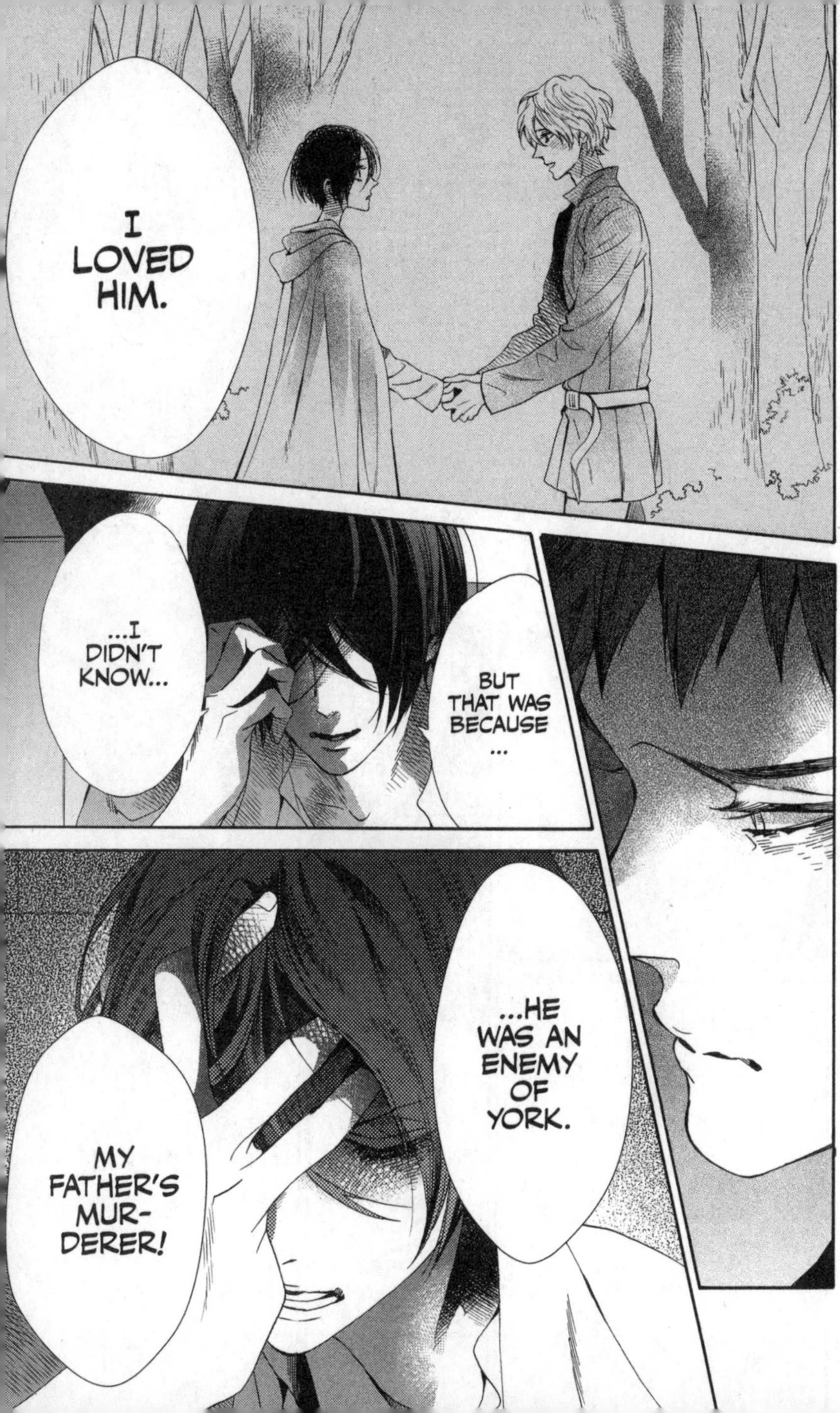
I LOVED HIM.
...I DIDN'T KNOW...
BUT THAT WAS BECAUSE ...
...HE WAS AN ENEMY OF YORK.
MY FATHER'S MUR- DERER!

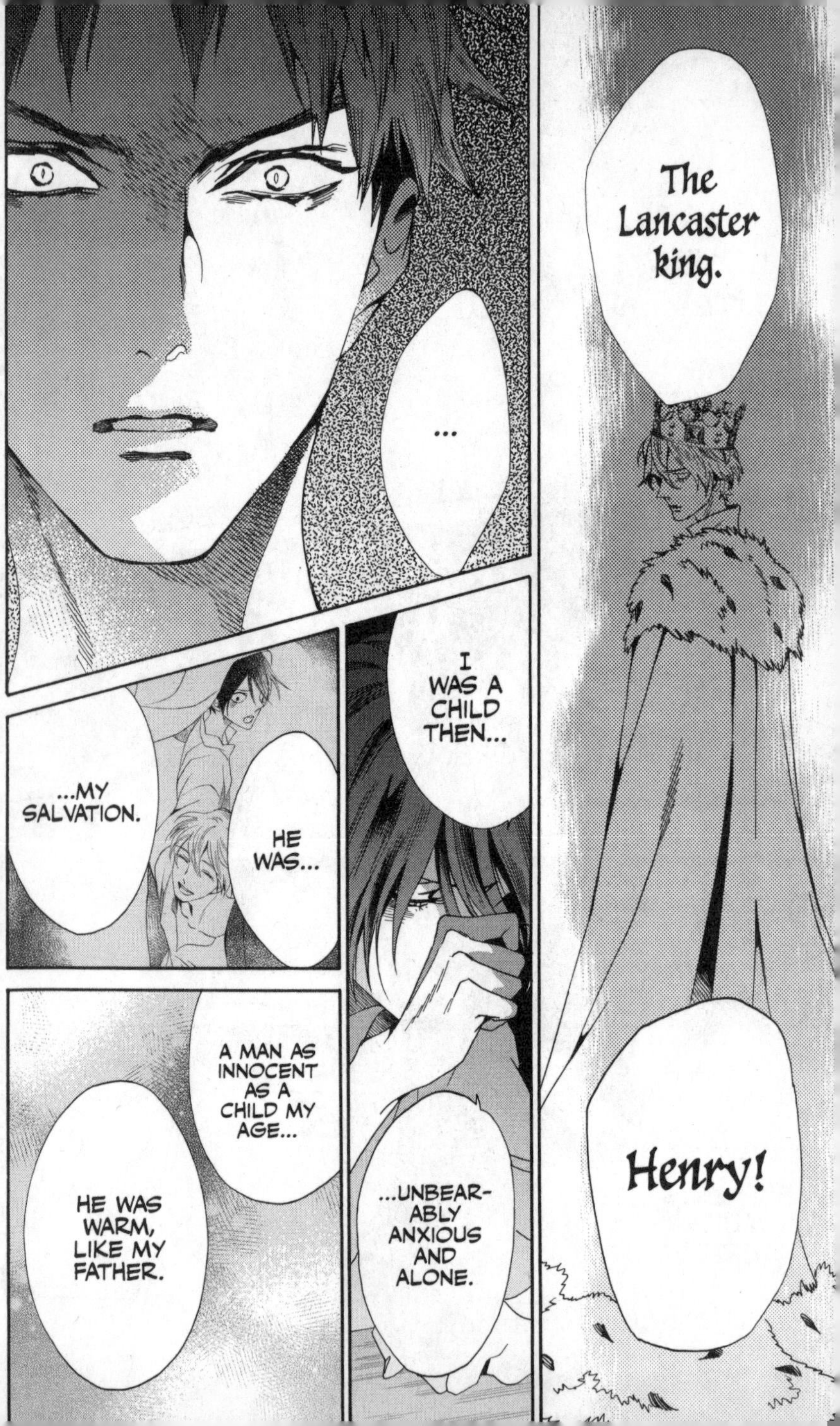
The Lancaster king.
Henry!
...
I WAS A CHILD THEN...
...UNBEAR-ABLY ANXIOUS AND ALONE.
HE WAS...
...MY SALVATION.
A MAN AS INNOCENT AS A CHILD MY AGE...
HE WAS WARM, LIKE MY FATHER.

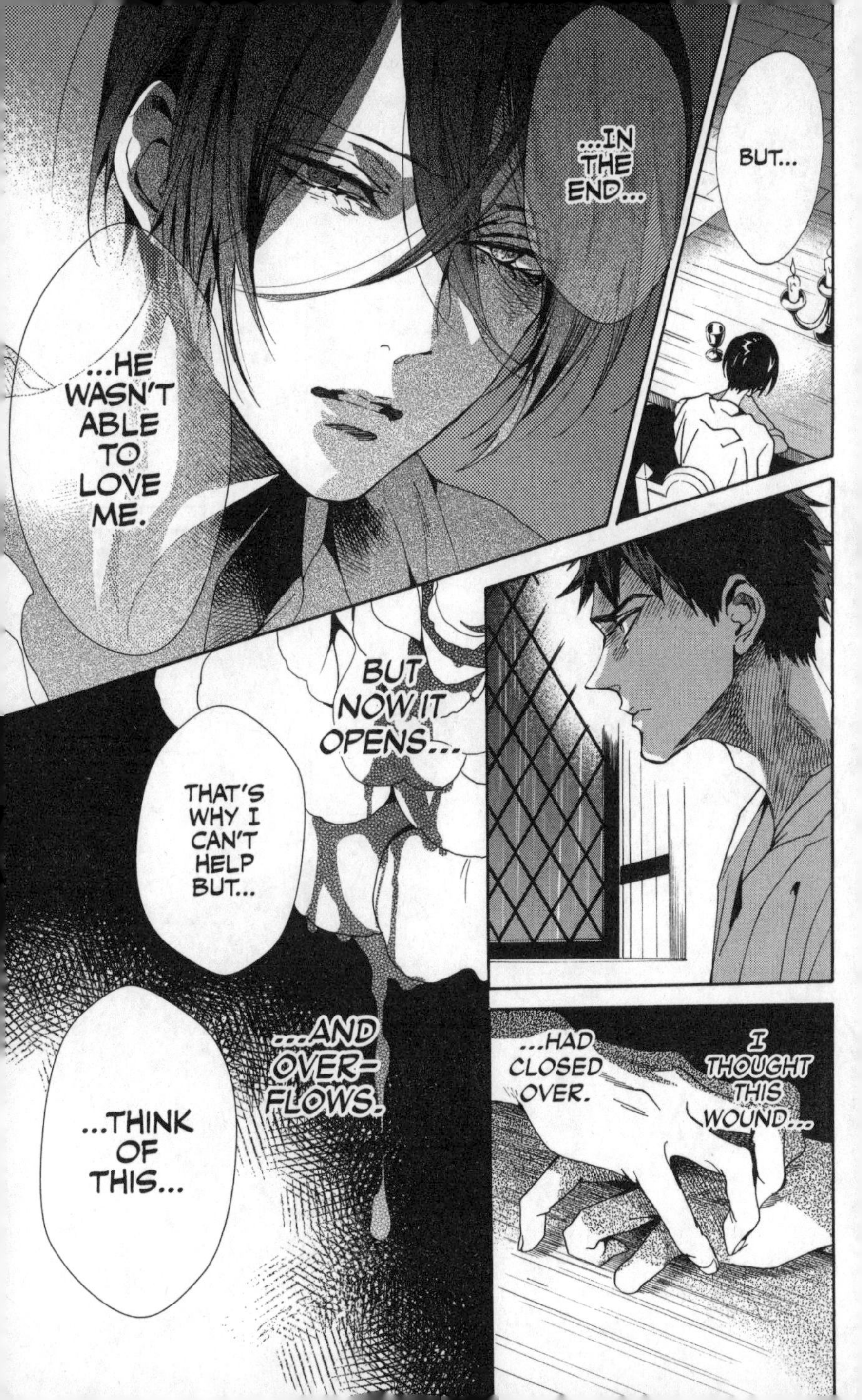
BUT...
...IN THE END...
...HE WASN'T ABLE TO LOVE ME.
I THOUGHT THIS WOUND...
...HAD CLOSED OVER.
BUT NOW IT OPENS...
...AND OVER-FLOWS.
THAT'S WHY I CAN'T HELP BUT...
...THINK OF THIS...

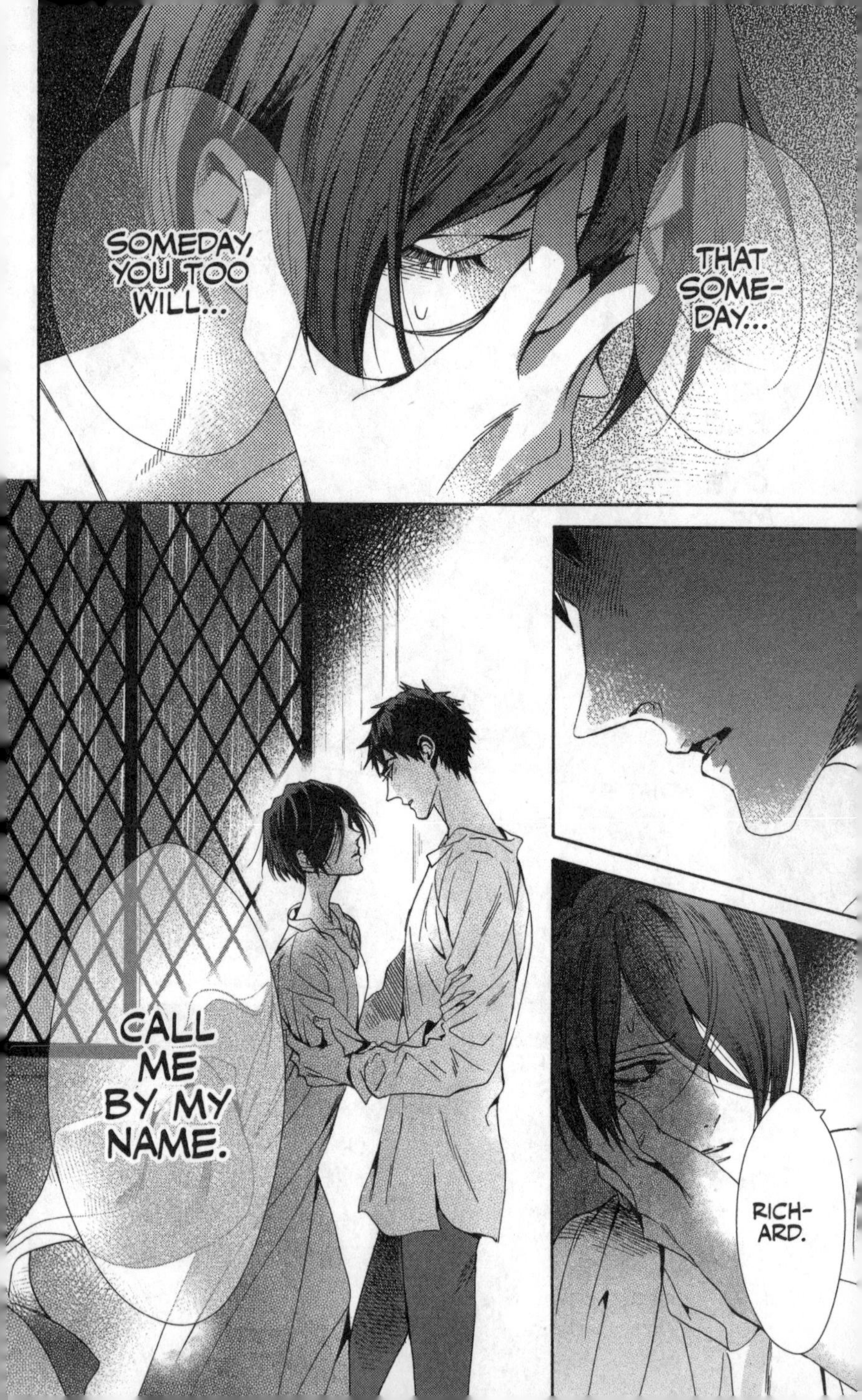
THAT SOME-DAY...
SOMEDAY, YOU TOO WILL...
RICH-ARD.
CALL ME BY MY NAME.

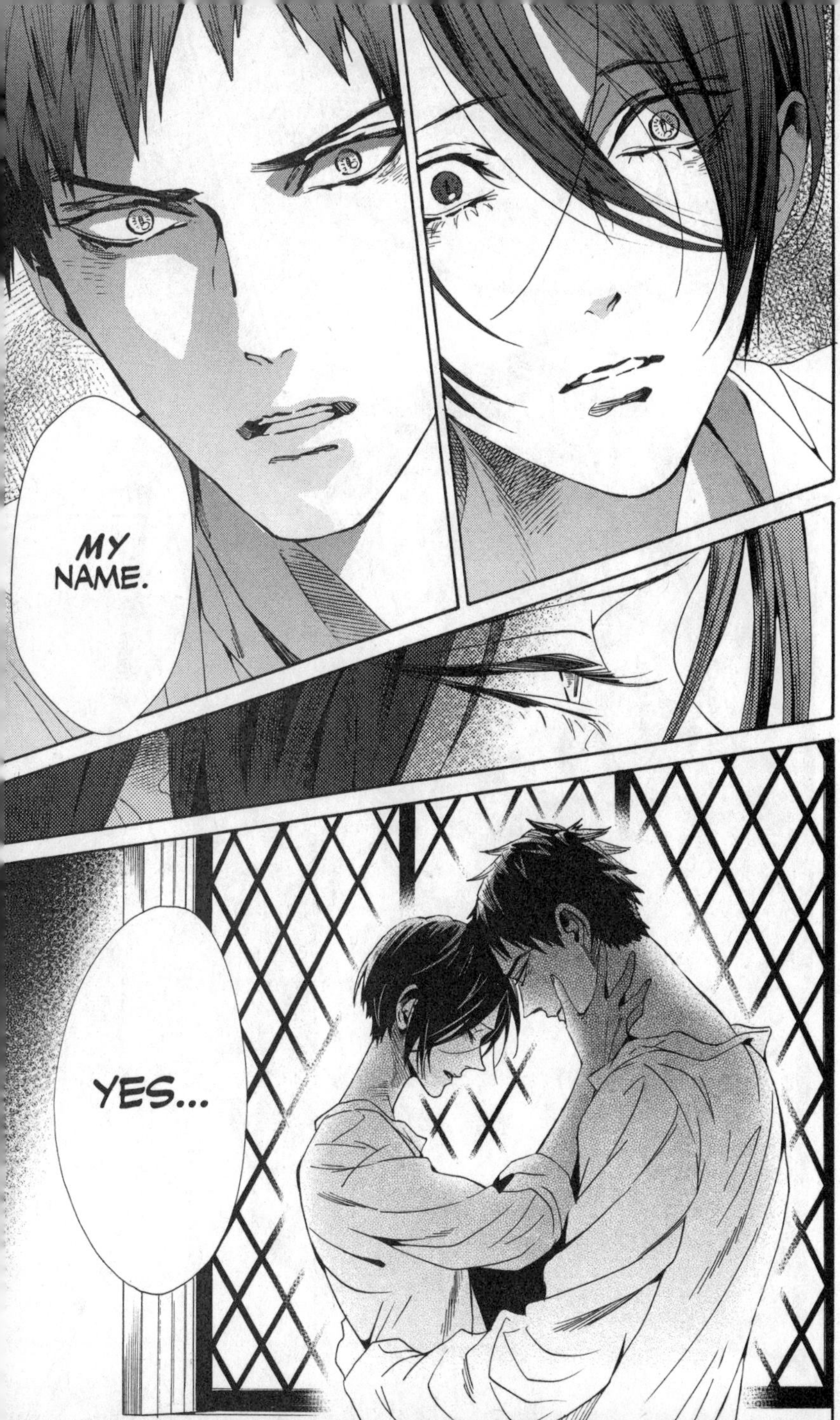
MY NAME.
YES...

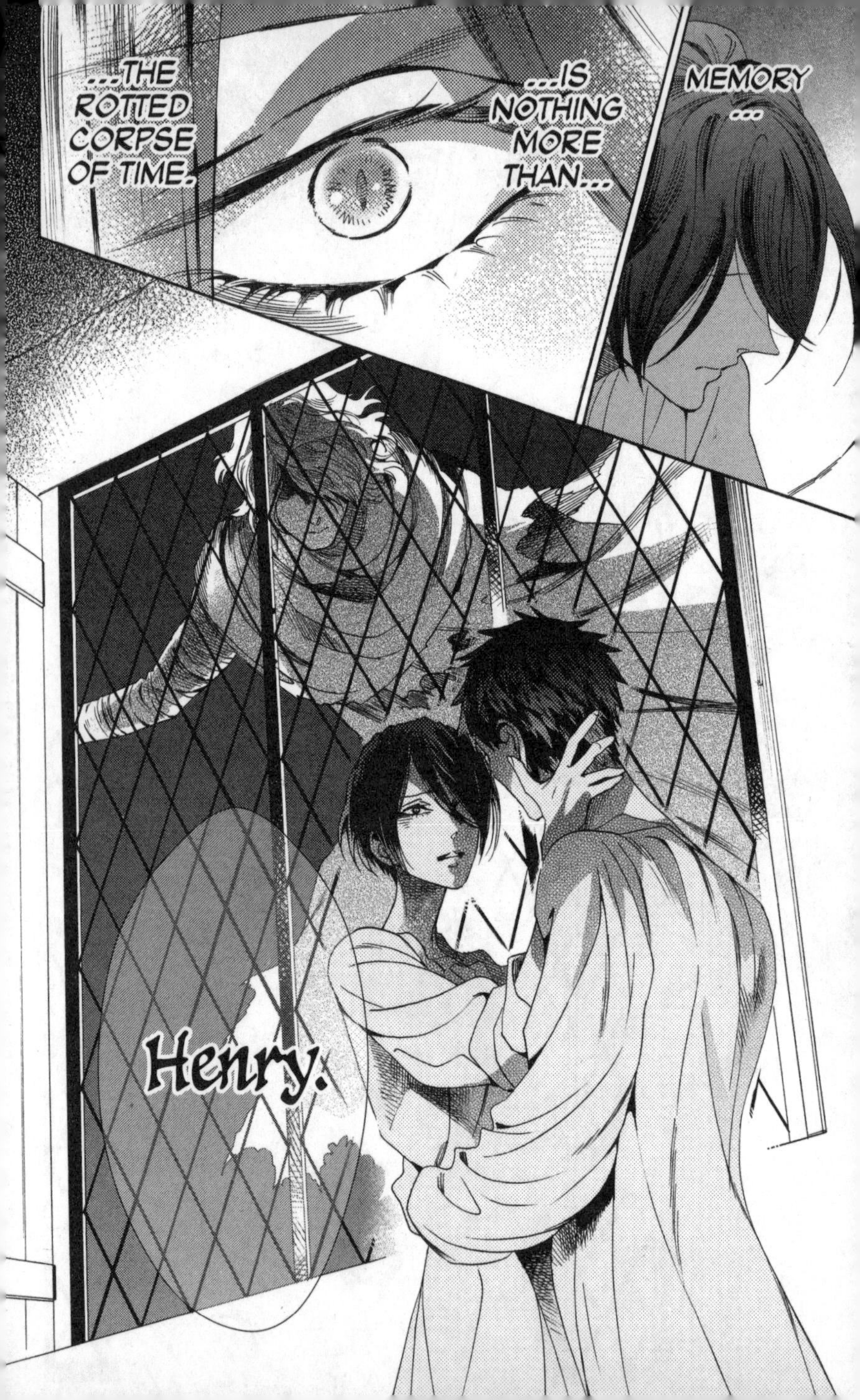
MEMORY...
...IS NOTHING MORE THAN...
...THE ROTTED CORPSE OF TIME.
Henry.

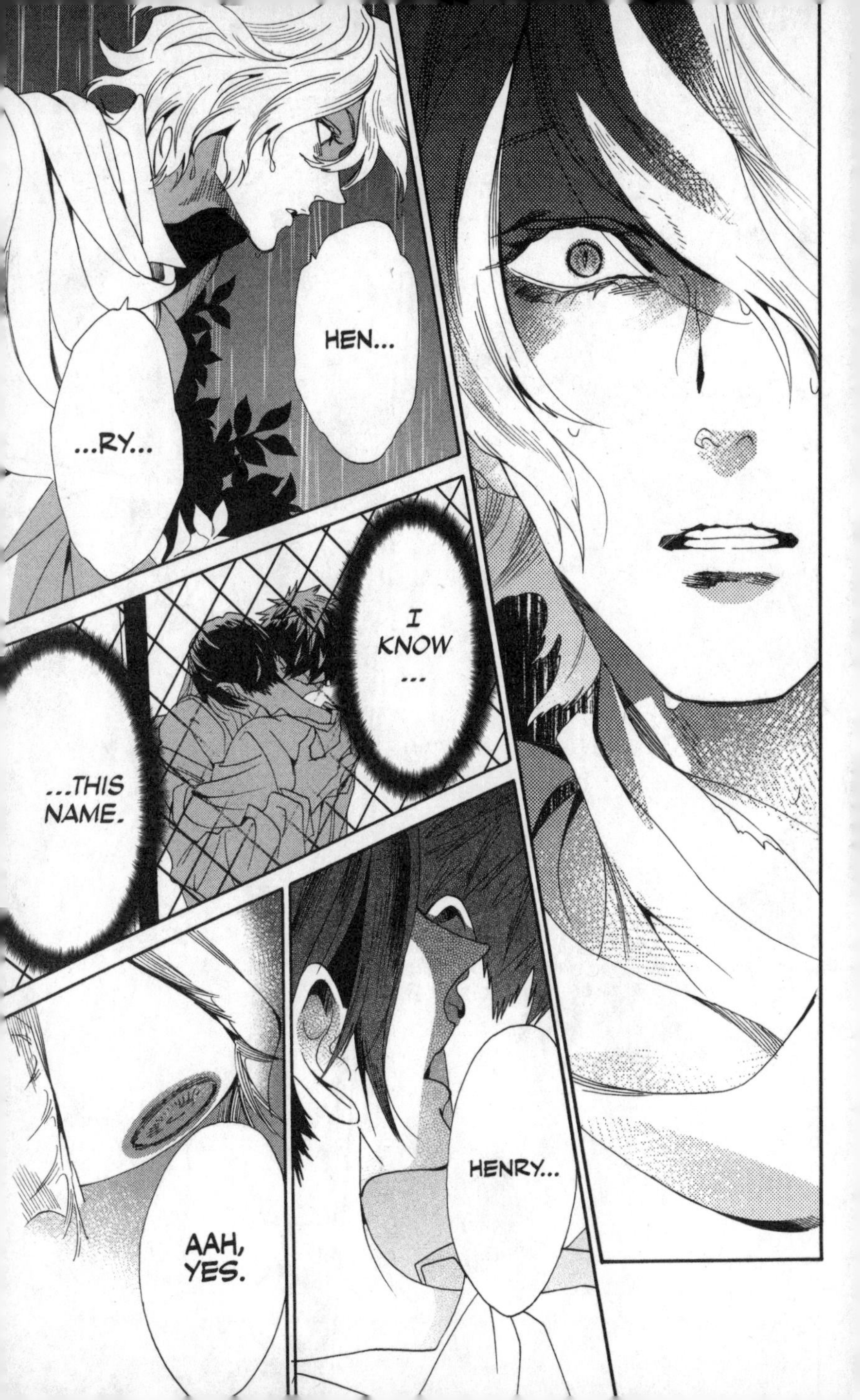
HEN...
...RY...
I KNOW ...
...THIS NAME.
HENRY...
AAH, YES.

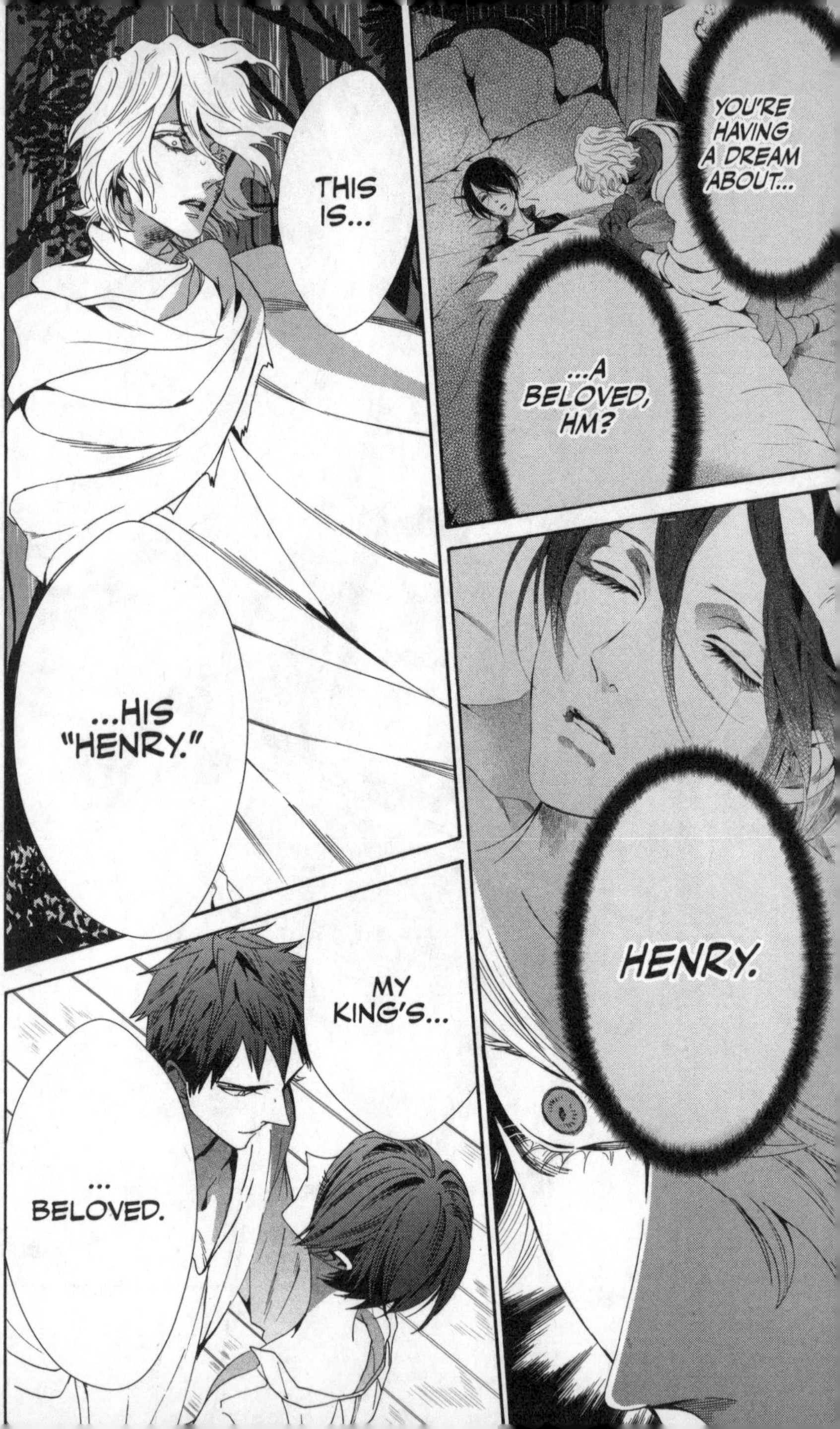
YOU'RE HAVING A DREAM ABOUT...
...A BELOVED, HM?
THIS IS...
...HIS "HENRY."
HENRY.
MY KING'S...
... BELOVED.

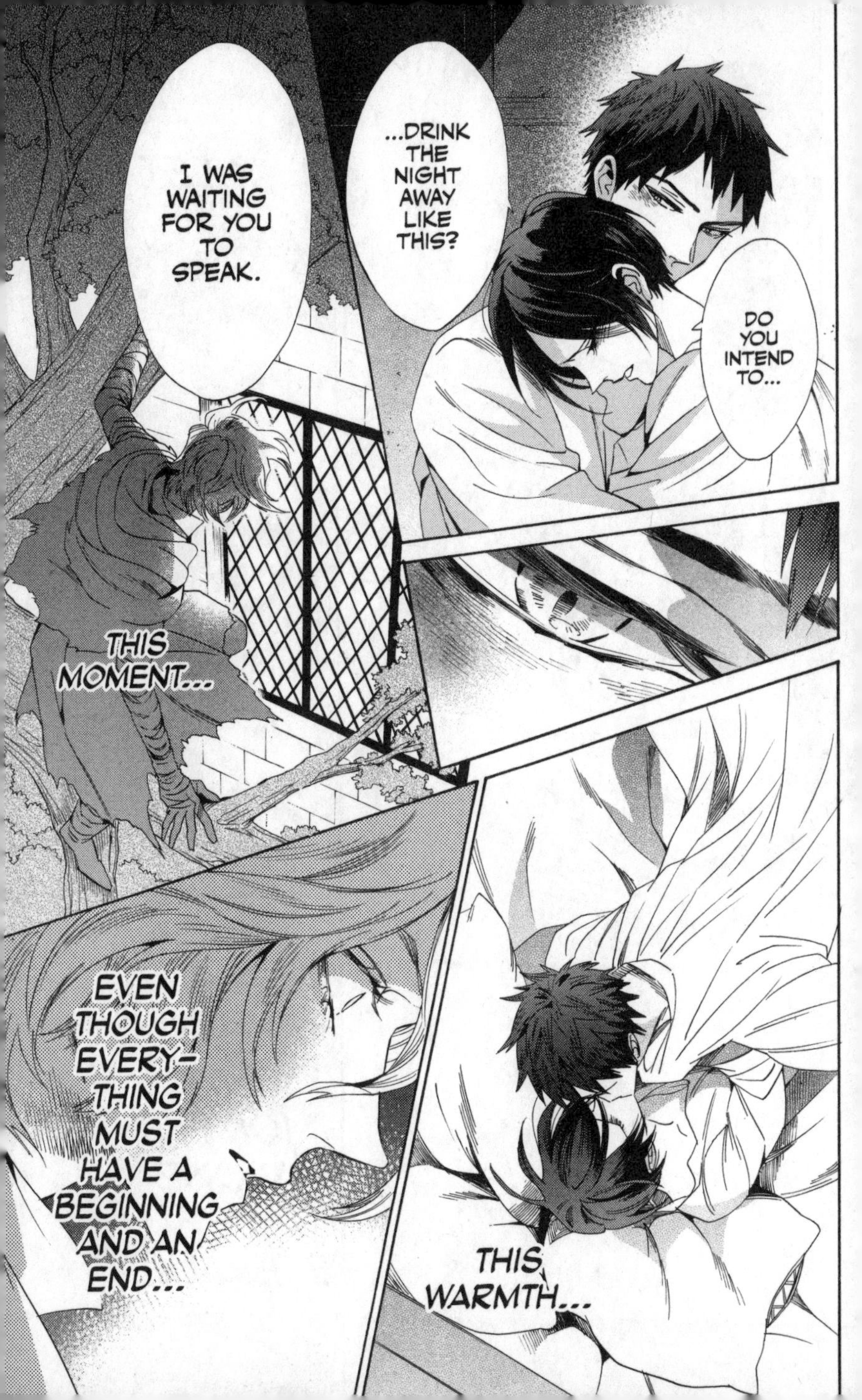
DO YOU INTEND TO...
...DRINK THE NIGHT AWAY LIKE THIS?
I WAS WAITING FOR YOU TO SPEAK.
THIS MOMENT...
THIS WARMTH...
EVEN THOUGH EVERY-THING MUST HAVE A BEGINNING AND AN END...

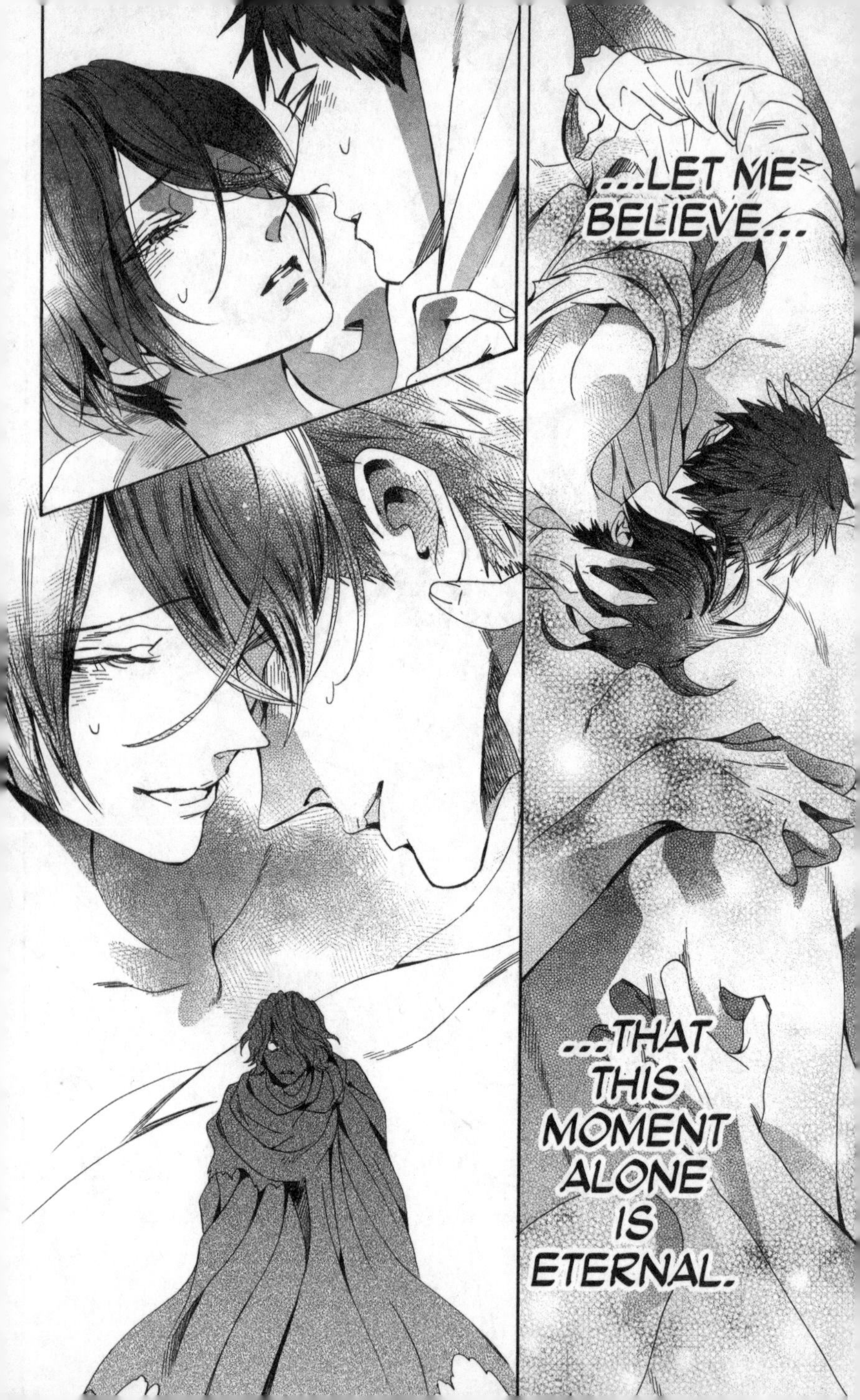
...LET ME BELIEVE...
...THAT THIS MOMENT ALONE IS ETERNAL.

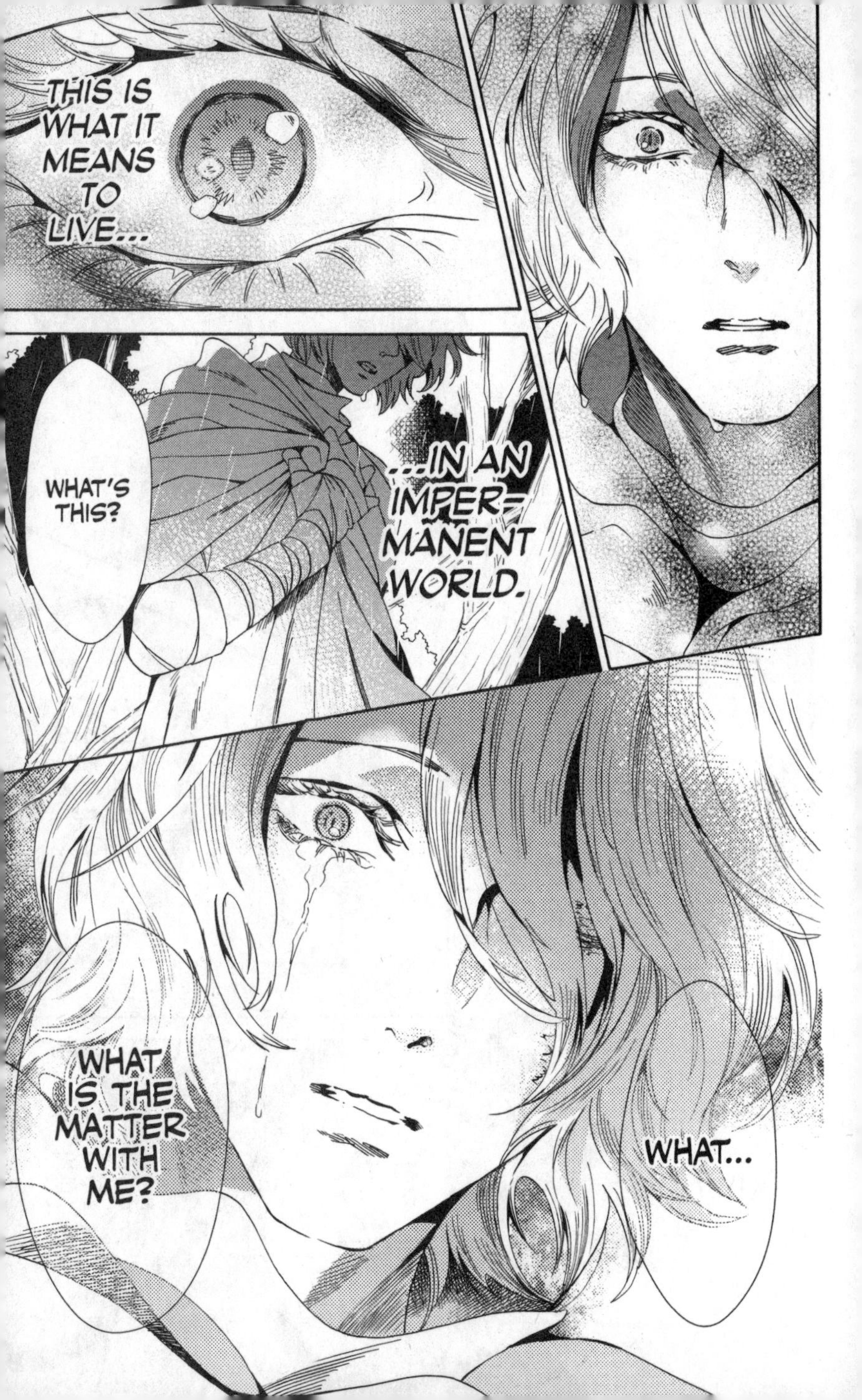
THIS IS WHAT IT MEANS TO LIVE...
...IN AN IMPER-MANENT WORLD.
WHAT'S THIS?
WHAT...
WHAT IS THE MATTER WITH ME?

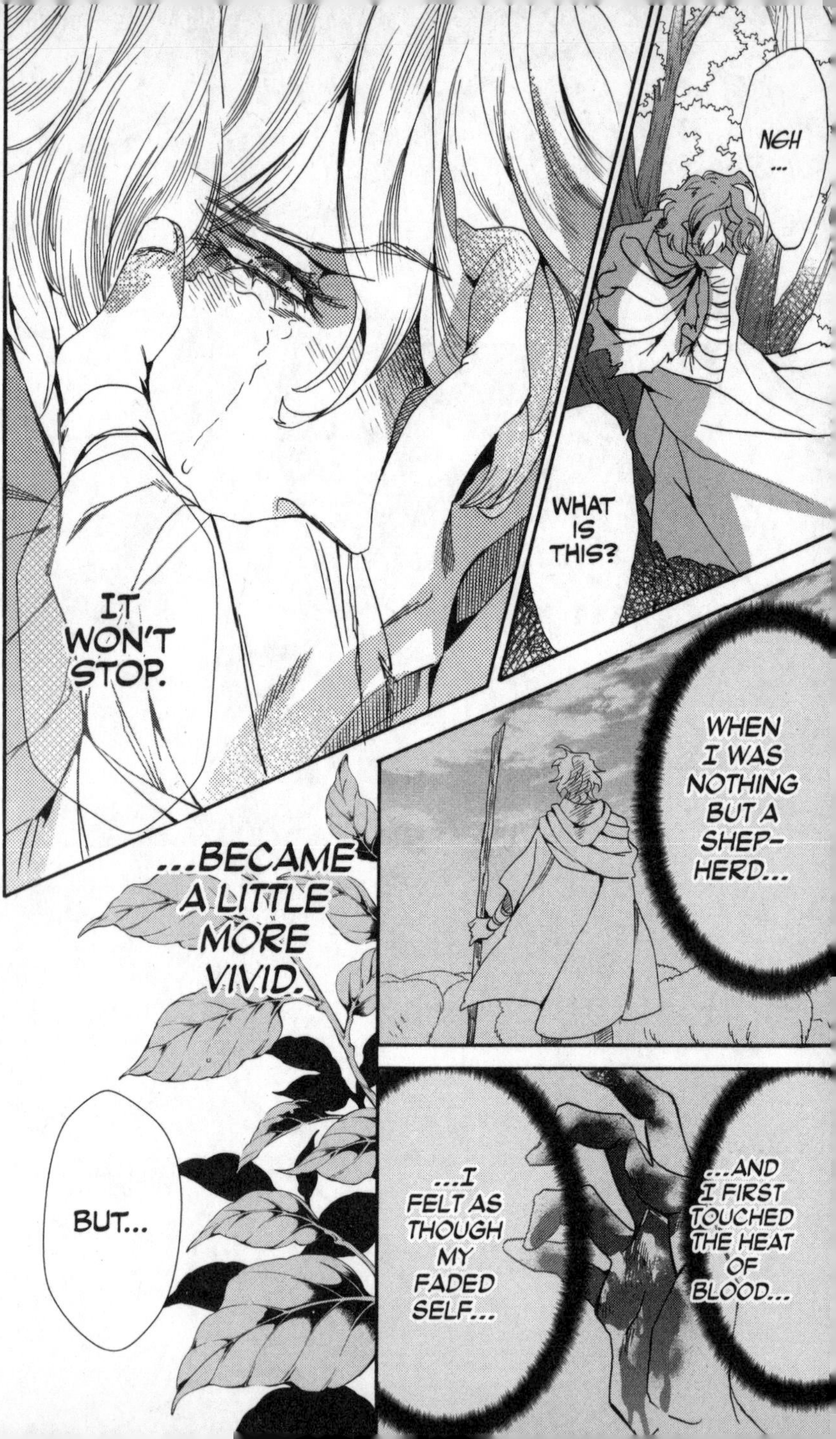
NGH ...
WHAT IS THIS?
IT WON'T STOP.
WHEN I WAS NOTHING BUT A SHEP-HERD...
...AND I FIRST TOUCHED THE HEAT OF BLOOD...
...I FELT AS THOUGH MY FADED SELF...
...BECAME A LITTLE MORE VIVID.
BUT...

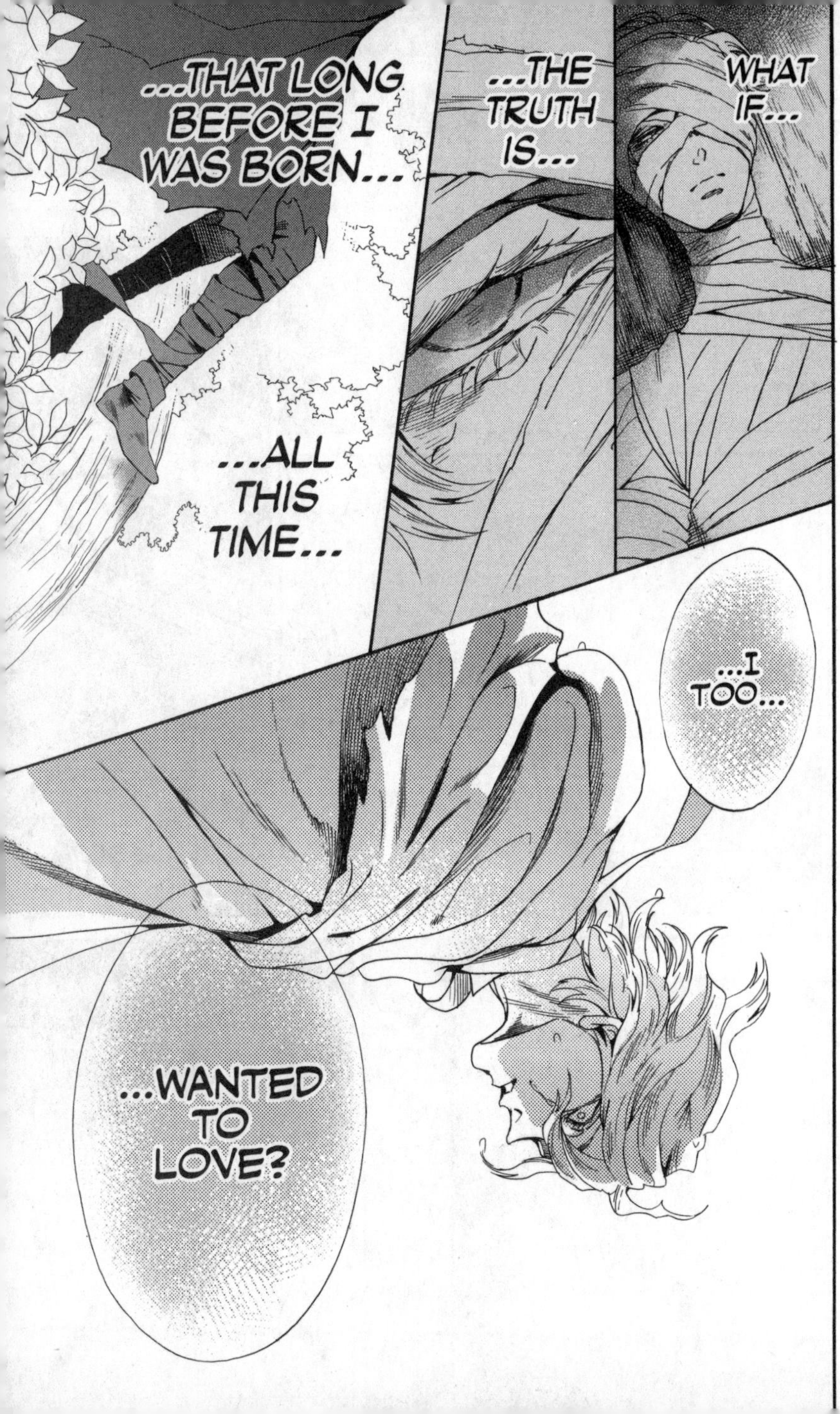
WHAT IF...
...THE TRUTH IS...
...THAT LONG BEFORE I WAS BORN...
...ALL THIS TIME...
...I TOO...
...WANTED TO LOVE?

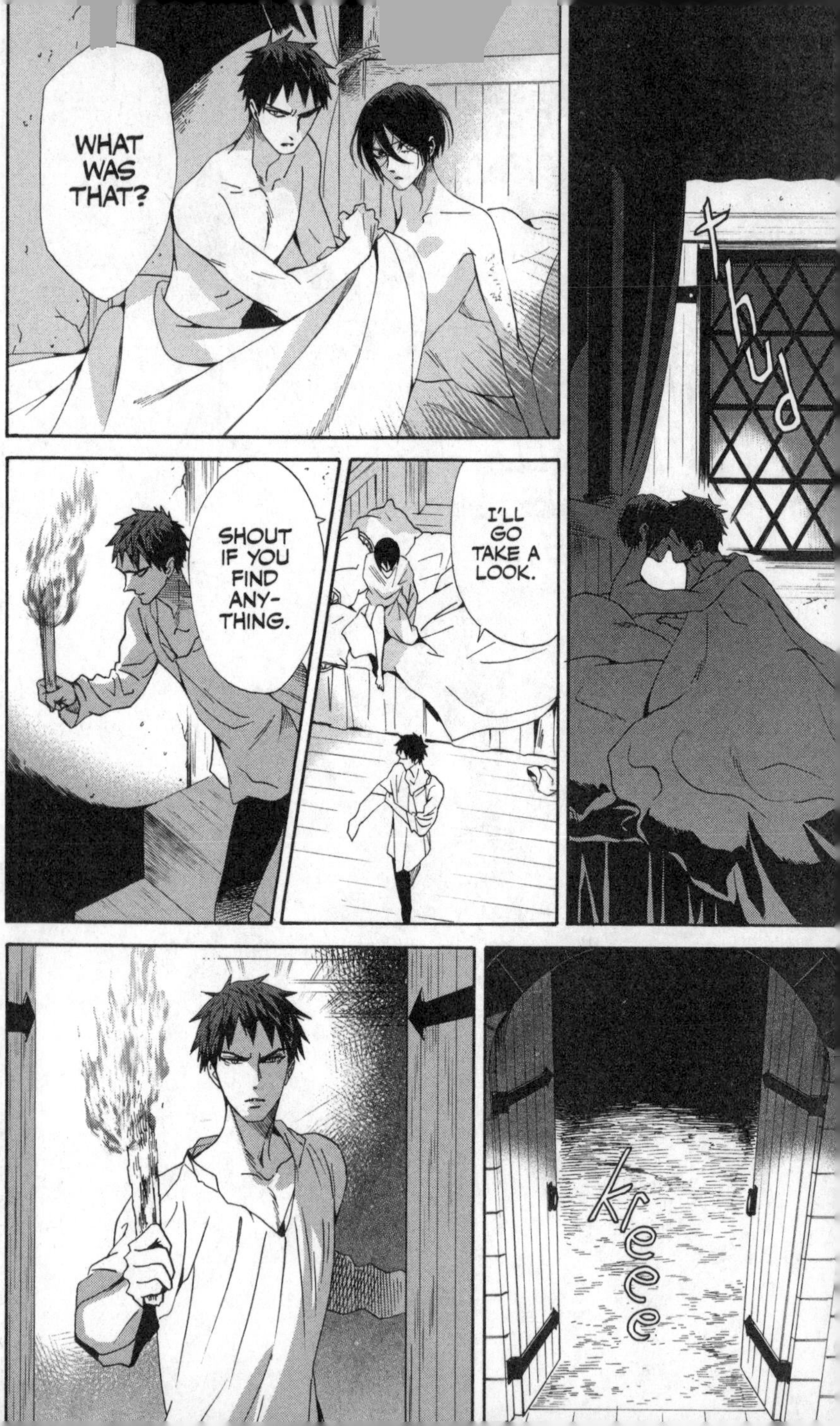
thud
WHAT WAS THAT?
I'LL GO TAKE A LOOK.
SHOUT IF YOU FIND ANY-THING.
kreee

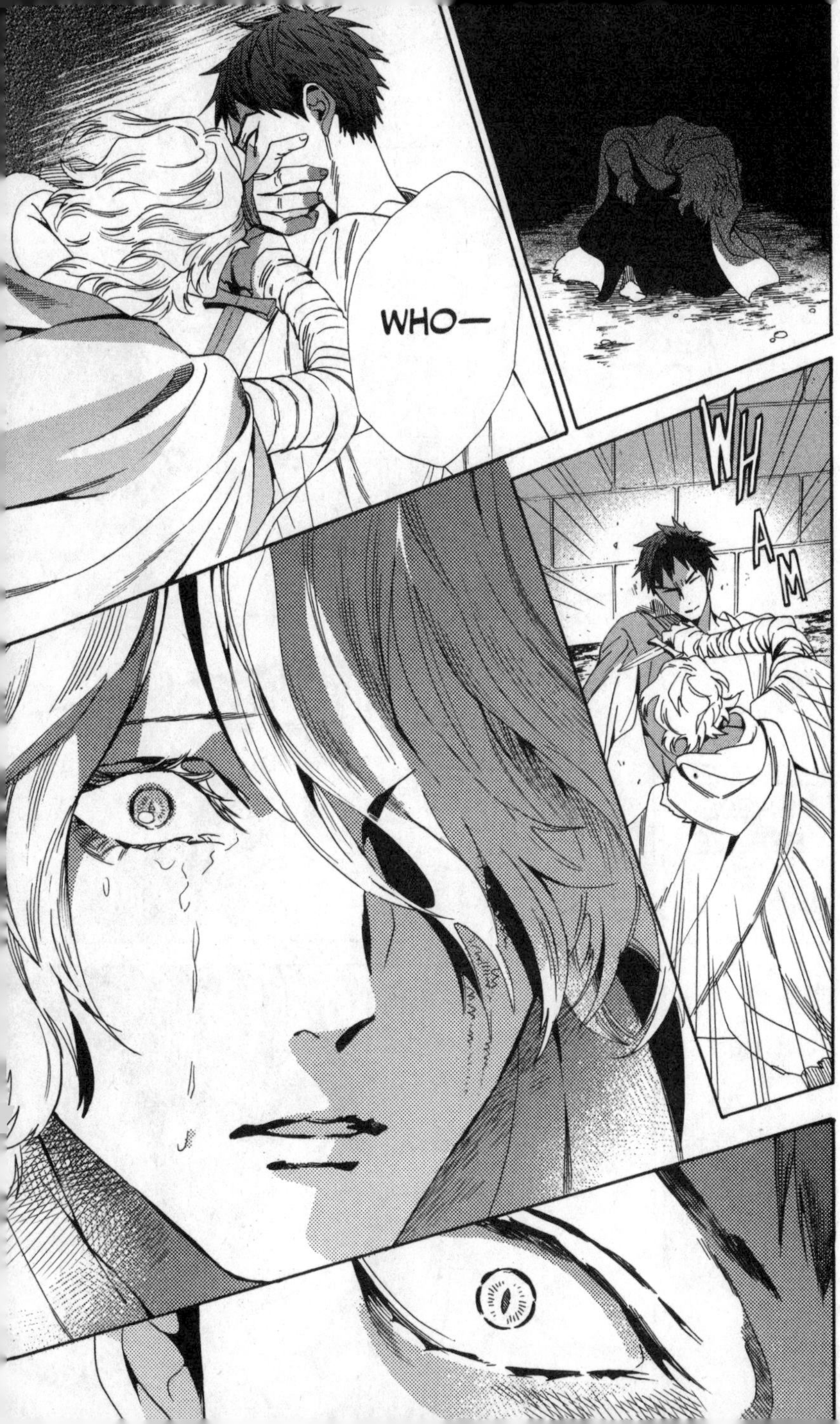
WHO—
WHAM

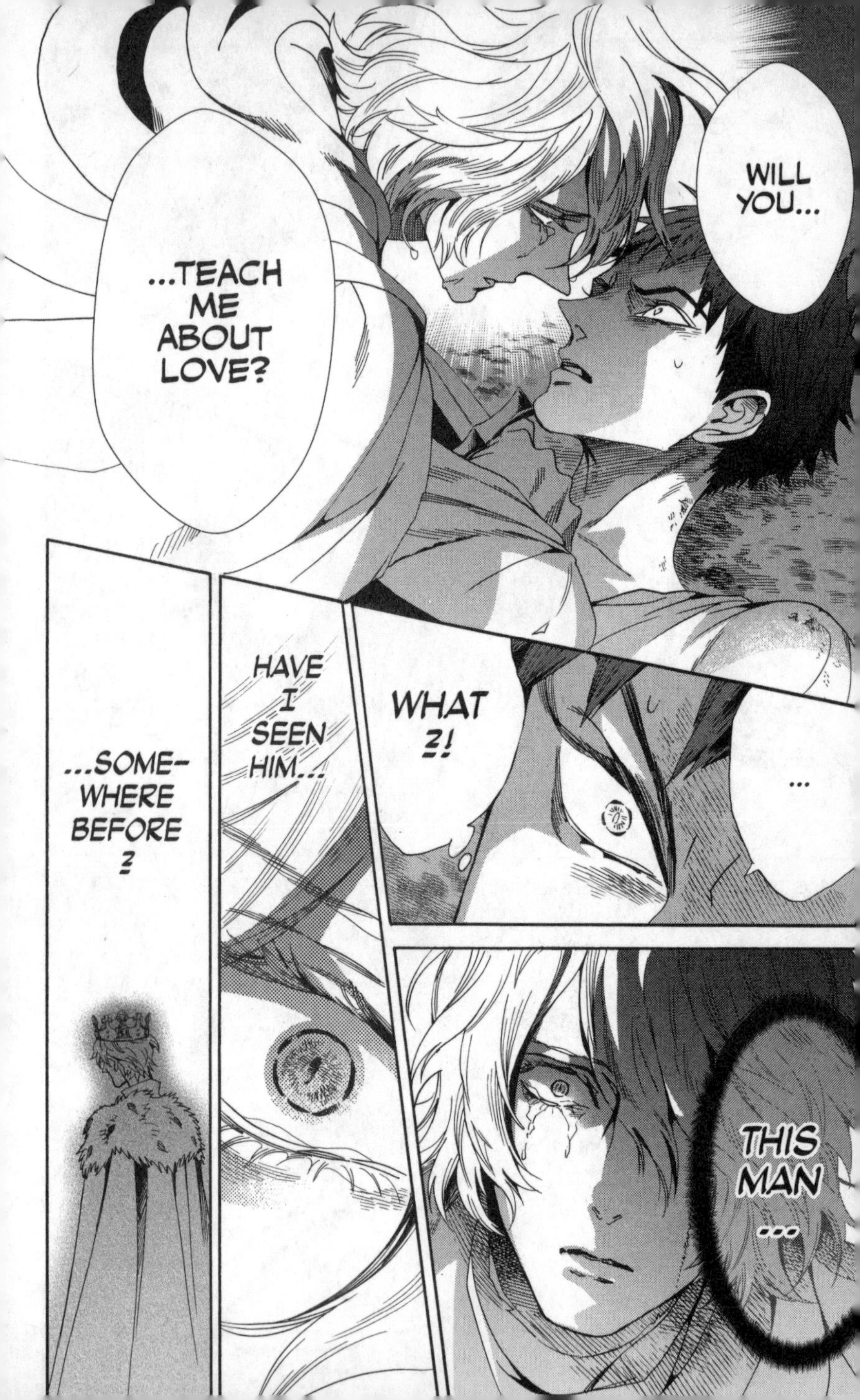
WILL YOU...
...TEACH ME ABOUT LOVE?
...
WHAT ?!
THIS MAN ...
HAVE I SEEN HIM...
...SOME-WHERE BEFORE ?

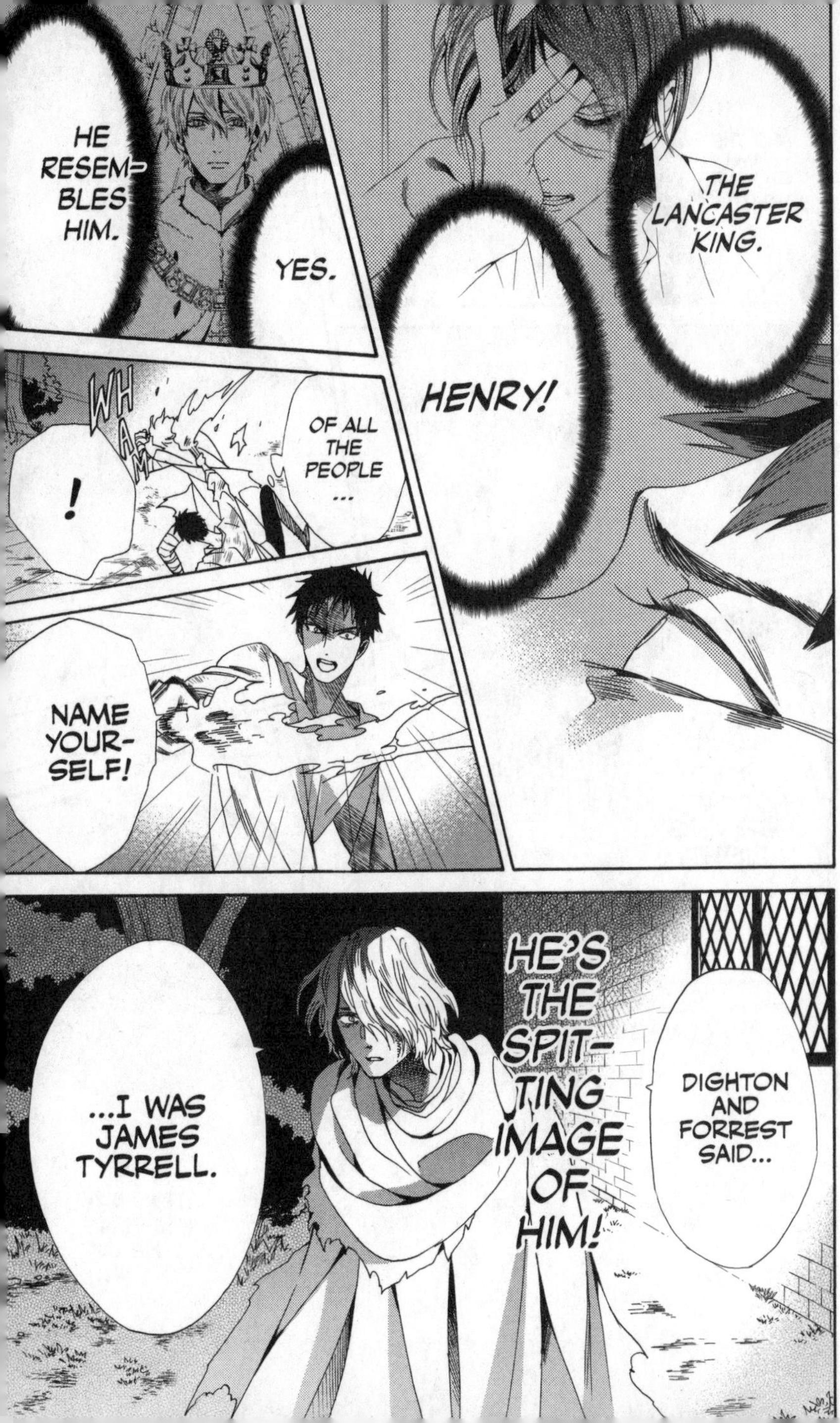
THE LANCASTER KING.
HENRY!
HE RESEMBLES HIM.
YES.
OF ALL THE PEOPLE ...
WHAM
!
NAME YOURSELF!
DIGHTON AND FORREST SAID...
HE'S THE SPITTING IMAGE OF HIM!
...I WAS JAMES TYRRELL.

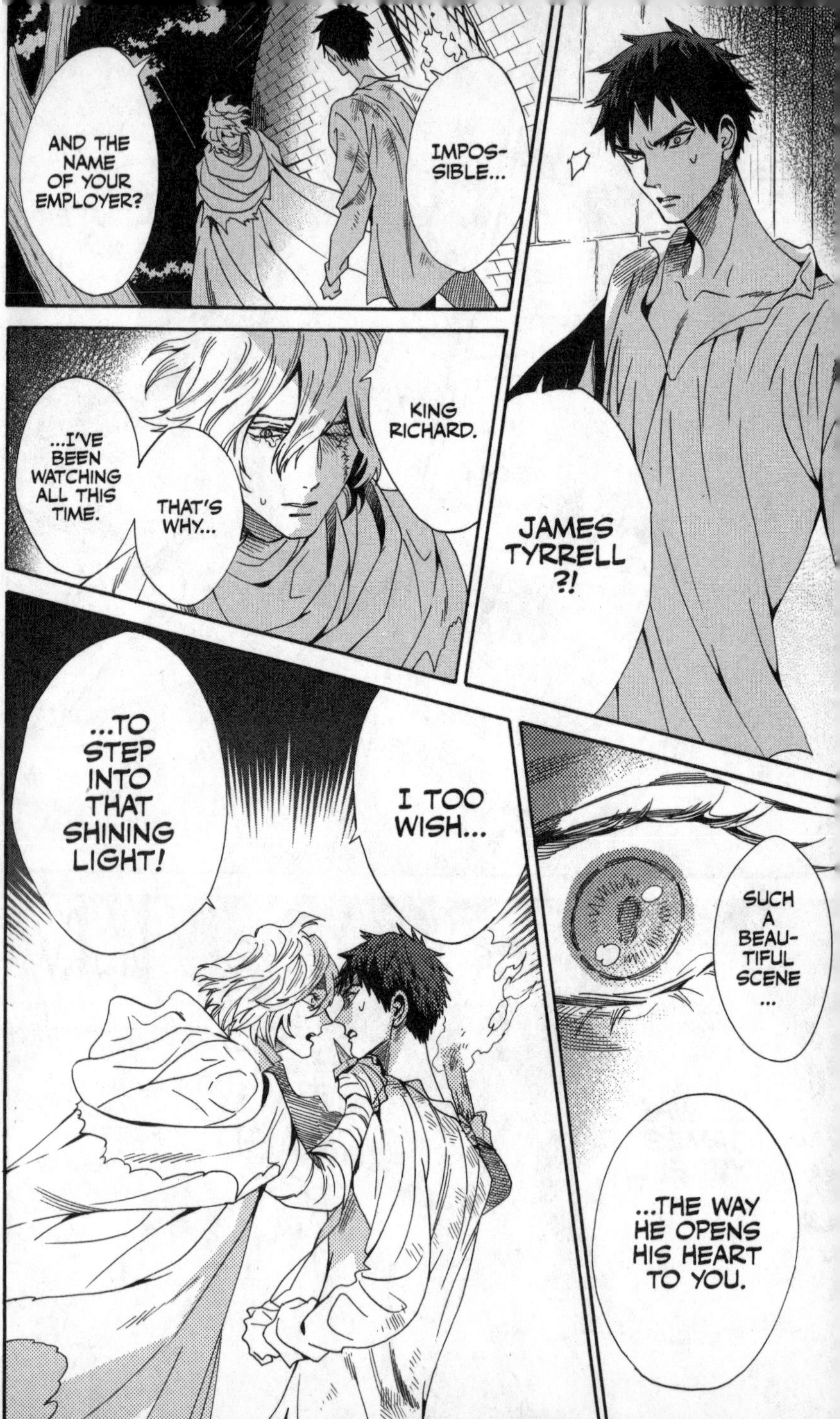
JAMES TYRRELL ?!
IMPOS- SIBLE...
AND THE NAME OF YOUR EMPLOYER?
KING RICHARD.
...I'VE BEEN WATCHING ALL THIS TIME.
THAT'S WHY...
SUCH A BEAU- TIFUL SCENE ...
...THE WAY HE OPENS HIS HEART TO YOU.
I TOO WISH...
...TO STEP INTO THAT SHINING LIGHT!

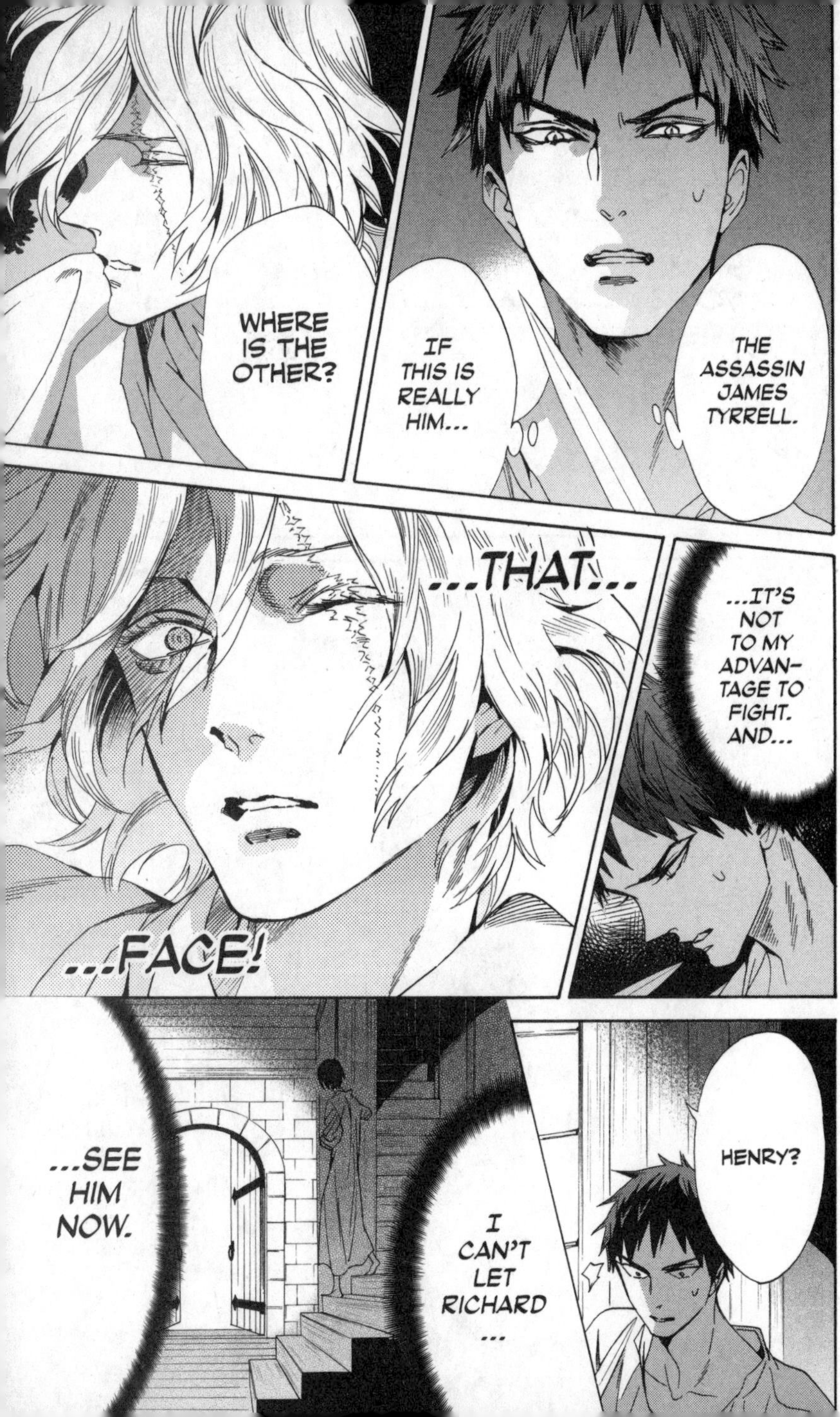
THE ASSASSIN JAMES TYRRELL.
IF THIS IS REALLY HIM...
WHERE IS THE OTHER?
...IT'S NOT TO MY ADVANTAGE TO FIGHT. AND...
...THAT...
...FACE!
HENRY?
I CAN'T LET RICHARD ...
...SEE HIM NOW.

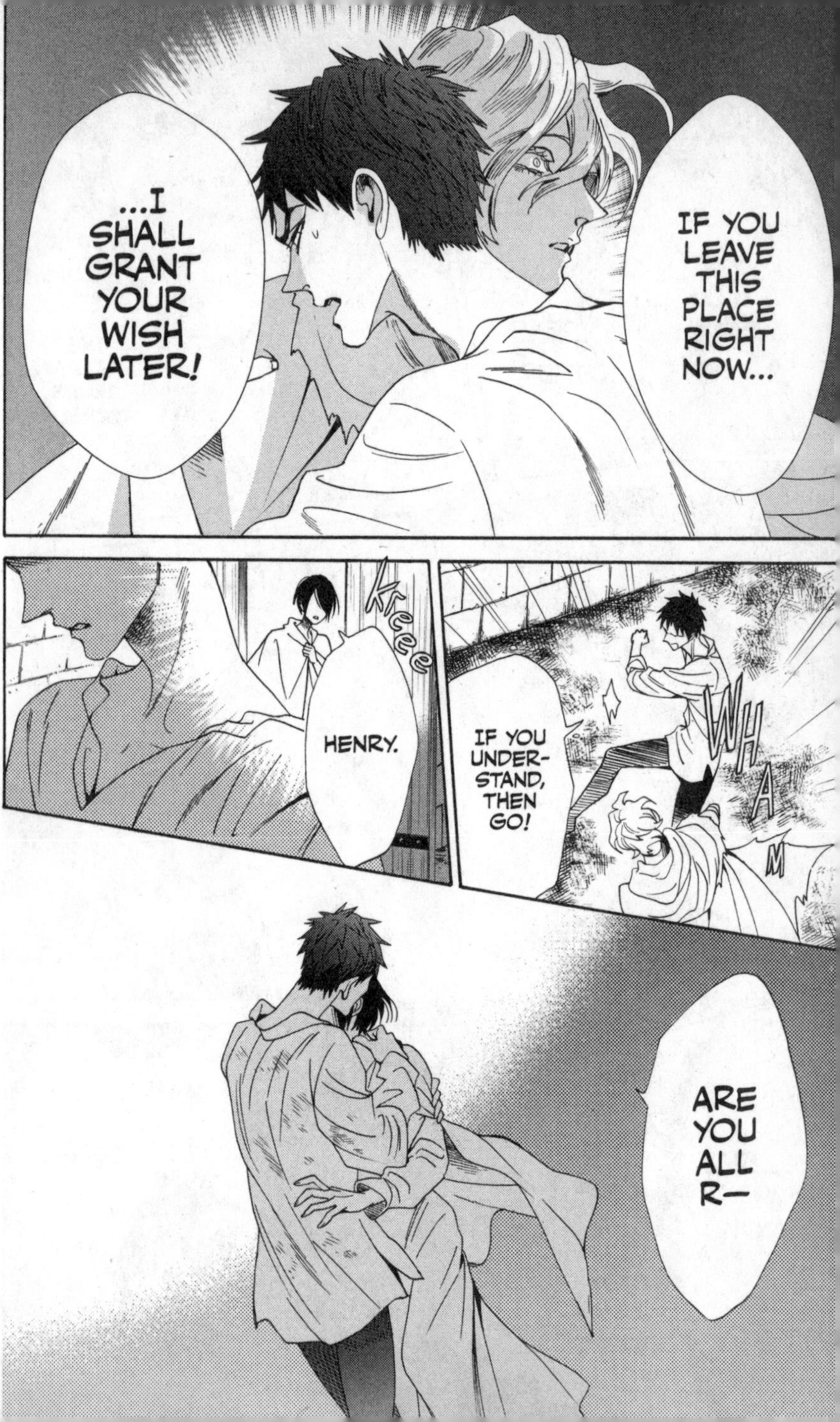
IF YOU LEAVE THIS PLACE RIGHT NOW...
...I SHALL GRANT YOUR WISH LATER!
WHAM
IF YOU UNDER-STAND, THEN GO!
kreee
HENRY.
ARE YOU ALL R—

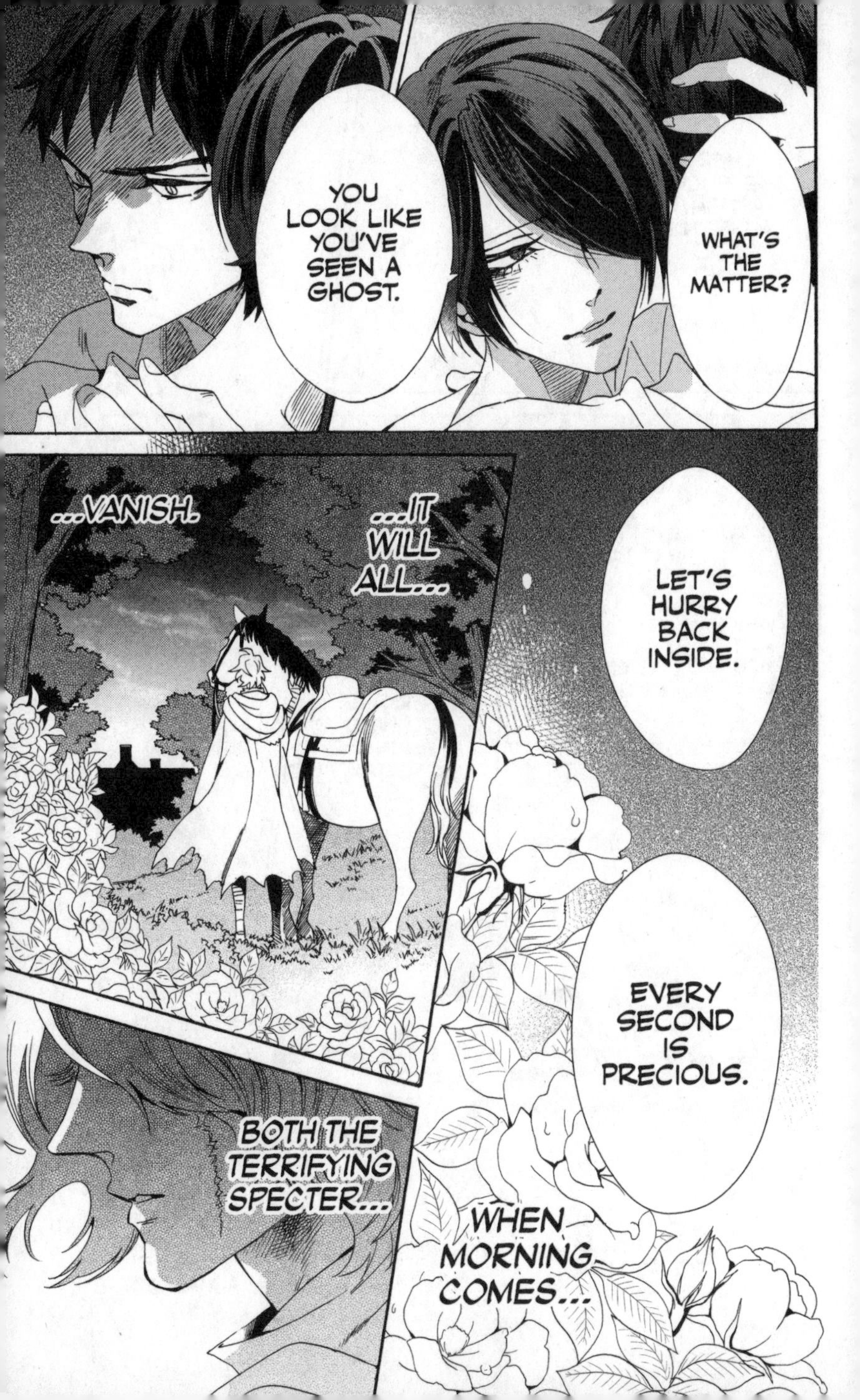
WHAT'S THE MATTER?
YOU LOOK LIKE YOU'VE SEEN A GHOST.
LET'S HURRY BACK INSIDE.
EVERY SECOND IS PRECIOUS.
WHEN MORNING COMES...
BOTH THE TERRIFYING SPECTER...
...IT WILL ALL...
...VANISH.

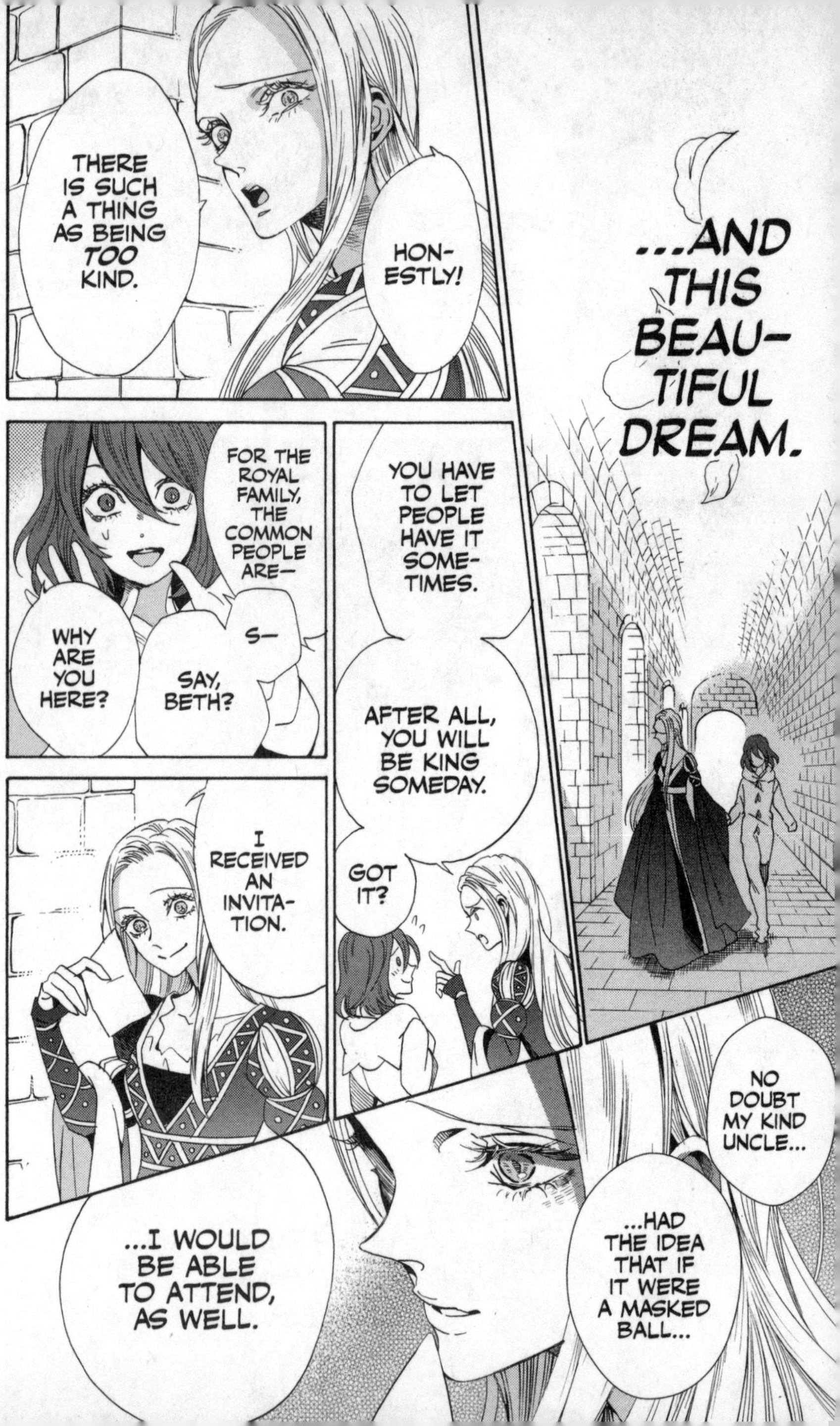
...AND THIS BEAUTIFUL DREAM.
HON-ESTLY!
THERE IS SUCH A THING AS BEING *TOO* KIND.
YOU HAVE TO LET PEOPLE HAVE IT SOME-TIMES.
AFTER ALL, YOU WILL BE KING SOMEDAY.
GOT IT?
FOR THE ROYAL FAMILY, THE COMMON PEOPLE ARE—
S—
SAY, BETH?
WHY ARE YOU HERE?
I RECEIVED AN INVITA-TION.
NO DOUBT MY KIND UNCLE...
...HAD THE IDEA THAT IF IT WERE A MASKED BALL...
...I WOULD BE ABLE TO ATTEND, AS WELL.

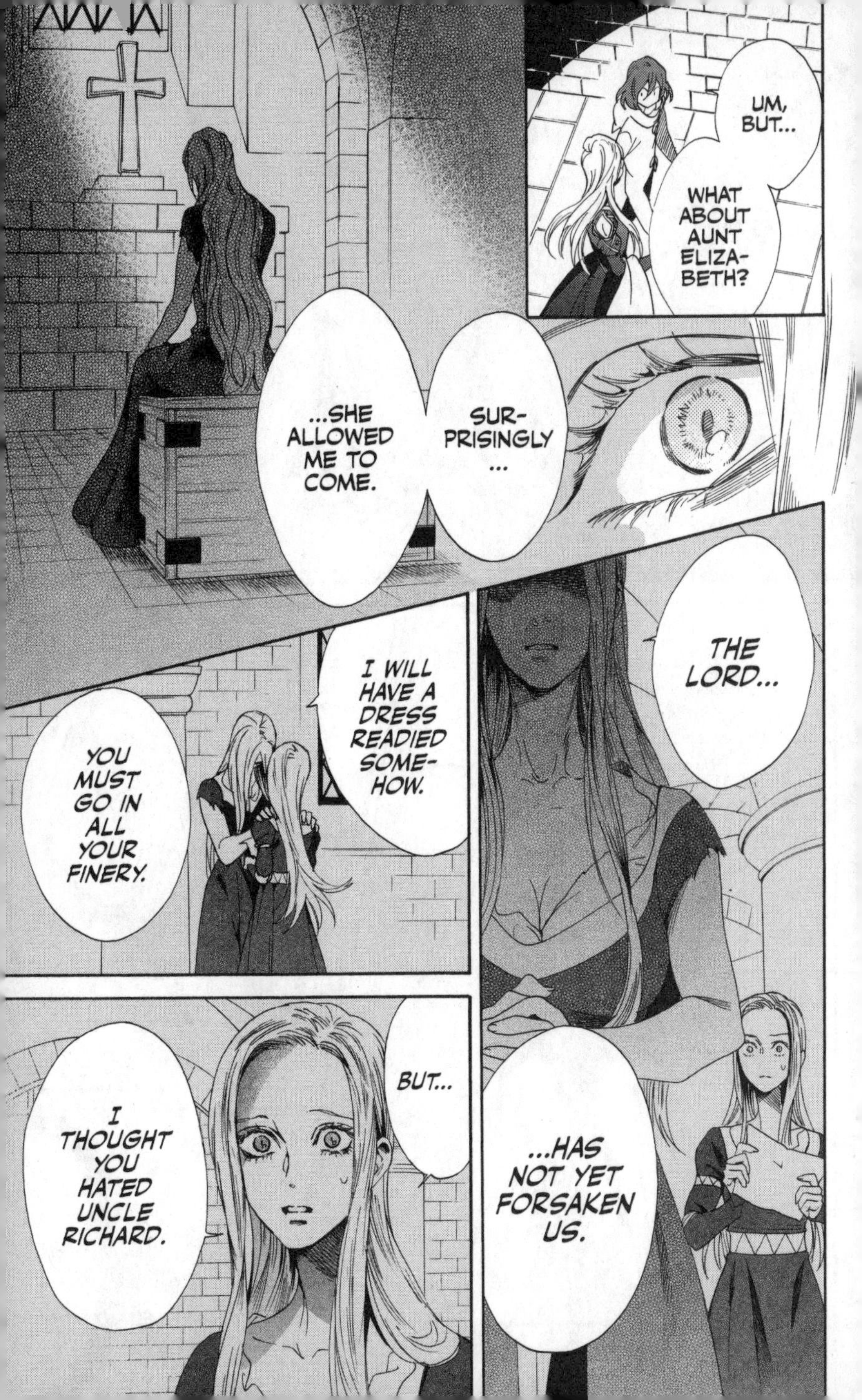
UM, BUT...
WHAT ABOUT AUNT ELIZA-BETH?
SUR-PRISINGLY ...
...SHE ALLOWED ME TO COME.
THE LORD...
...HAS NOT YET FORSAKEN US.
I WILL HAVE A DRESS READIED SOME-HOW.
YOU MUST GO IN ALL YOUR FINERY.
BUT...
I THOUGHT YOU HATED UNCLE RICHARD.

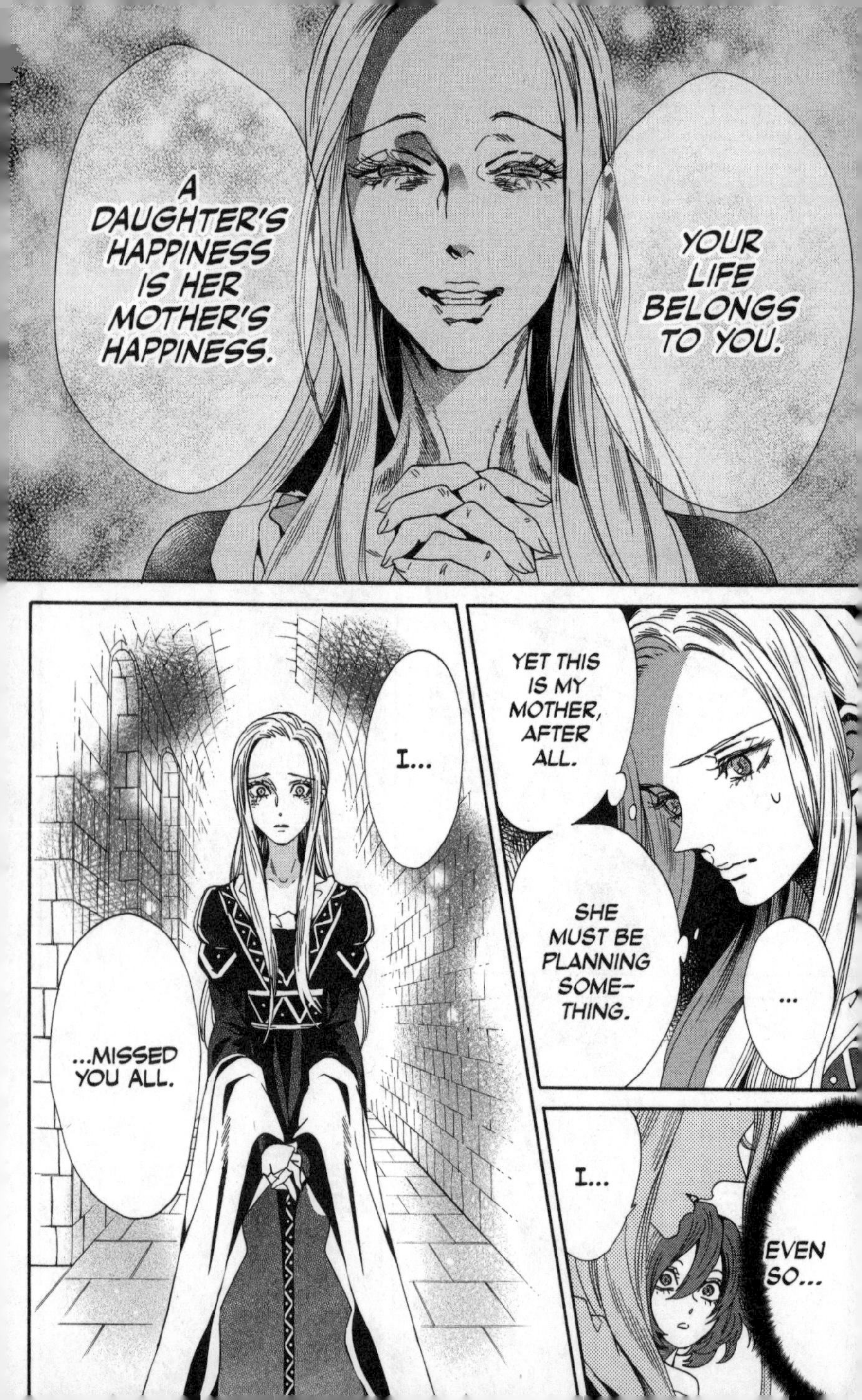
YOUR LIFE BELONGS TO YOU.
A DAUGHTER'S HAPPINESS IS HER MOTHER'S HAPPINESS.
YET THIS IS MY MOTHER, AFTER ALL.
SHE MUST BE PLANNING SOME-THING.
...
EVEN SO...
I...
I...
...MISSED YOU ALL.

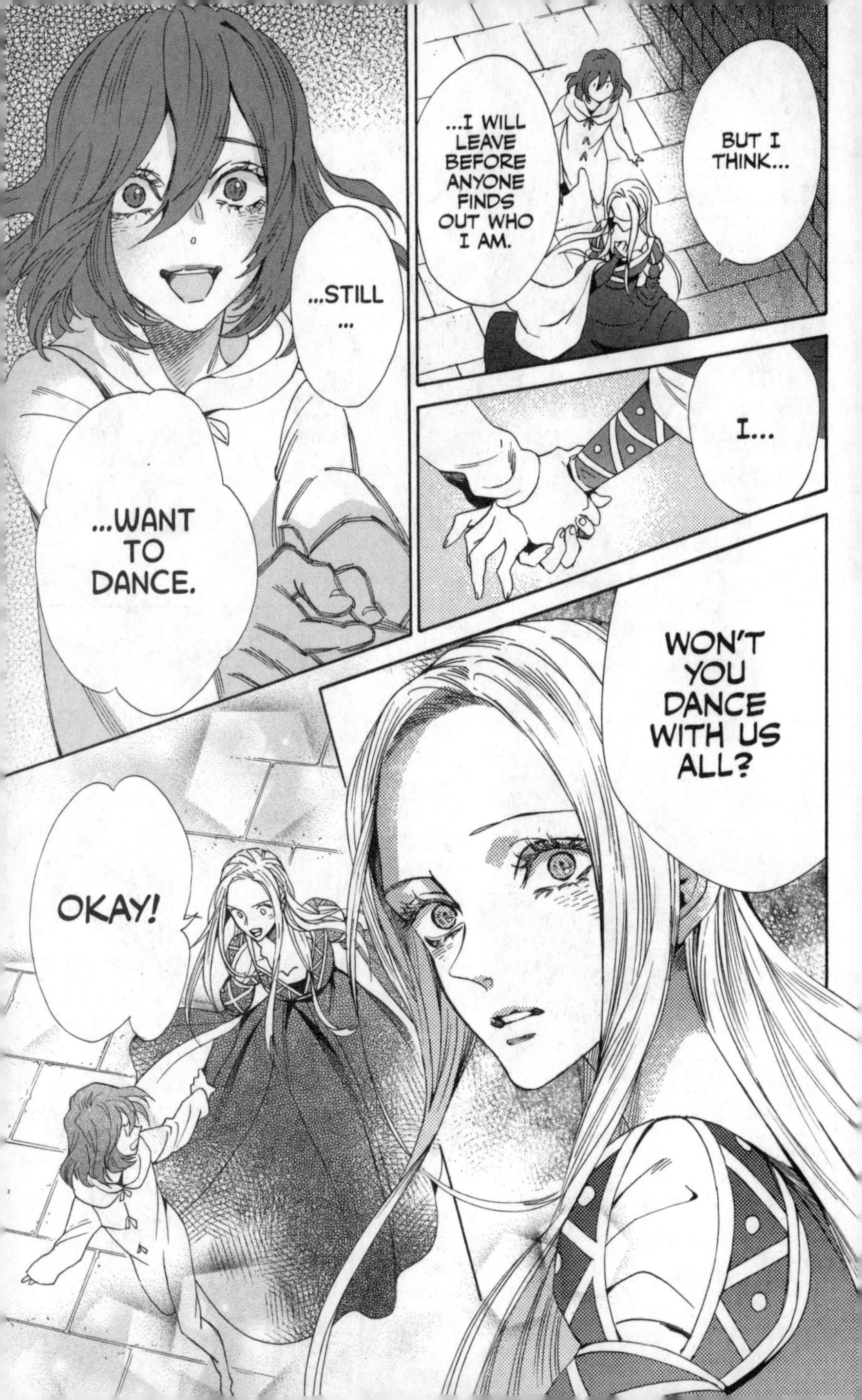

BUT I THINK...
...I WILL LEAVE BEFORE ANYONE FINDS OUT WHO I AM.
I...
...STILL ...
...WANT TO DANCE.
WON'T YOU DANCE WITH US ALL?
OKAY!

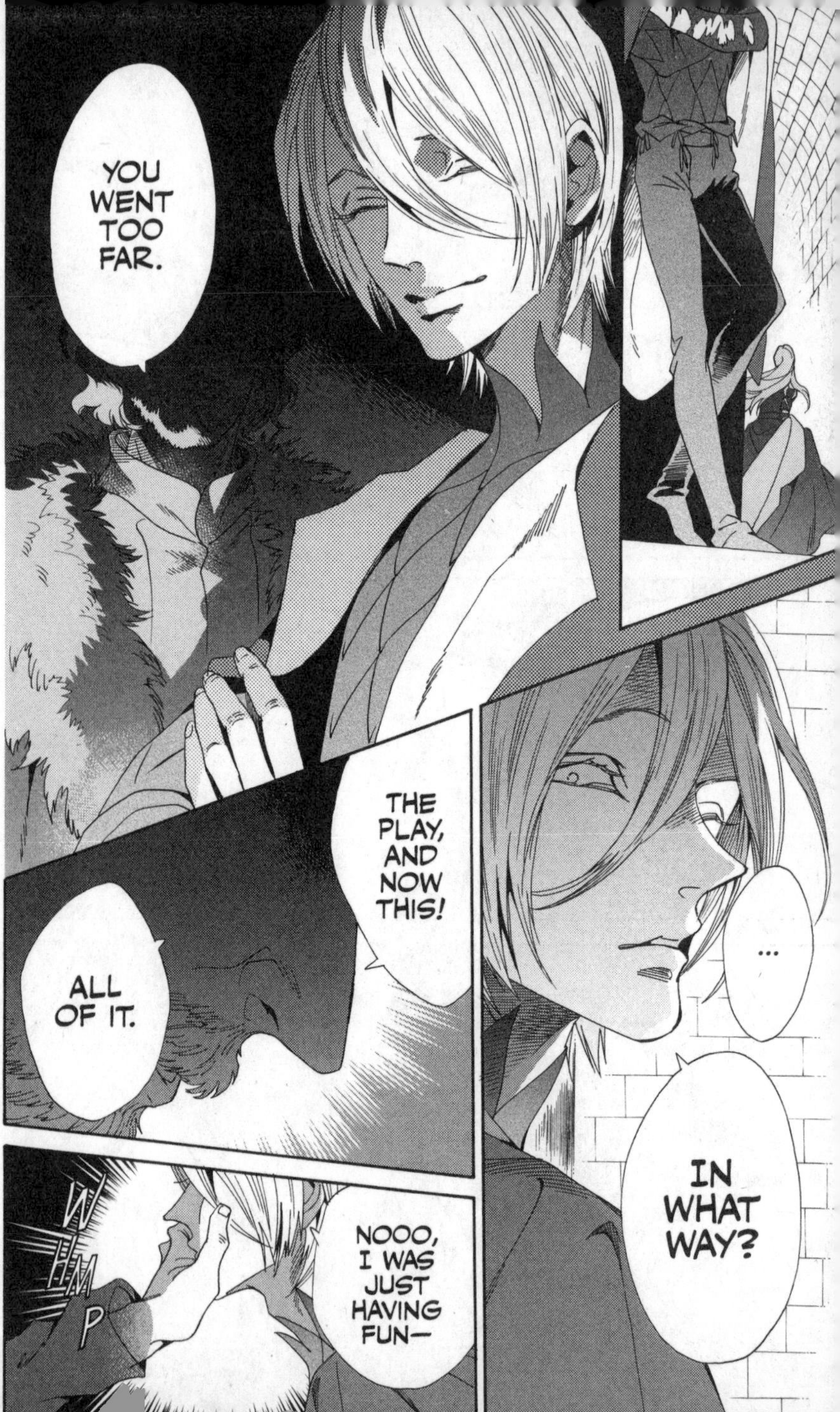
YOU WENT TOO FAR.
...
IN WHAT WAY?
THE PLAY, AND NOW THIS!
ALL OF IT.
NOOO, I WAS JUST HAVING FUN—
WHMP

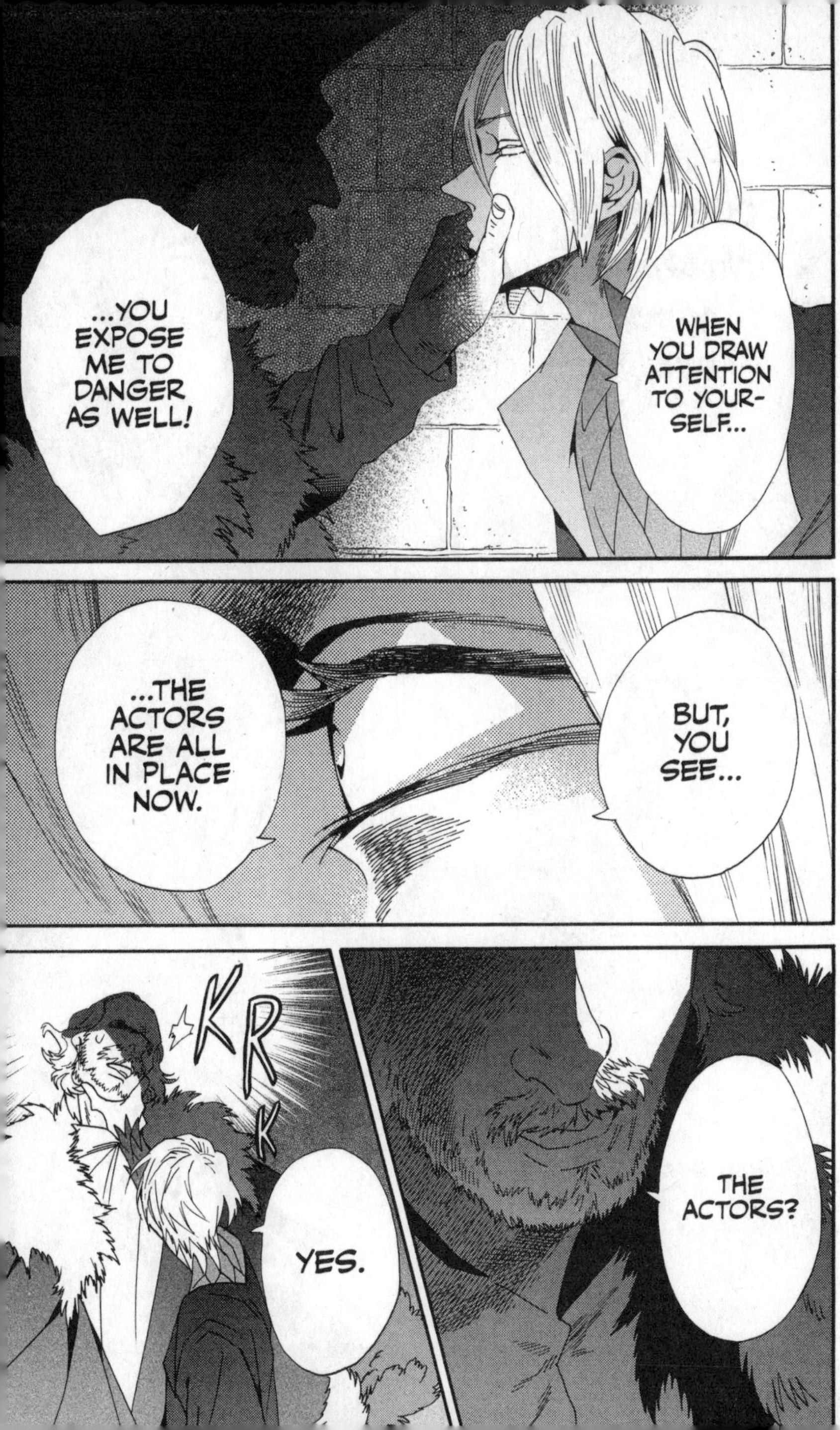
WHEN YOU DRAW ATTENTION TO YOUR-SELF...
...YOU EXPOSE ME TO DANGER AS WELL!
BUT, YOU SEE...
...THE ACTORS ARE ALL IN PLACE NOW.
THE ACTORS?
KRK
YES.

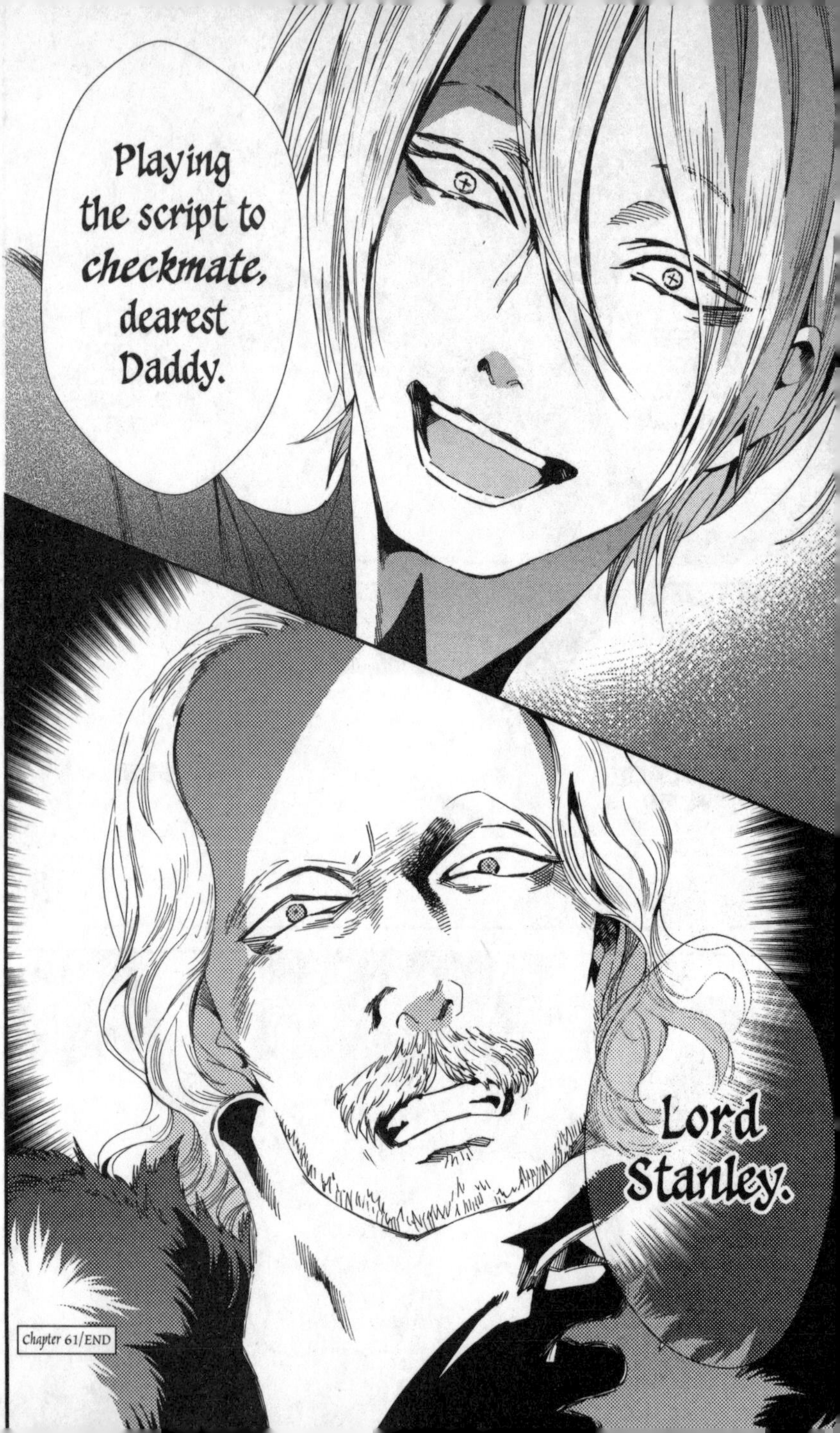
Playing the script to checkmate, dearest Daddy.
Lord Stanley.
Chapter 61/END

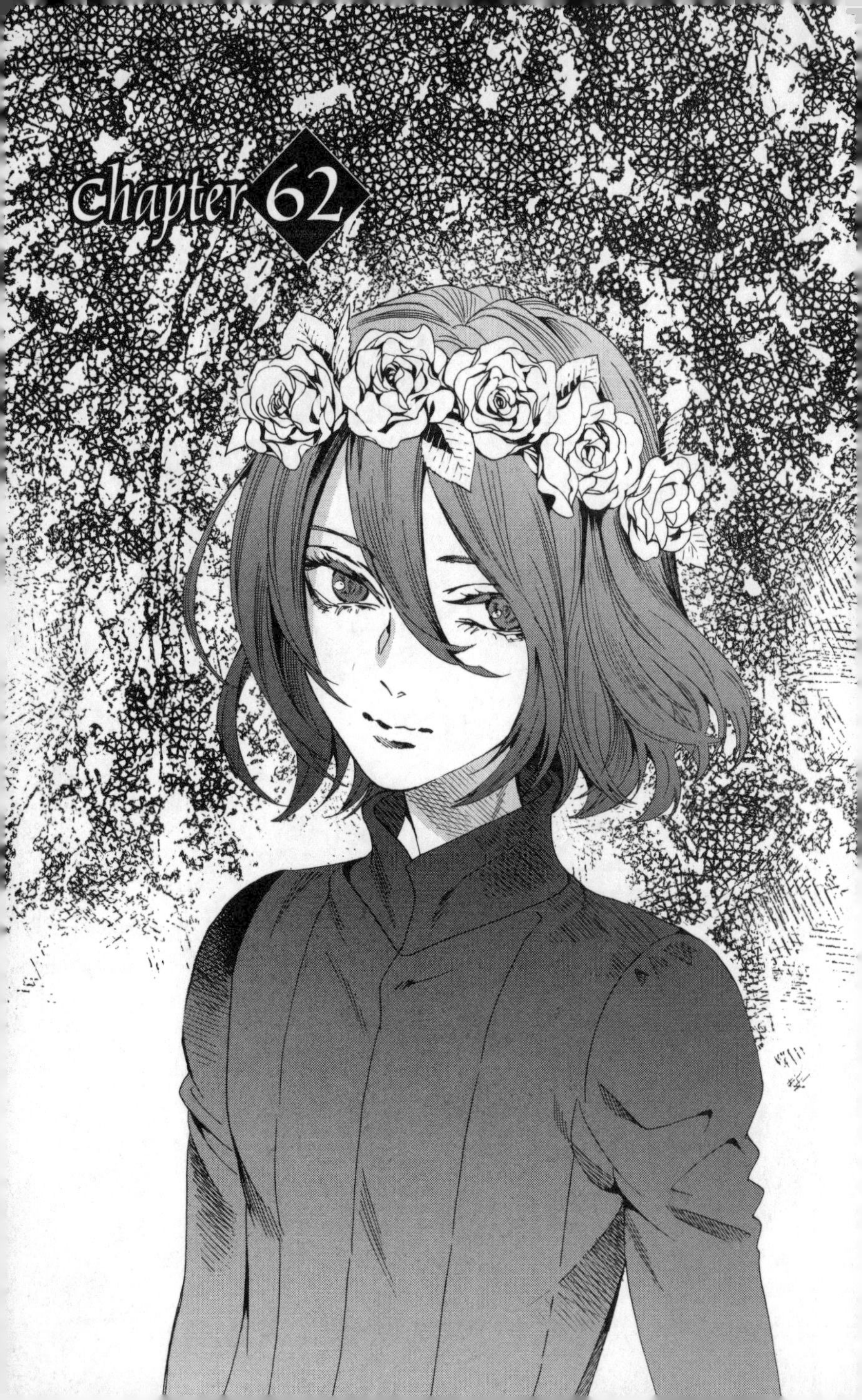
Chapter 62

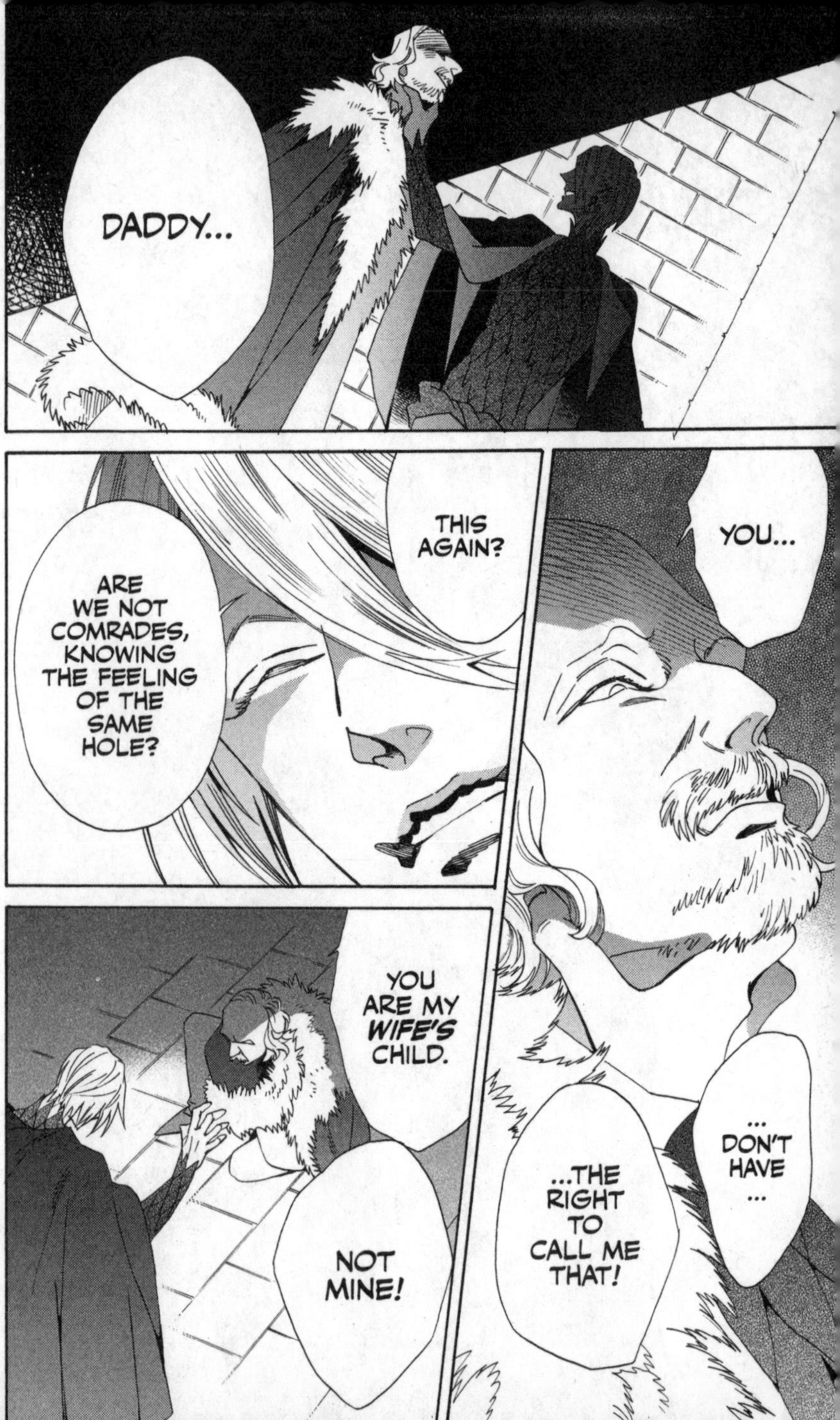
DADDY...
YOU...
... DON'T HAVE ...
...THE RIGHT TO CALL ME THAT!
THIS AGAIN?
ARE WE NOT COMRADES, KNOWING THE FEELING OF THE SAME HOLE?
YOU ARE MY *WIFE'S* CHILD.
NOT MINE!

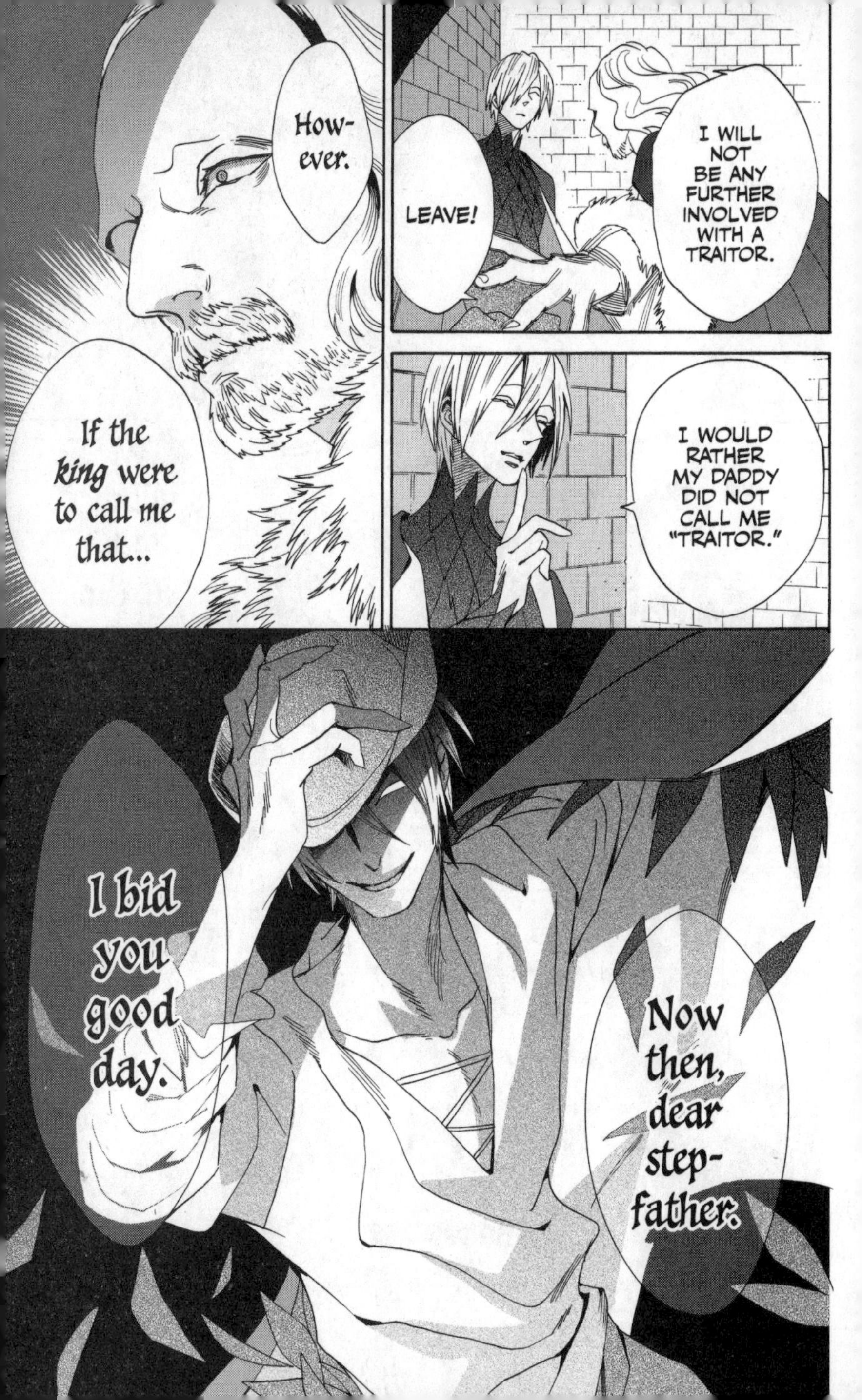
I WILL NOT BE ANY FURTHER INVOLVED WITH A TRAITOR.
LEAVE!
I WOULD RATHER MY DADDY DID NOT CALL ME "TRAITOR."
However.
If the *king* were to call me that...
Now then, dear stepfather.
I bid you good day.

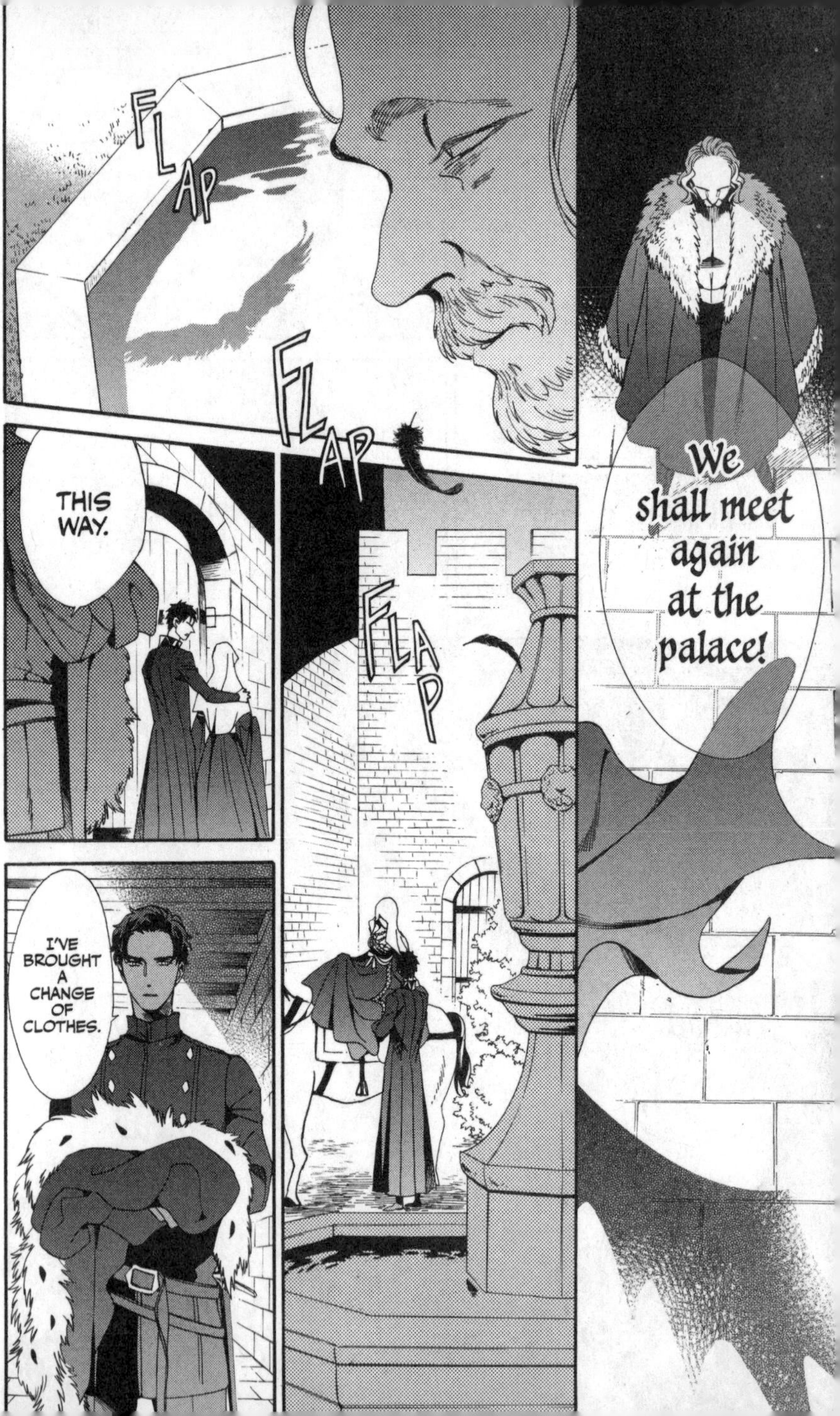
We shall meet again at the palace!
FLAP
FLAP
FLAP
THIS WAY.
I'VE BROUGHT A CHANGE OF CLOTHES.

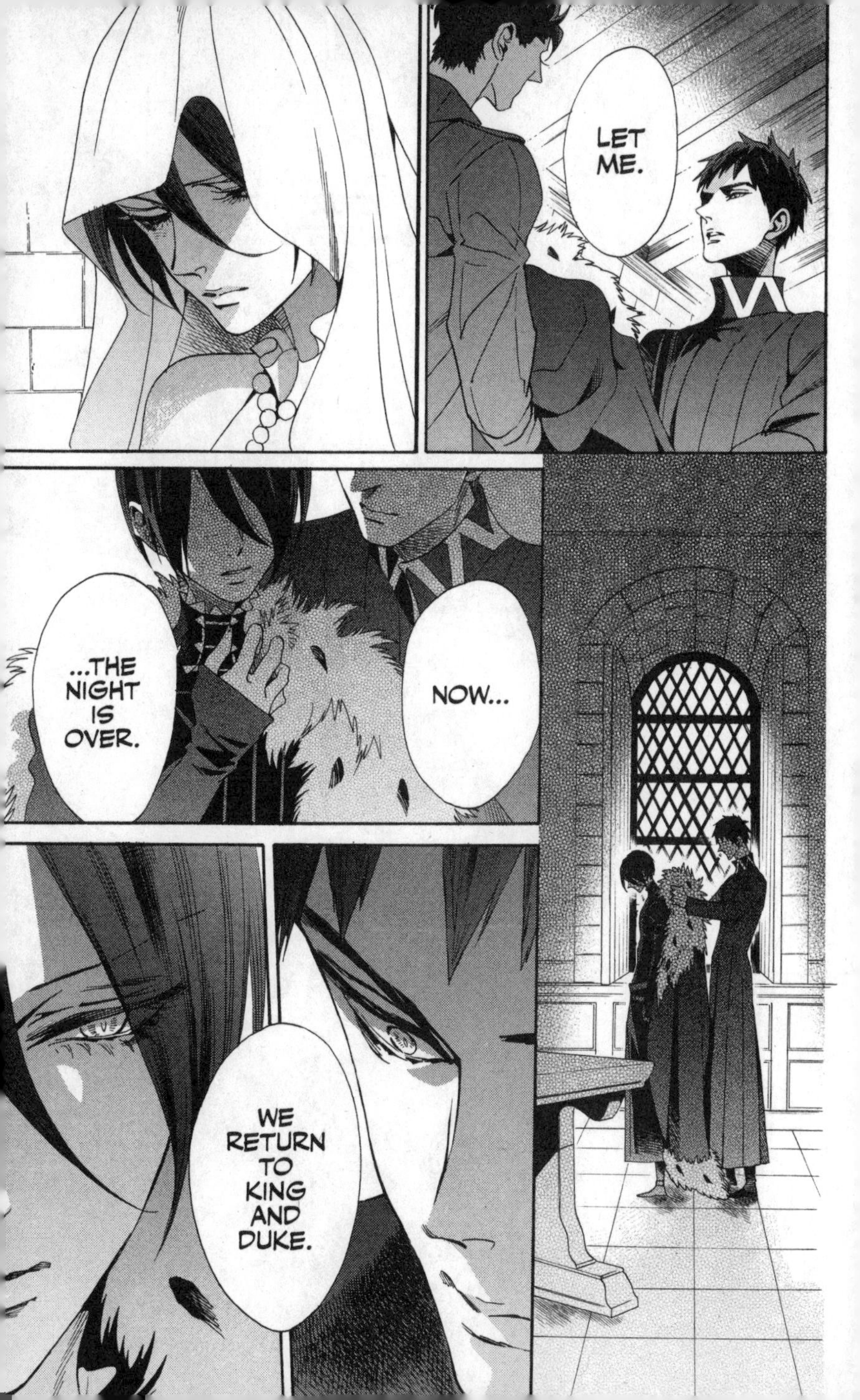
LET ME.
NOW...
...THE NIGHT IS OVER.
WE RETURN TO KING AND DUKE.

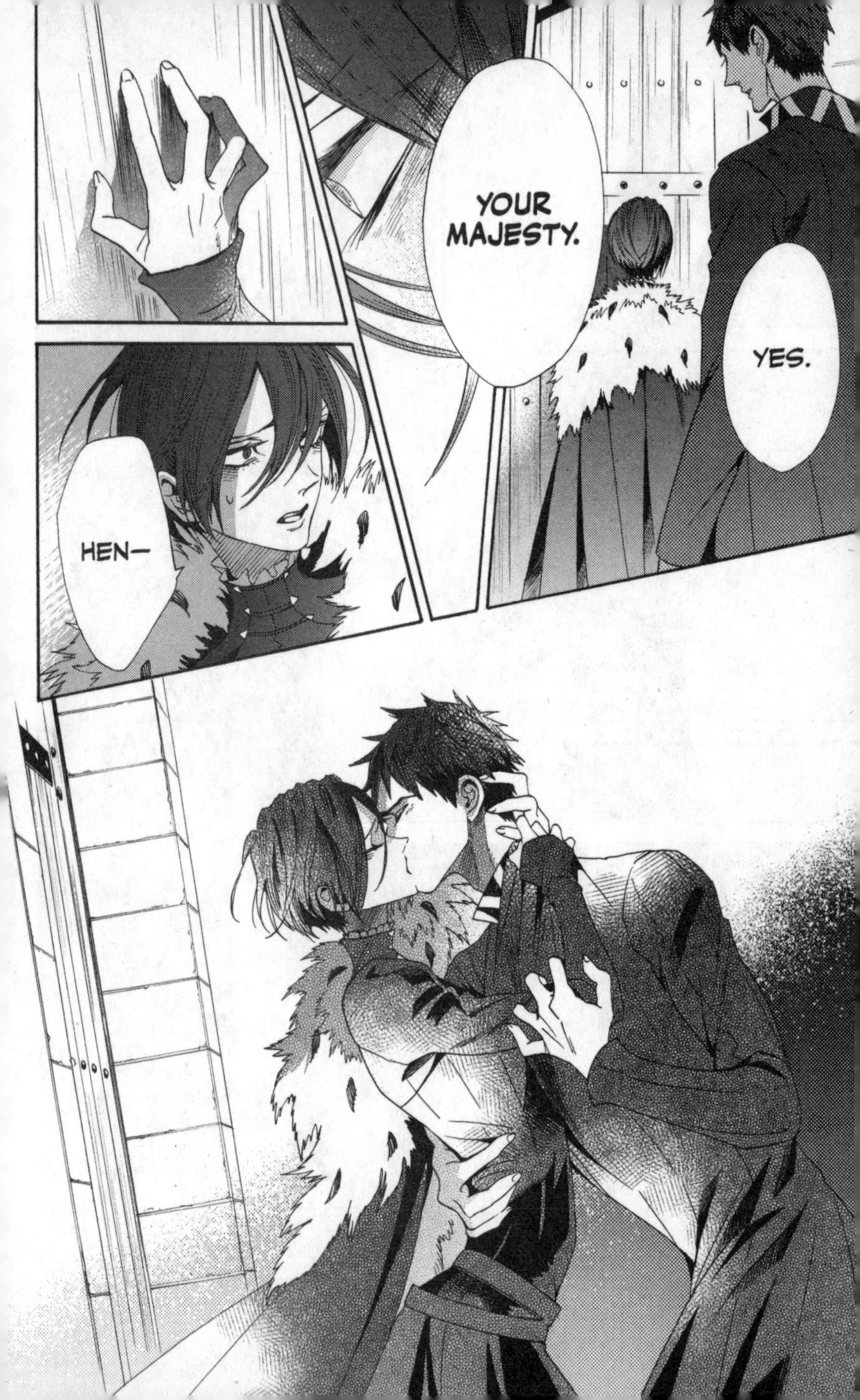
YOUR MAJESTY.
YES.
HEN—

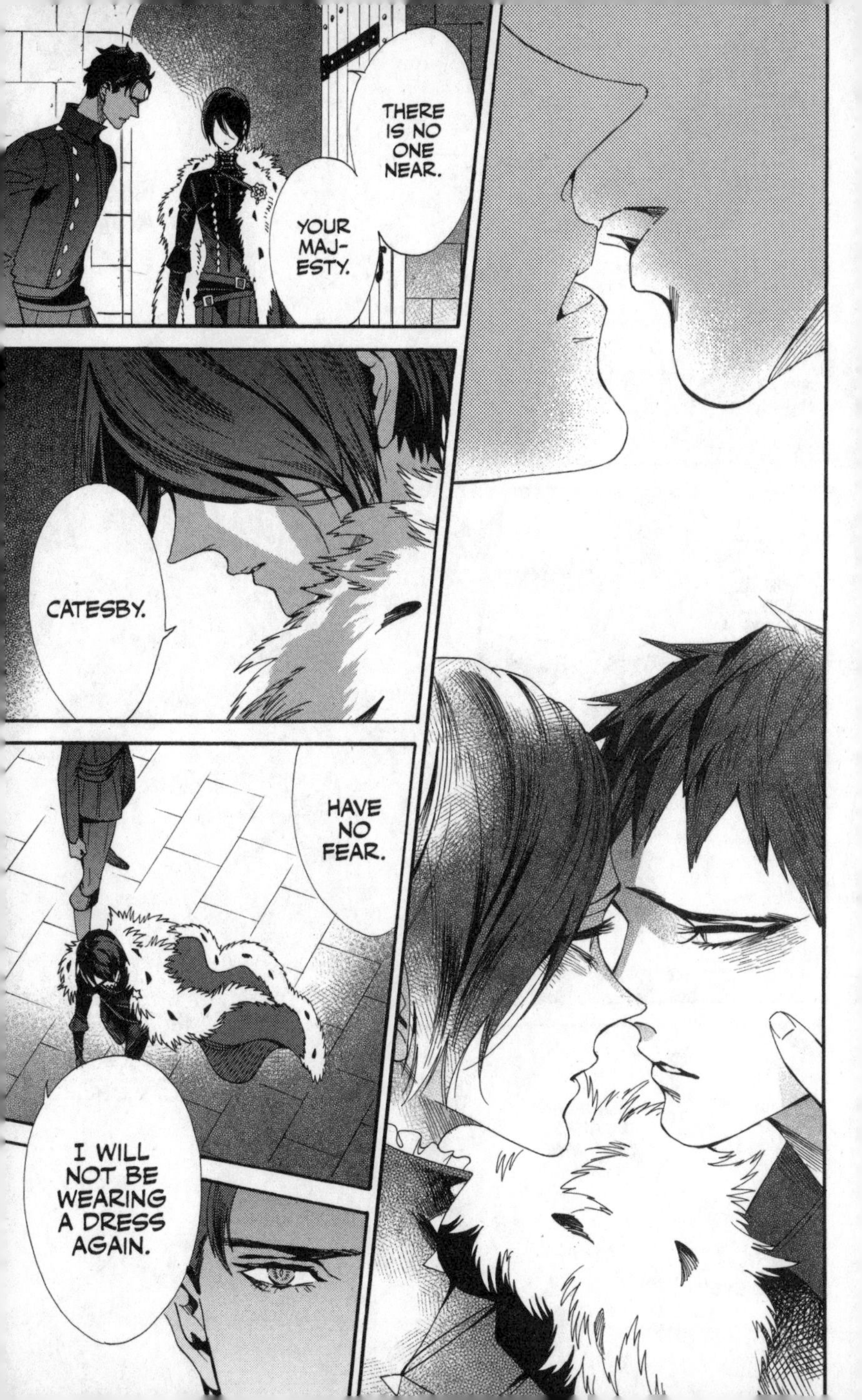
THERE IS NO ONE NEAR.
YOUR MAJESTY.
CATESBY.
HAVE NO FEAR.
I WILL NOT BE WEARING A DRESS AGAIN.

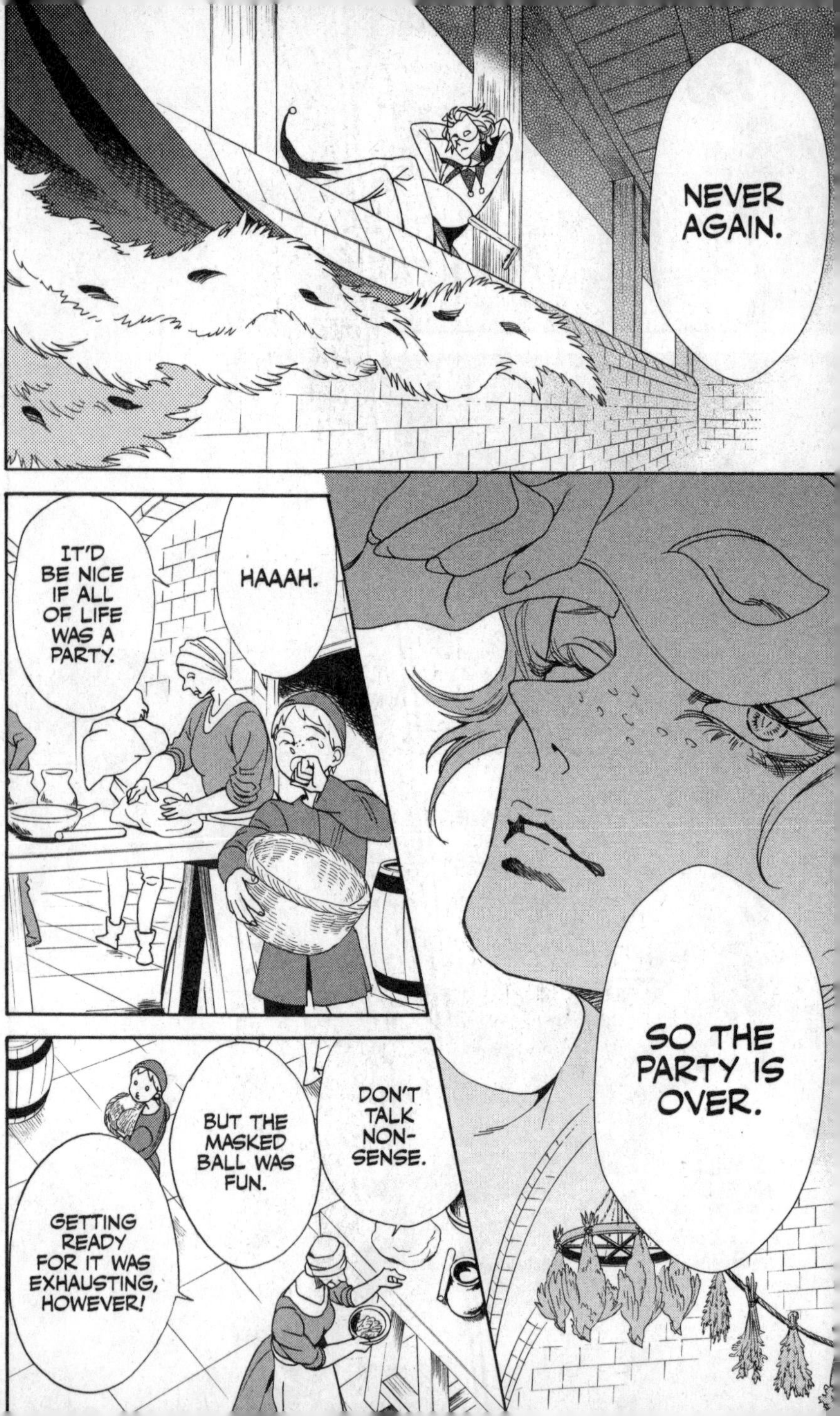
NEVER AGAIN.
SO THE PARTY IS OVER.
HAAAH.
IT'D BE NICE IF ALL OF LIFE WAS A PARTY.
DON'T TALK NON-SENSE.
BUT THE MASKED BALL WAS FUN.
GETTING READY FOR IT WAS EXHAUSTING, HOWEVER!

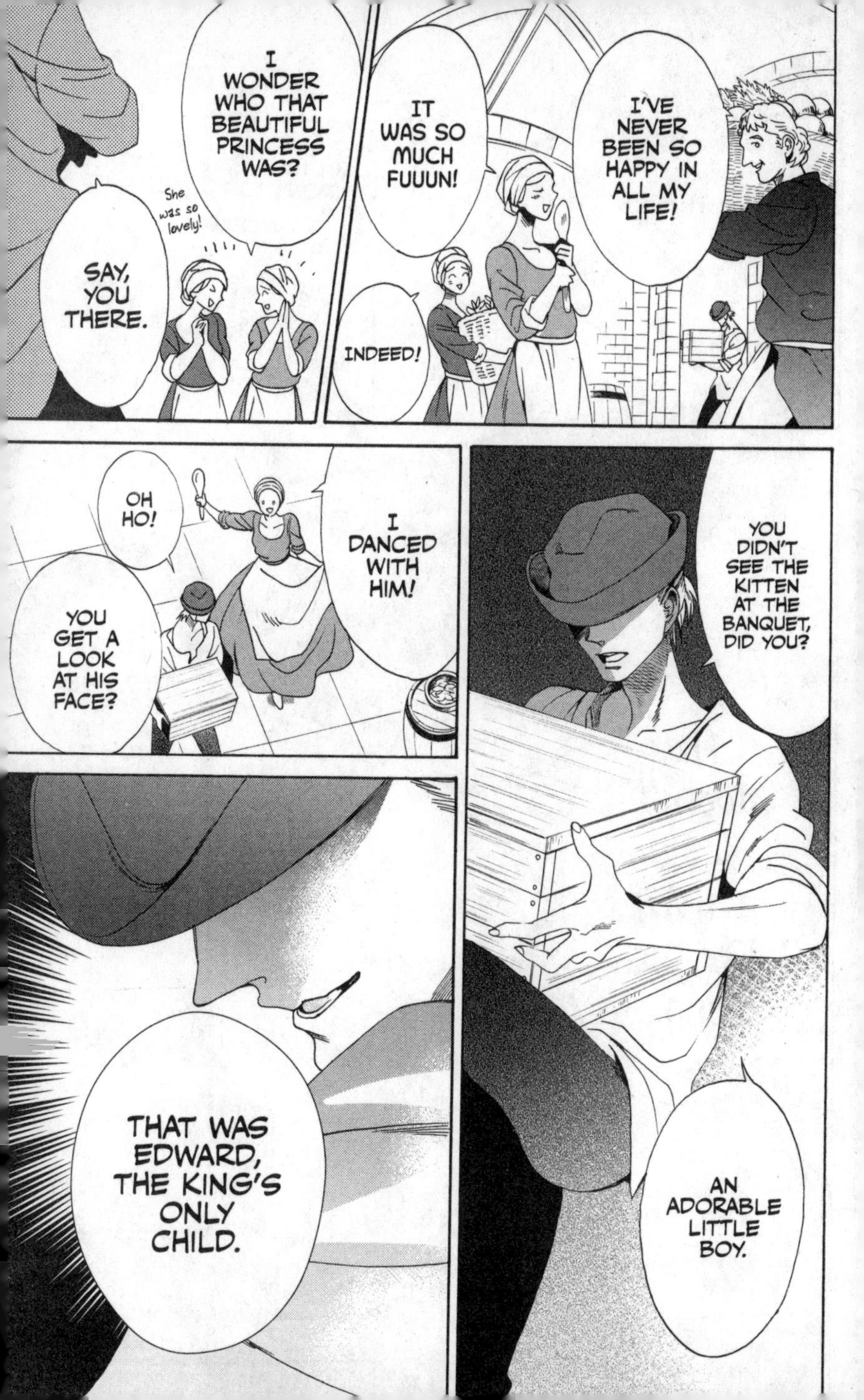
I'VE NEVER BEEN SO HAPPY IN ALL MY LIFE!
IT WAS SO MUCH FUUUN!
INDEED!
I WONDER WHO THAT BEAUTIFUL PRINCESS WAS?
She was so lovely!
SAY, YOU THERE.
YOU DIDN'T SEE THE KITTEN AT THE BANQUET, DID YOU?
AN ADORABLE LITTLE BOY.
I DANCED WITH HIM!
OH HO!
YOU GET A LOOK AT HIS FACE?
THAT WAS EDWARD, THE KING'S ONLY CHILD.

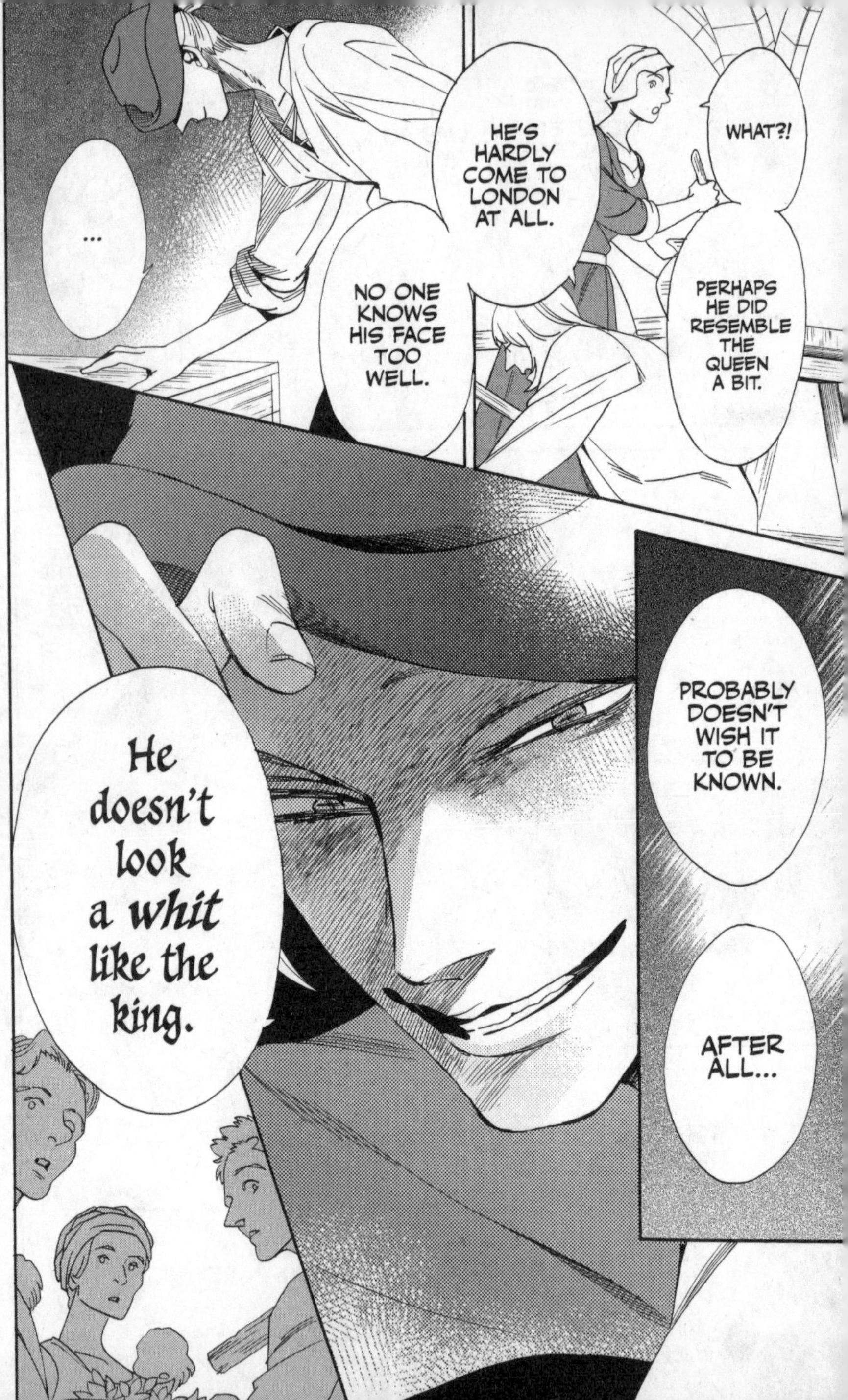
WHAT?!
PERHAPS HE DID RESEMBLE THE QUEEN A BIT.
HE'S HARDLY COME TO LONDON AT ALL.
NO ONE KNOWS HIS FACE TOO WELL.
...
PROBABLY DOESN'T WISH IT TO BE KNOWN.
AFTER ALL...
He doesn't look a *whit* like the king.

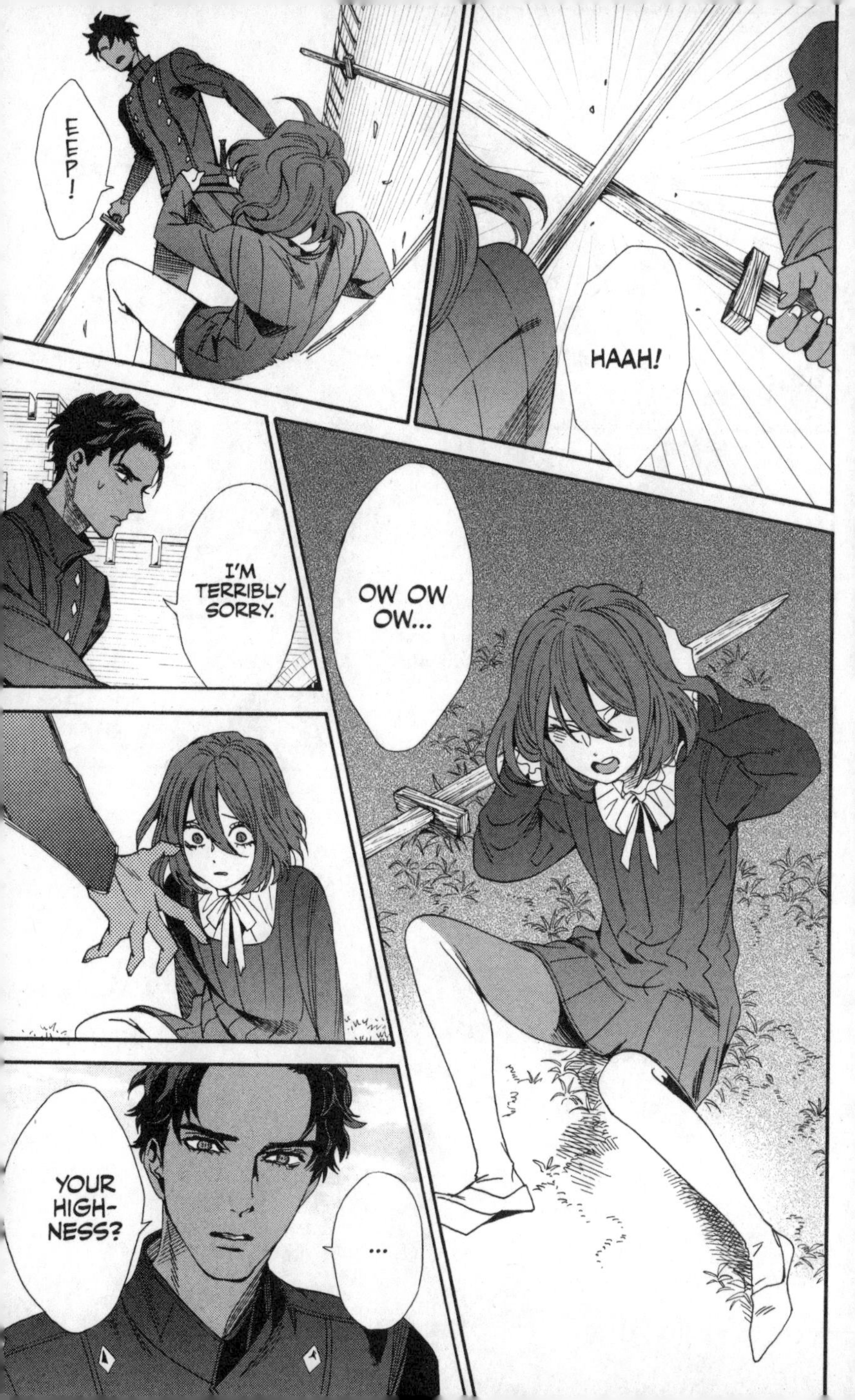
HAAH!
EEP!
OW OW OW...
I'M TERRIBLY SORRY.
YOUR HIGHNESS?
...

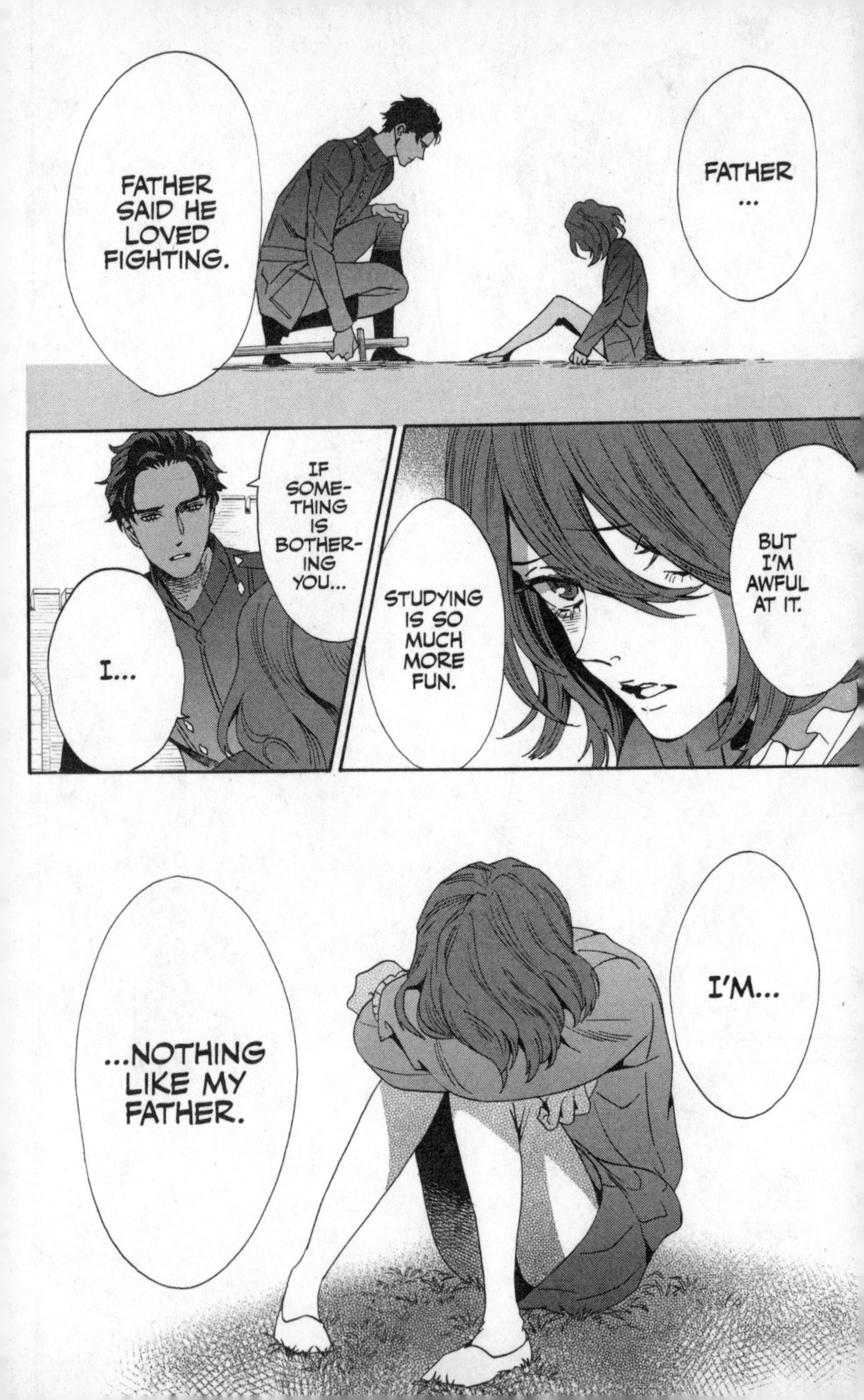
FATHER ...
FATHER SAID HE LOVED FIGHTING.
BUT I'M AWFUL AT IT.
STUDYING IS SO MUCH MORE FUN.
IF SOME-THING IS BOTHER-ING YOU...
I...
I'M...
...NOTHING LIKE MY FATHER.

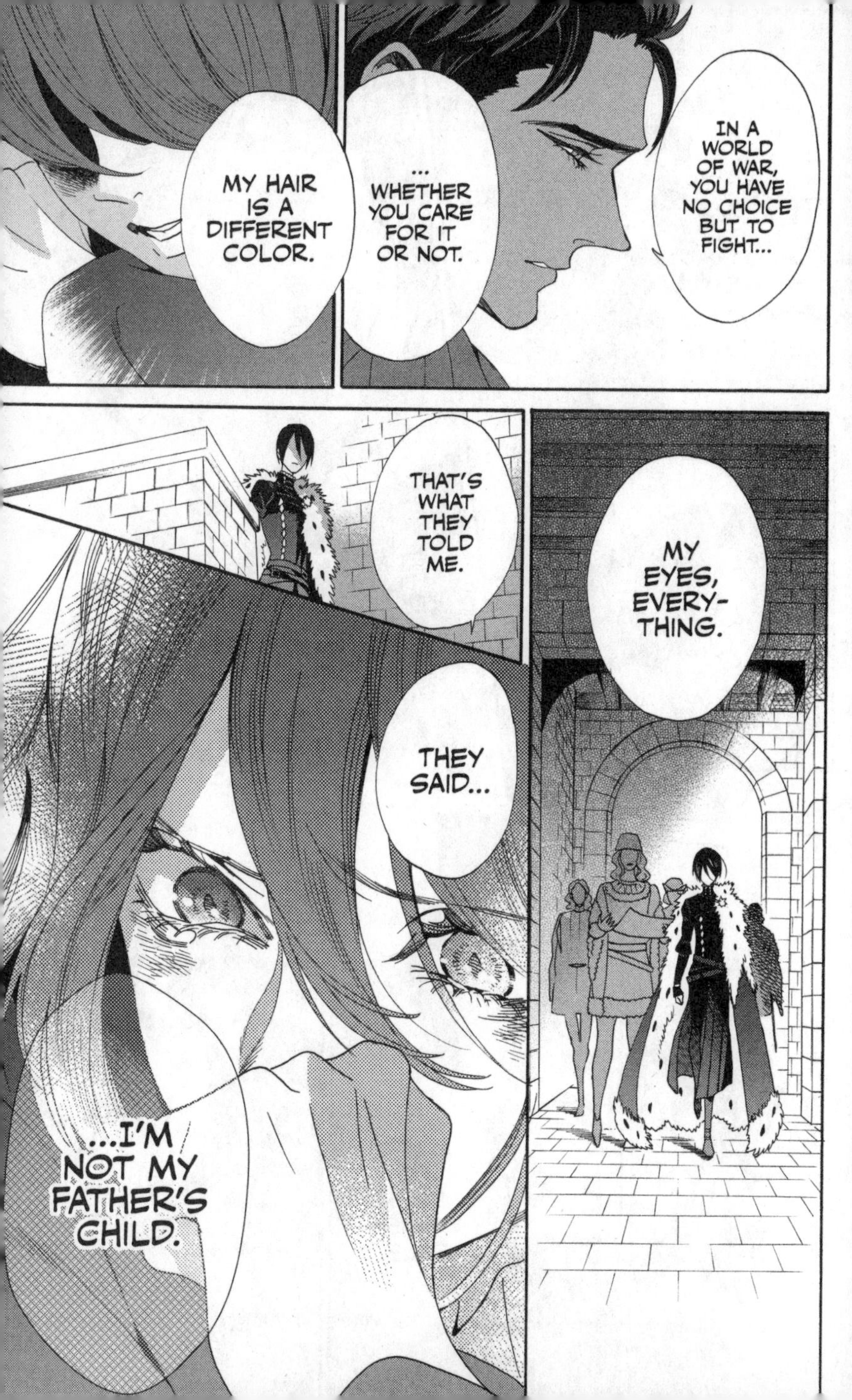
IN A WORLD OF WAR, YOU HAVE NO CHOICE BUT TO FIGHT...
...WHETHER YOU CARE FOR IT OR NOT.
MY HAIR IS A DIFFERENT COLOR.
MY EYES, EVERYTHING.
THAT'S WHAT THEY TOLD ME.
THEY SAID...
...I'M NOT MY FATHER'S CHILD.

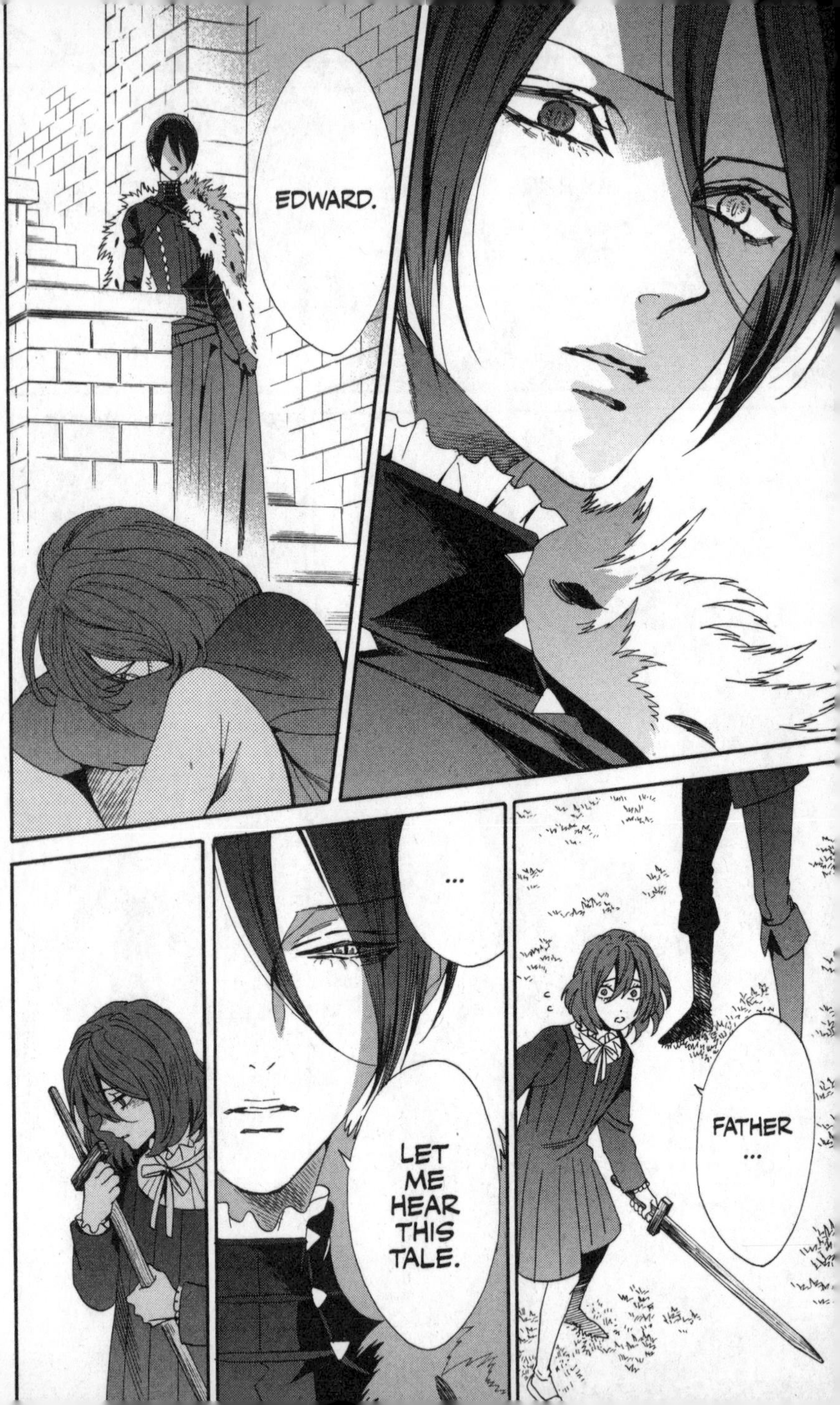
EDWARD.
FATHER ...
...
LET ME HEAR THIS TALE.

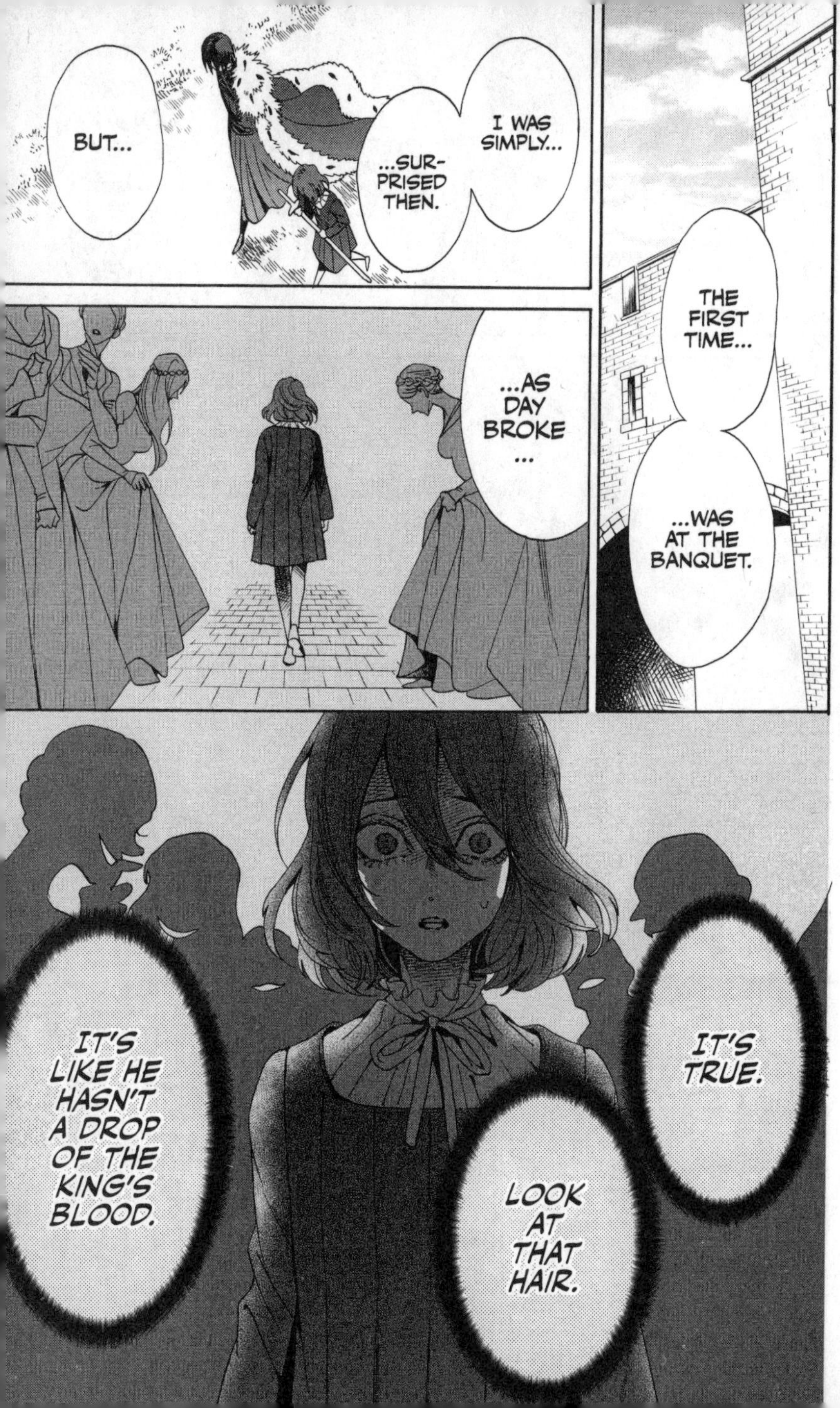
THE FIRST TIME...
...WAS AT THE BANQUET.
I WAS SIMPLY...
...SUR-PRISED THEN.
BUT...
...AS DAY BROKE...
IT'S TRUE.
LOOK AT THAT HAIR.
IT'S LIKE HE HASN'T A DROP OF THE KING'S BLOOD.

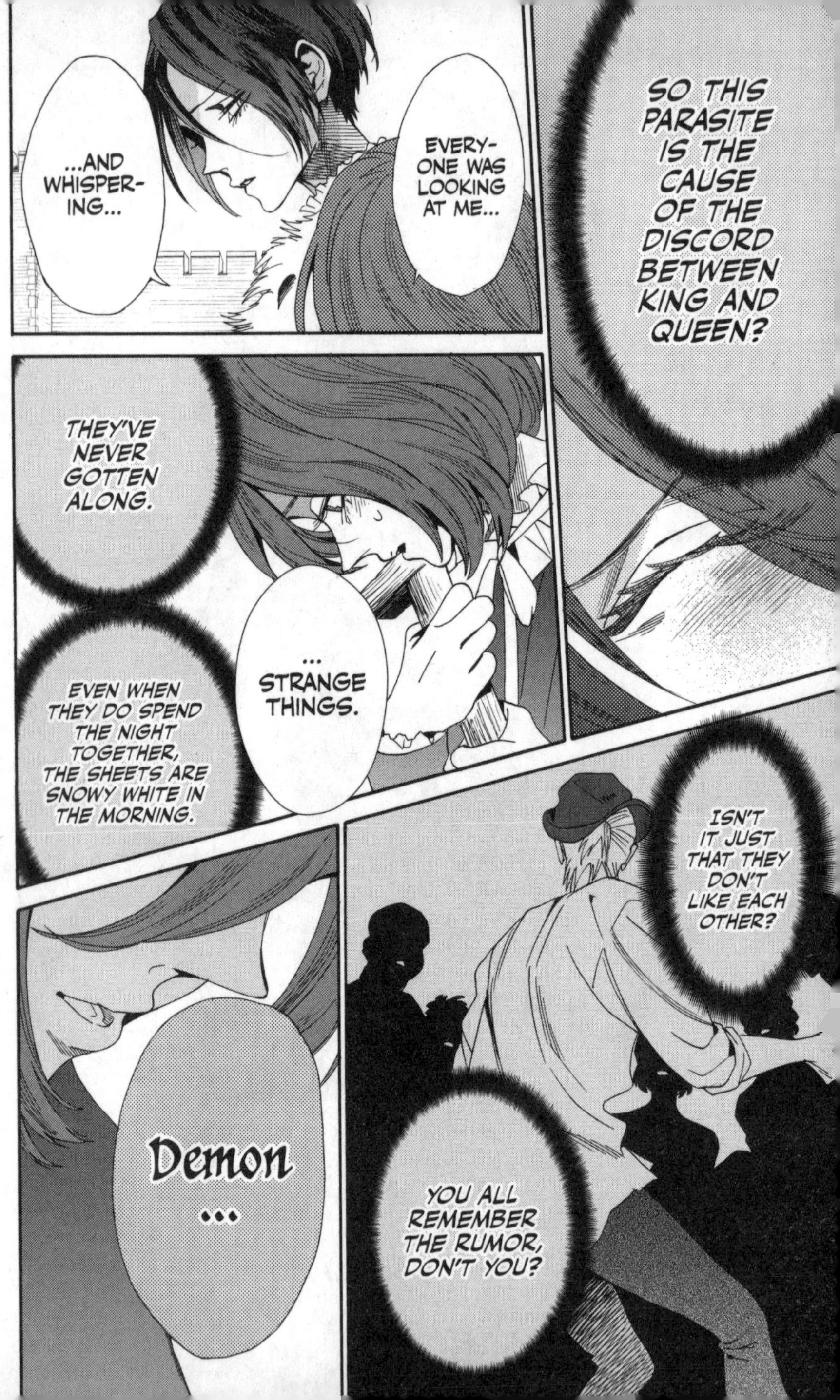
SO THIS PARASITE IS THE CAUSE OF THE DISCORD BETWEEN KING AND QUEEN?
EVERY-ONE WAS LOOKING AT ME...
...AND WHISPER-ING...
THEY'VE NEVER GOTTEN ALONG.
... STRANGE THINGS.
EVEN WHEN THEY DO SPEND THE NIGHT TOGETHER, THE SHEETS ARE SNOWY WHITE IN THE MORNING.
ISN'T IT JUST THAT THEY DON'T LIKE EACH OTHER?
YOU ALL REMEMBER THE RUMOR, DON'T YOU?
Demon ...

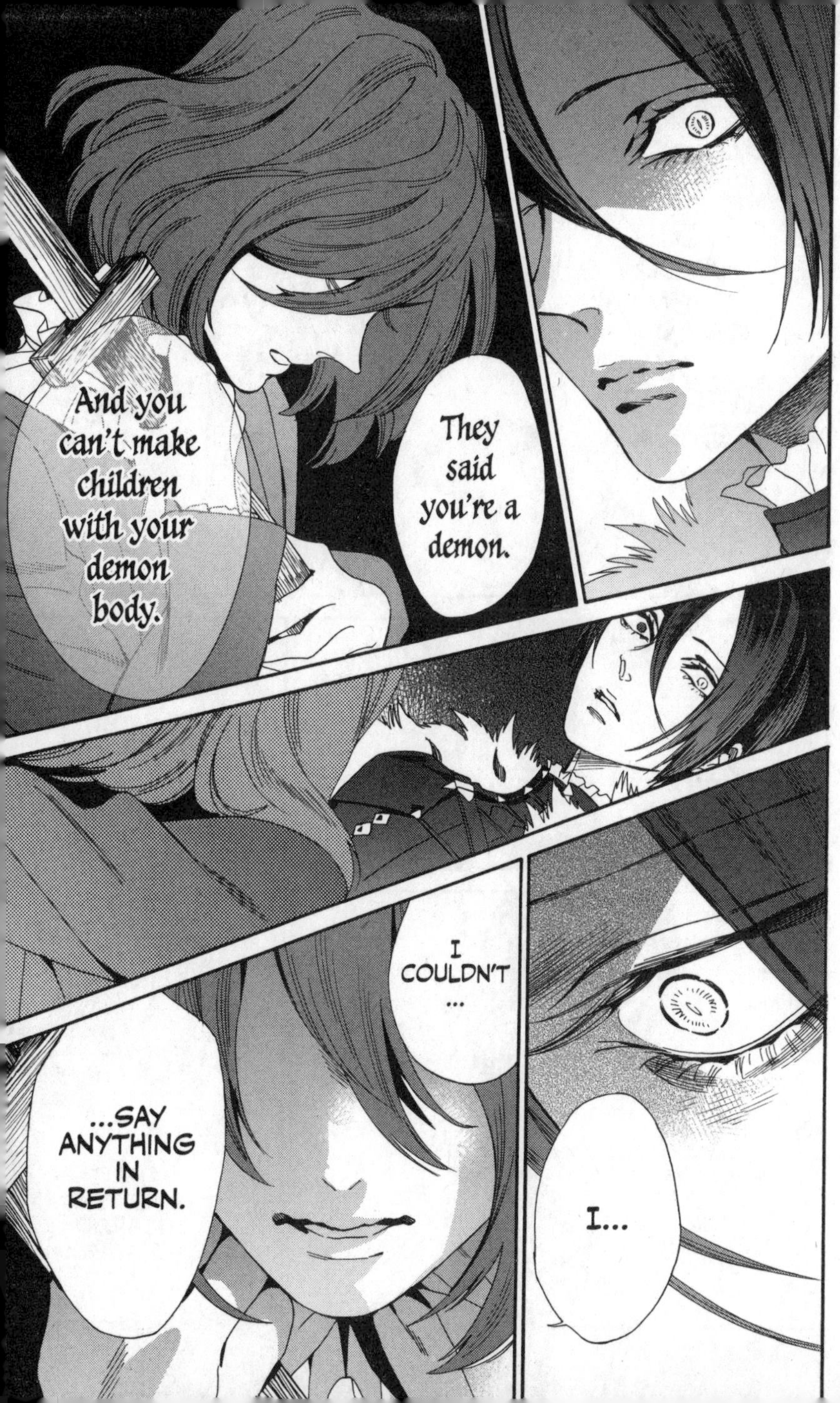
They said you're a demon.
And you can't make children with your demon body.
I...
I COULDN'T ...
...SAY ANYTHING IN RETURN.

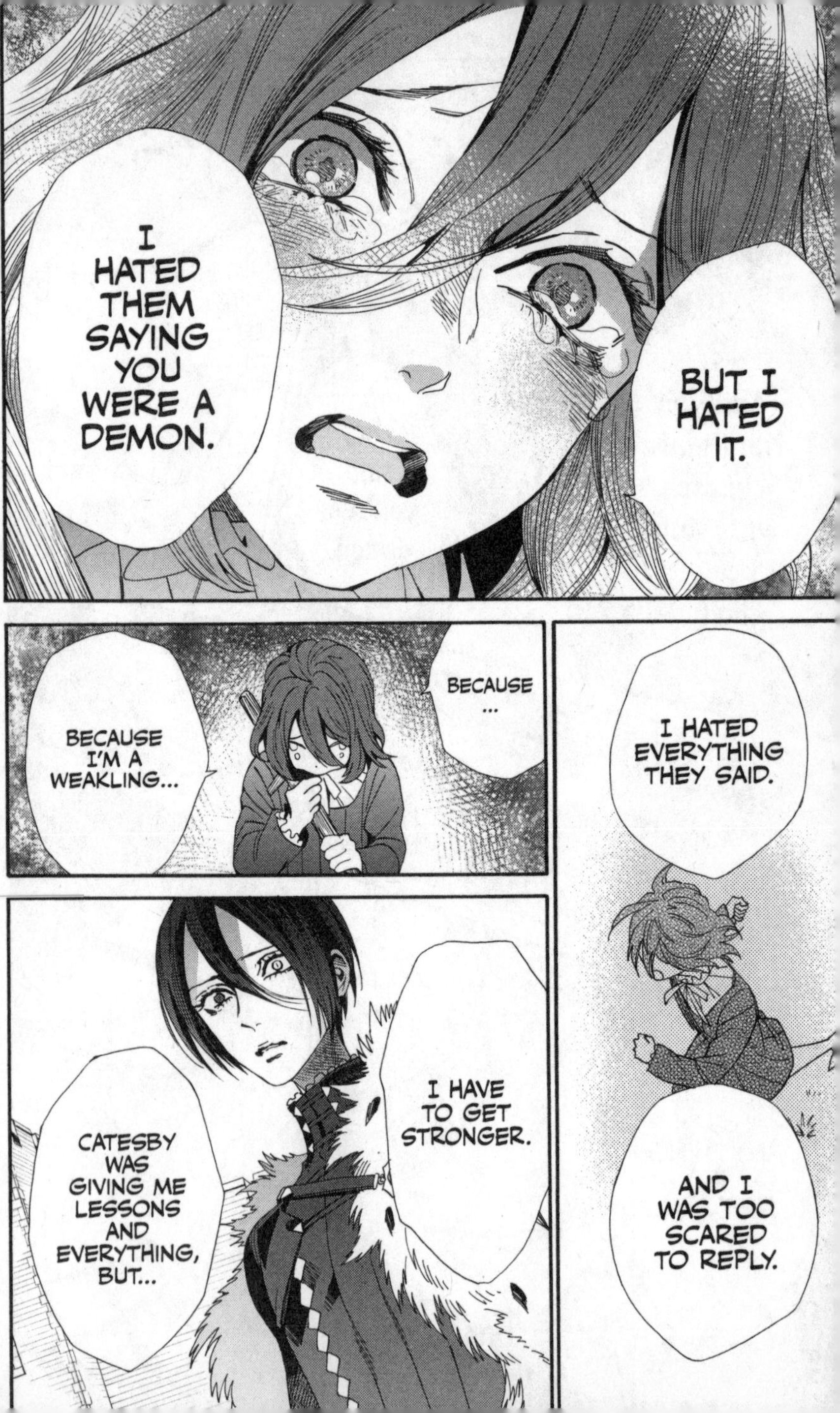
BUT I HATED IT.
I HATED THEM SAYING YOU WERE A DEMON.
I HATED EVERYTHING THEY SAID.
AND I WAS TOO SCARED TO REPLY.
BECAUSE...
BECAUSE I'M A WEAKLING...
I HAVE TO GET STRONGER.
CATESBY WAS GIVING ME LESSONS AND EVERYTHING, BUT...

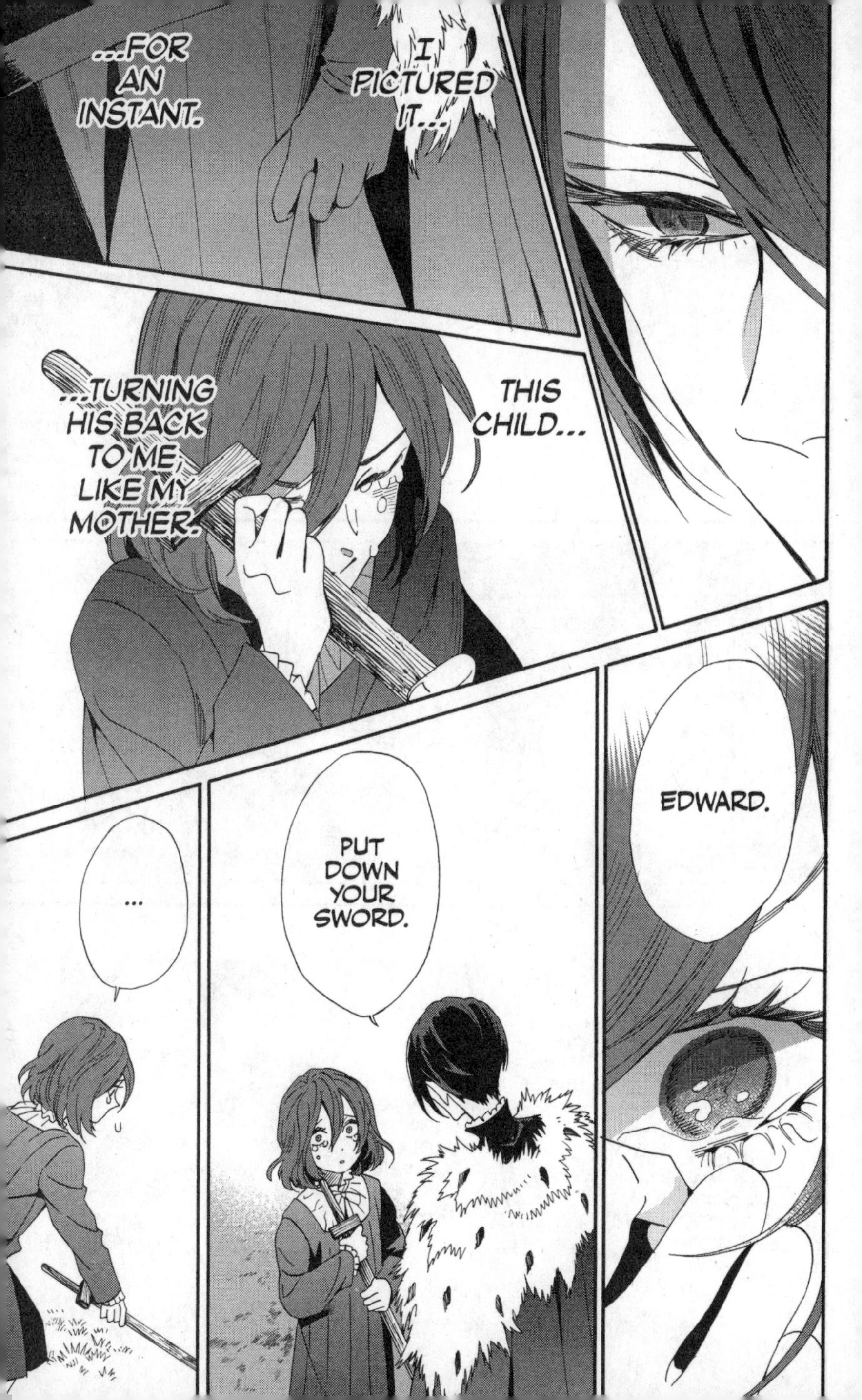
I PICTURED IT...
...FOR AN INSTANT.
THIS CHILD...
...TURNING HIS BACK TO ME, LIKE MY MOTHER.
EDWARD.
PUT DOWN YOUR SWORD.
...

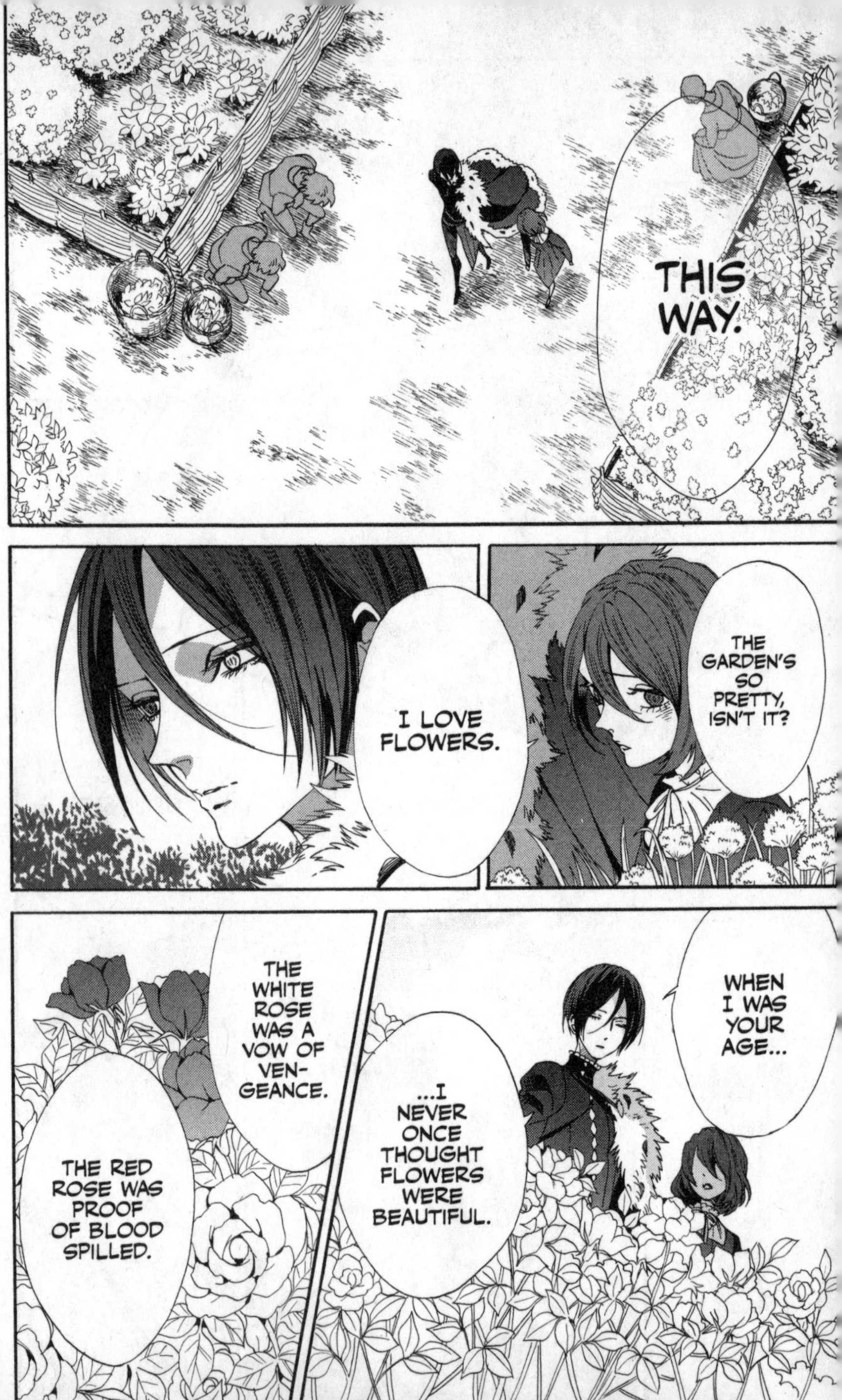
THIS WAY.
THE GARDEN'S SO PRETTY, ISN'T IT?
I LOVE FLOWERS.
WHEN I WAS YOUR AGE...
...I NEVER ONCE THOUGHT FLOWERS WERE BEAUTIFUL.
THE WHITE ROSE WAS A VOW OF VEN-GEANCE.
THE RED ROSE WAS PROOF OF BLOOD SPILLED.

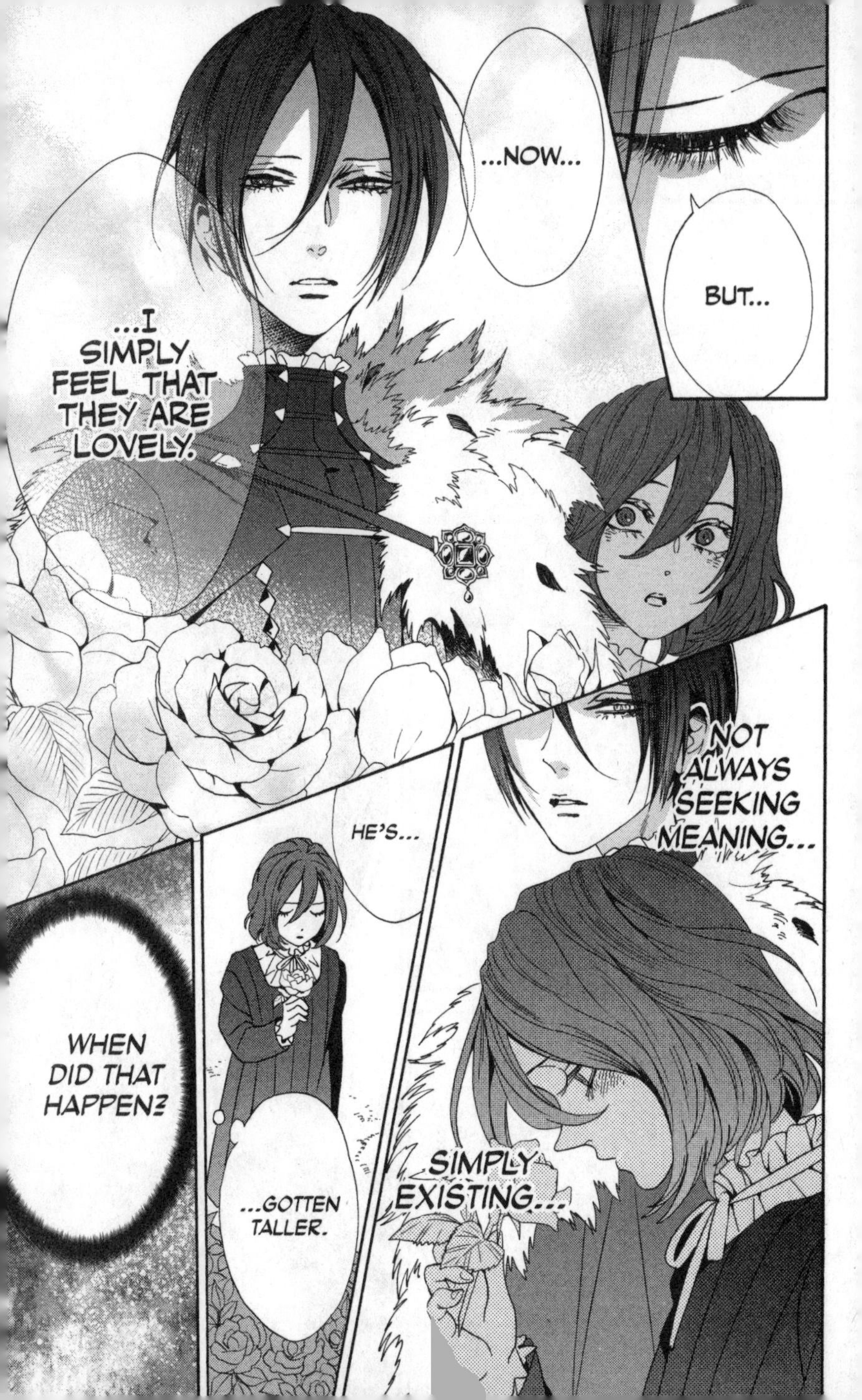
BUT...
...NOW...
...I SIMPLY FEEL THAT THEY ARE LOVELY.
NOT ALWAYS SEEKING MEANING...
SIMPLY EXISTING...
HE'S...
...GOTTEN TALLER.
WHEN DID THAT HAPPEN?

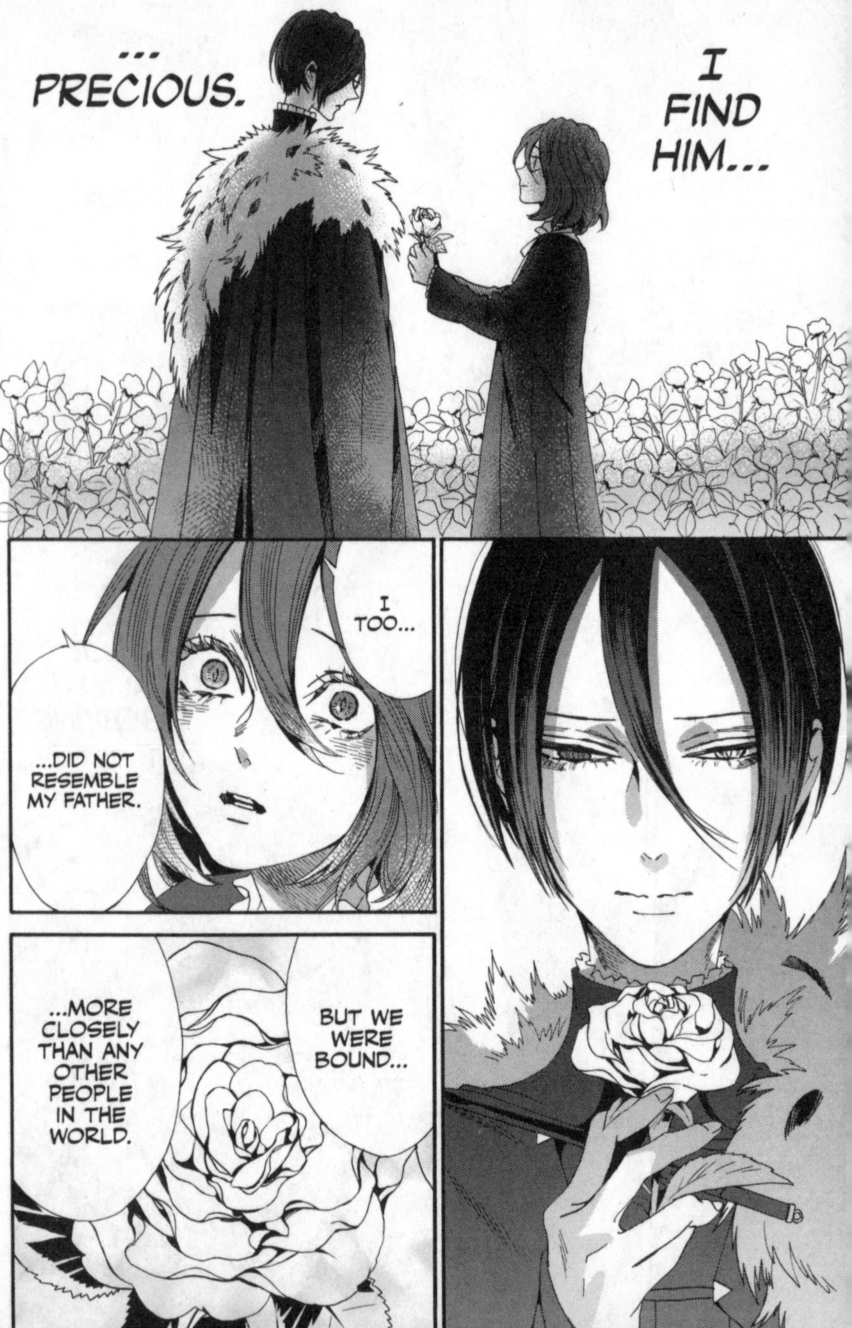
I FIND HIM...
...PRECIOUS.
I TOO...
...DID NOT RESEMBLE MY FATHER.
BUT WE WERE BOUND...
...MORE CLOSELY THAN ANY OTHER PEOPLE IN THE WORLD.

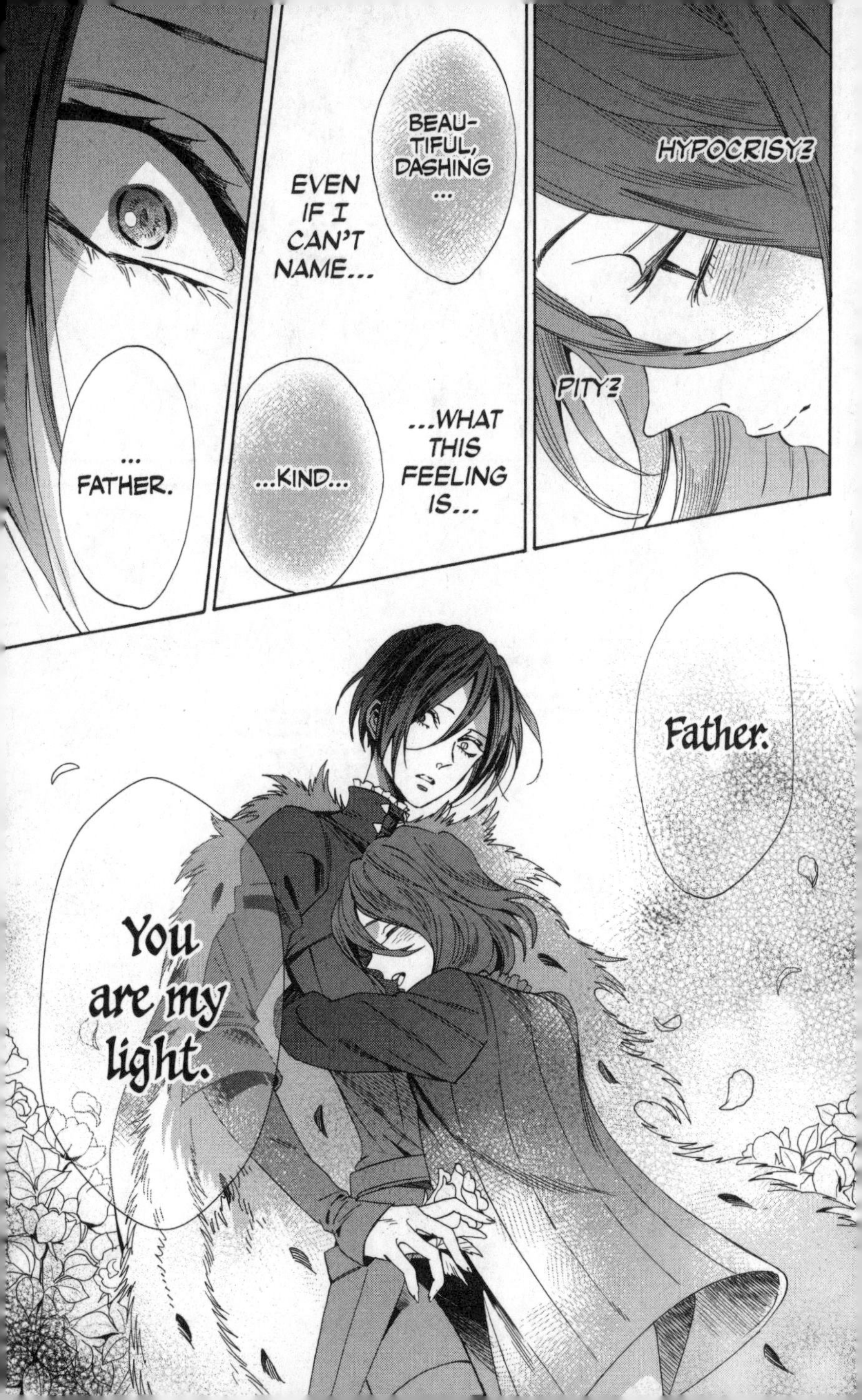
HYPOCRISY?
PITY?
BEAU-TIFUL, DASHING ...
EVEN IF I CAN'T NAME...
...WHAT THIS FEELING IS...
...KIND...
... FATHER.
Father.
You are my light.

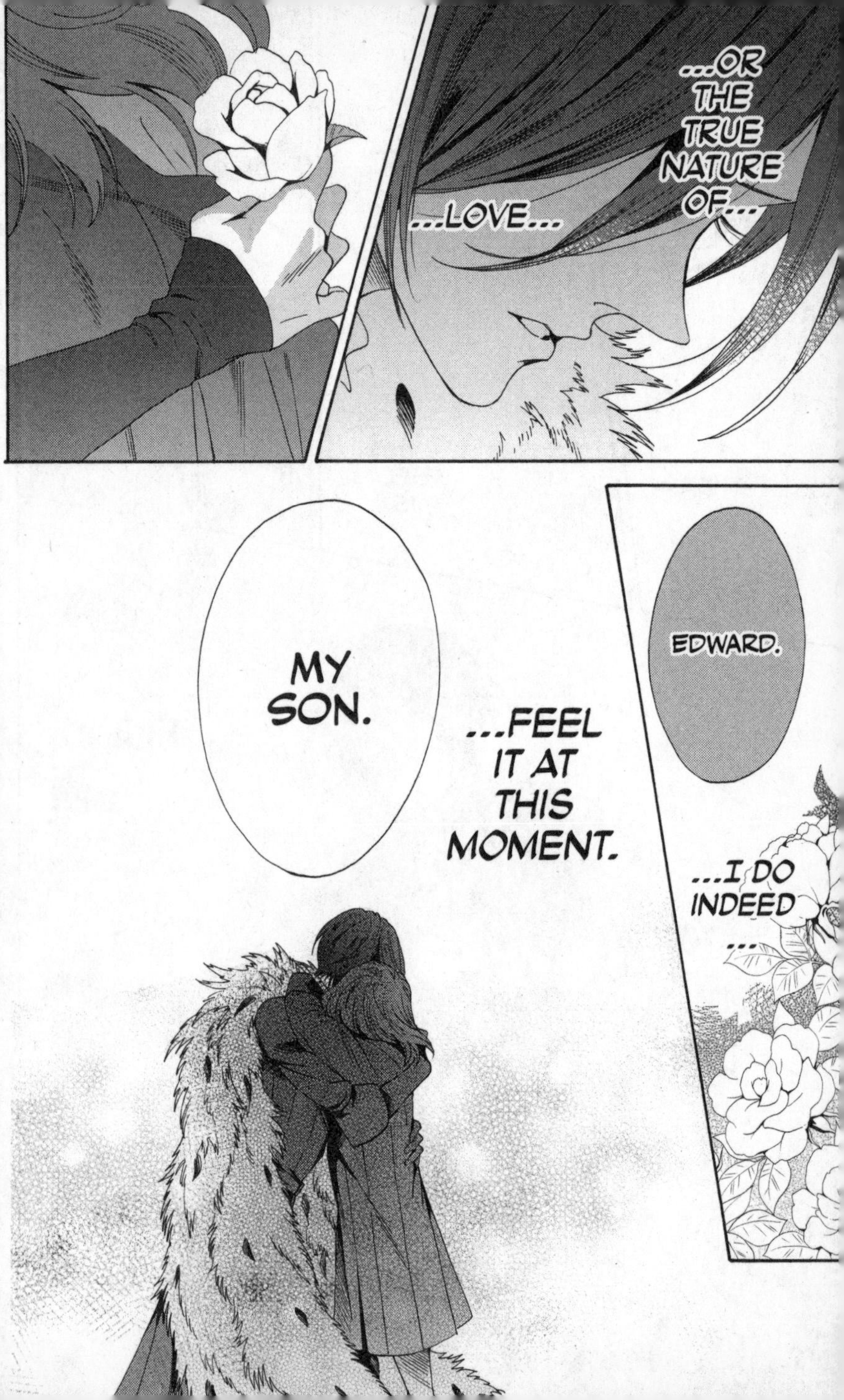
...OR THE TRUE NATURE OF...
...LOVE...
EDWARD.
...I DO INDEED ...
...FEEL IT AT THIS MOMENT.
MY SON.

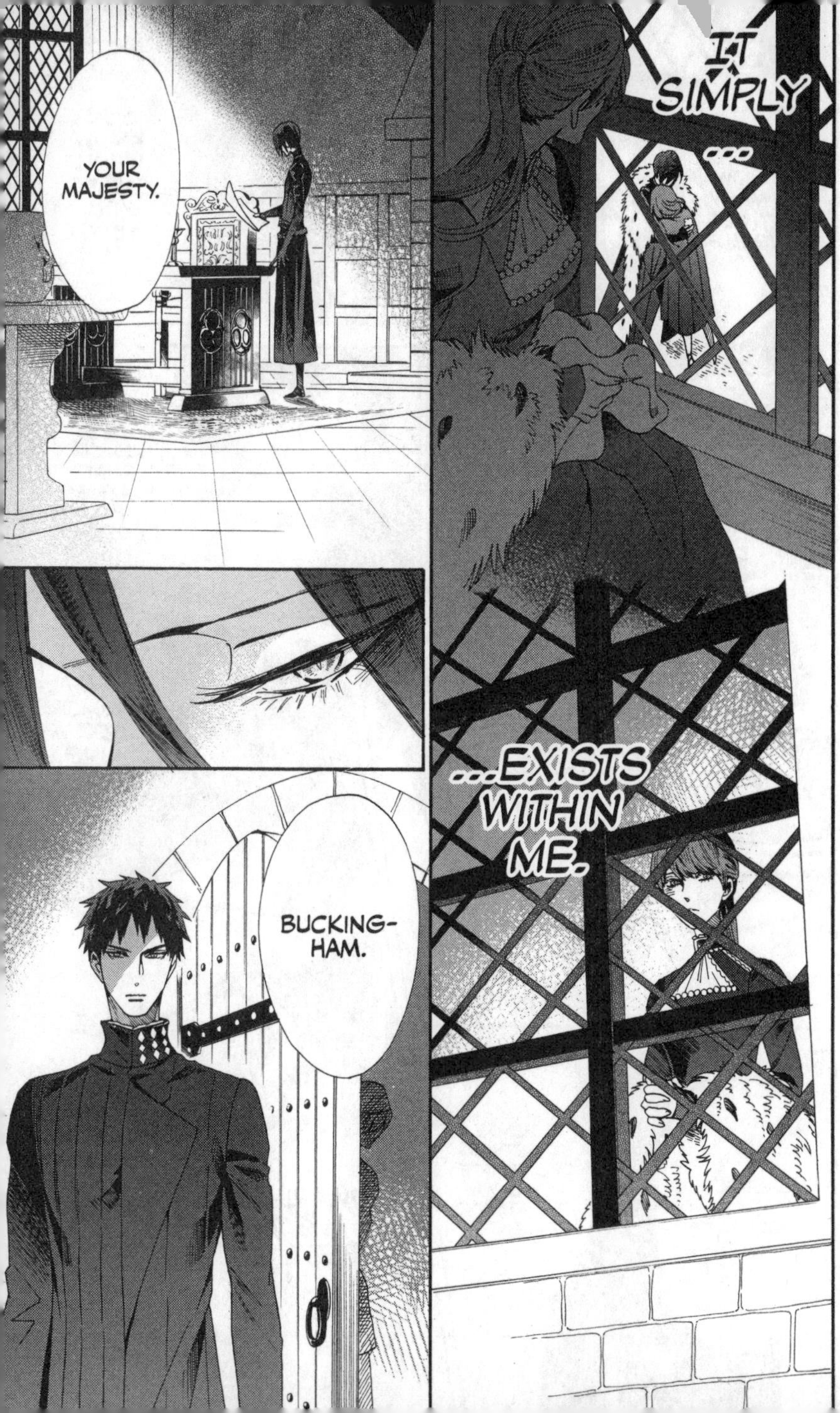
IT SIMPLY ...
...EXISTS WITHIN ME.
YOUR MAJESTY.
BUCKING-HAM.

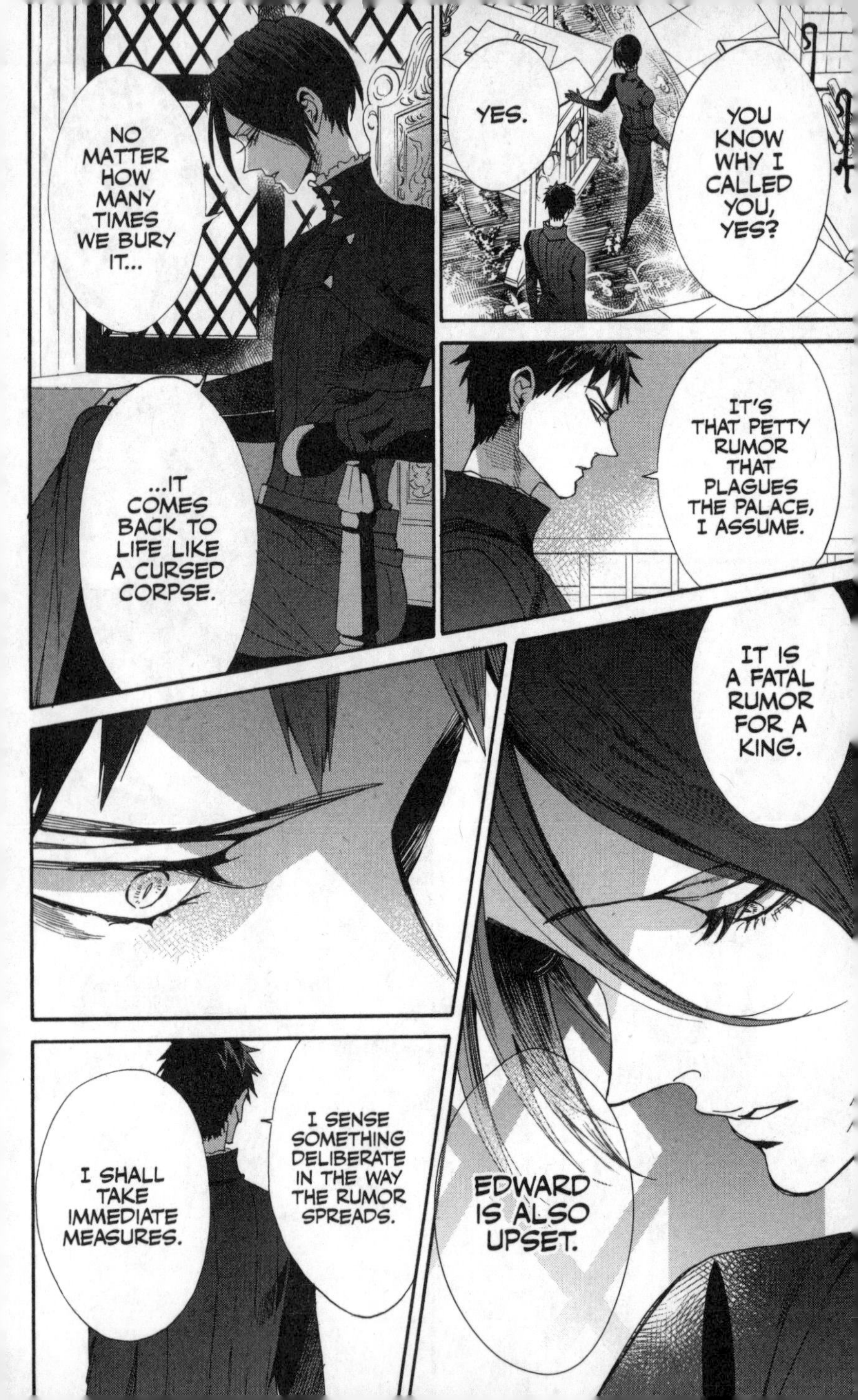
YOU KNOW WHY I CALLED YOU, YES?
YES.
IT'S THAT PETTY RUMOR THAT PLAGUES THE PALACE, I ASSUME.
NO MATTER HOW MANY TIMES WE BURY IT...
...IT COMES BACK TO LIFE LIKE A CURSED CORPSE.
IT IS A FATAL RUMOR FOR A KING.
EDWARD IS ALSO UPSET.
I SENSE SOMETHING DELIBERATE IN THE WAY THE RUMOR SPREADS.
I SHALL TAKE IMMEDIATE MEASURES.

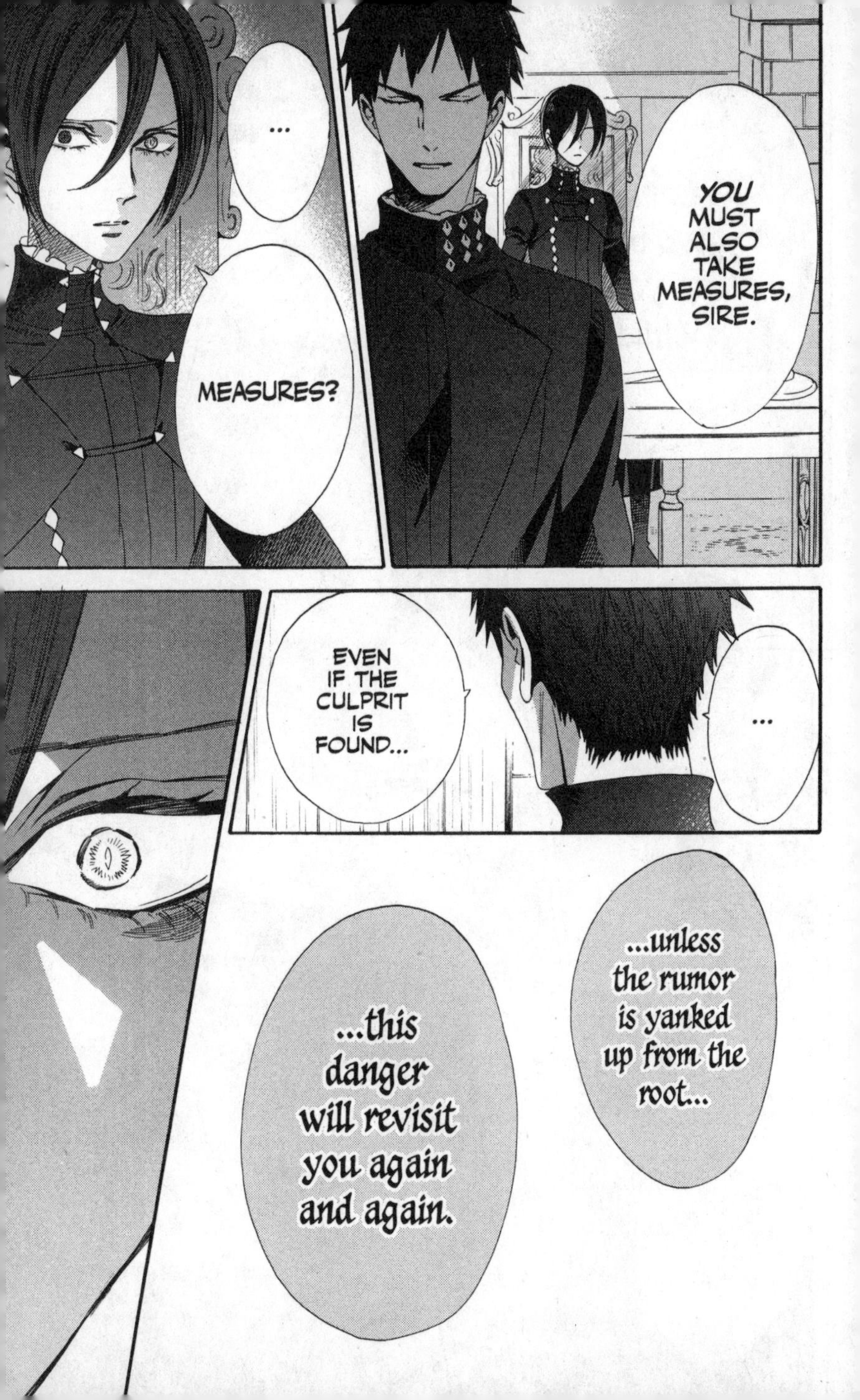
YOU MUST ALSO TAKE MEASURES, SIRE.
...
MEASURES?
...
EVEN IF THE CULPRIT IS FOUND...
...unless the rumor is yanked up from the root...
...this danger will revisit you again and again.

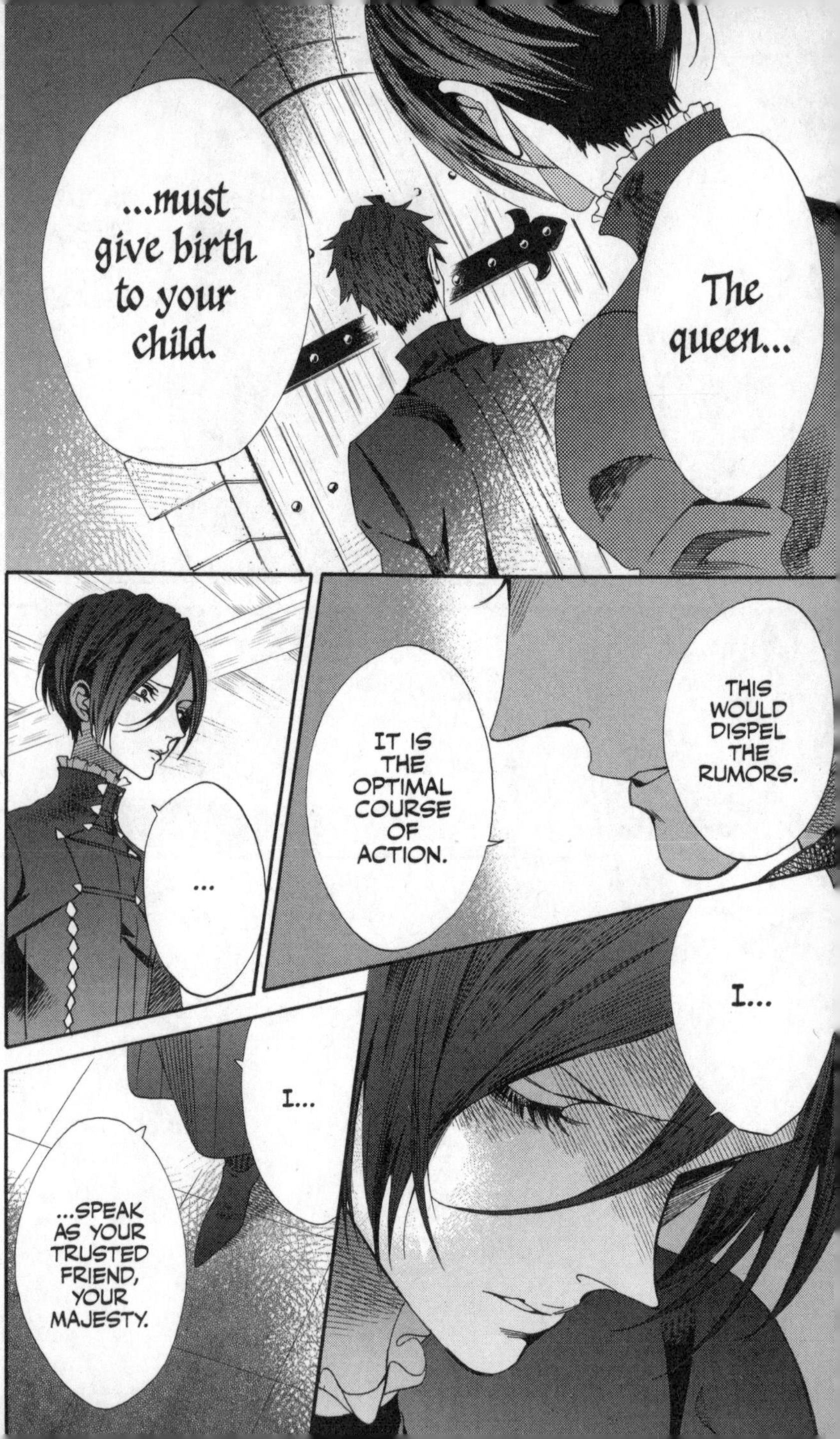
The queen...
...must give birth to your child.
THIS WOULD DISPEL THE RUMORS.
IT IS THE OPTIMAL COURSE OF ACTION.
...
I...
I...
...SPEAK AS YOUR TRUSTED FRIEND, YOUR MAJESTY.

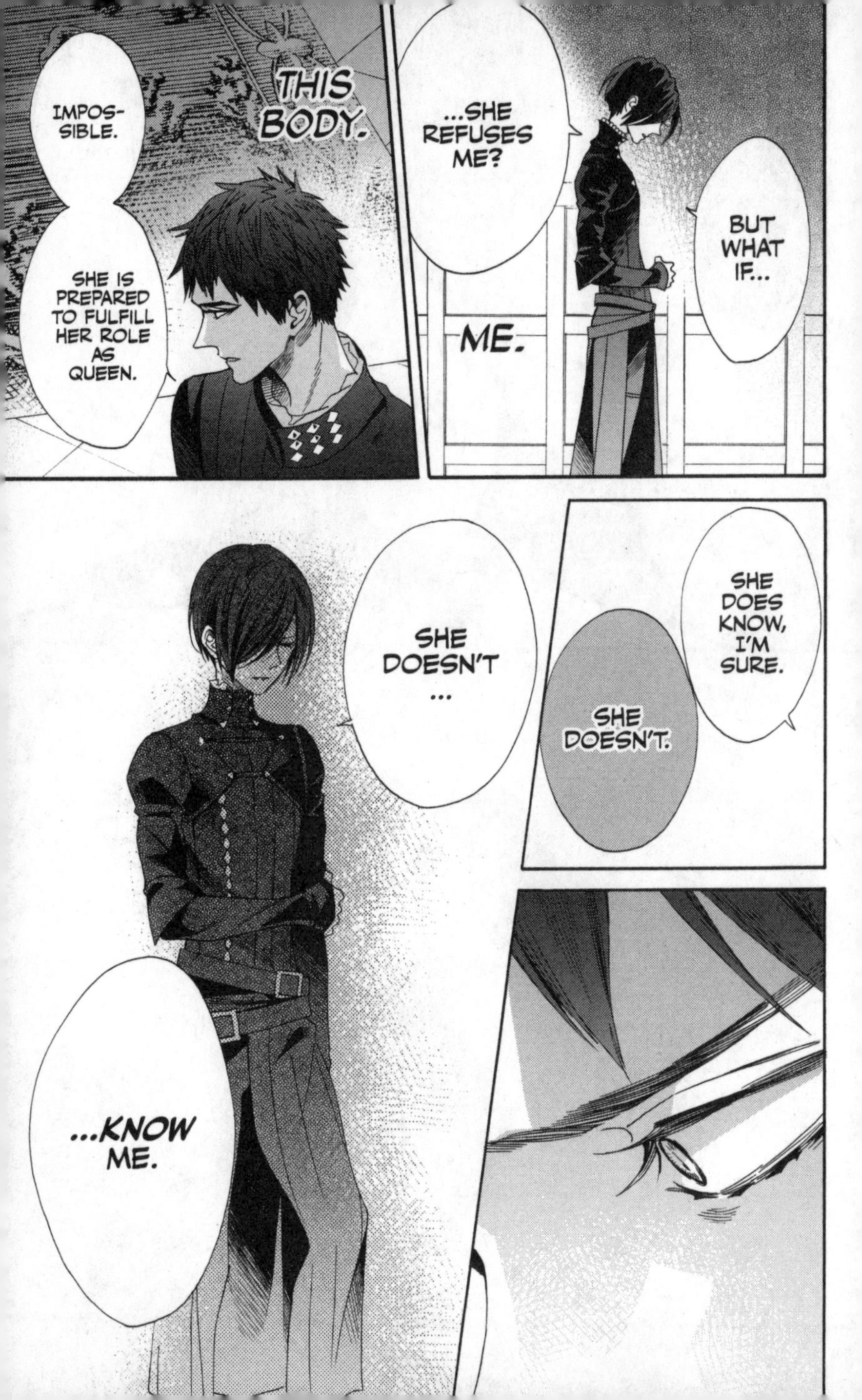
BUT WHAT IF...
...SHE REFUSES ME?
ME.
THIS BODY.
IMPOSSIBLE.
SHE IS PREPARED TO FULFILL HER ROLE AS QUEEN.
SHE DOES KNOW, I'M SURE.
SHE DOESN'T.
SHE DOESN'T ...
...KNOW ME.

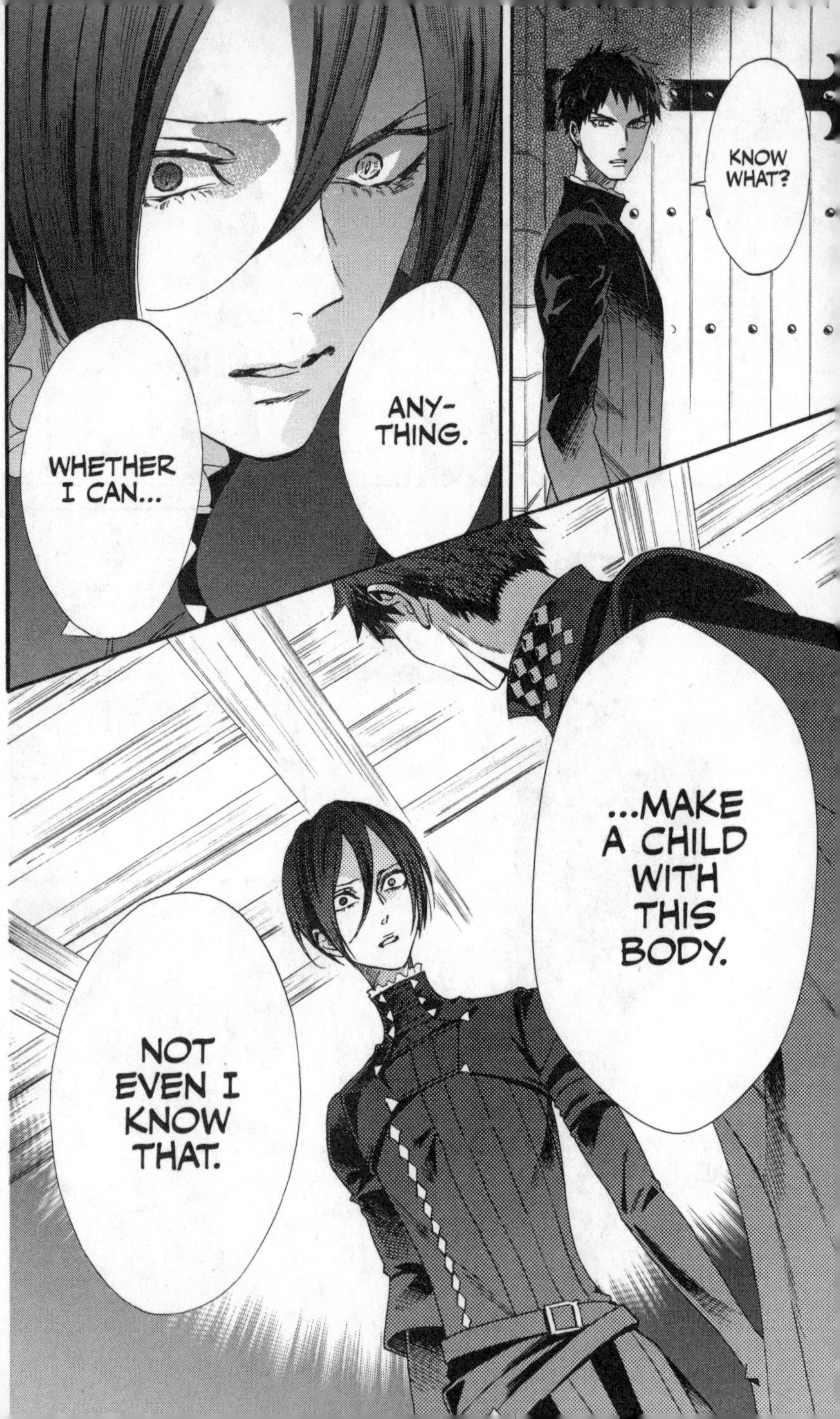
KNOW WHAT?
ANY-THING.
WHETHER I CAN...
...MAKE A CHILD WITH THIS BODY.
NOT EVEN I KNOW THAT.

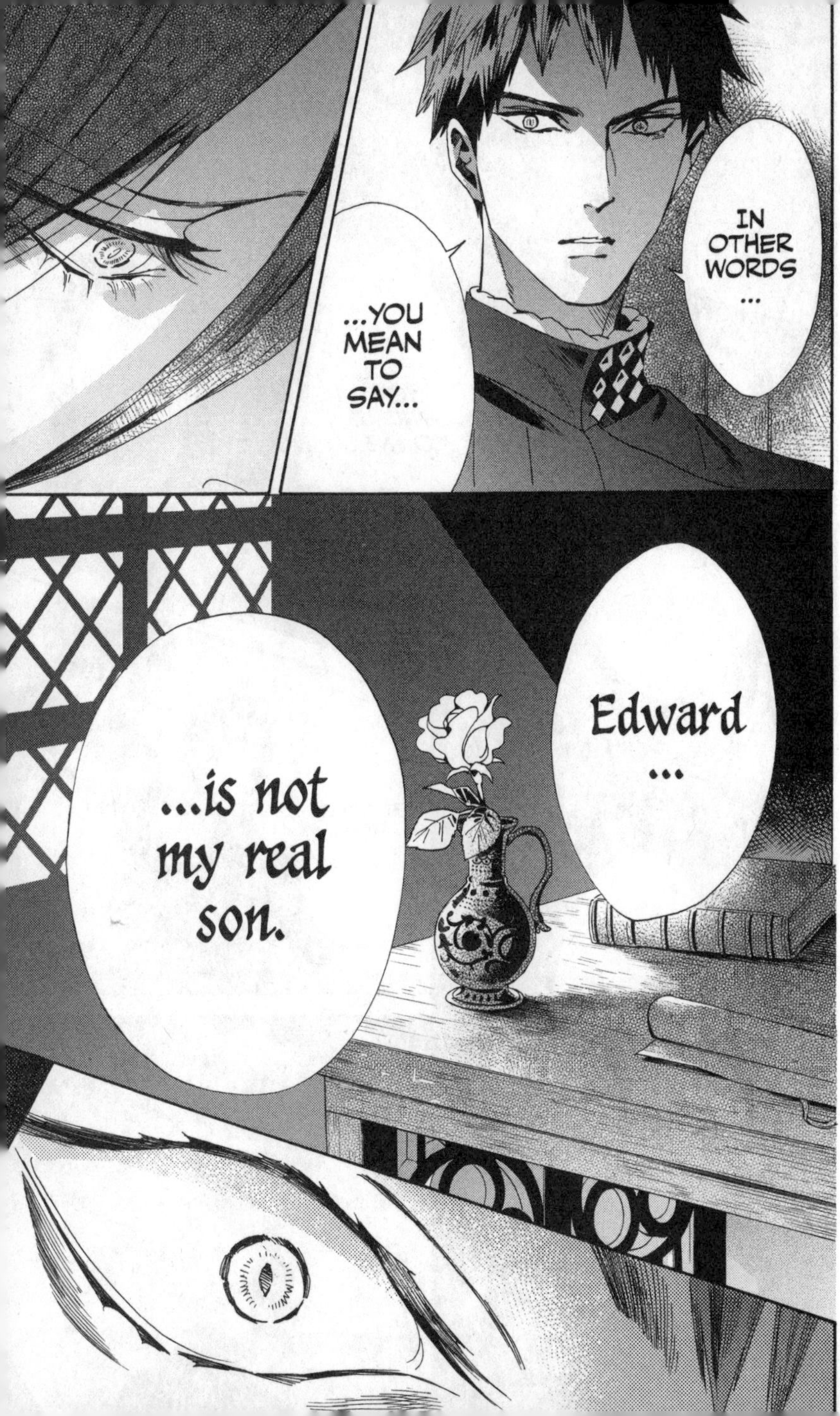
IN OTHER WORDS...
...YOU MEAN TO SAY...
Edward...
...is not my real son.

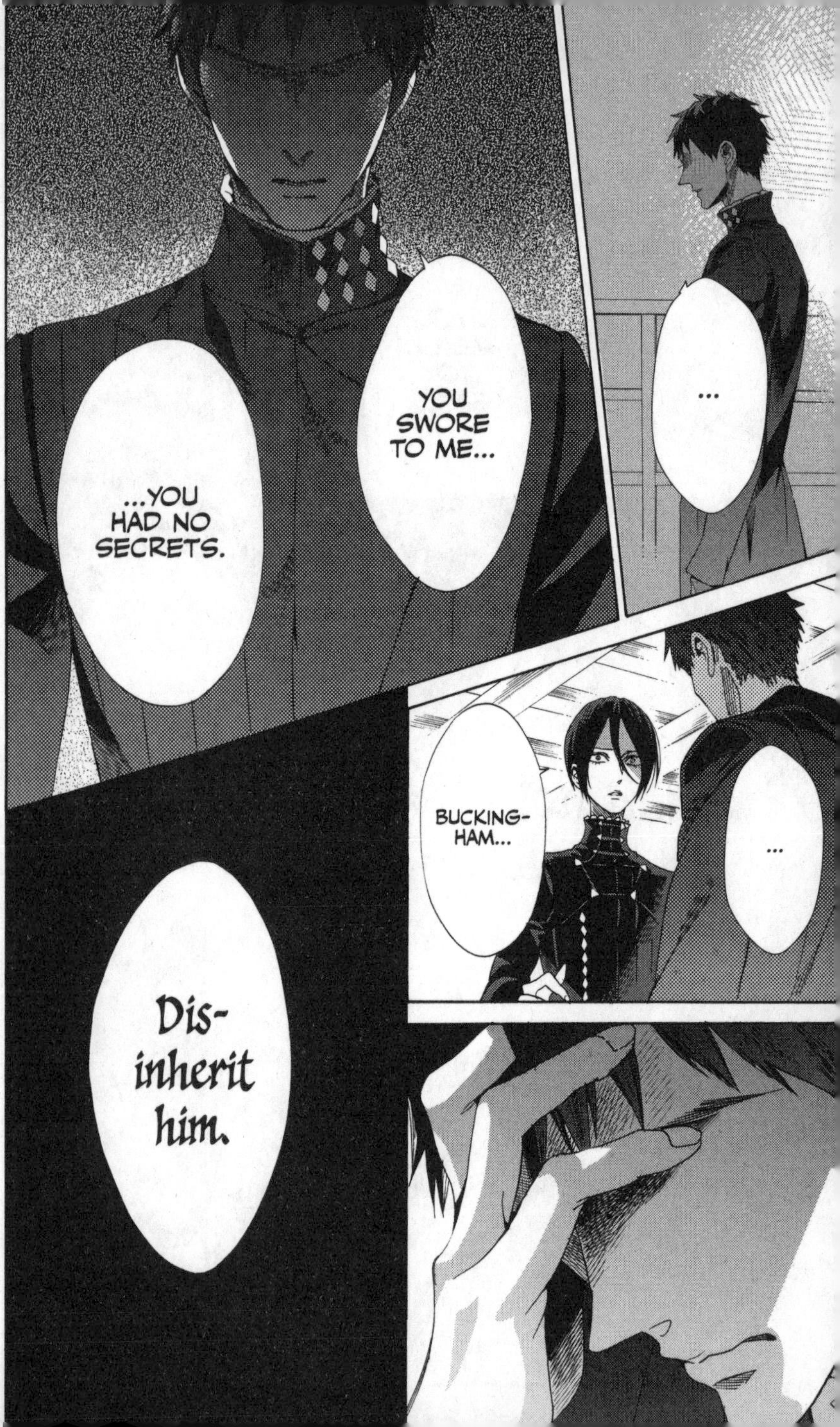
...
YOU SWORE TO ME...
...YOU HAD NO SECRETS.
...
BUCKING-HAM...
Dis-inherit him.

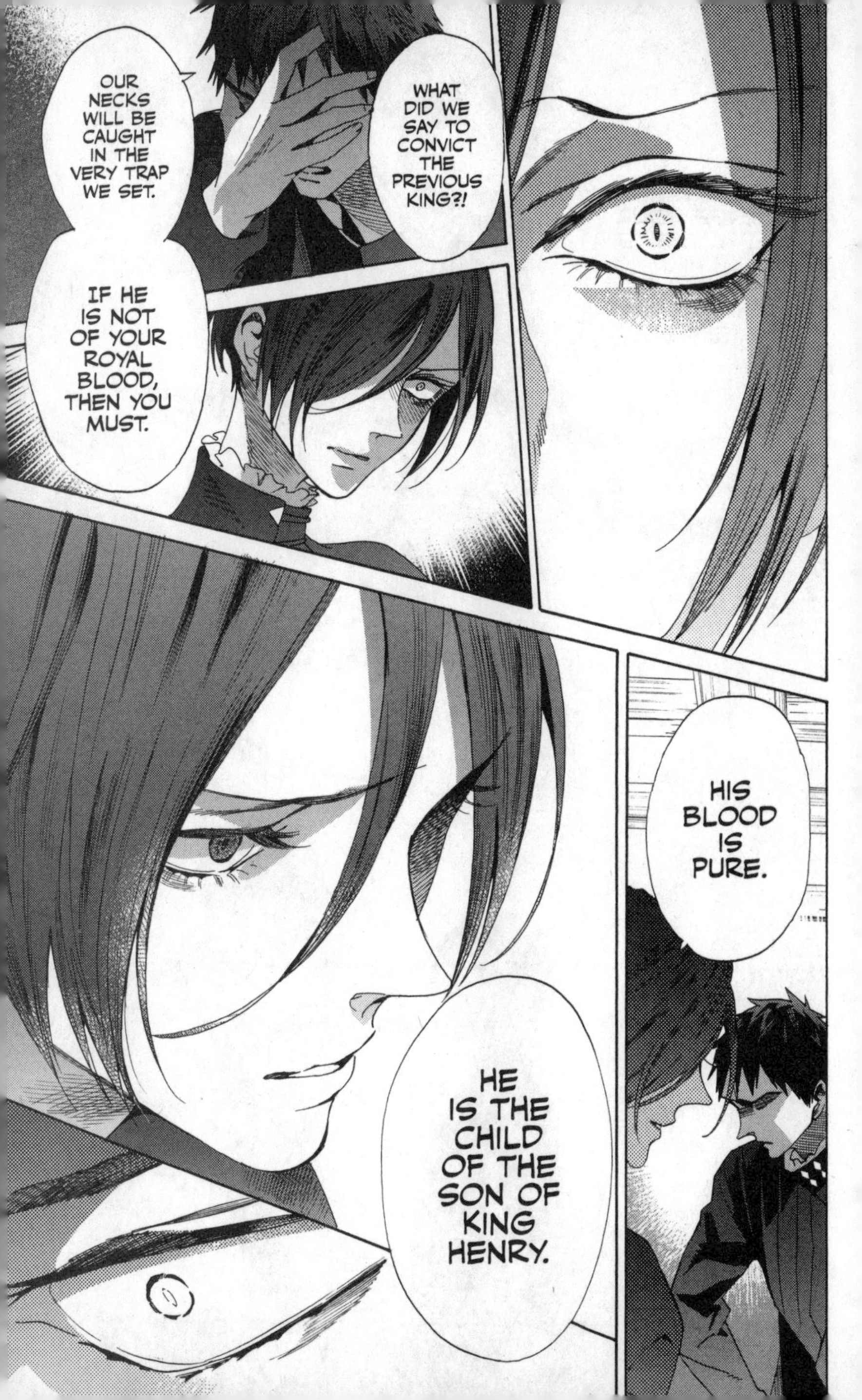
WHAT DID WE SAY TO CONVICT THE PREVIOUS KING?!
OUR NECKS WILL BE CAUGHT IN THE VERY TRAP WE SET.
IF HE IS NOT OF YOUR ROYAL BLOOD, THEN YOU MUST.
HIS BLOOD IS PURE.
HE IS THE CHILD OF THE SON OF KING HENRY.

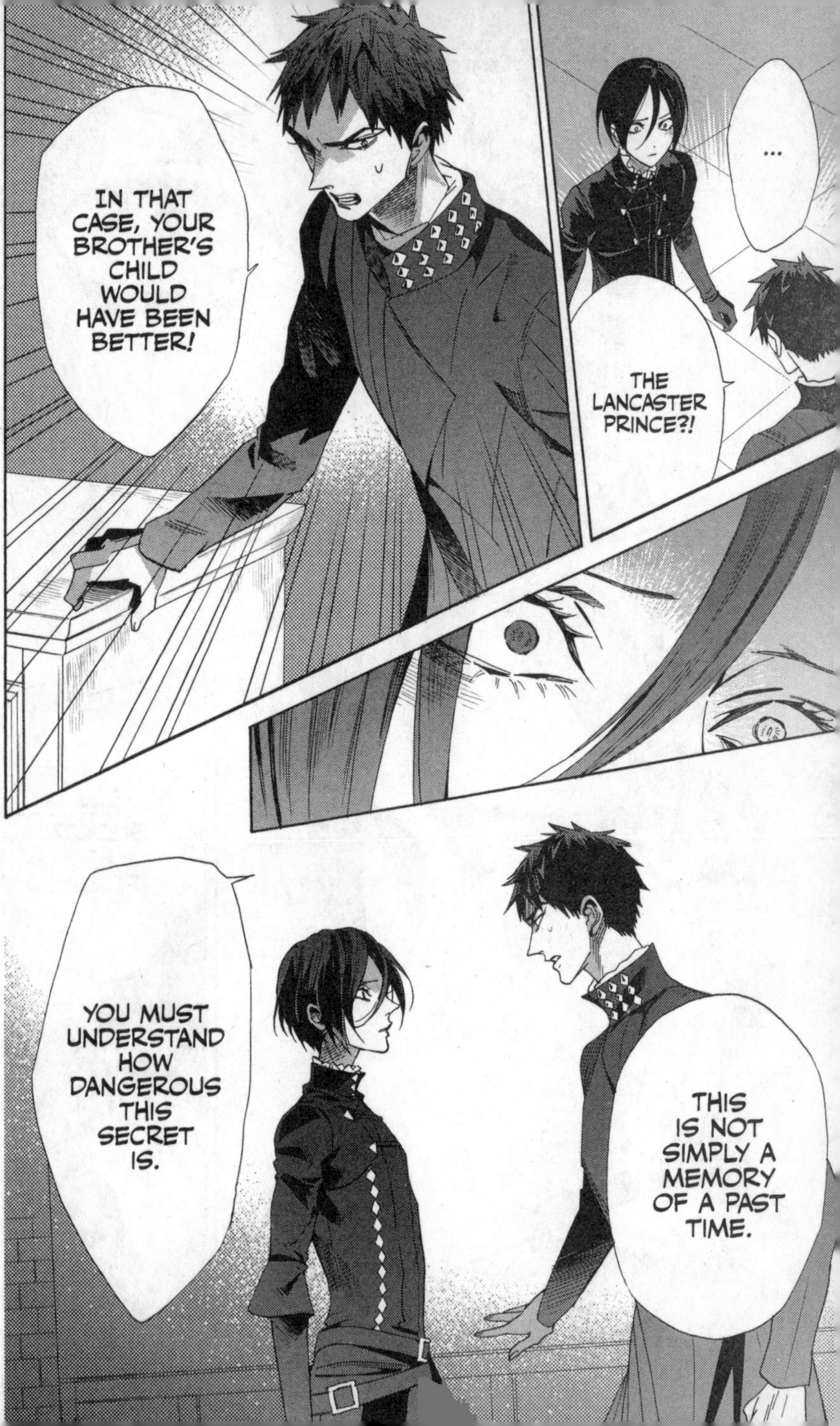
...
THE LANCASTER PRINCE?!
IN THAT CASE, YOUR BROTHER'S CHILD WOULD HAVE BEEN BETTER!
THIS IS NOT SIMPLY A MEMORY OF A PAST TIME.
YOU MUST UNDERSTAND HOW DANGEROUS THIS SECRET IS.

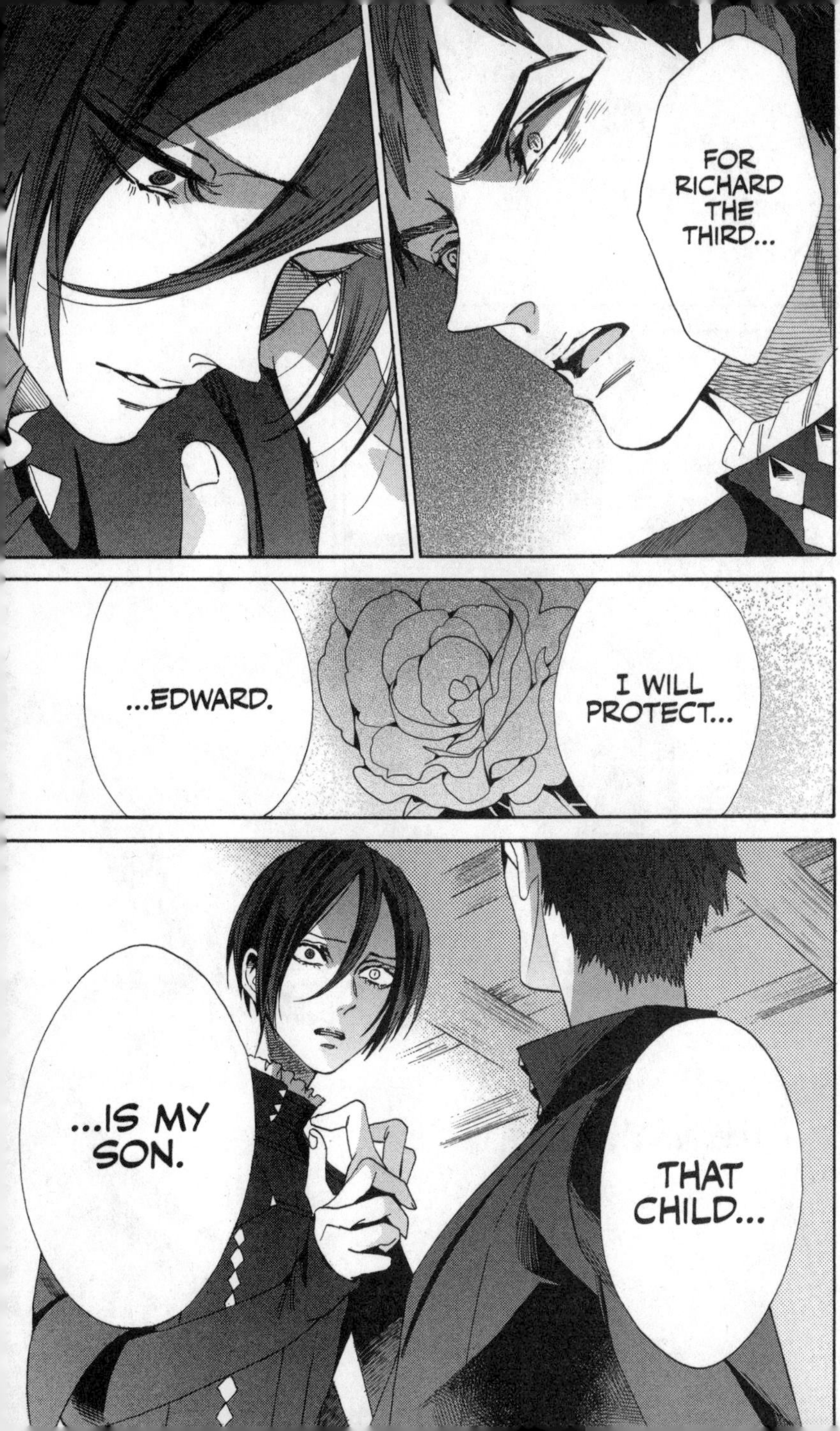
FOR RICHARD THE THIRD...
I WILL PROTECT...
...EDWARD.
THAT CHILD...
...IS MY SON.

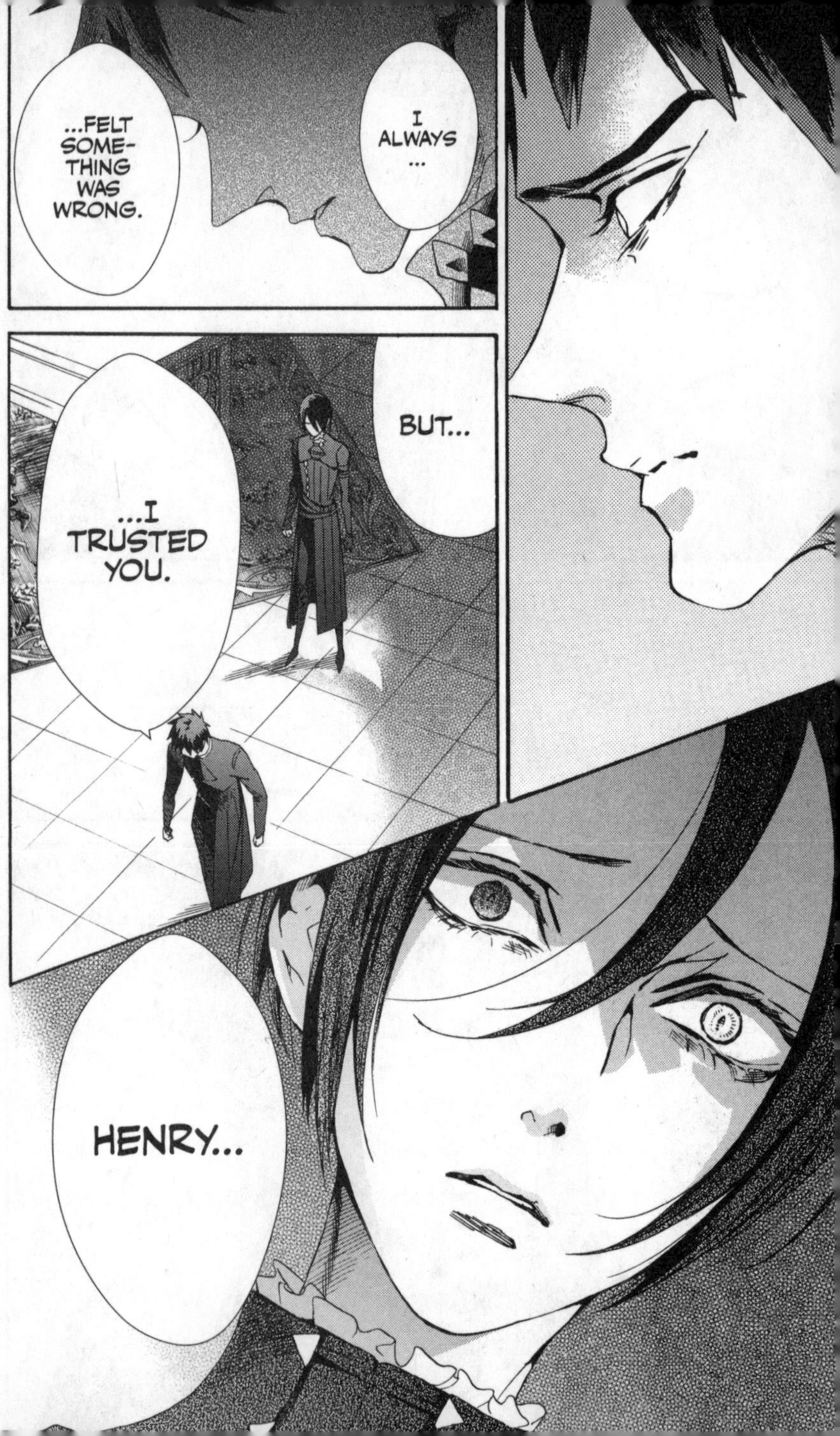
I ALWAYS ...
...FELT SOMETHING WAS WRONG.
BUT...
...I TRUSTED YOU.
HENRY...

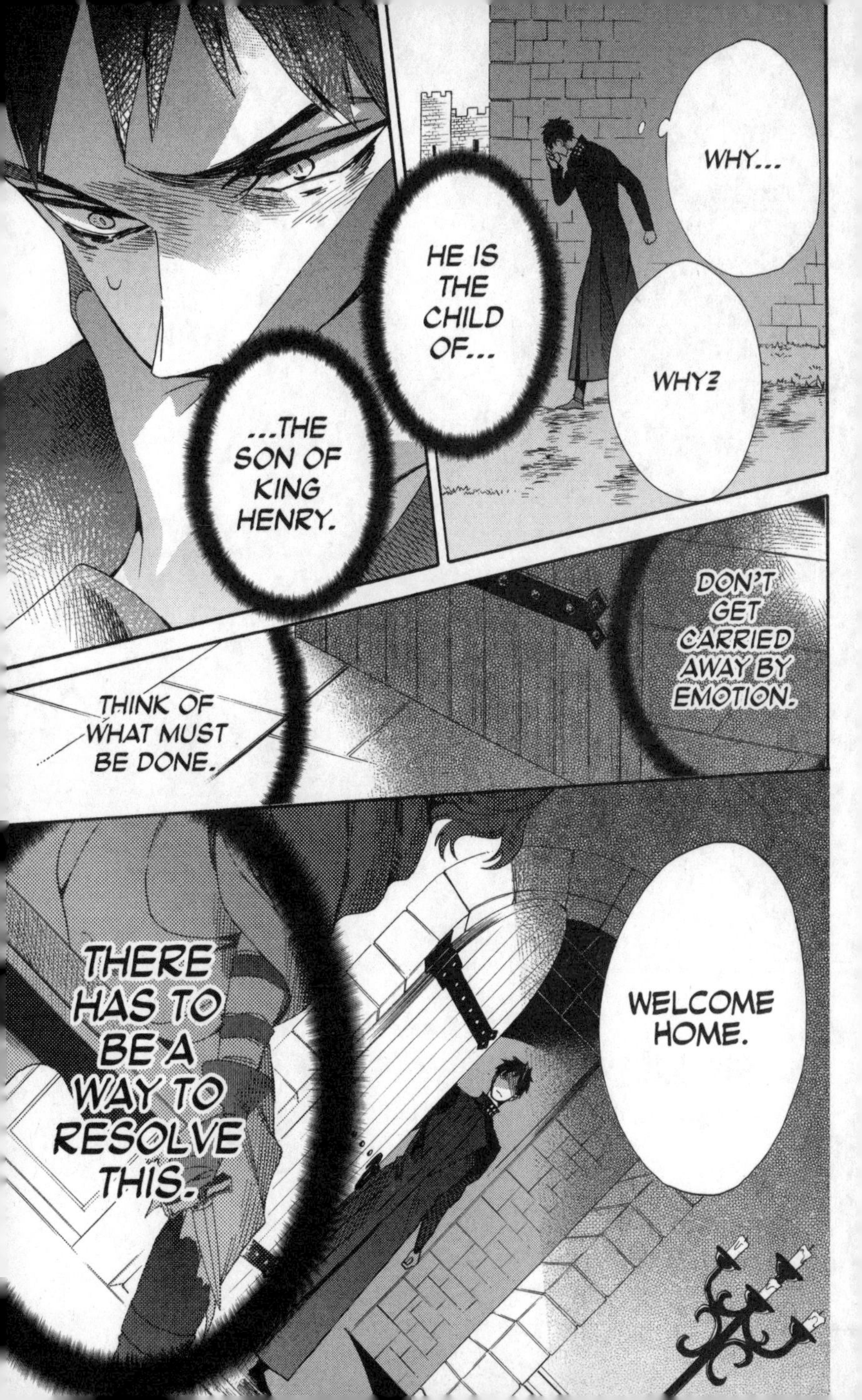
WHY...
WHY?
HE IS THE CHILD OF...
...THE SON OF KING HENRY.
DON'T GET CARRIED AWAY BY EMOTION.
THINK OF WHAT MUST BE DONE.
WELCOME HOME.
THERE HAS TO BE A WAY TO RESOLVE THIS.

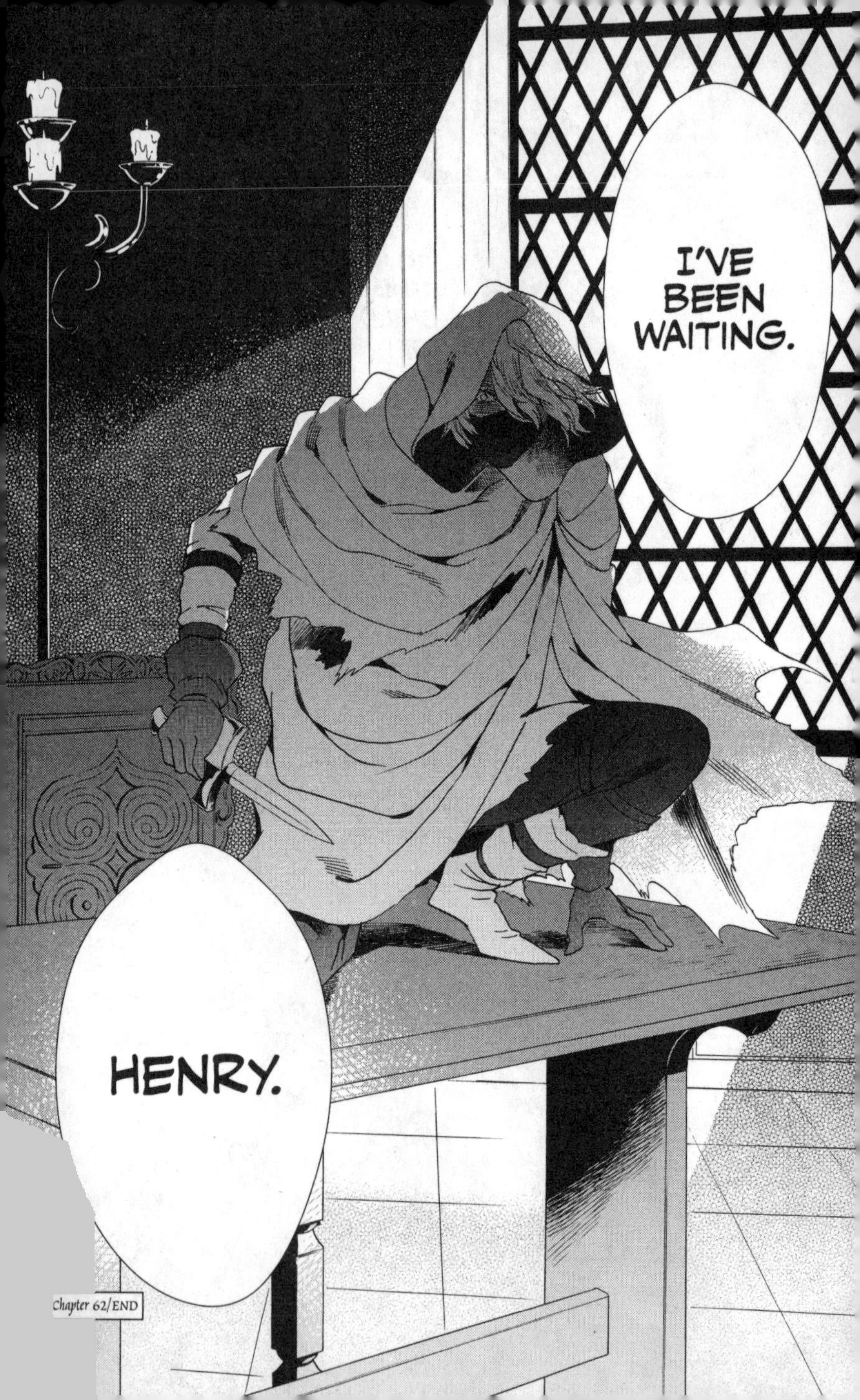
I'VE BEEN WAITING.
HENRY.
Chapter 62/END

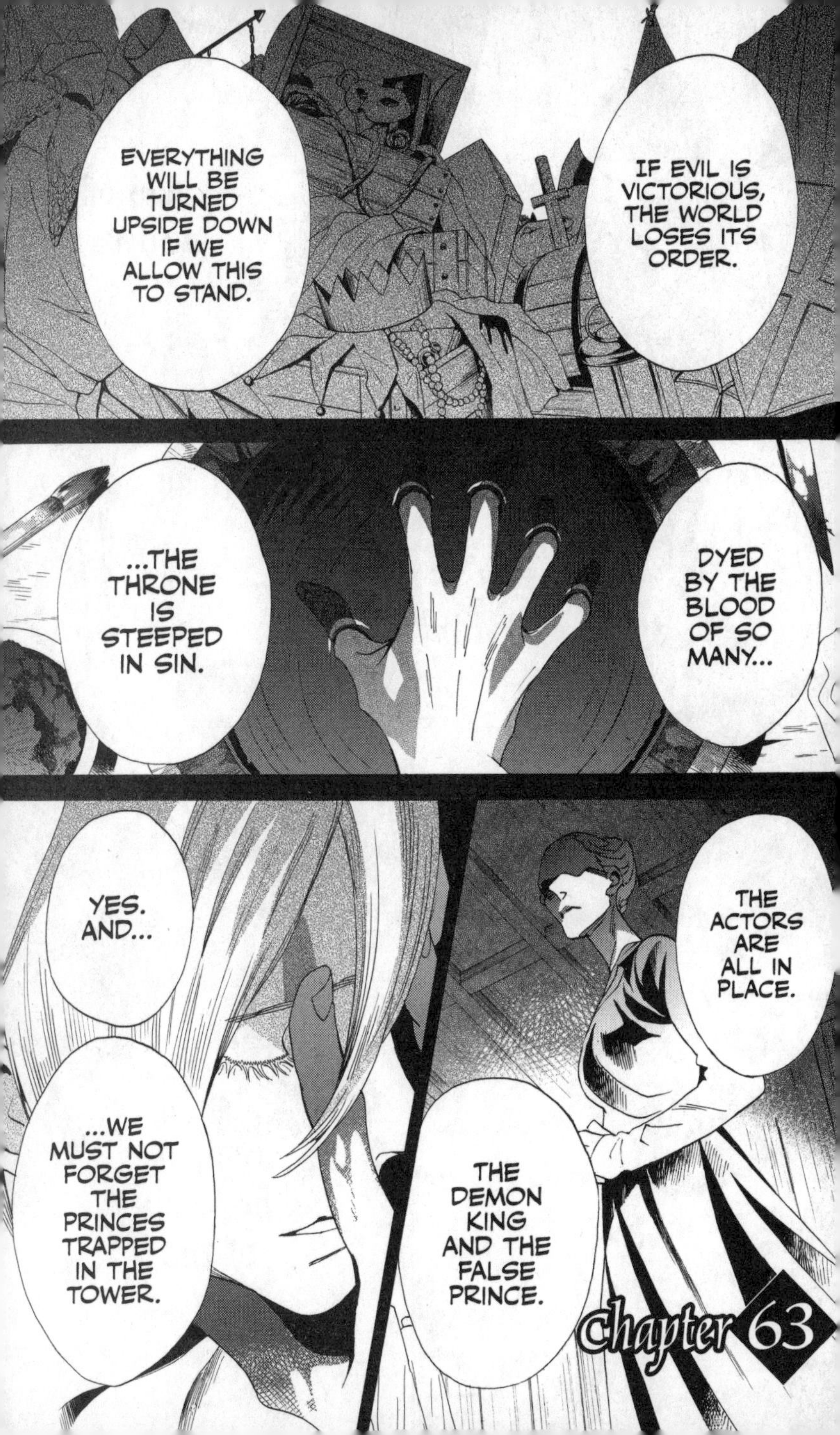
IF EVIL IS VICTORIOUS, THE WORLD LOSES ITS ORDER.
EVERYTHING WILL BE TURNED UPSIDE DOWN IF WE ALLOW THIS TO STAND.
DYED BY THE BLOOD OF SO MANY...
...THE THRONE IS STEEPED IN SIN.
THE ACTORS ARE ALL IN PLACE.
THE DEMON KING AND THE FALSE PRINCE.
YES. AND...
...WE MUST NOT FORGET THE PRINCES TRAPPED IN THE TOWER.
Chapter 63

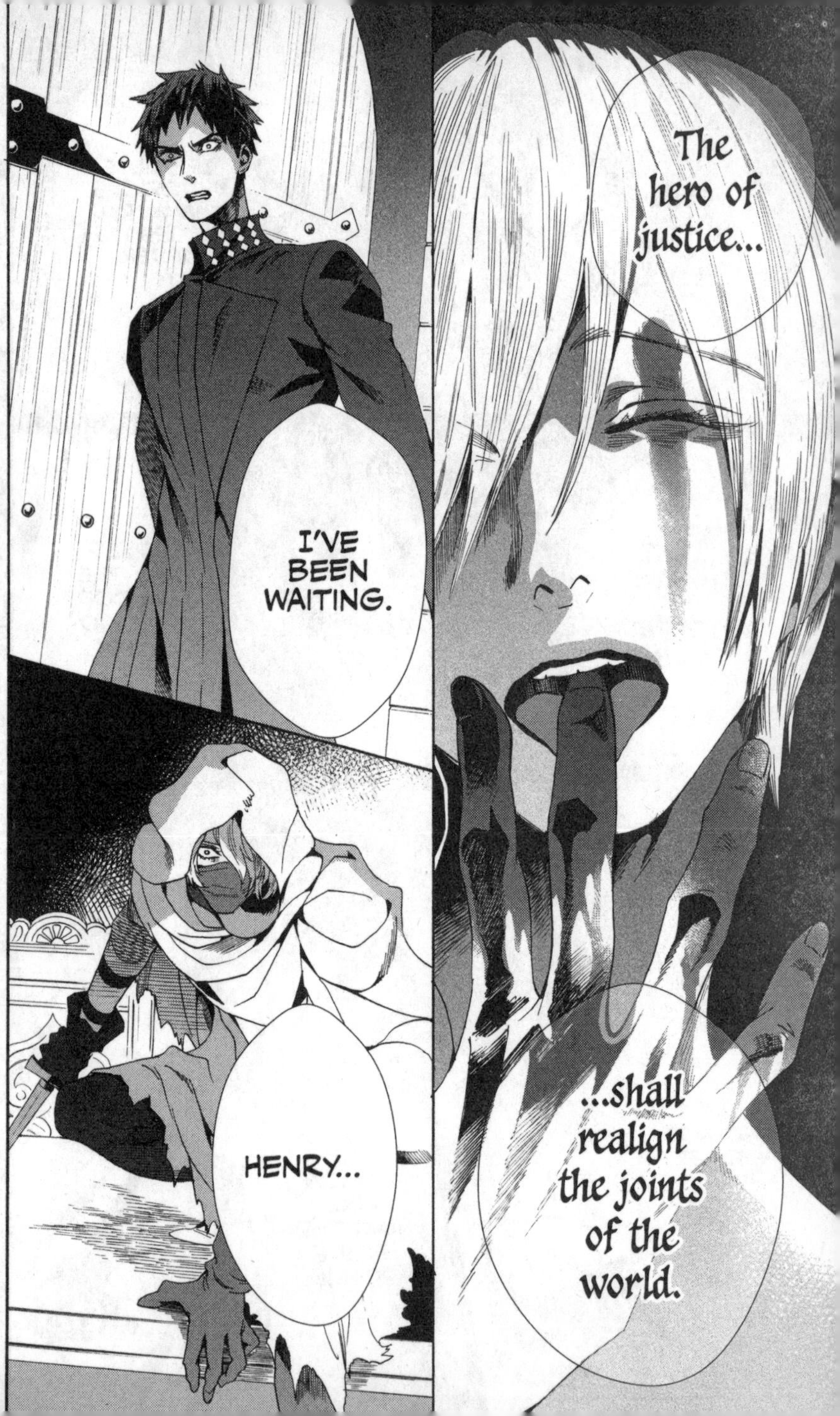
The hero of justice...
...shall realign the joints of the world.
I'VE BEEN WAITING.
HENRY...

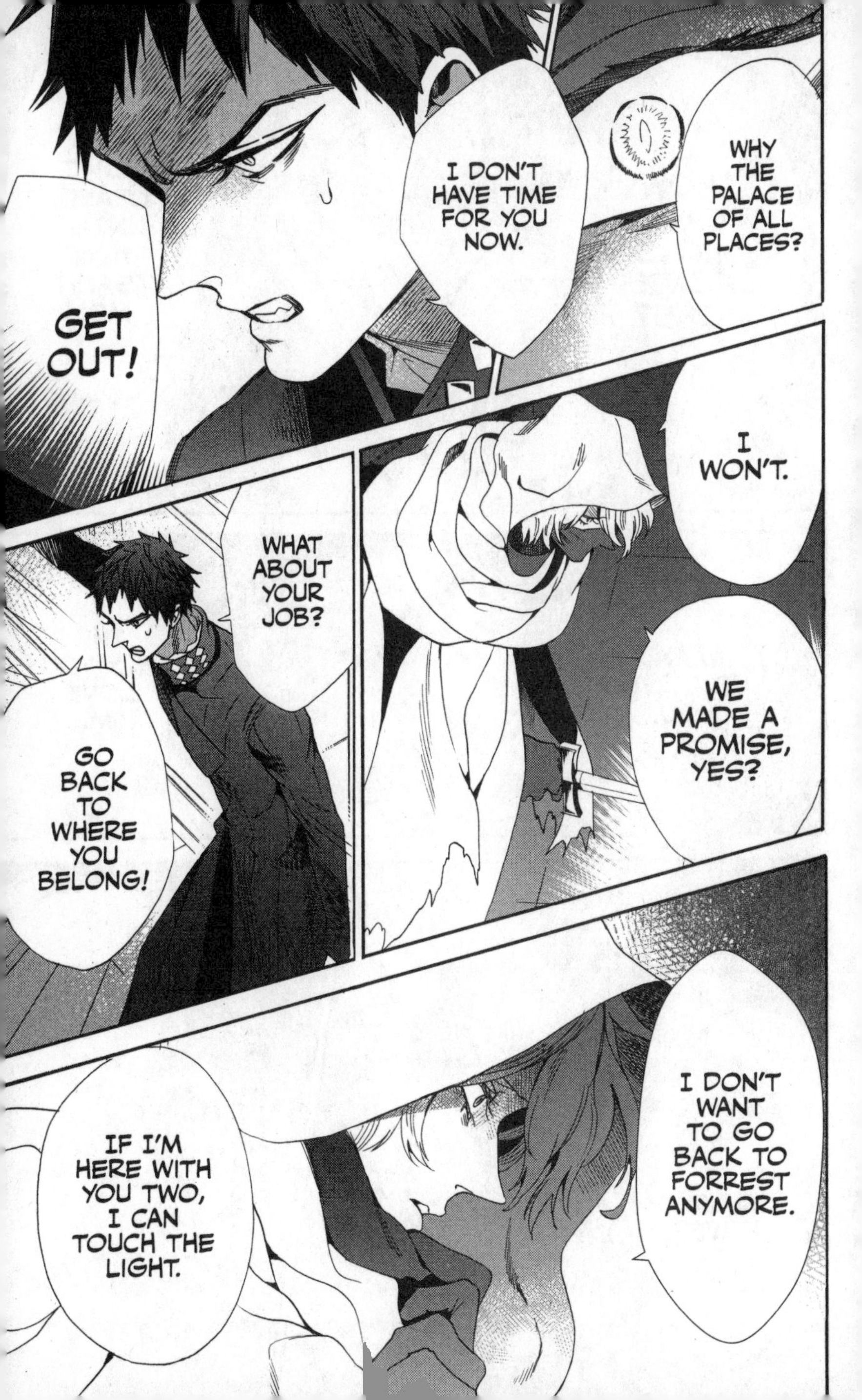
WHY THE PALACE OF ALL PLACES?
I DON'T HAVE TIME FOR YOU NOW.
GET OUT!
I WON'T.
WE MADE A PROMISE, YES?
WHAT ABOUT YOUR JOB?
GO BACK TO WHERE YOU BELONG!
I DON'T WANT TO GO BACK TO FORREST ANYMORE.
IF I'M HERE WITH YOU TWO, I CAN TOUCH THE LIGHT.

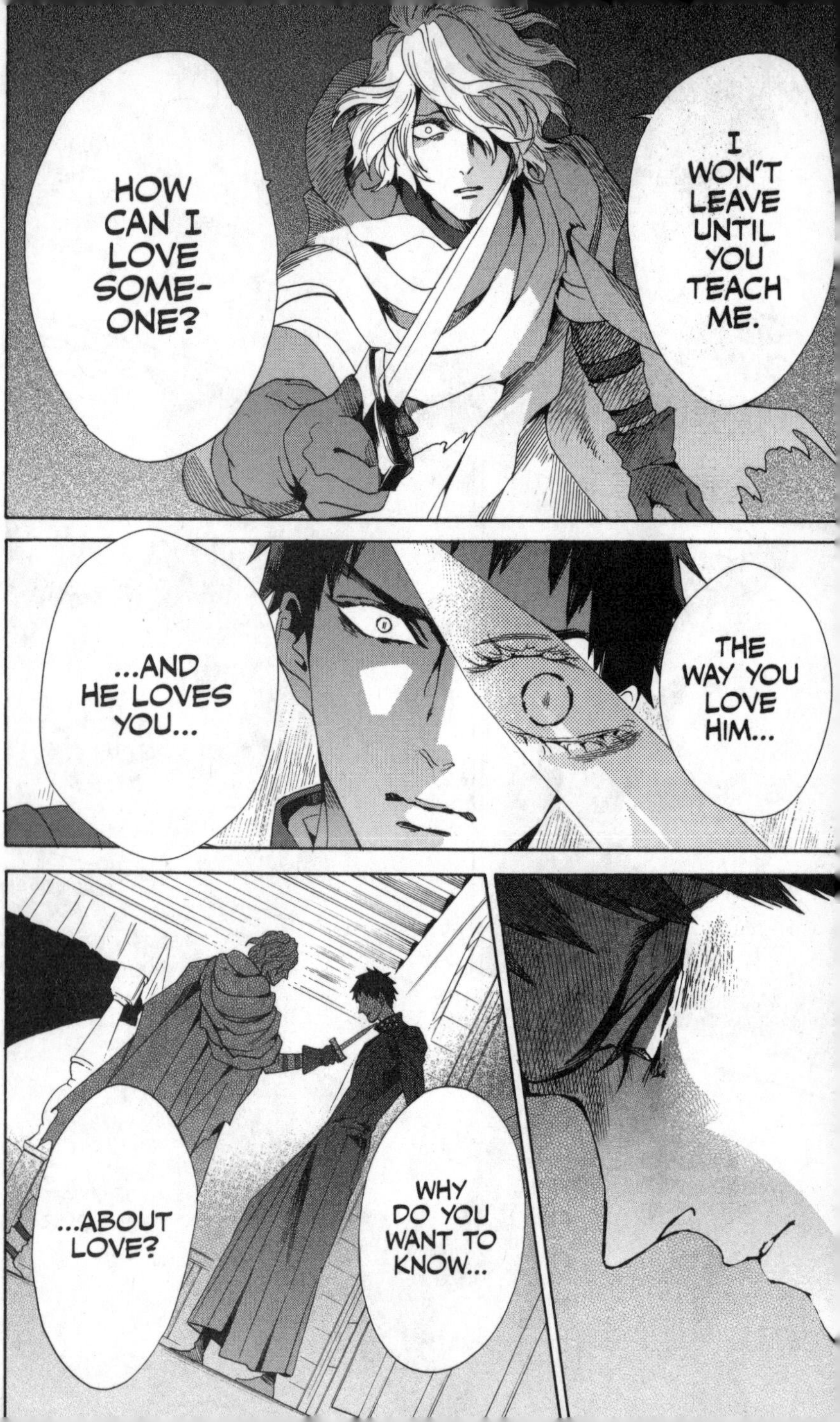
I WON'T LEAVE UNTIL YOU TEACH ME.
HOW CAN I LOVE SOME-ONE?
THE WAY YOU LOVE HIM...
...AND HE LOVES YOU...
WHY DO YOU WANT TO KNOW...
...ABOUT LOVE?

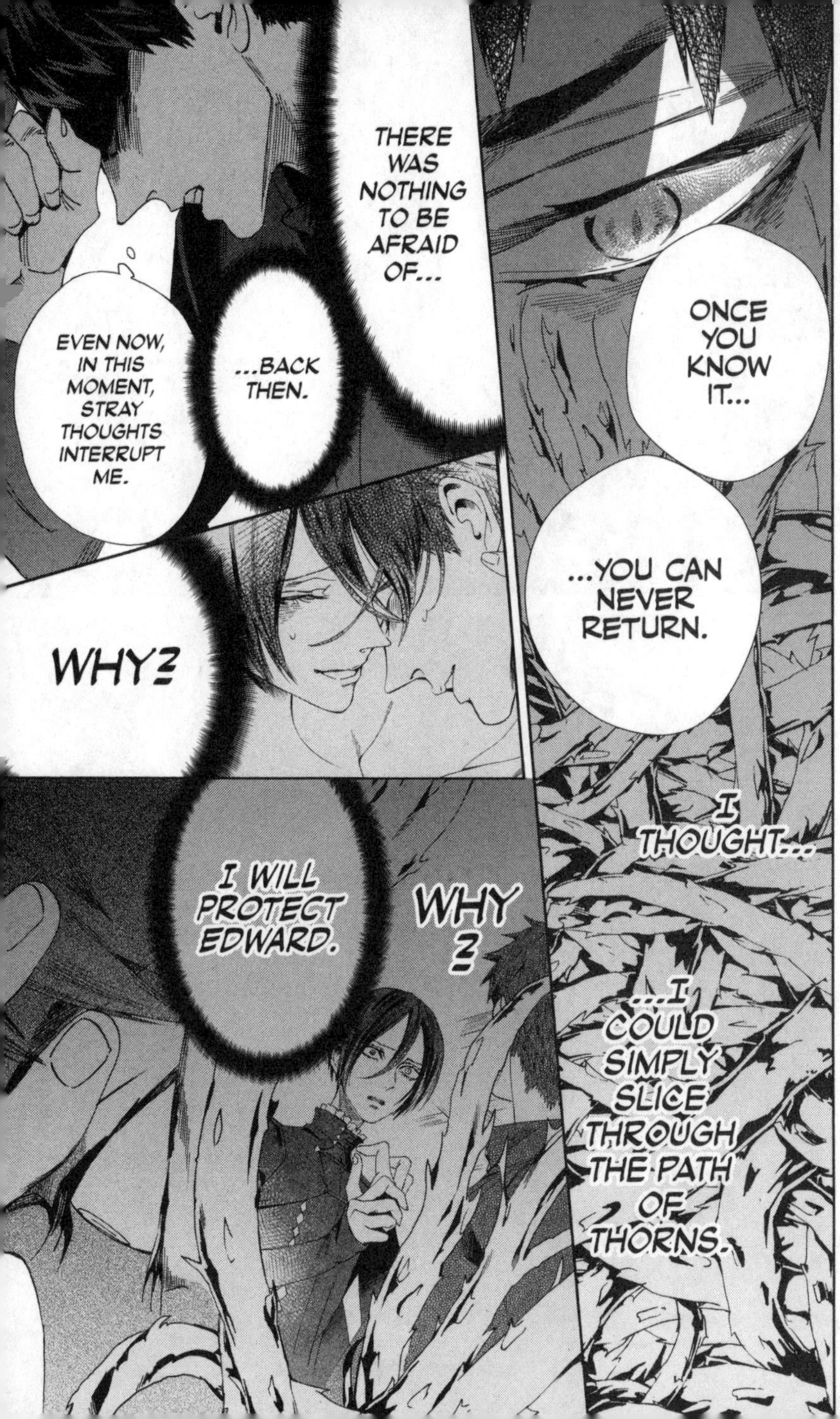
ONCE YOU KNOW IT...
...YOU CAN NEVER RETURN.
THERE WAS NOTHING TO BE AFRAID OF...
...BACK THEN.
EVEN NOW, IN THIS MOMENT, STRAY THOUGHTS INTERRUPT ME.
WHY?
I THOUGHT...
...I COULD SIMPLY SLICE THROUGH THE PATH OF THORNS.
I WILL PROTECT EDWARD.
WHY?

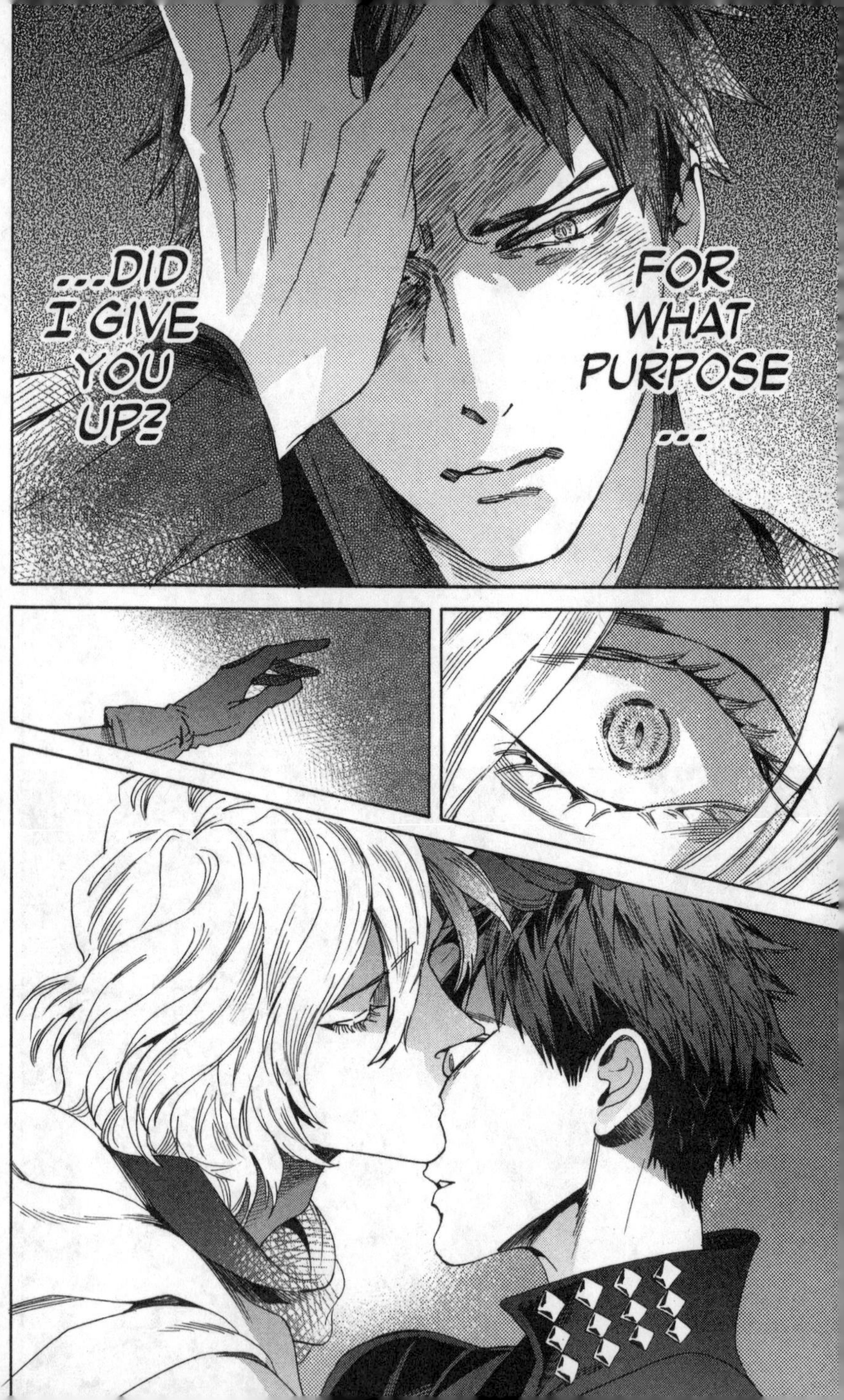
FOR WHAT PURPOSE...
...DID I GIVE YOU UP?

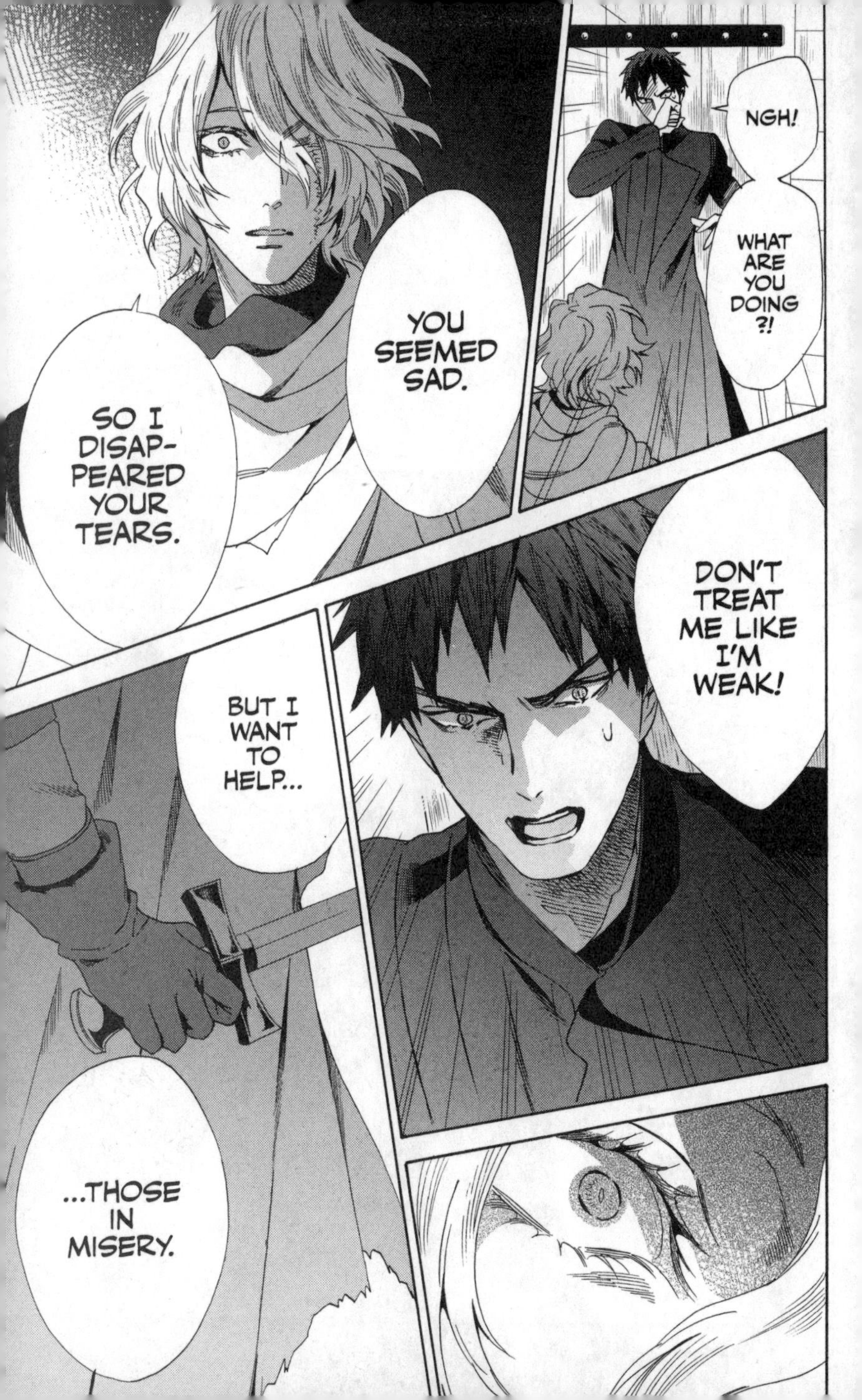
NGH!
WHAT ARE YOU DOING?!
YOU SEEMED SAD.
SO I DISAPPEARED YOUR TEARS.
DON'T TREAT ME LIKE I'M WEAK!
BUT I WANT TO HELP...
...THOSE IN MISERY.

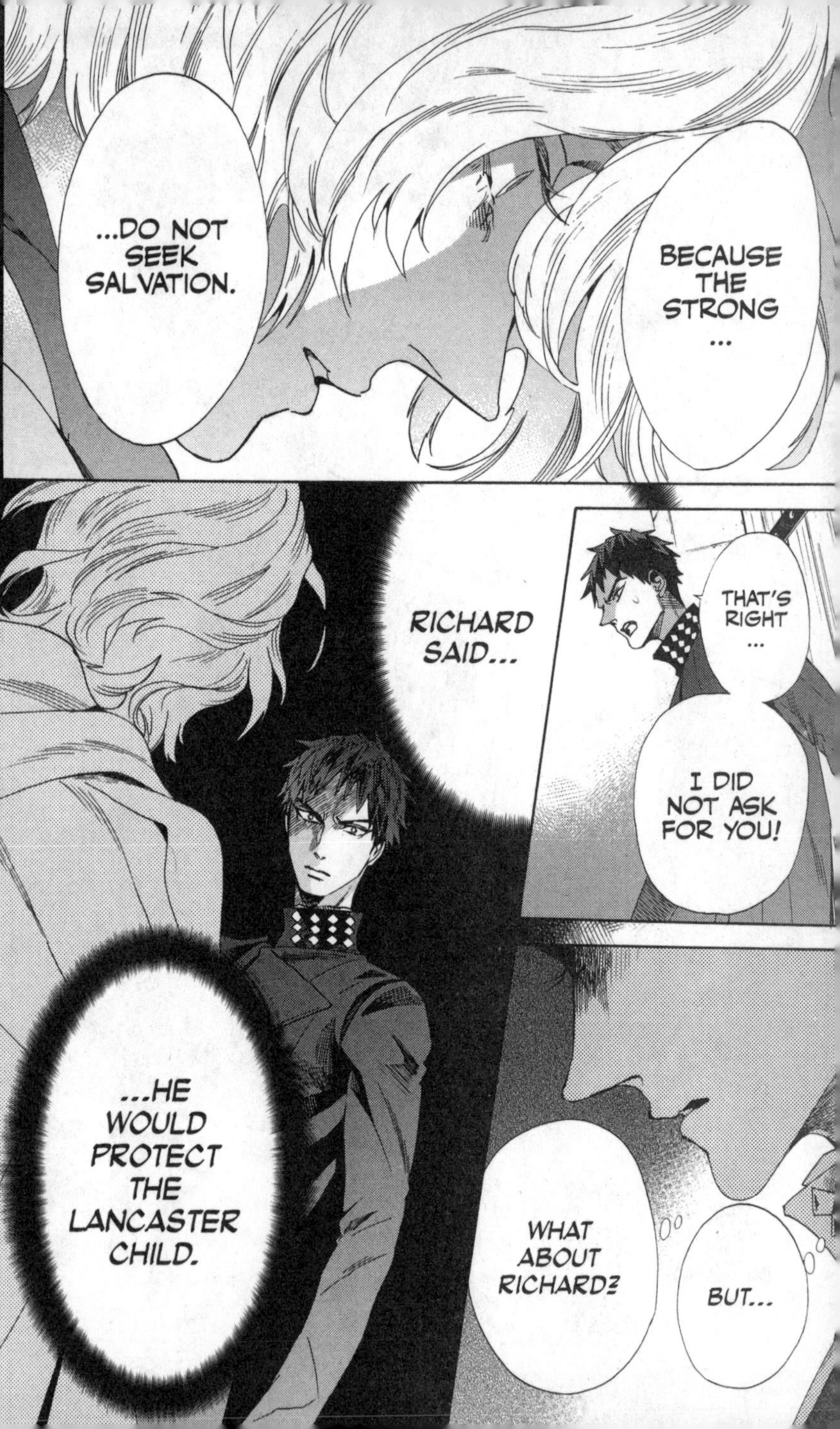
BECAUSE THE STRONG ...
...DO NOT SEEK SALVATION.
THAT'S RIGHT ...
I DID NOT ASK FOR YOU!
BUT...
WHAT ABOUT RICHARD?
RICHARD SAID...
...HE WOULD PROTECT THE LANCASTER CHILD.

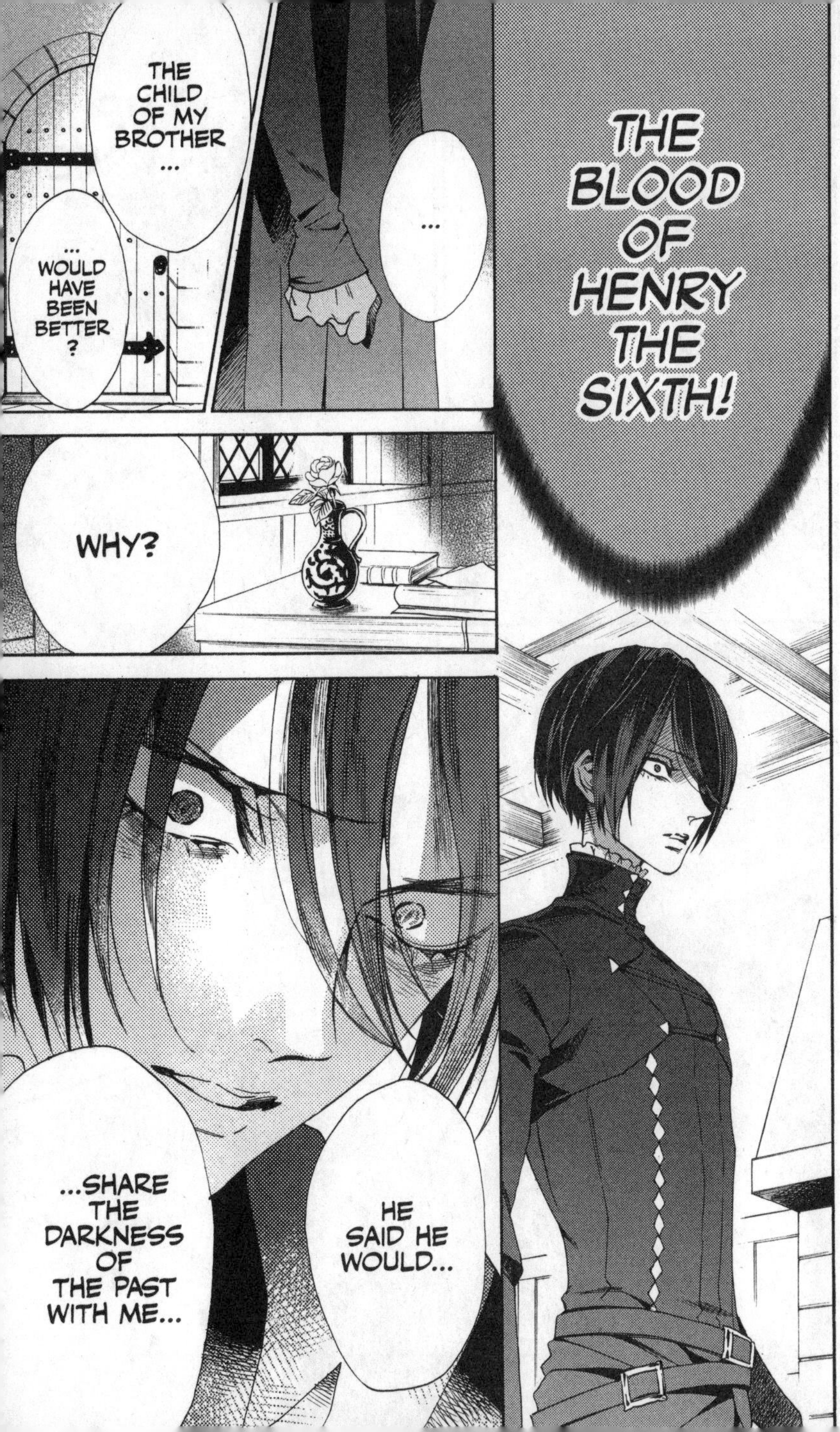
THE BLOOD OF HENRY THE SIXTH!
...
THE CHILD OF MY BROTHER ...
... WOULD HAVE BEEN BETTER ?
WHY?
HE SAID HE WOULD...
...SHARE THE DARKNESS OF THE PAST WITH ME...

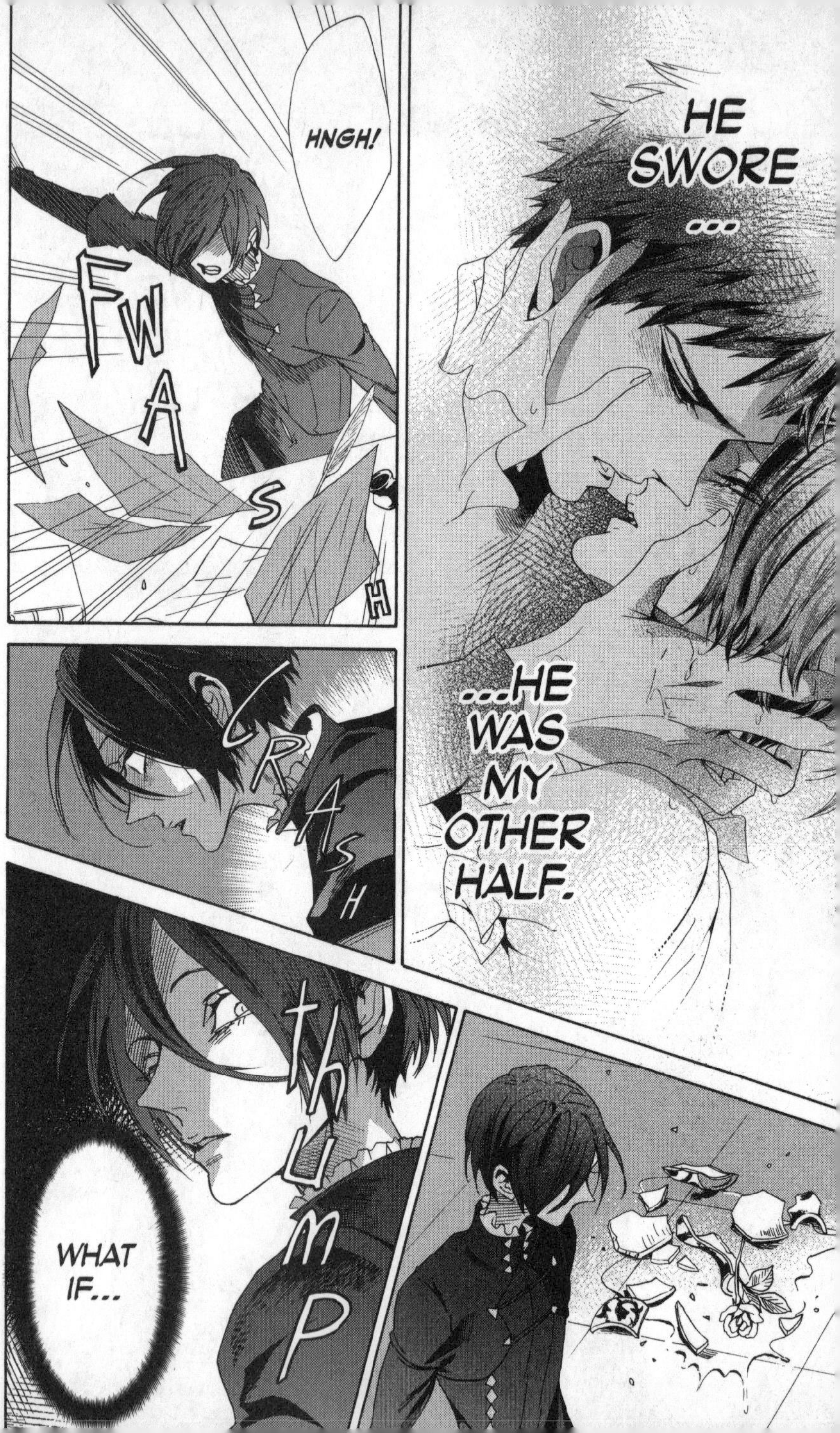
HE SWORE...
...HE WAS MY OTHER HALF.
HNGH!
FWASH
CRASH
thUMP
WHAT IF...

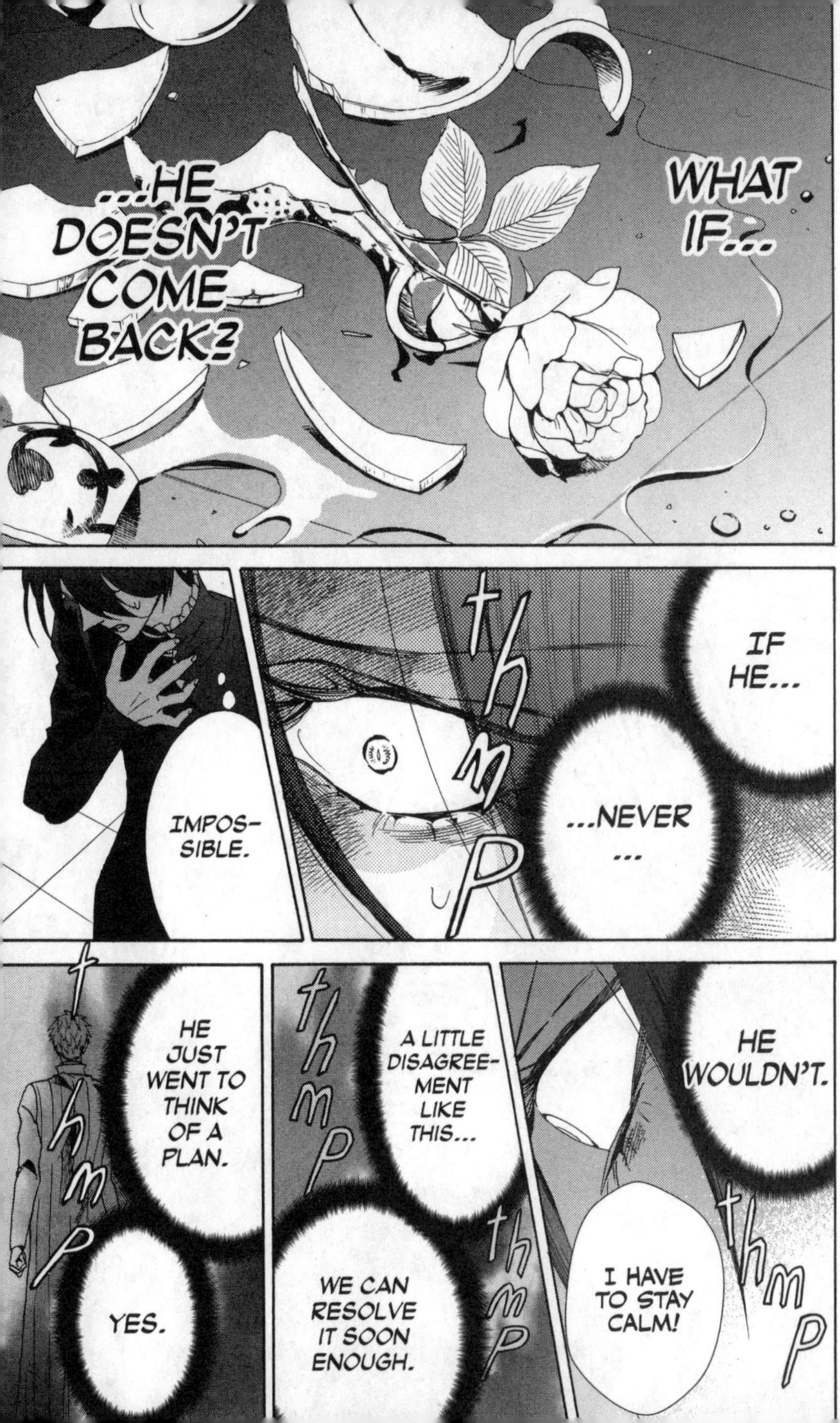
WHAT IF...
...HE DOESN'T COME BACK?
IF HE...
thmp
...NEVER ...
IMPOSSIBLE.
HE WOULDN'T.
thmp
I HAVE TO STAY CALM!
thmp
A LITTLE DISAGREEMENT LIKE THIS...
thmp
WE CAN RESOLVE IT SOON ENOUGH.
thmp
HE JUST WENT TO THINK OF A PLAN.
YES.

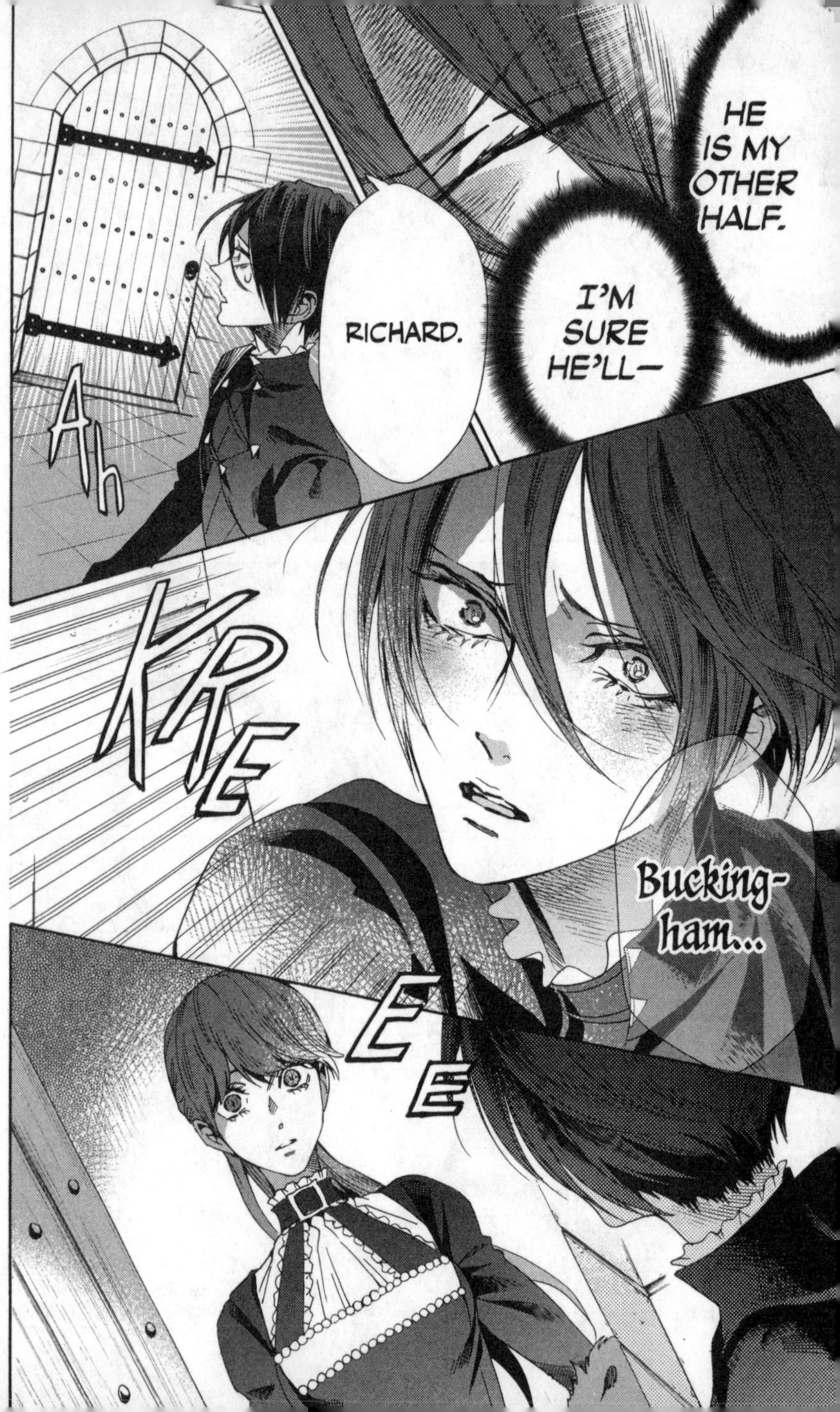
HE IS MY OTHER HALF.
I'M SURE HE'LL—
RICHARD.
Ah
Bucking-ham...
KREEEE

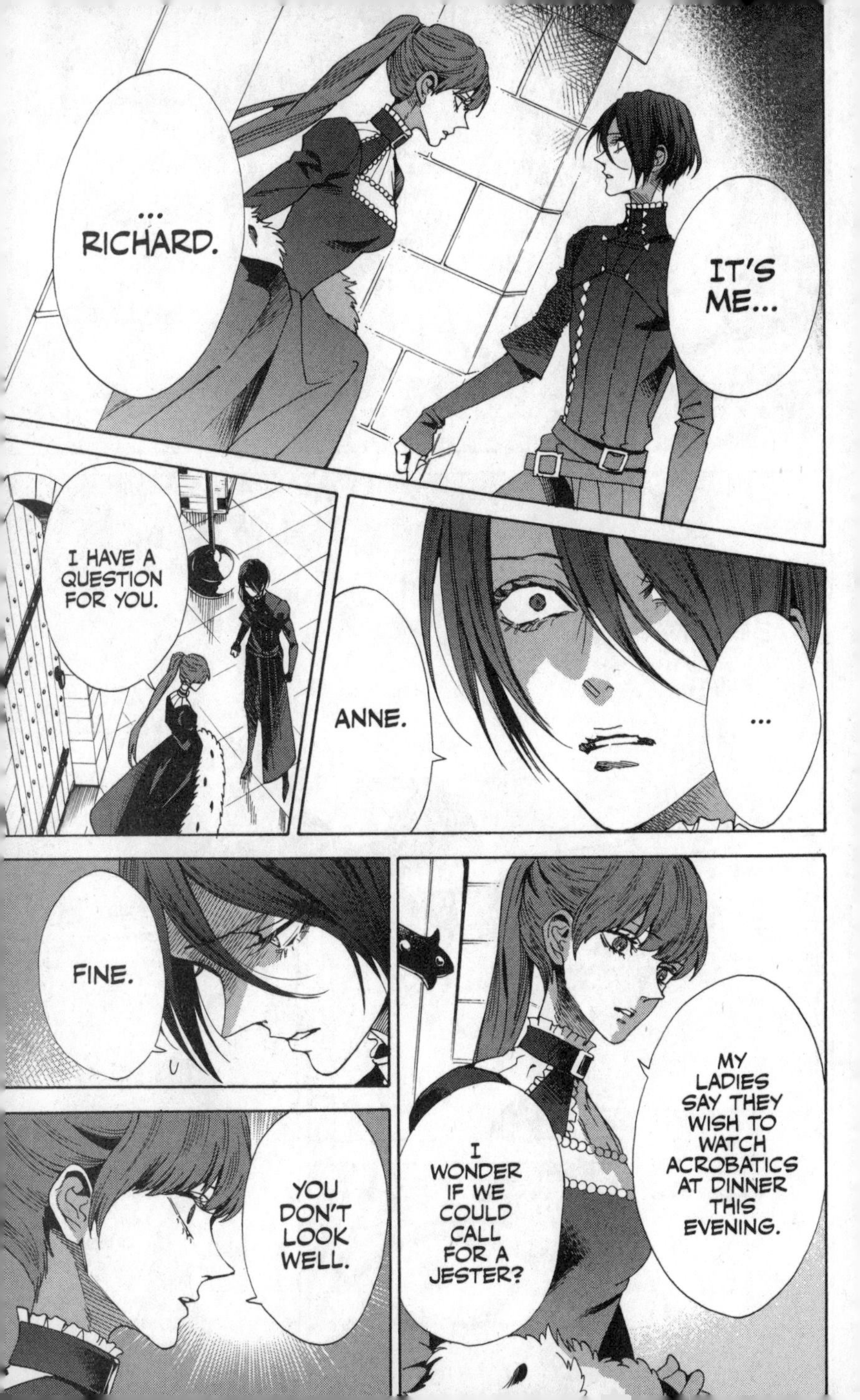
IT'S ME...
... RICHARD.
...
ANNE.
I HAVE A QUESTION FOR YOU.
MY LADIES SAY THEY WISH TO WATCH ACROBATICS AT DINNER THIS EVENING.
I WONDER IF WE COULD CALL FOR A JESTER?
FINE.
YOU DON'T LOOK WELL.

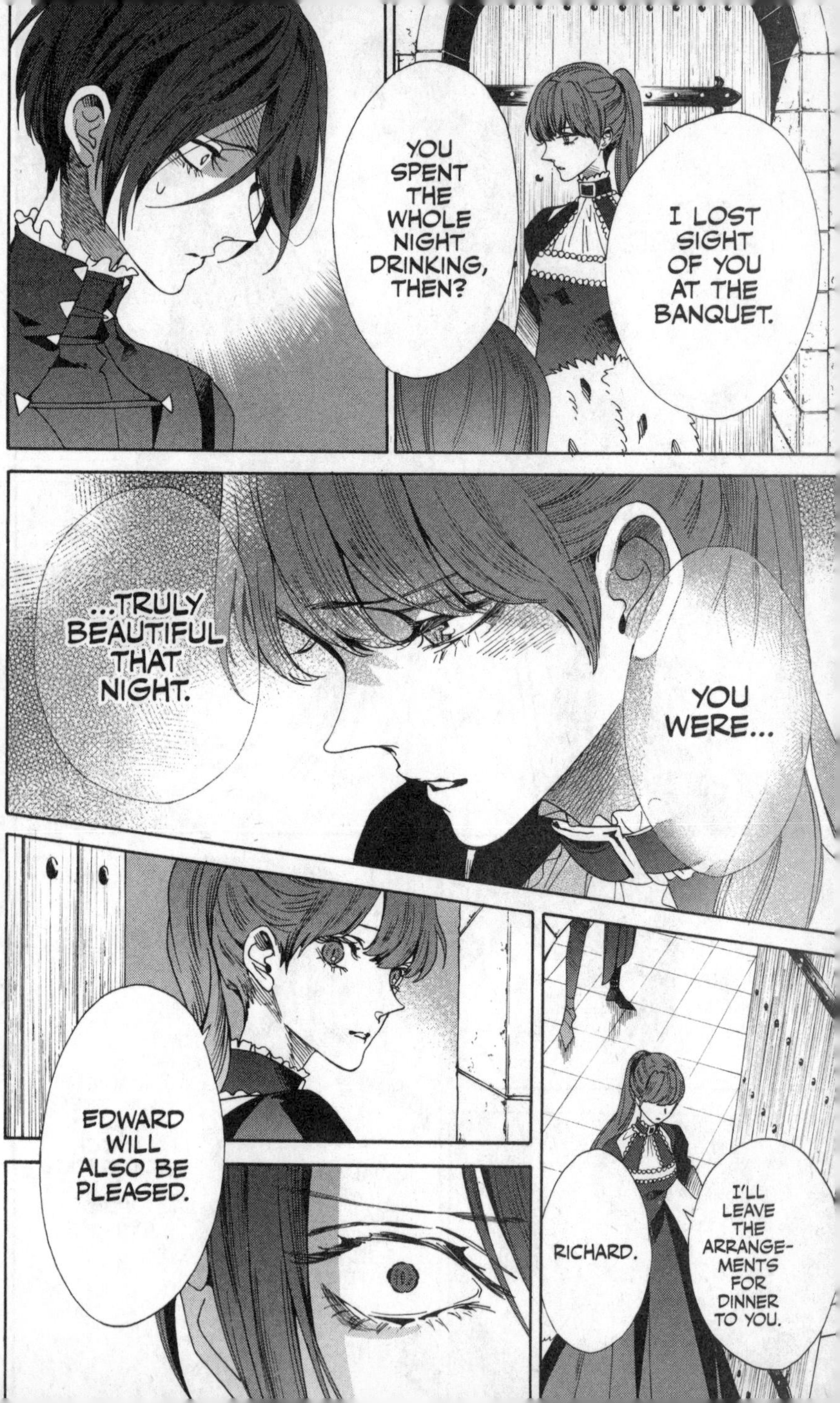
I LOST SIGHT OF YOU AT THE BANQUET.
YOU SPENT THE WHOLE NIGHT DRINKING, THEN?
YOU WERE...
...TRULY BEAUTIFUL THAT NIGHT.
I'LL LEAVE THE ARRANGE-MENTS FOR DINNER TO YOU.
RICHARD.
EDWARD WILL ALSO BE PLEASED.

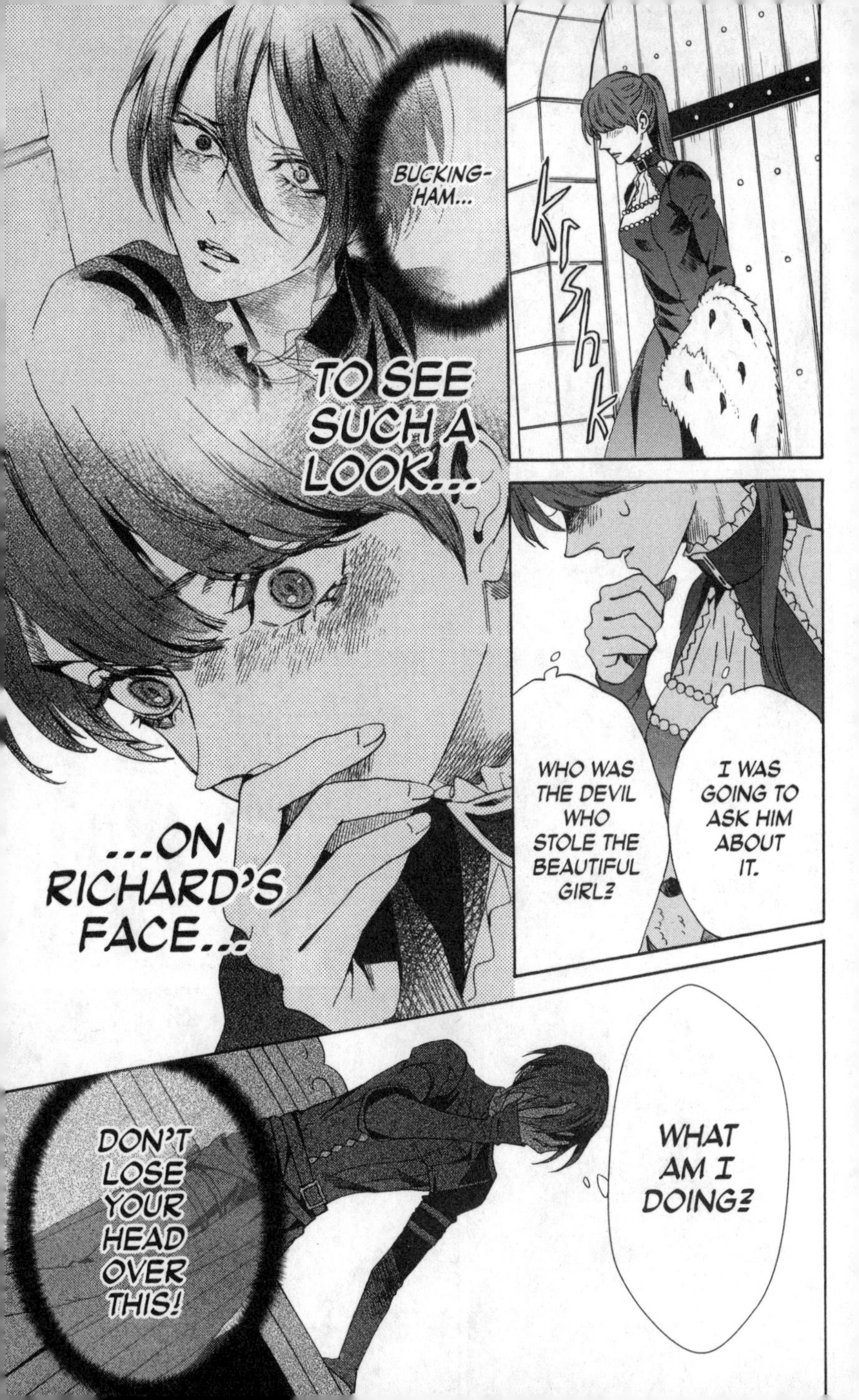
KSHK
I WAS GOING TO ASK HIM ABOUT IT.
WHO WAS THE DEVIL WHO STOLE THE BEAUTIFUL GIRL?
BUCKING-HAM...
TO SEE SUCH A LOOK...
...ON RICHARD'S FACE...
WHAT AM I DOING?
DON'T LOSE YOUR HEAD OVER THIS!

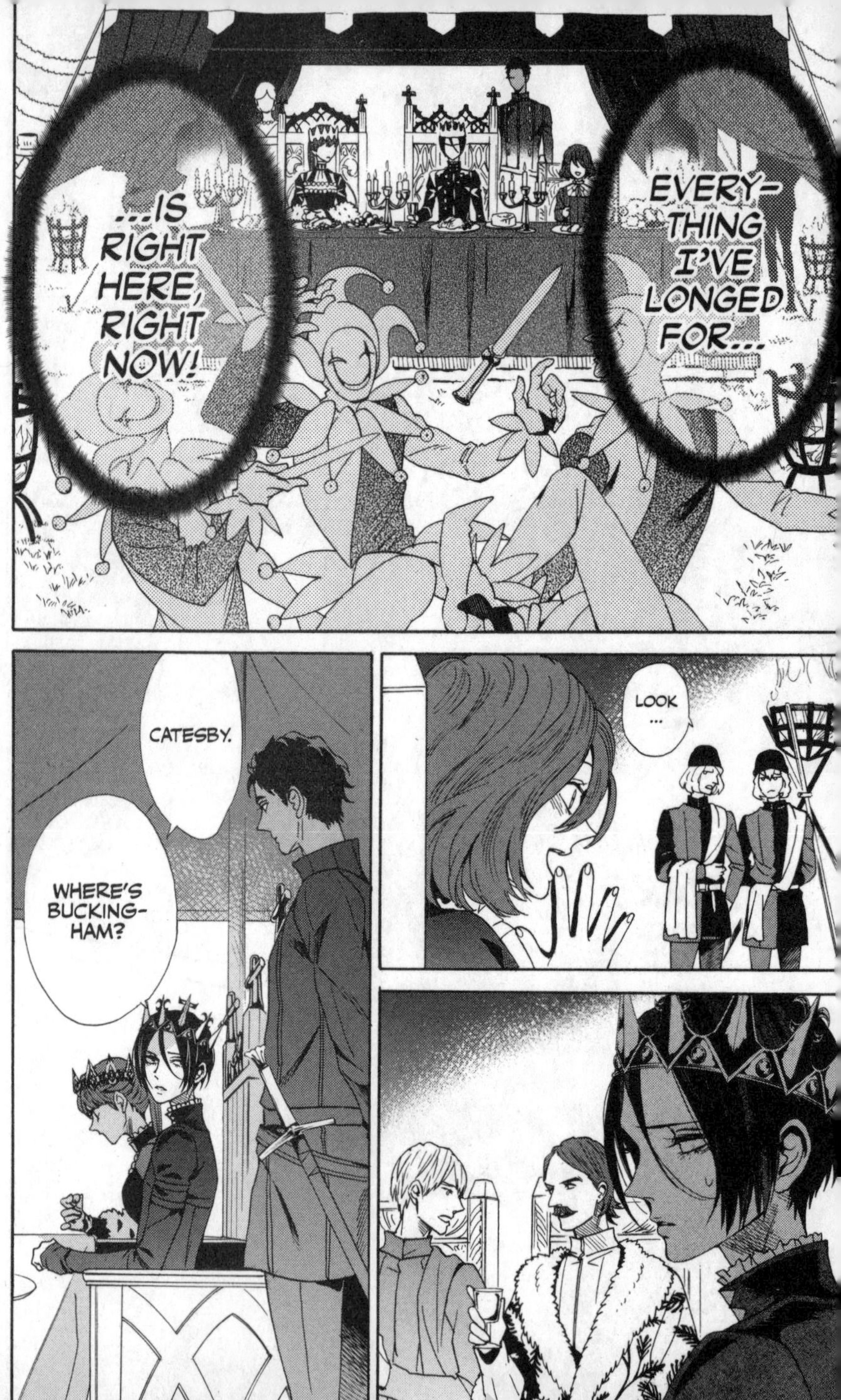
EVERY-THING I'VE LONGED FOR...
...IS RIGHT HERE, RIGHT NOW!
LOOK ...
CATESBY.
WHERE'S BUCKING-HAM?

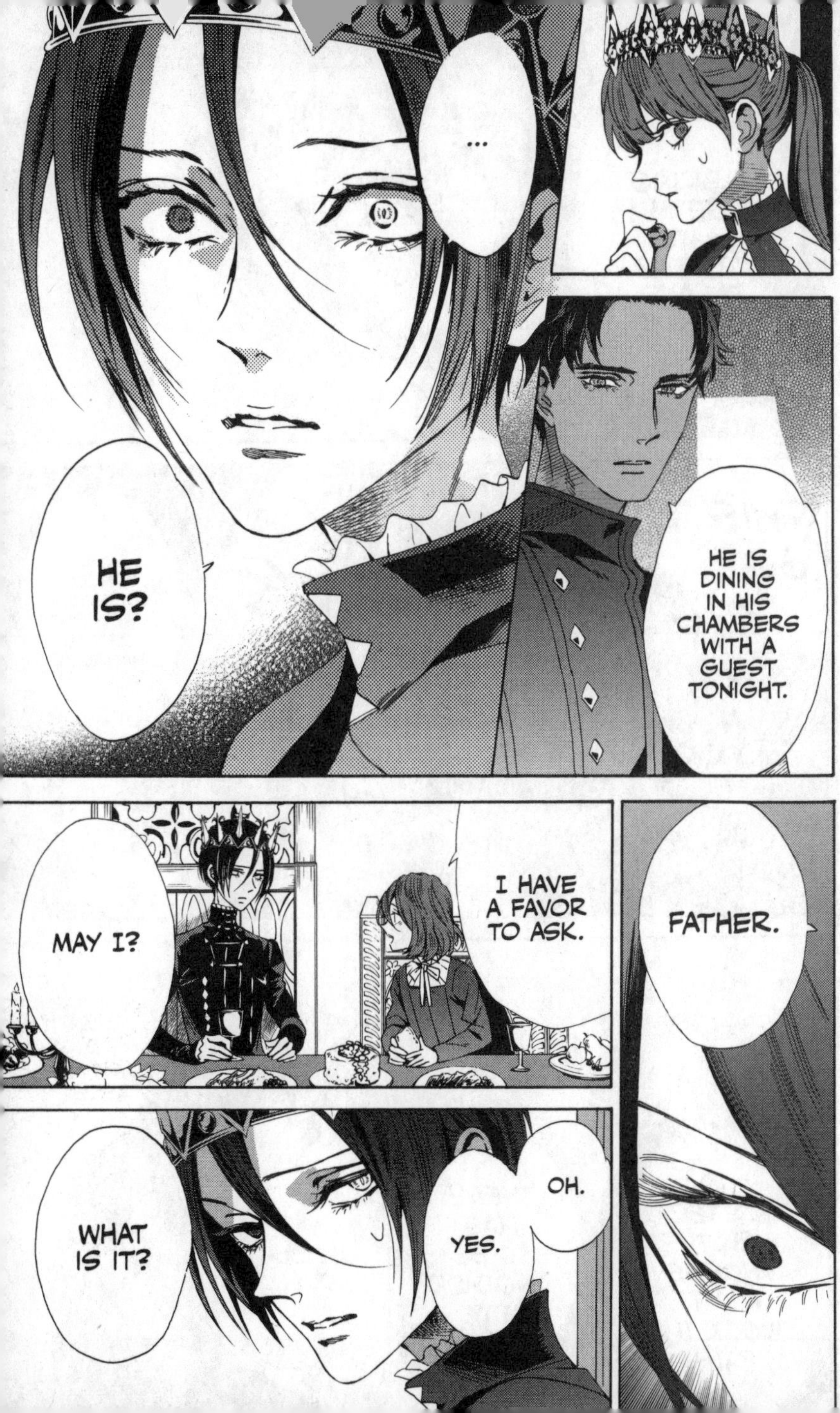
...
HE IS DINING IN HIS CHAMBERS WITH A GUEST TONIGHT.
HE IS?
FATHER.
I HAVE A FAVOR TO ASK.
MAY I?
OH.
YES.
WHAT IS IT?

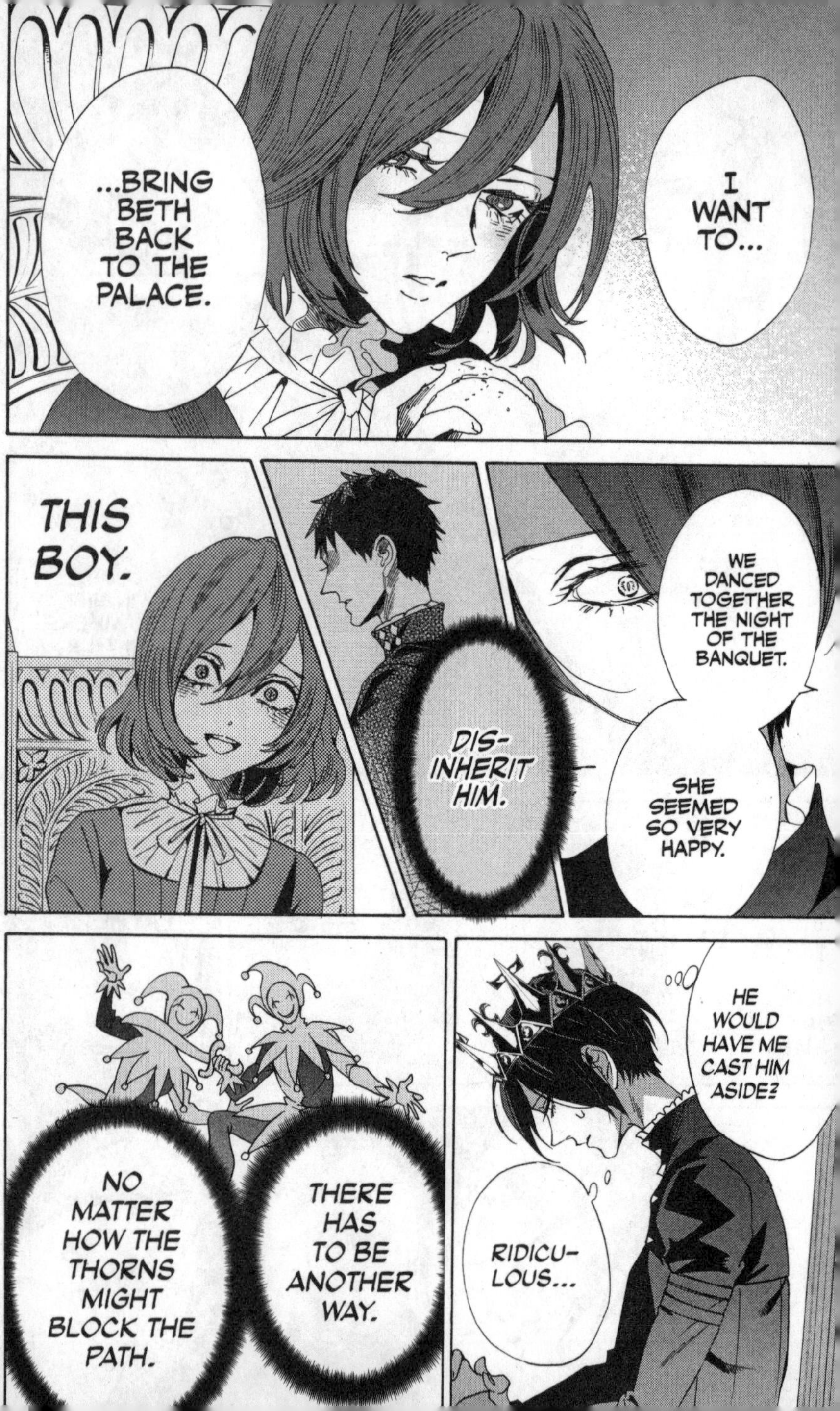
I WANT TO...
...BRING BETH BACK TO THE PALACE.
WE DANCED TOGETHER THE NIGHT OF THE BANQUET.
SHE SEEMED SO VERY HAPPY.
DIS-INHERIT HIM.
THIS BOY.
HE WOULD HAVE ME CAST HIM ASIDE?
RIDICU-LOUS...
THERE HAS TO BE ANOTHER WAY.
NO MATTER HOW THE THORNS MIGHT BLOCK THE PATH.

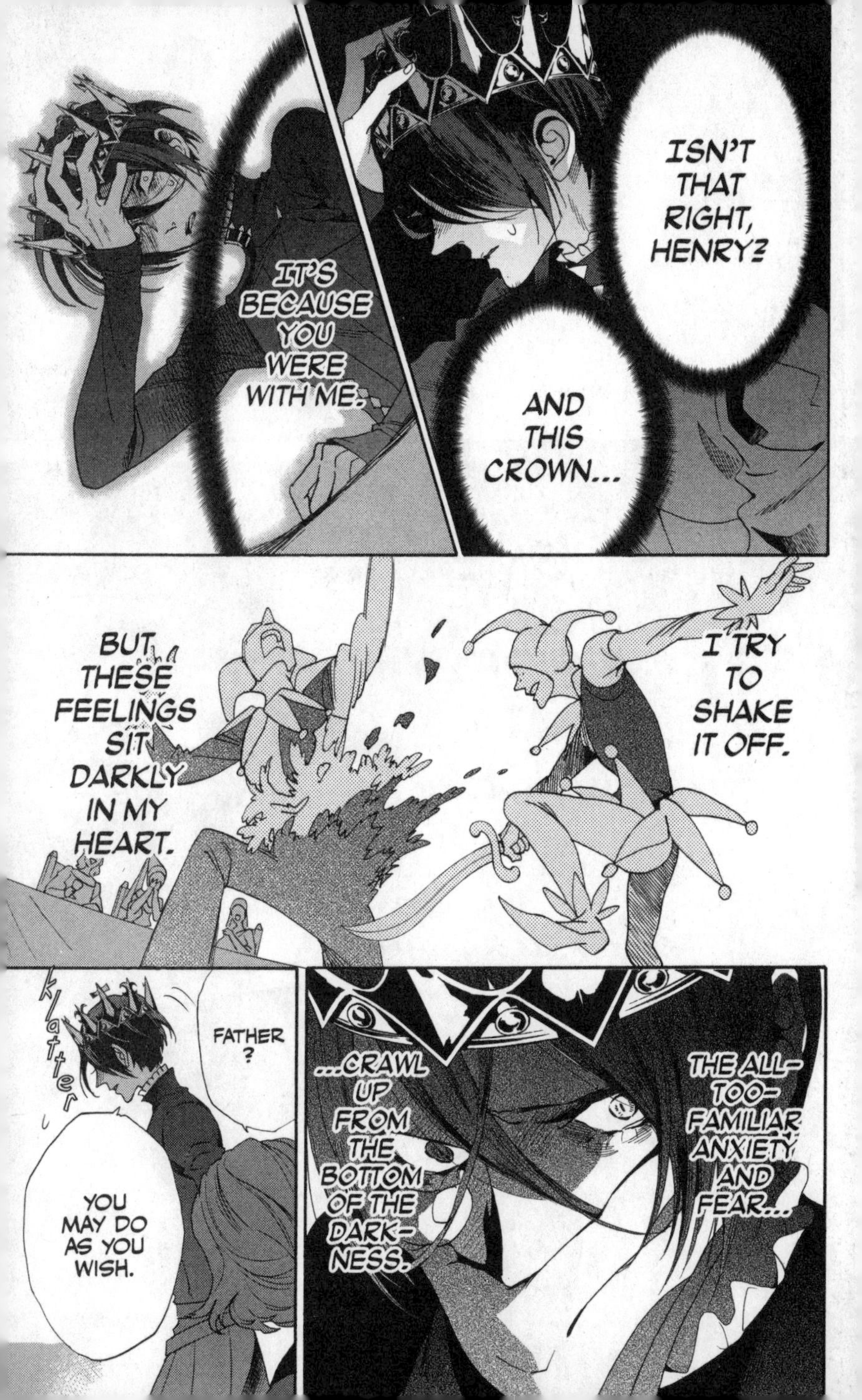
ISN'T THAT RIGHT, HENRY?
AND THIS CROWN...
IT'S BECAUSE YOU WERE WITH ME.
I TRY TO SHAKE IT OFF.
BUT THESE FEELINGS SIT DARKLY IN MY HEART.
THE ALL-TOO-FAMILIAR ANXIETY AND FEAR...
...CRAWL UP FROM THE BOTTOM OF THE DARK-NESS.
klatter
FATHER?
YOU MAY DO AS YOU WISH.

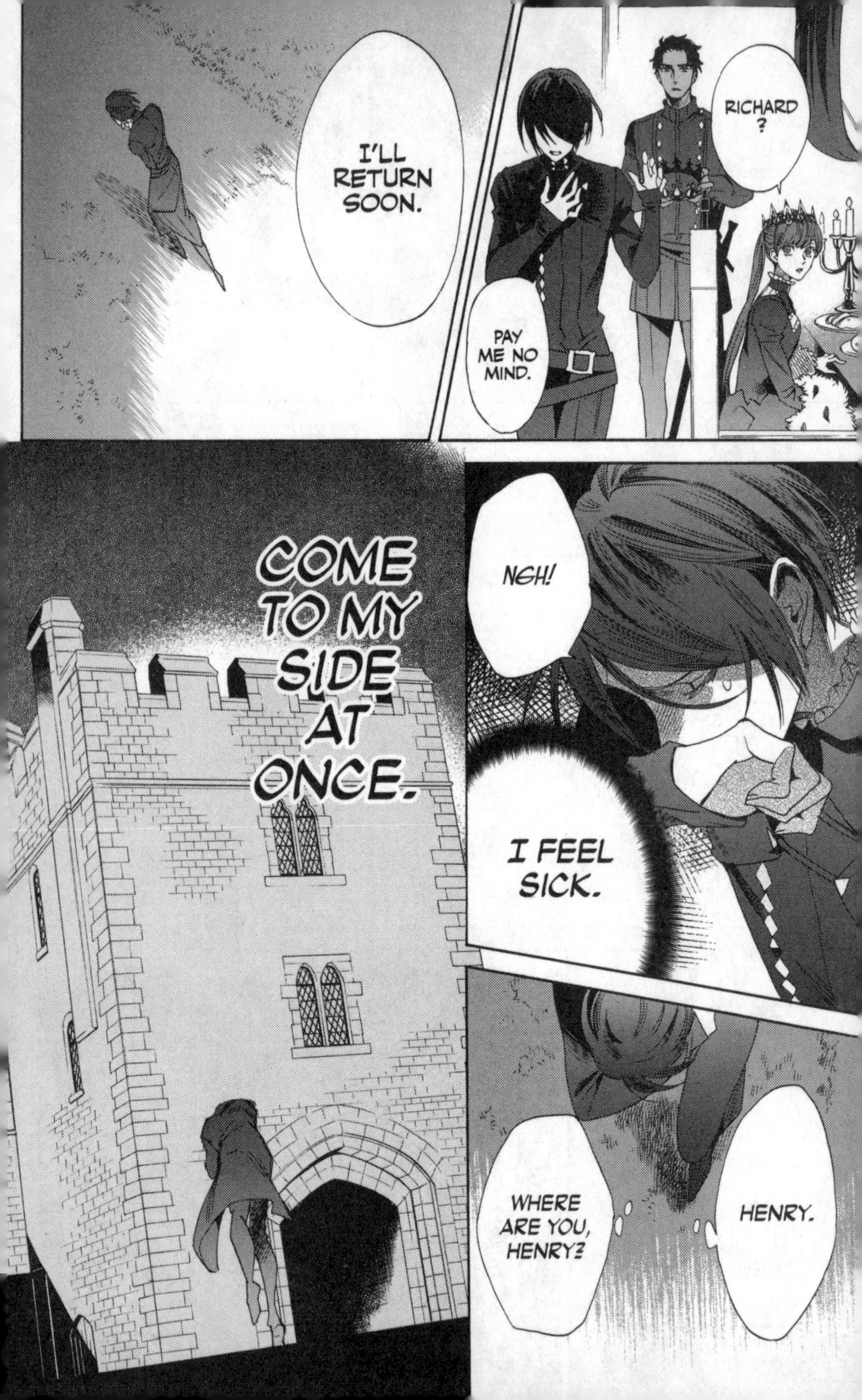
RICHARD?
PAY ME NO MIND.
I'LL RETURN SOON.
NGH!
I FEEL SICK.
HENRY.
WHERE ARE YOU, HENRY?
COME TO MY SIDE AT ONCE.

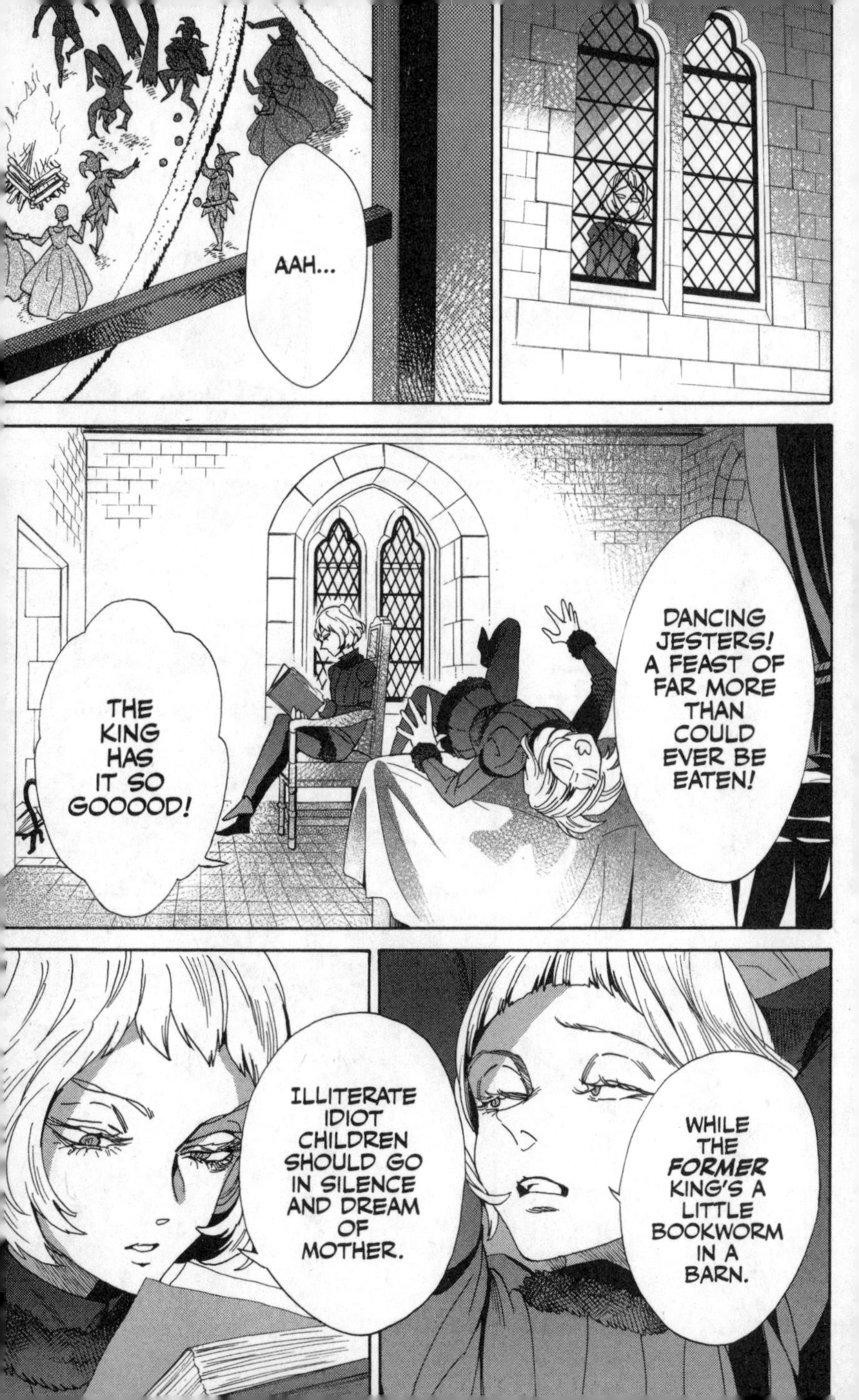
AAH...
DANCING JESTERS! A FEAST OF FAR MORE THAN COULD EVER BE EATEN!
THE KING HAS IT SO GOOOOD!
WHILE THE *FORMER* KING'S A LITTLE BOOKWORM IN A BARN.
ILLITERATE IDIOT CHILDREN SHOULD GO IN SILENCE AND DREAM OF MOTHER.

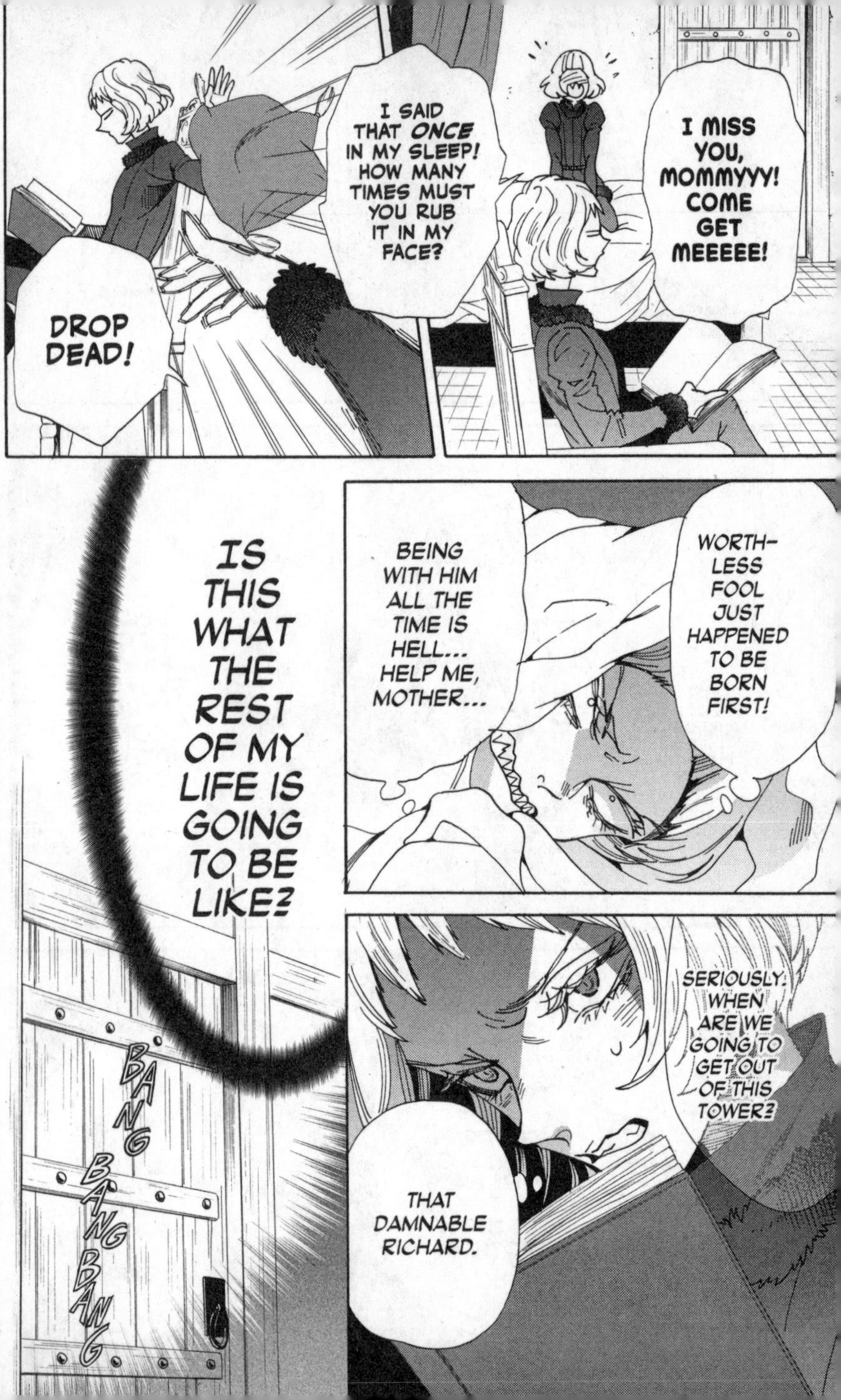
I MISS YOU, MOMMYYY! COME GET MEEEEE!
I SAID THAT *ONCE* IN MY SLEEP! HOW MANY TIMES MUST YOU RUB IT IN MY FACE?
DROP DEAD!
WORTH-LESS FOOL JUST HAPPENED TO BE BORN FIRST!
BEING WITH HIM ALL THE TIME IS HELL... HELP ME, MOTHER...
SERIOUSLY. WHEN ARE WE GOING TO GET OUT OF THIS TOWER?
THAT DAMNABLE RICHARD.
IS THIS WHAT THE REST OF MY LIFE IS GOING TO BE LIKE?
BANG BANG BANG BANG

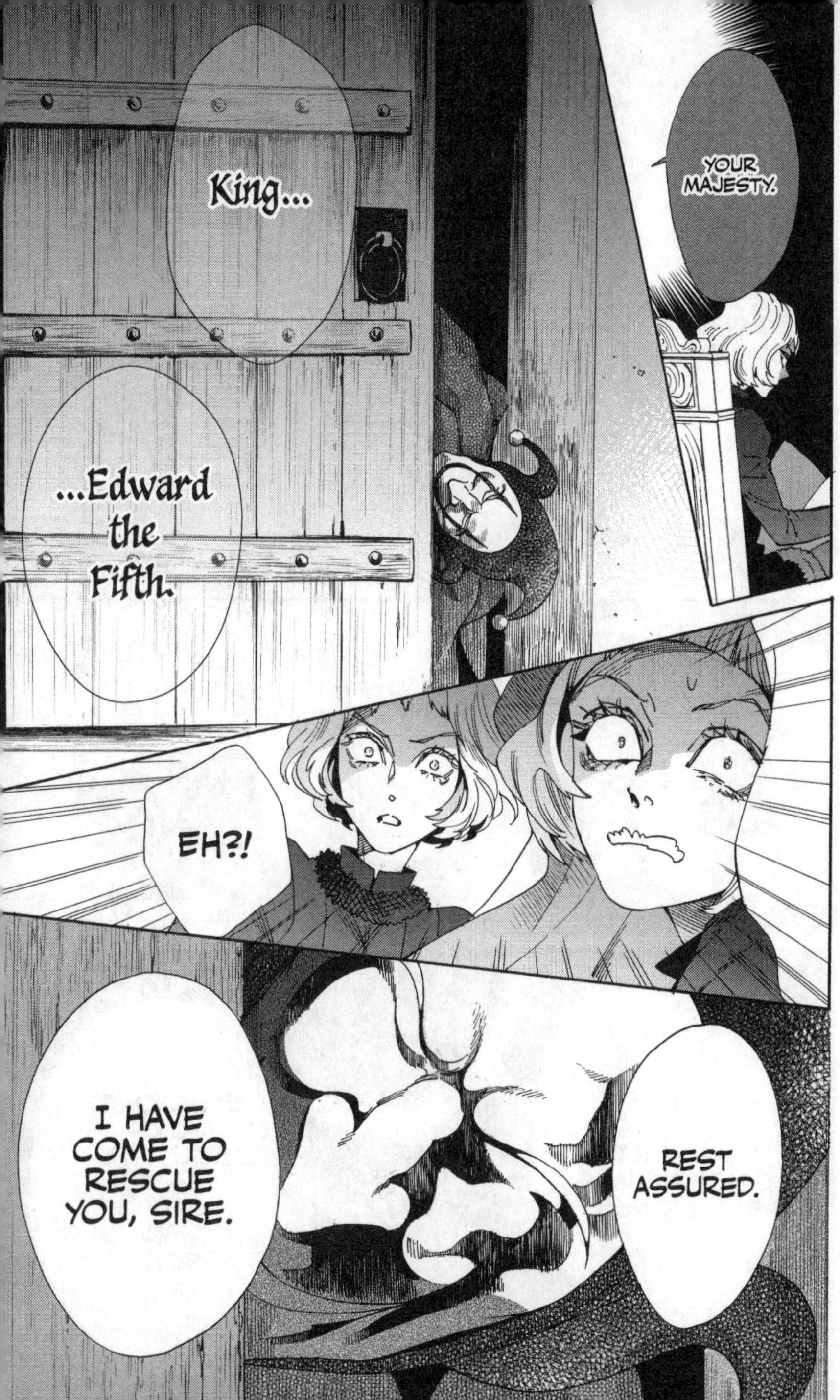
YOUR MAJESTY.
King...
...Edward the Fifth.
EH?!
REST ASSURED.
I HAVE COME TO RESCUE YOU, SIRE.

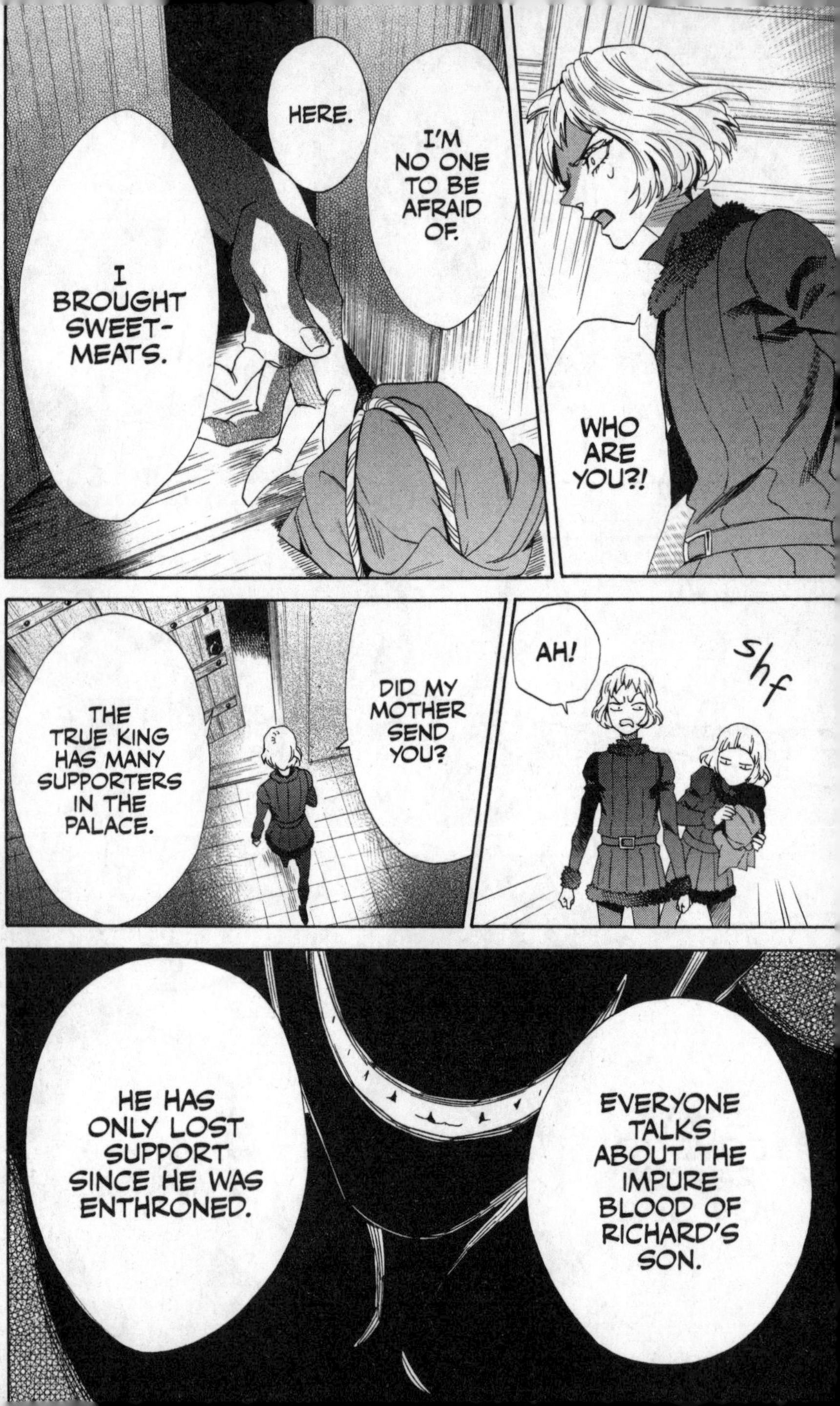
WHO ARE YOU?!
I'M NO ONE TO BE AFRAID OF.
HERE.
I BROUGHT SWEETMEATS.
AH!
shf
DID MY MOTHER SEND YOU?
THE TRUE KING HAS MANY SUPPORTERS IN THE PALACE.
EVERYONE TALKS ABOUT THE IMPURE BLOOD OF RICHARD'S SON.
HE HAS ONLY LOST SUPPORT SINCE HE WAS ENTHRONED.

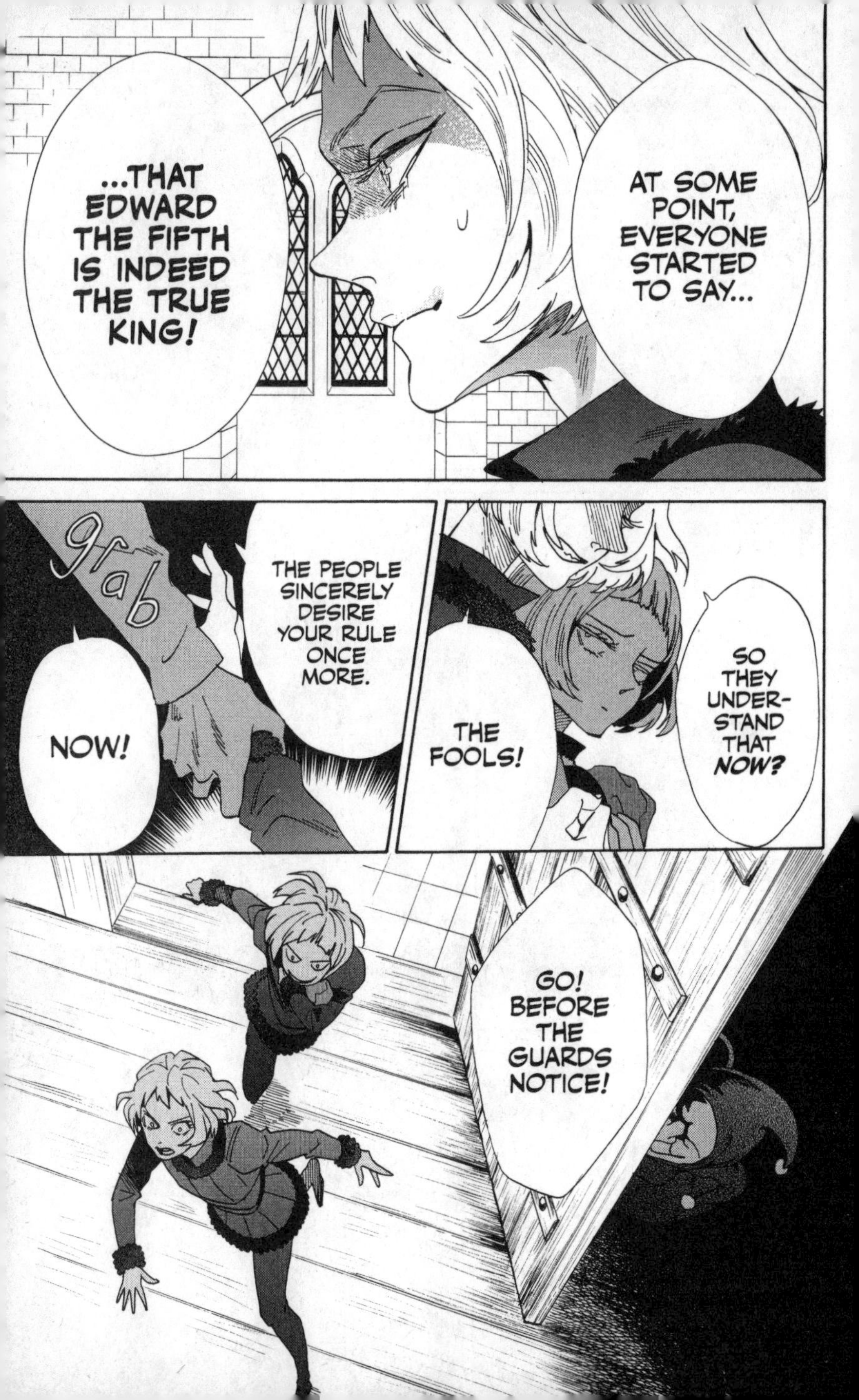
AT SOME POINT, EVERYONE STARTED TO SAY...
...THAT EDWARD THE FIFTH IS INDEED THE TRUE KING!
SO THEY UNDERSTAND THAT *NOW*?
THE FOOLS!
THE PEOPLE SINCERELY DESIRE YOUR RULE ONCE MORE.
grab
NOW!
GO! BEFORE THE GUARDS NOTICE!

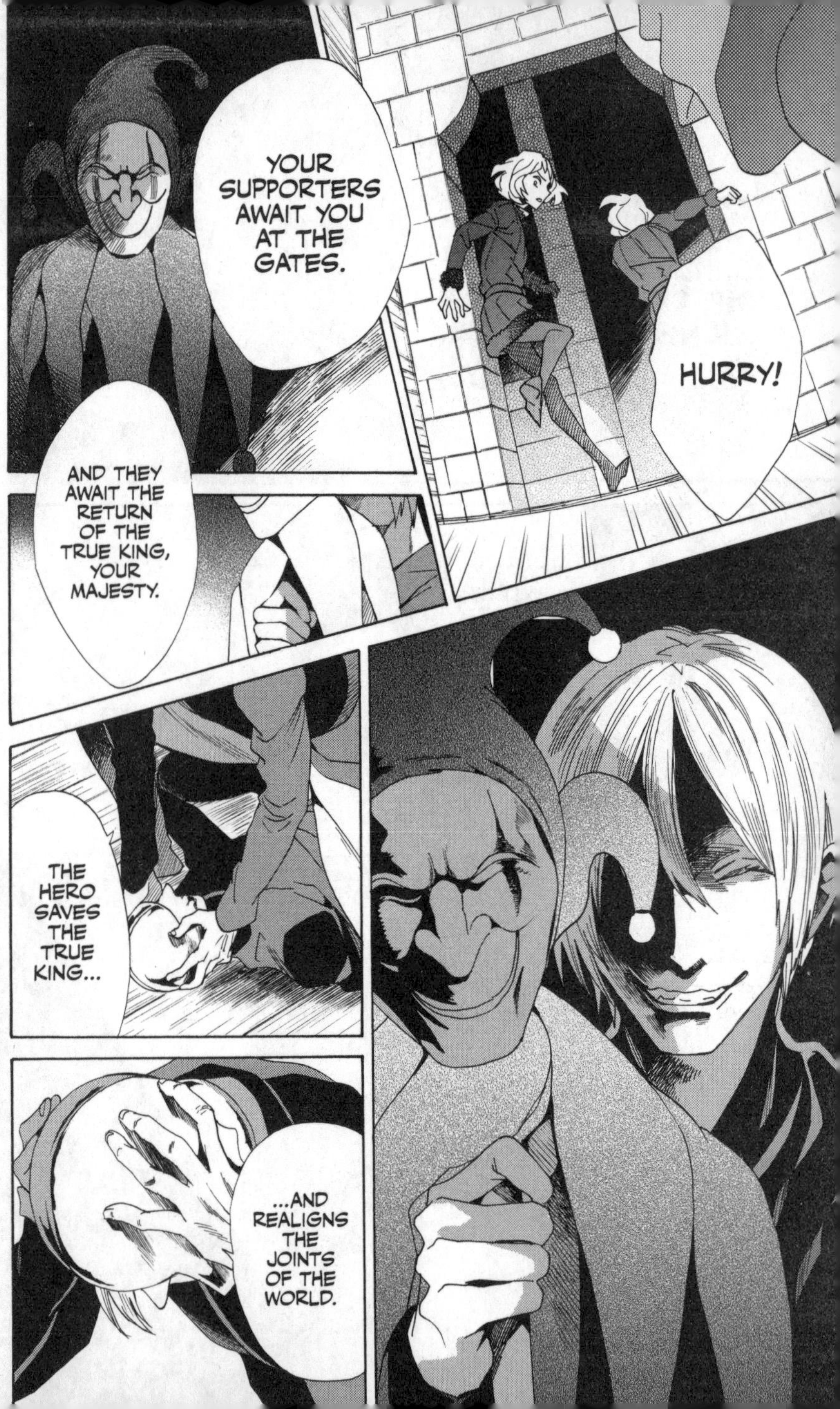
HURRY!
YOUR SUPPORTERS AWAIT YOU AT THE GATES.
AND THEY AWAIT THE RETURN OF THE TRUE KING, YOUR MAJESTY.
THE HERO SAVES THE TRUE KING...
...AND REALIGNS THE JOINTS OF THE WORLD.

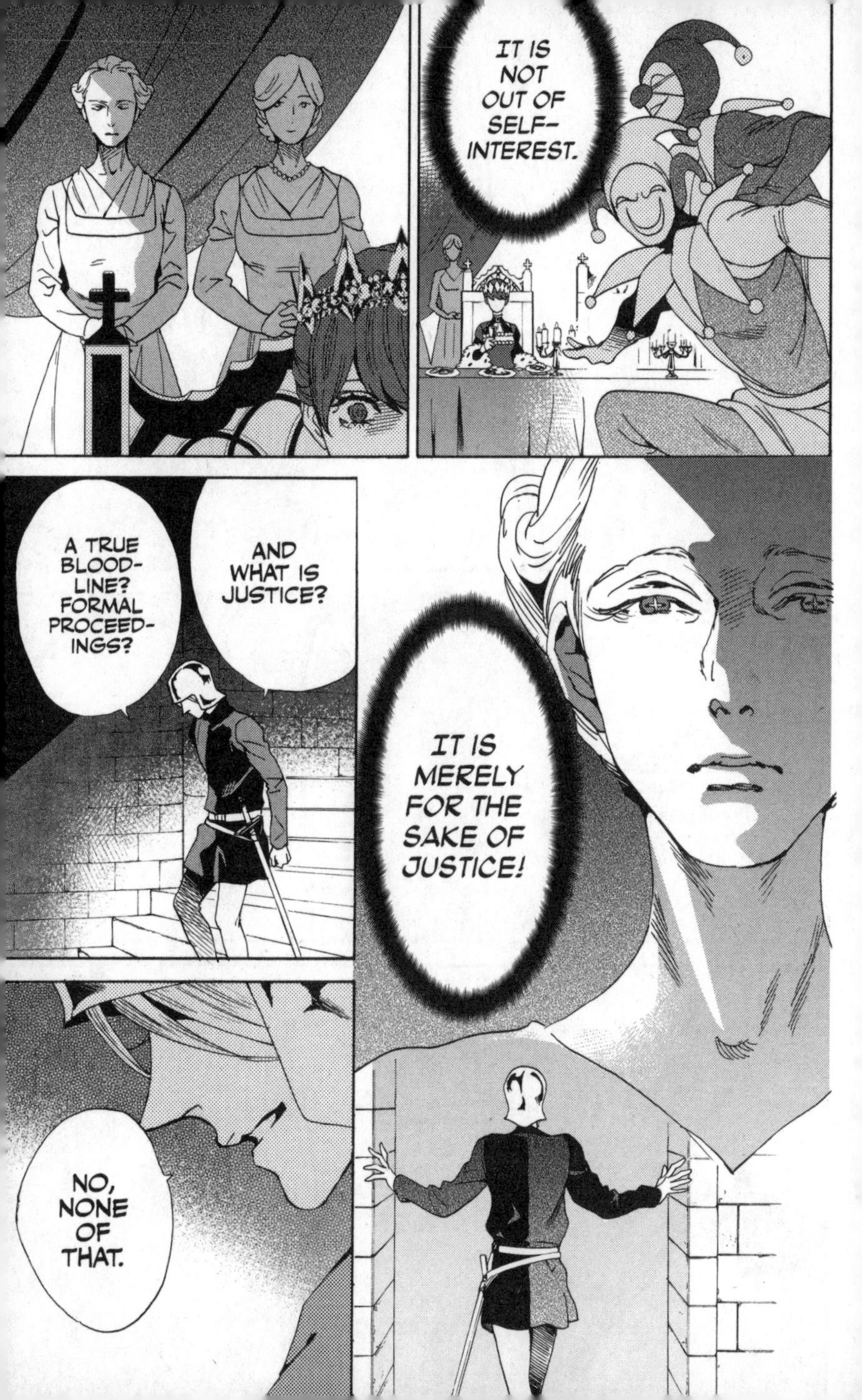
IT IS NOT OUT OF SELF-INTEREST.
IT IS MERELY FOR THE SAKE OF JUSTICE!
AND WHAT IS JUSTICE?
A TRUE BLOODLINE? FORMAL PROCEEDINGS?
NO, NONE OF THAT.

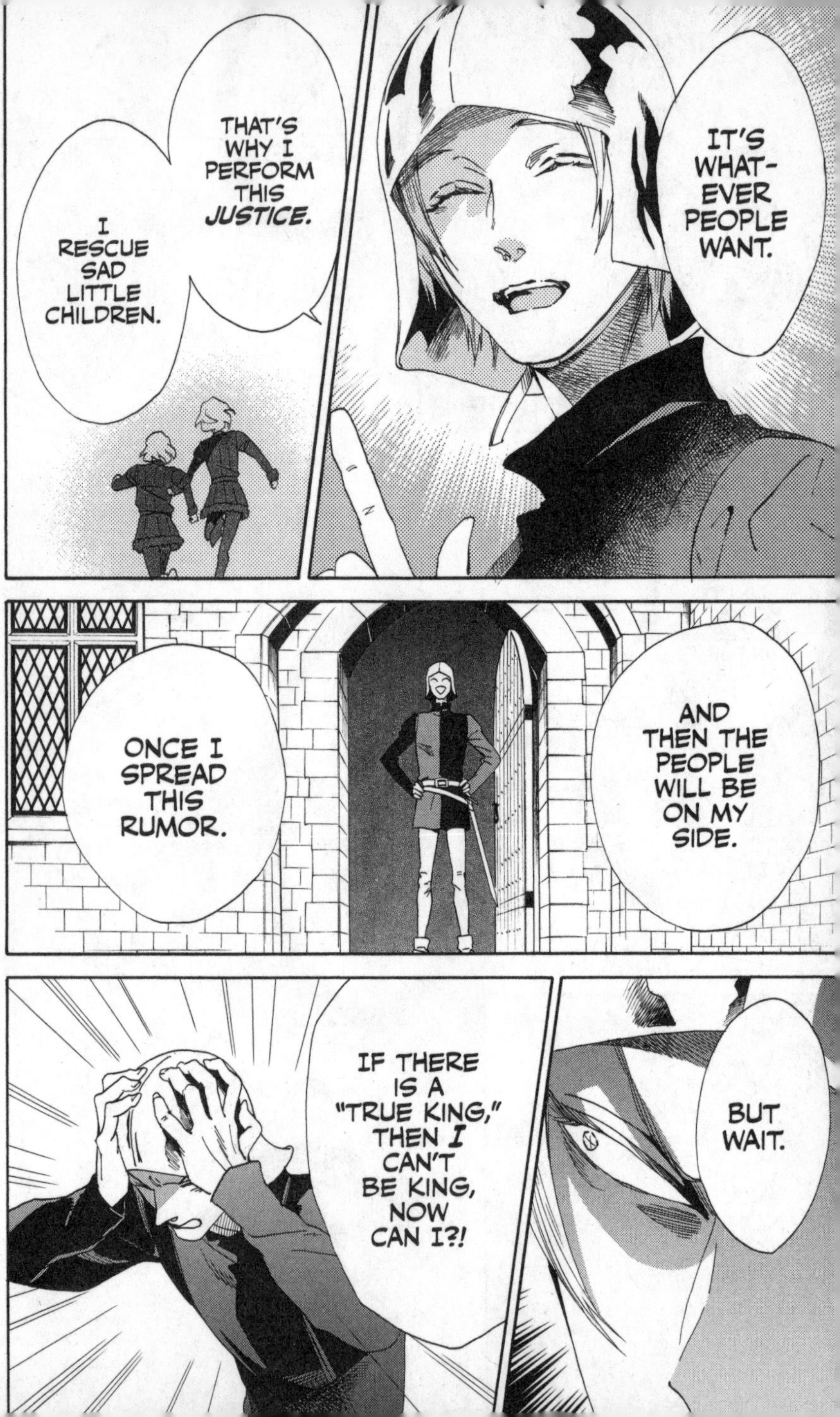
IT'S WHATEVER PEOPLE WANT.
THAT'S WHY I PERFORM THIS *JUSTICE.*
I RESCUE SAD LITTLE CHILDREN.
ONCE I SPREAD THIS RUMOR.
AND THEN THE PEOPLE WILL BE ON MY SIDE.
BUT WAIT.
IF THERE IS A "TRUE KING," THEN *I* CAN'T BE KING, NOW CAN I?!

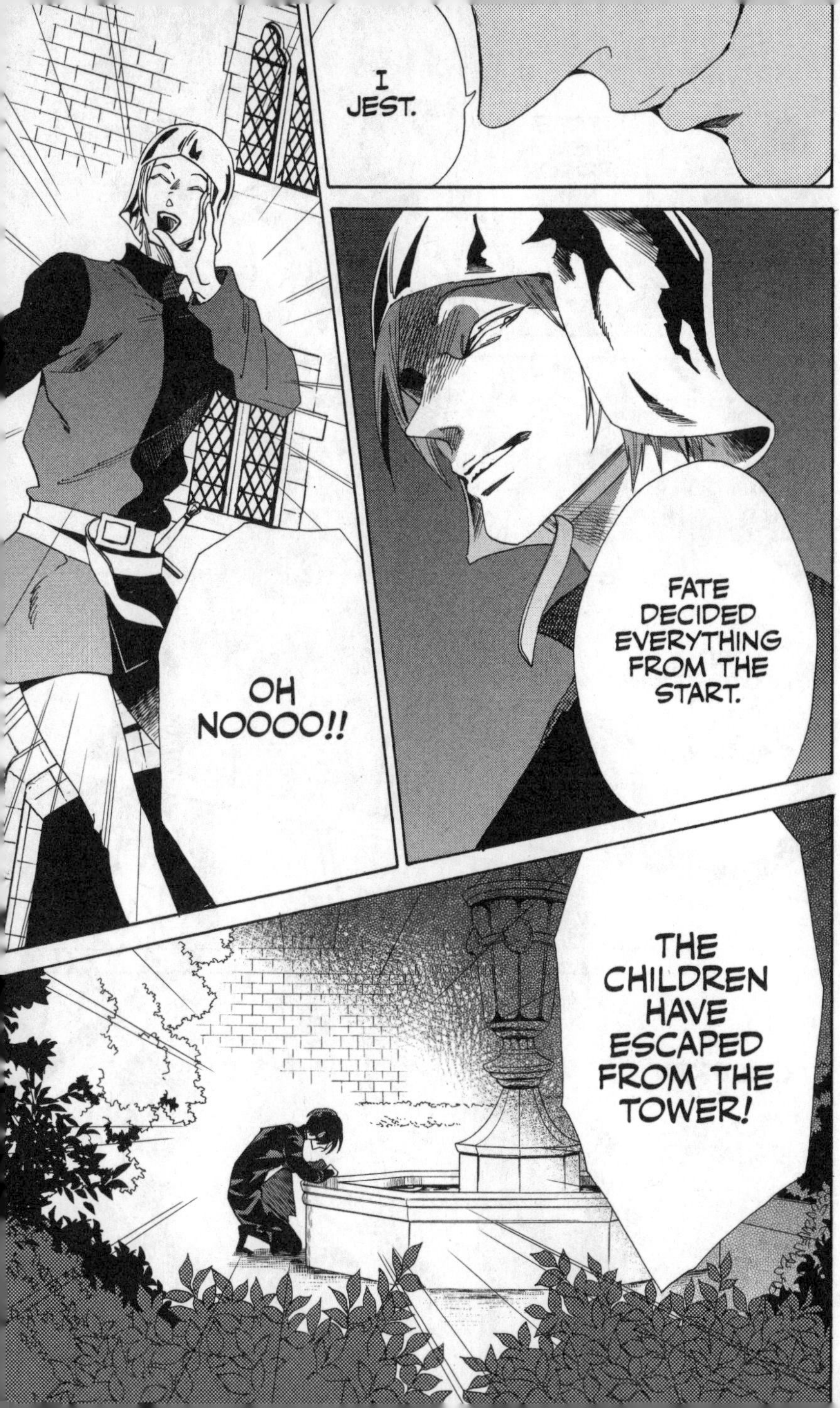
I JEST.
FATE DECIDED EVERYTHING FROM THE START.
OH NOOOO!!
THE CHILDREN HAVE ESCAPED FROM THE TOWER!

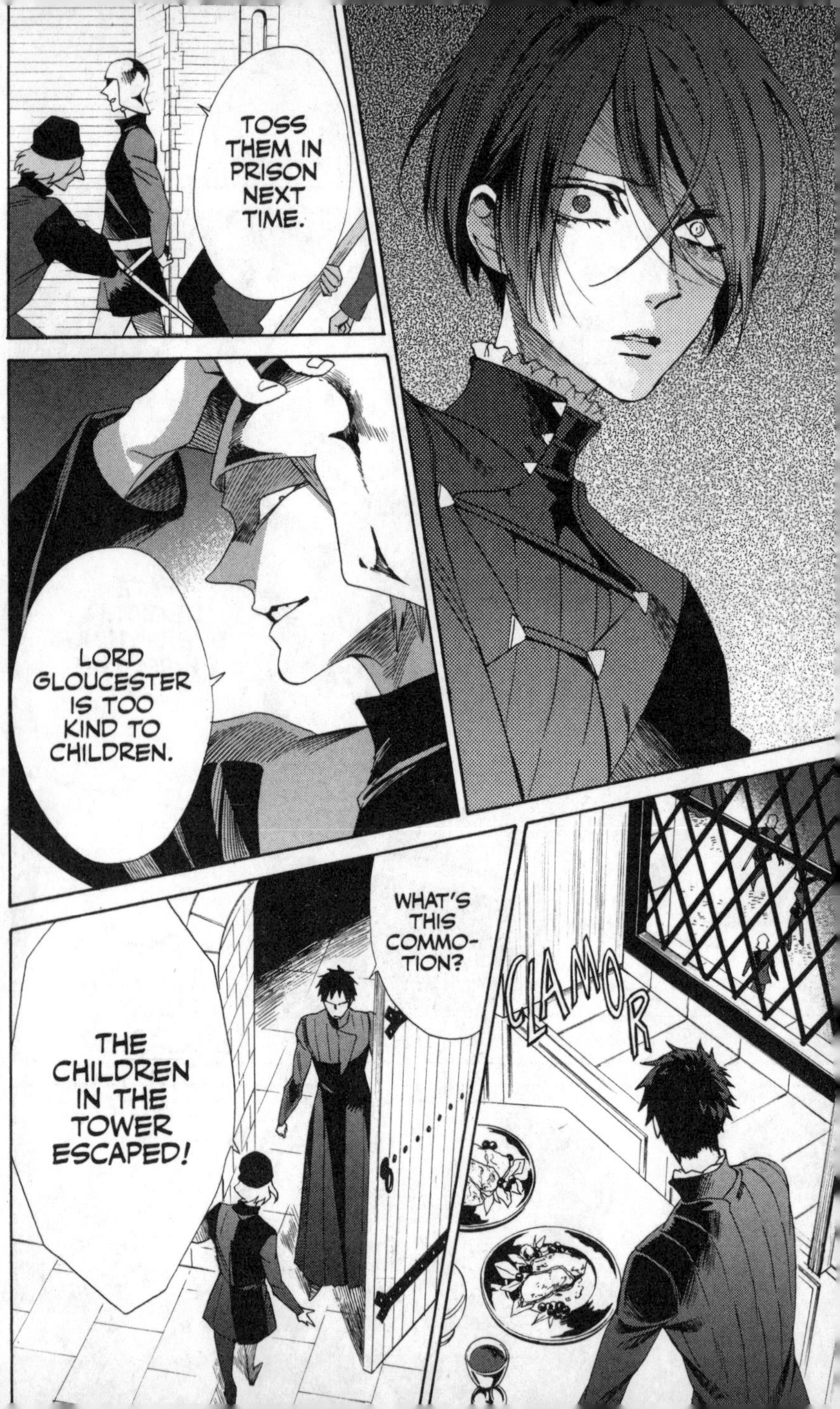
TOSS THEM IN PRISON NEXT TIME.
LORD GLOUCESTER IS TOO KIND TO CHILDREN.
CLAMOR
WHAT'S THIS COMMO-TION?
THE CHILDREN IN THE TOWER ESCAPED!

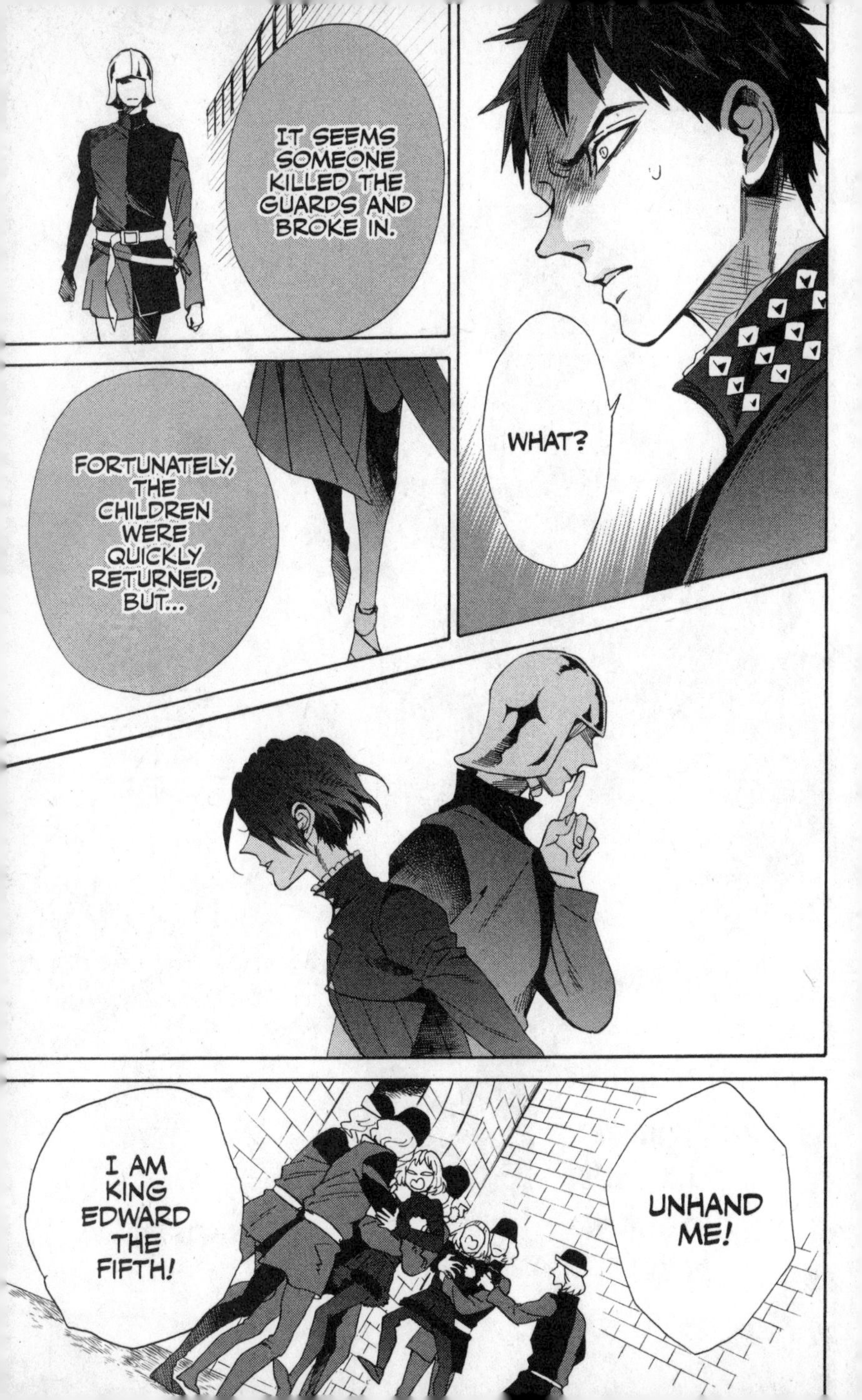
WHAT?
IT SEEMS SOMEONE KILLED THE GUARDS AND BROKE IN.
FORTUNATELY, THE CHILDREN WERE QUICKLY RETURNED, BUT...
UNHAND ME!
I AM KING EDWARD THE FIFTH!

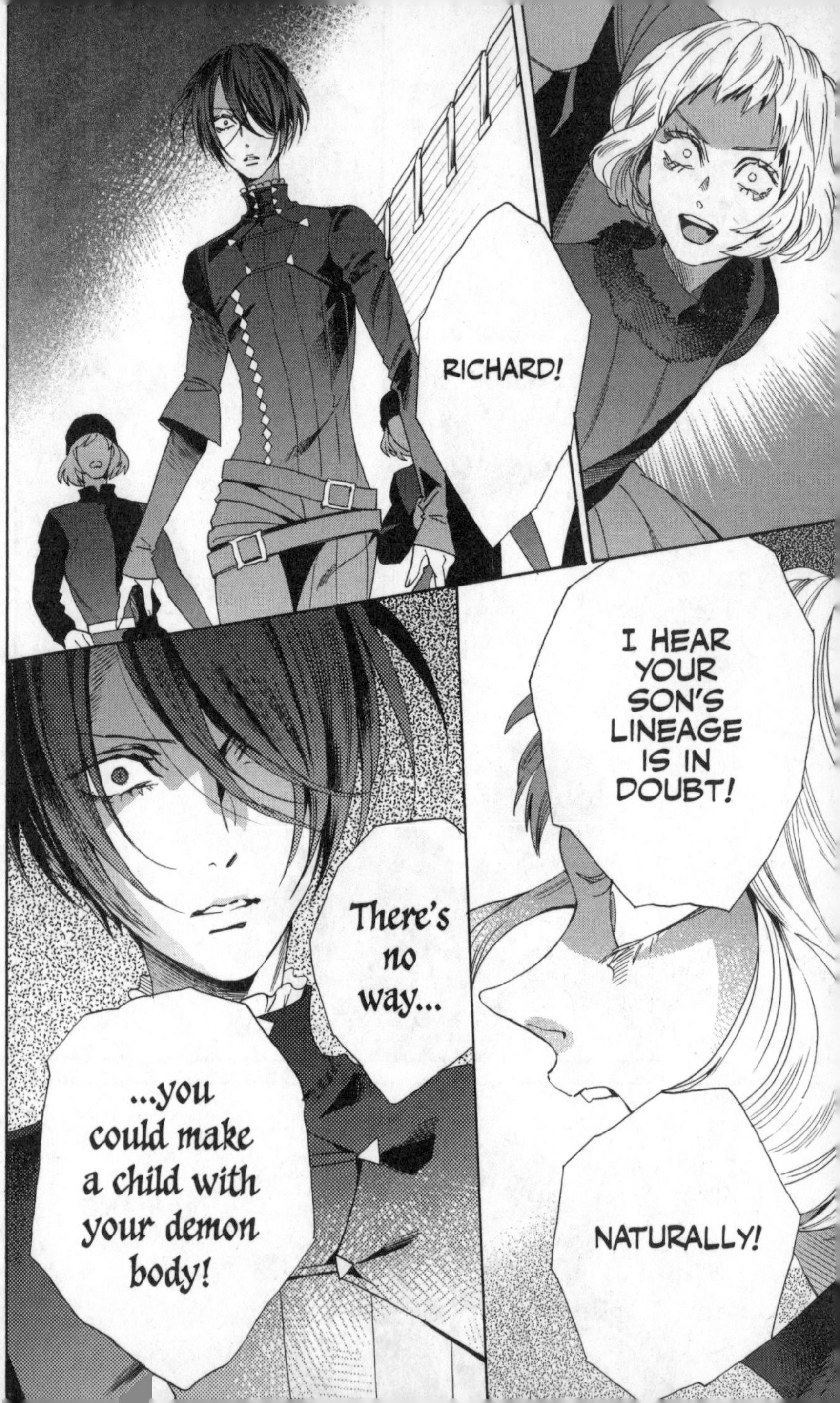
RICHARD!
I HEAR YOUR SON'S LINEAGE IS IN DOUBT!
NATURALLY!
There's no way...
...you could make a child with your demon body!

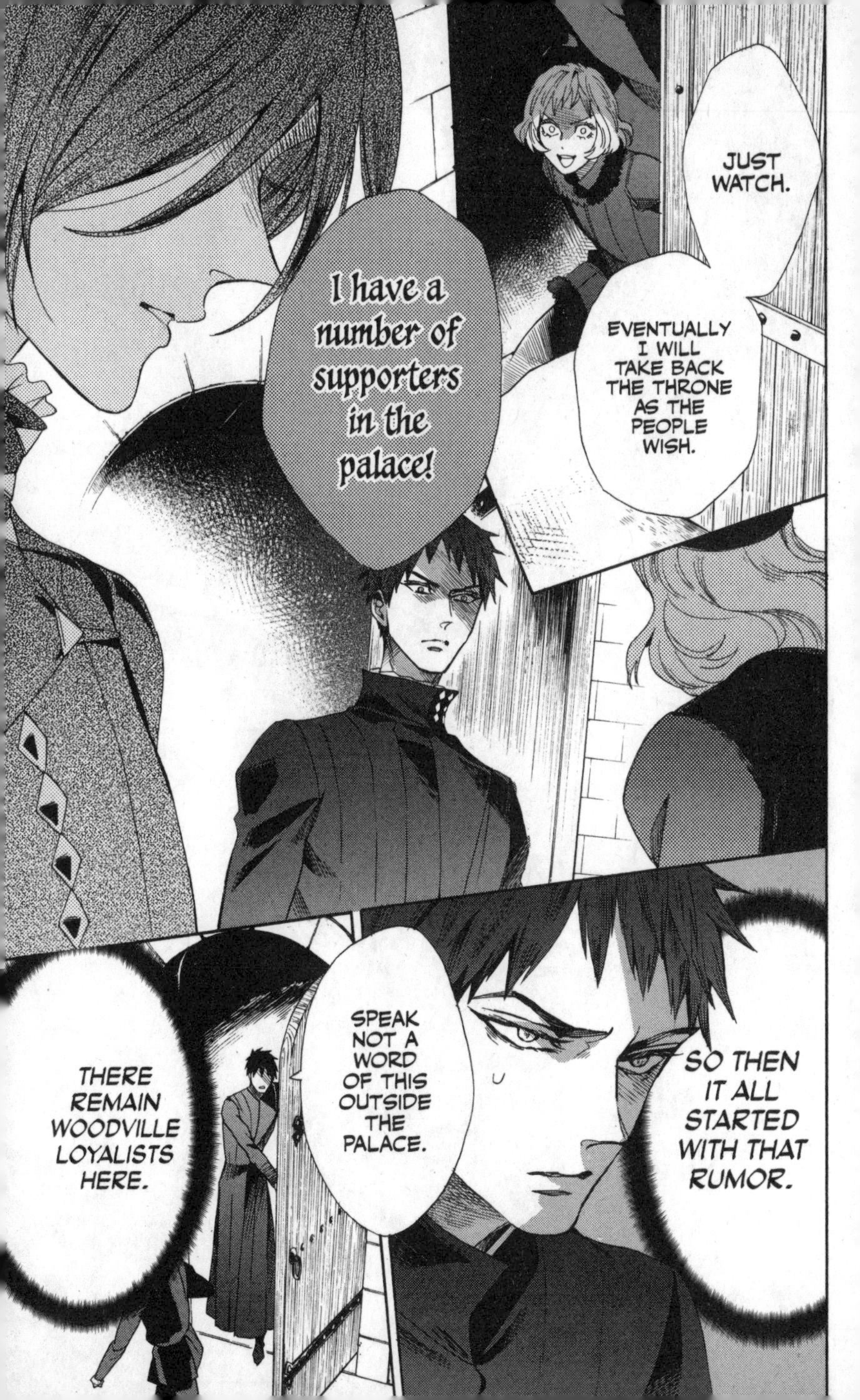
JUST WATCH.
EVENTUALLY I WILL TAKE BACK THE THRONE AS THE PEOPLE WISH.
I have a number of supporters in the palace!
SO THEN IT ALL STARTED WITH THAT RUMOR.
SPEAK NOT A WORD OF THIS OUTSIDE THE PALACE.
THERE REMAIN WOODVILLE LOYALISTS HERE.

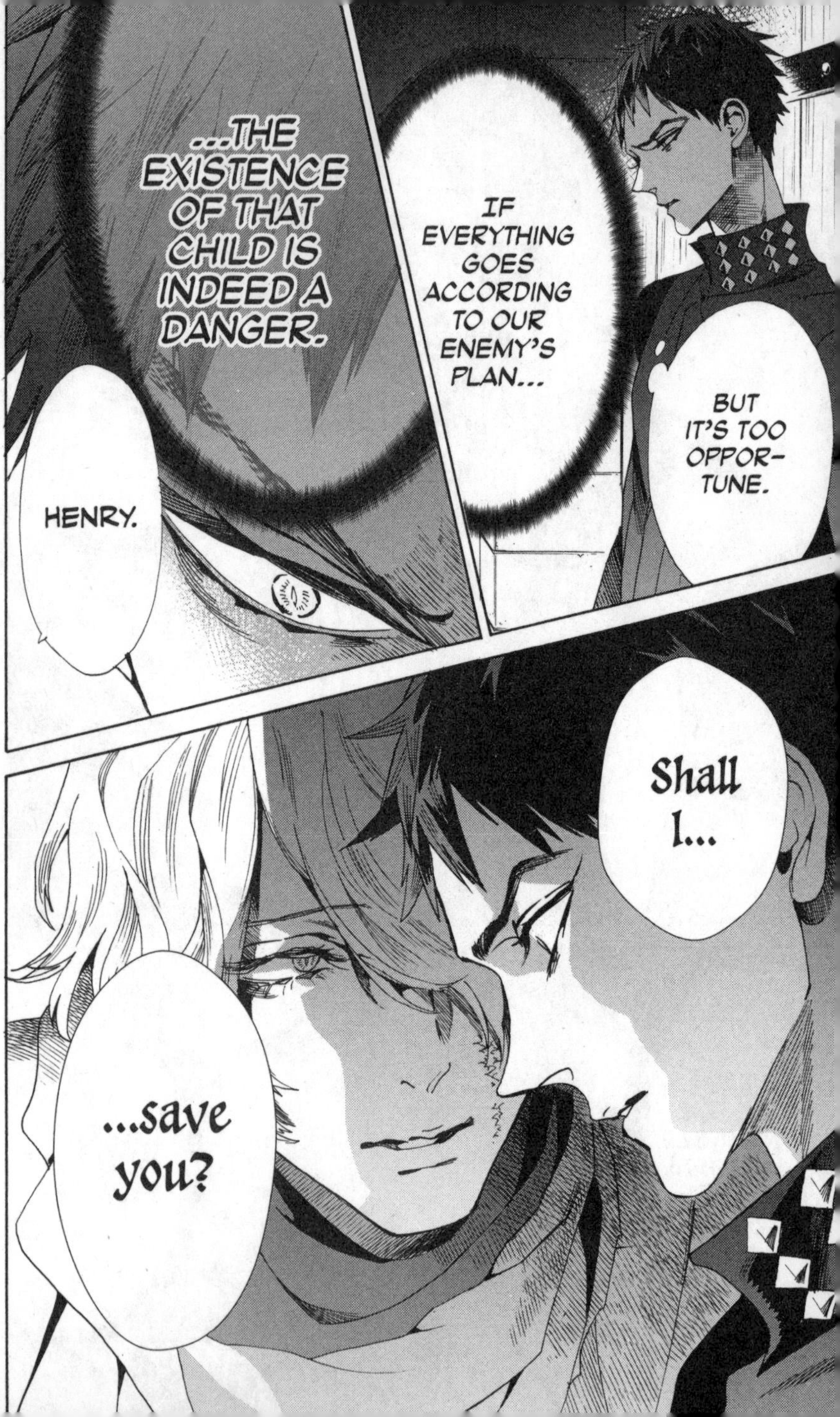
BUT IT'S TOO OPPOR-TUNE.
IF EVERYTHING GOES ACCORDING TO OUR ENEMY'S PLAN...
...THE EXISTENCE OF THAT CHILD IS INDEED A DANGER.
HENRY.
Shall I...
...save you?

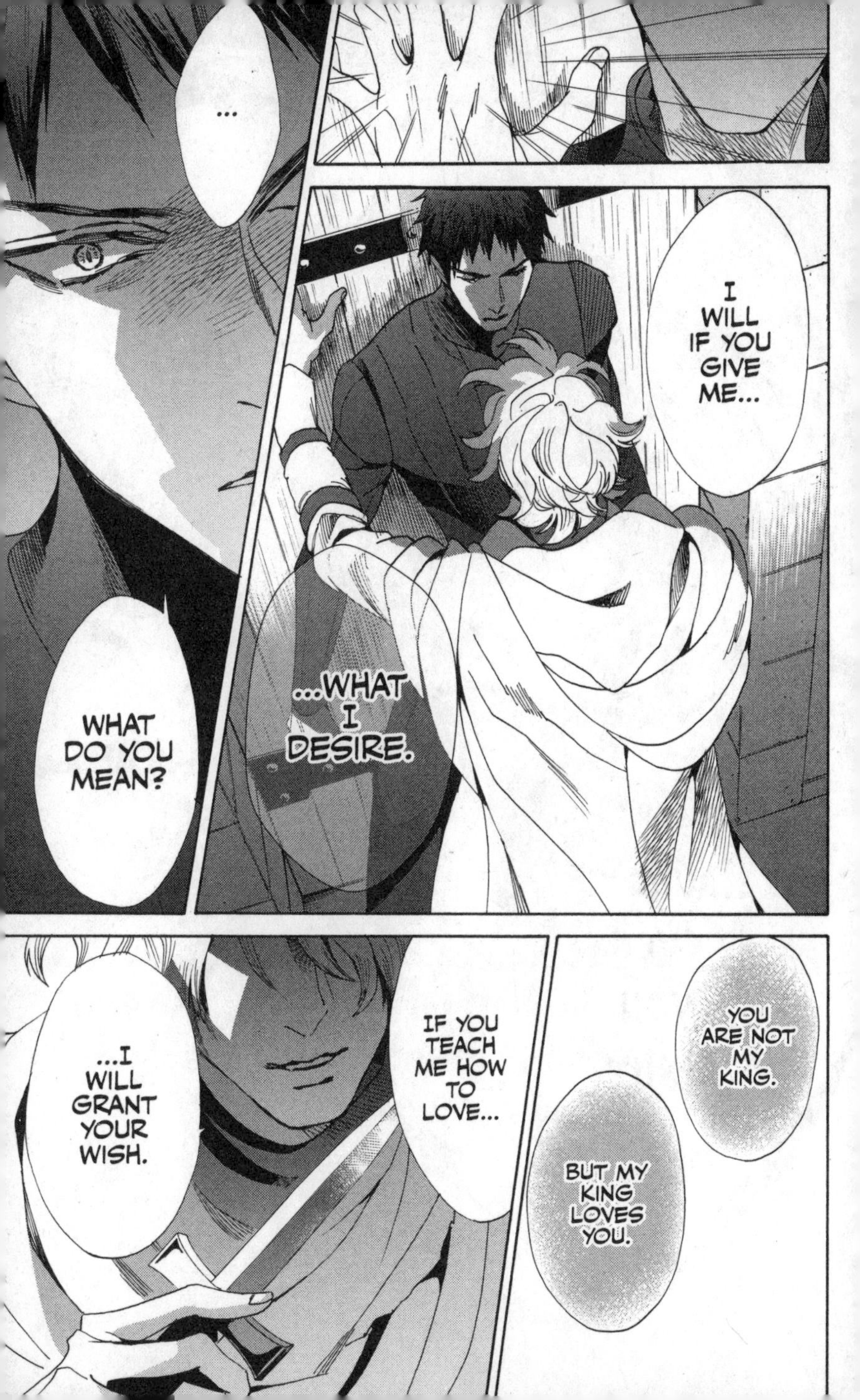
I WILL IF YOU GIVE ME...
...WHAT I DESIRE.
...
WHAT DO YOU MEAN?
YOU ARE NOT MY KING.
BUT MY KING LOVES YOU.
IF YOU TEACH ME HOW TO LOVE...
...I WILL GRANT YOUR WISH.

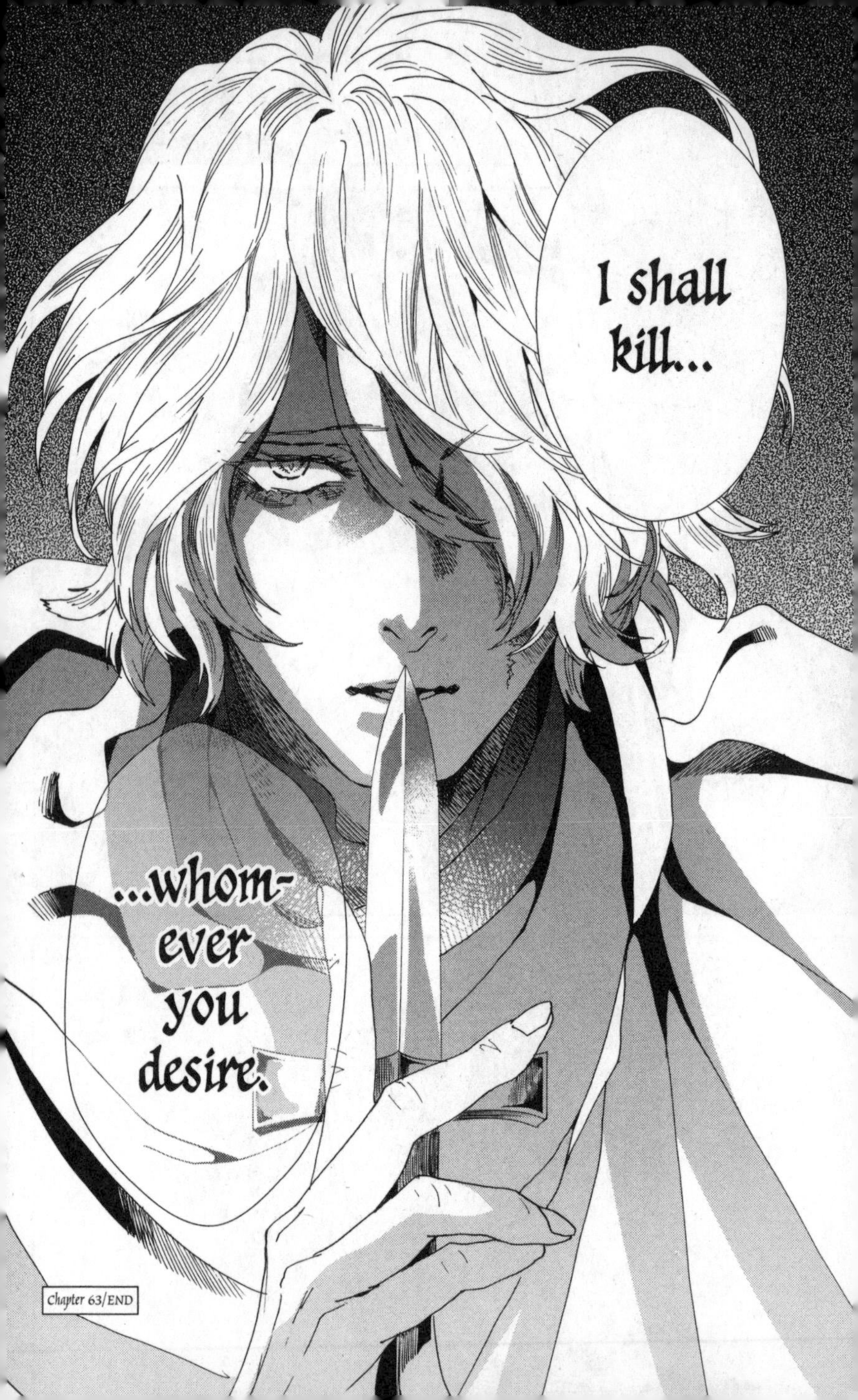
I shall kill...
...whom-ever you desire.
Chapter 63/END

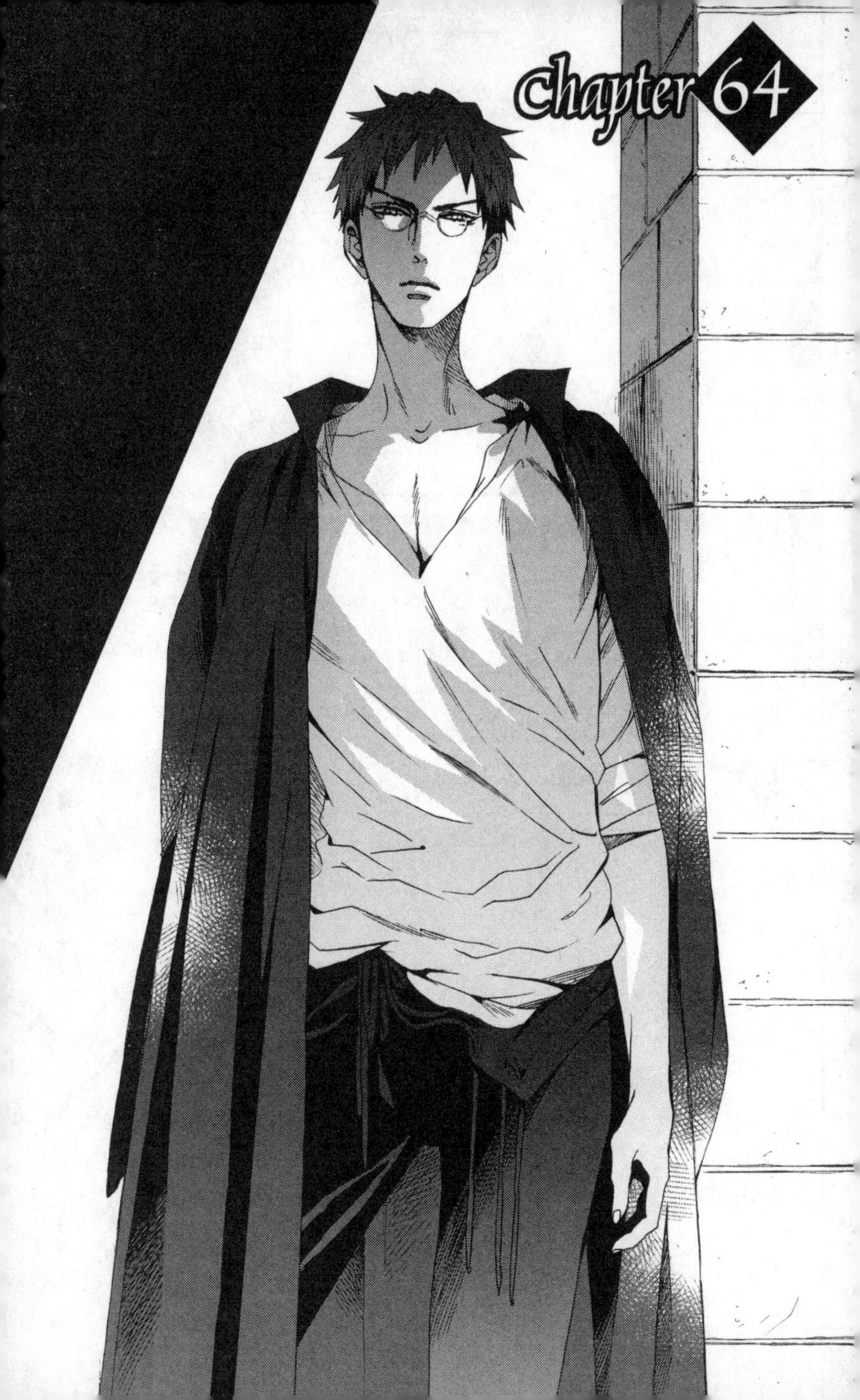
Chapter 64

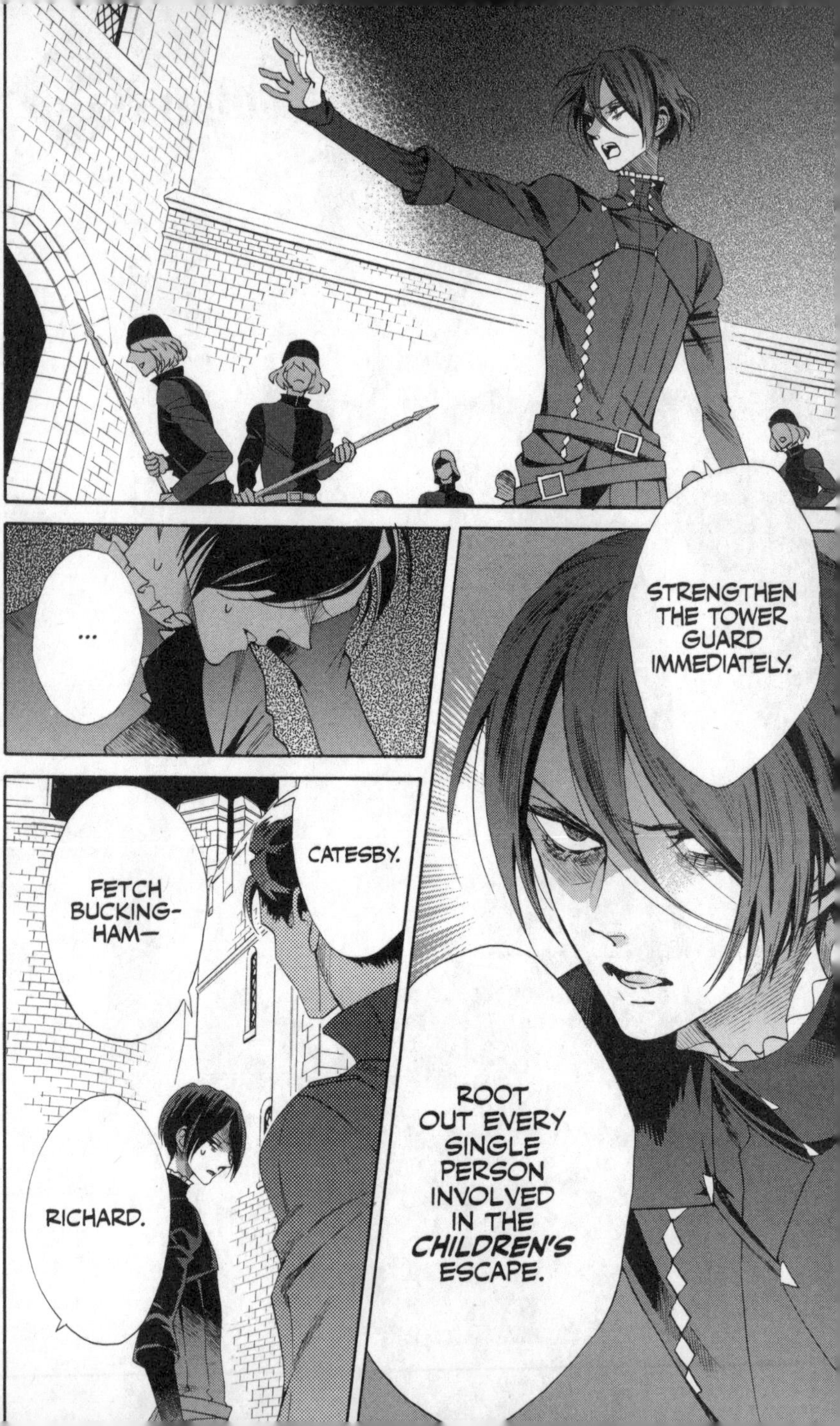

STRENGTHEN THE TOWER GUARD IMMEDIATELY.
ROOT OUT EVERY SINGLE PERSON INVOLVED IN THE *CHILDREN'S* ESCAPE.
...
CATESBY.
FETCH BUCKING-HAM—
RICHARD.

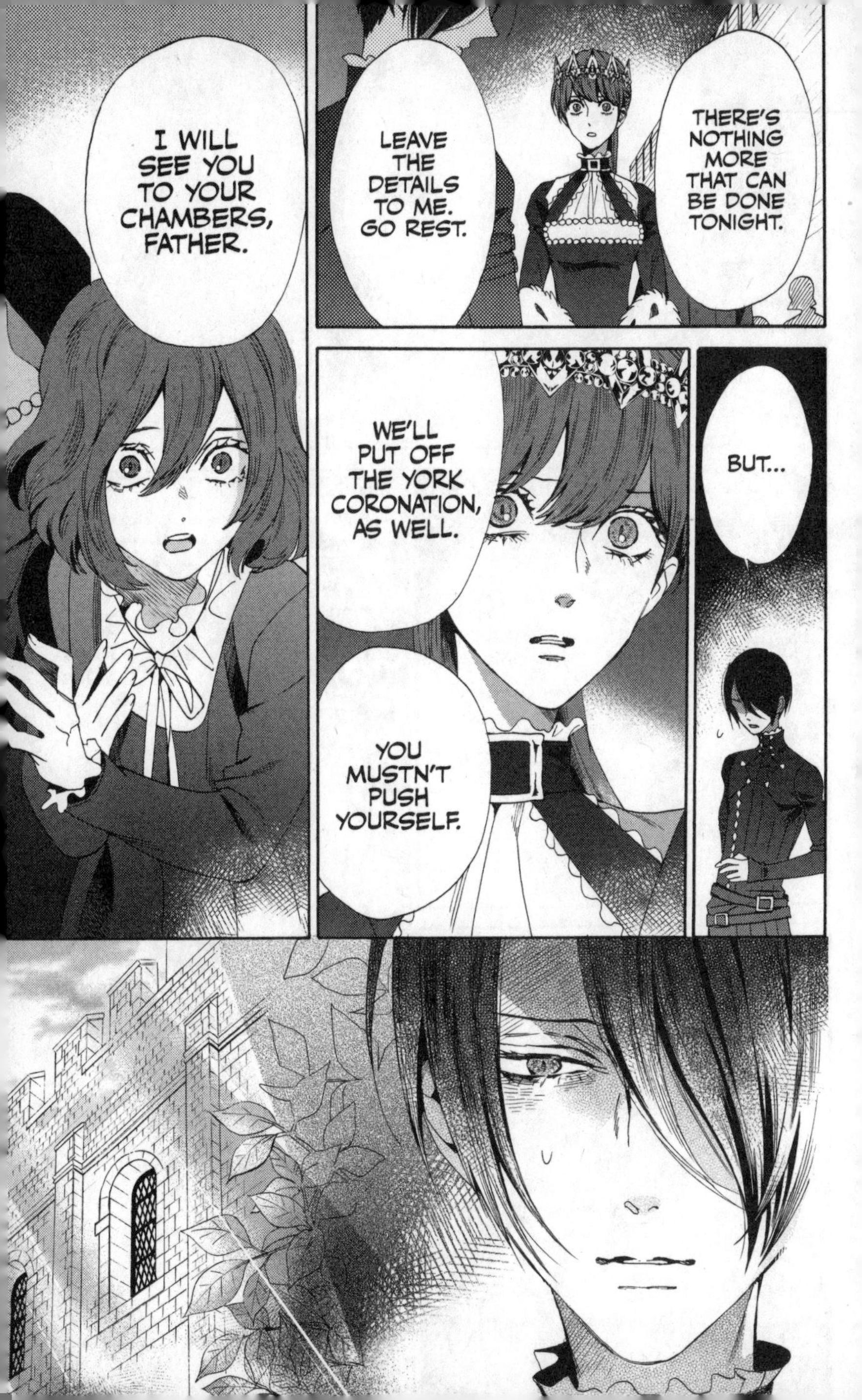
THERE'S NOTHING MORE THAT CAN BE DONE TONIGHT.
LEAVE THE DETAILS TO ME. GO REST.
BUT...
WE'LL PUT OFF THE YORK CORONATION, AS WELL.
YOU MUSTN'T PUSH YOURSELF.
I WILL SEE YOU TO YOUR CHAMBERS, FATHER.

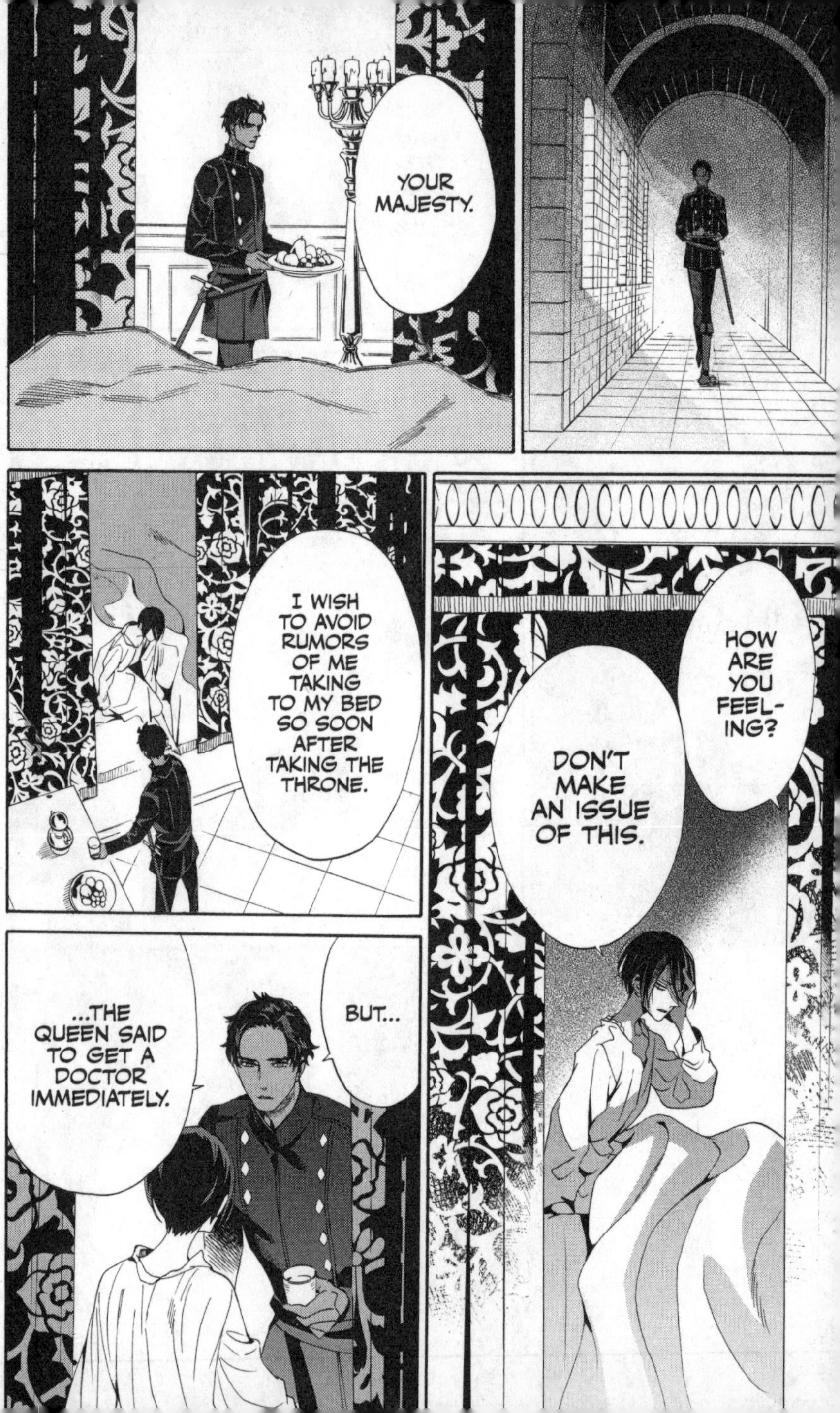
YOUR MAJESTY.
HOW ARE YOU FEEL-ING?
DON'T MAKE AN ISSUE OF THIS.
I WISH TO AVOID RUMORS OF ME TAKING TO MY BED SO SOON AFTER TAKING THE THRONE.
BUT...
...THE QUEEN SAID TO GET A DOCTOR IMMEDIATELY.

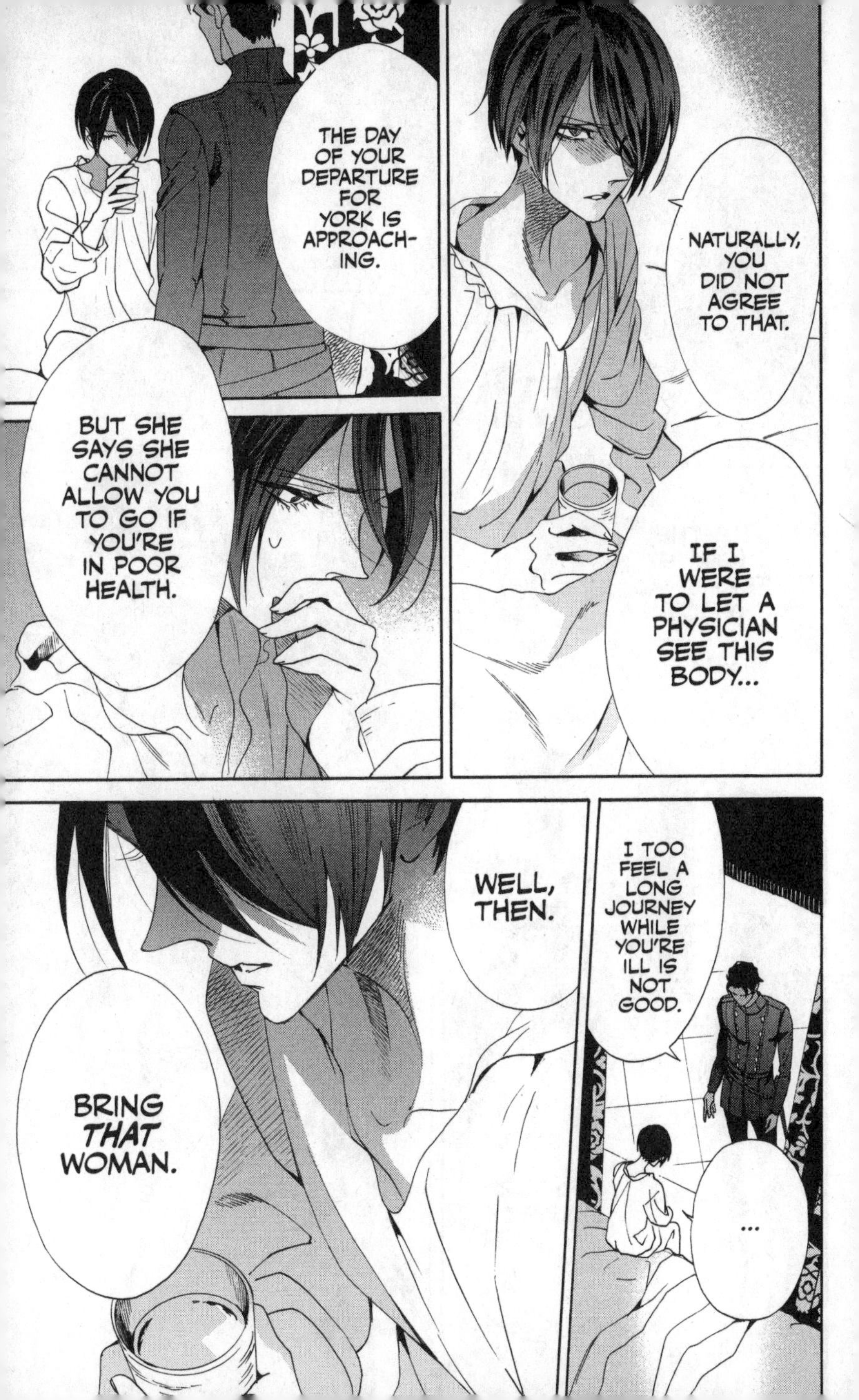
NATURALLY, YOU DID NOT AGREE TO THAT.
IF I WERE TO LET A PHYSICIAN SEE THIS BODY...
THE DAY OF YOUR DEPARTURE FOR YORK IS APPROACH-ING.
BUT SHE SAYS SHE CANNOT ALLOW YOU TO GO IF YOU'RE IN POOR HEALTH.
I TOO FEEL A LONG JOURNEY WHILE YOU'RE ILL IS NOT GOOD.
...
WELL, THEN.
BRING *THAT* WOMAN.

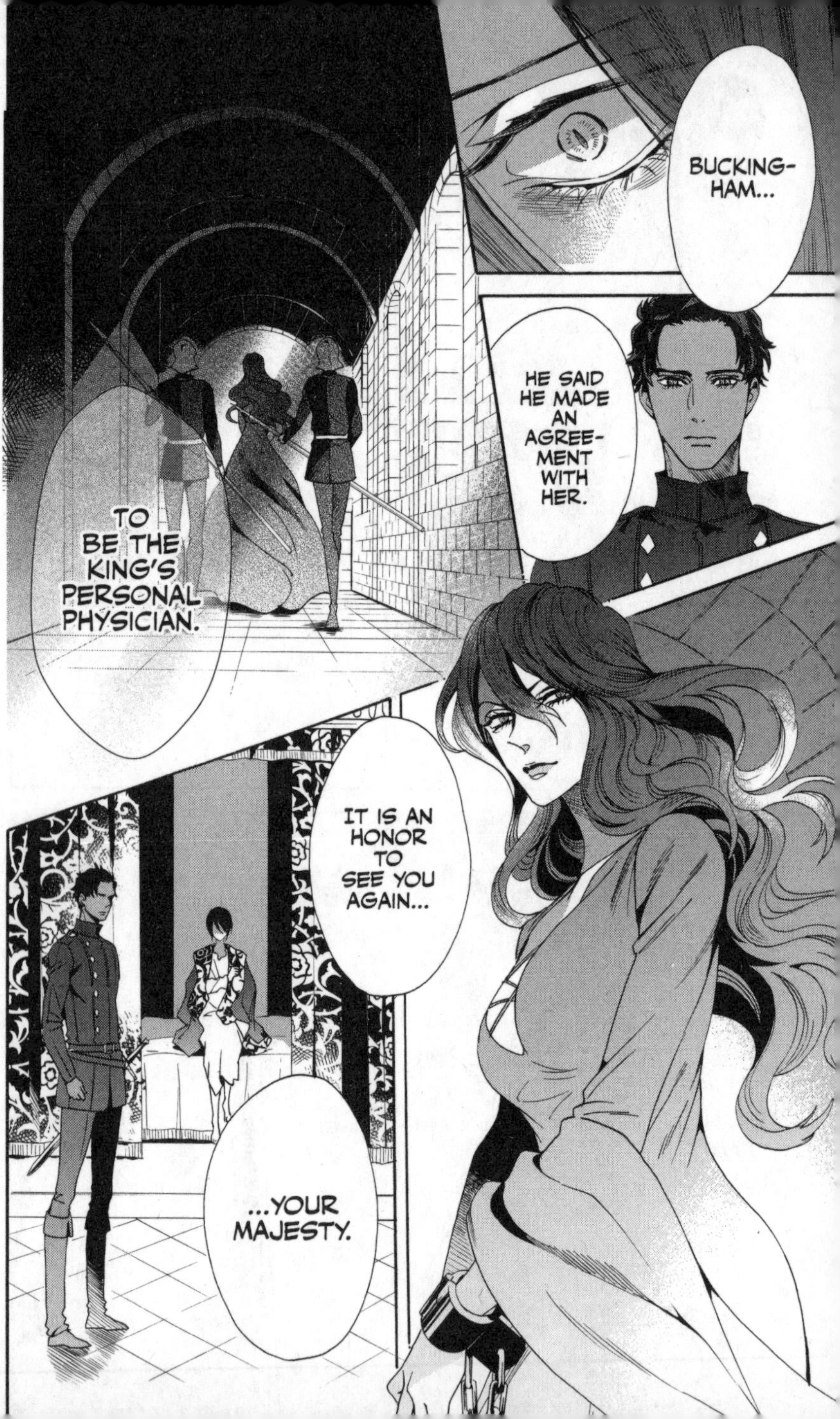
BUCKING-HAM...
HE SAID HE MADE AN AGREE-MENT WITH HER.
TO BE THE KING'S PERSONAL PHYSICIAN.
IT IS AN HONOR TO SEE YOU AGAIN...
...YOUR MAJESTY.

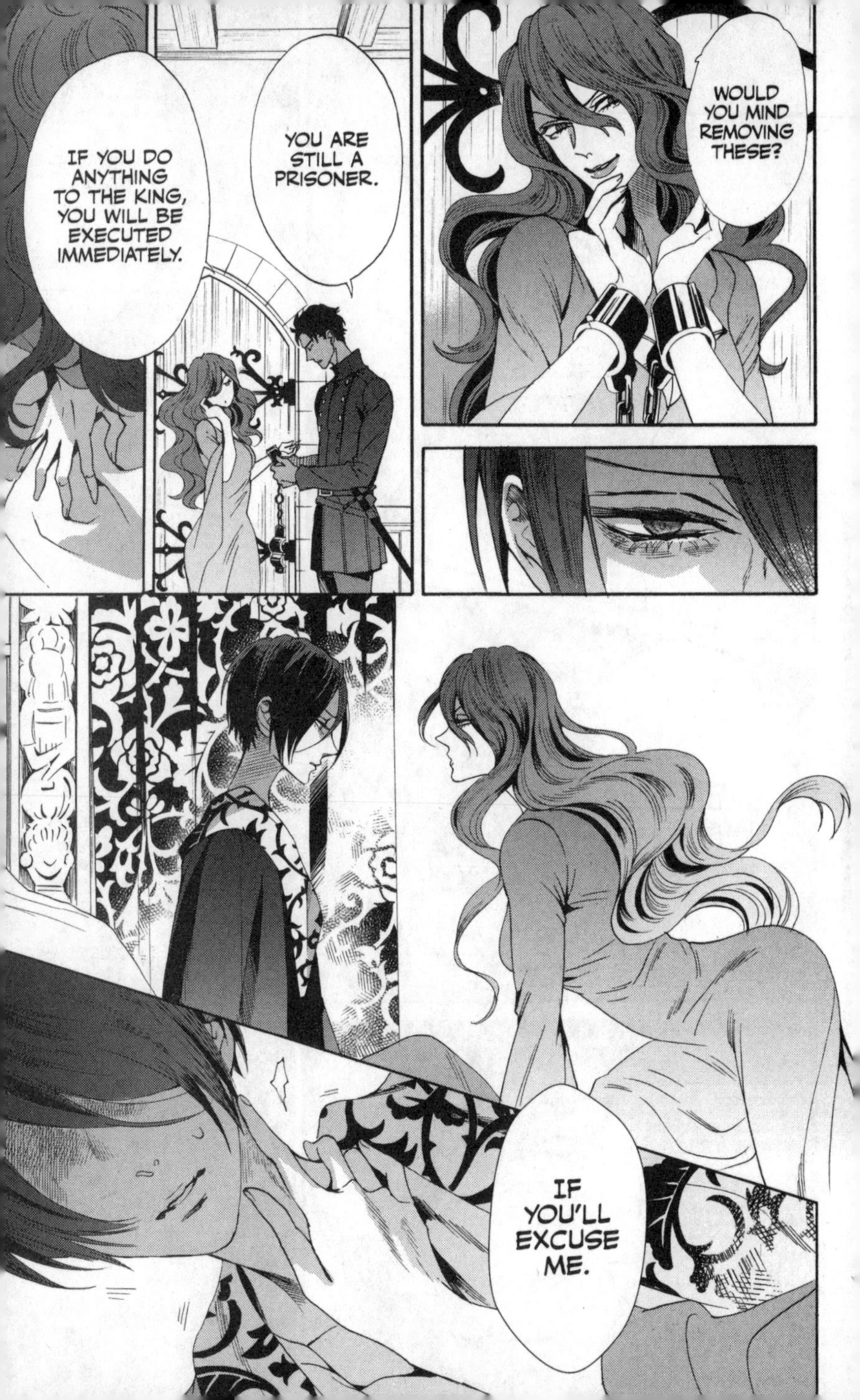
WOULD YOU MIND REMOVING THESE?
YOU ARE STILL A PRISONER.
IF YOU DO ANYTHING TO THE KING, YOU WILL BE EXECUTED IMMEDIATELY.
IF YOU'LL EXCUSE ME.

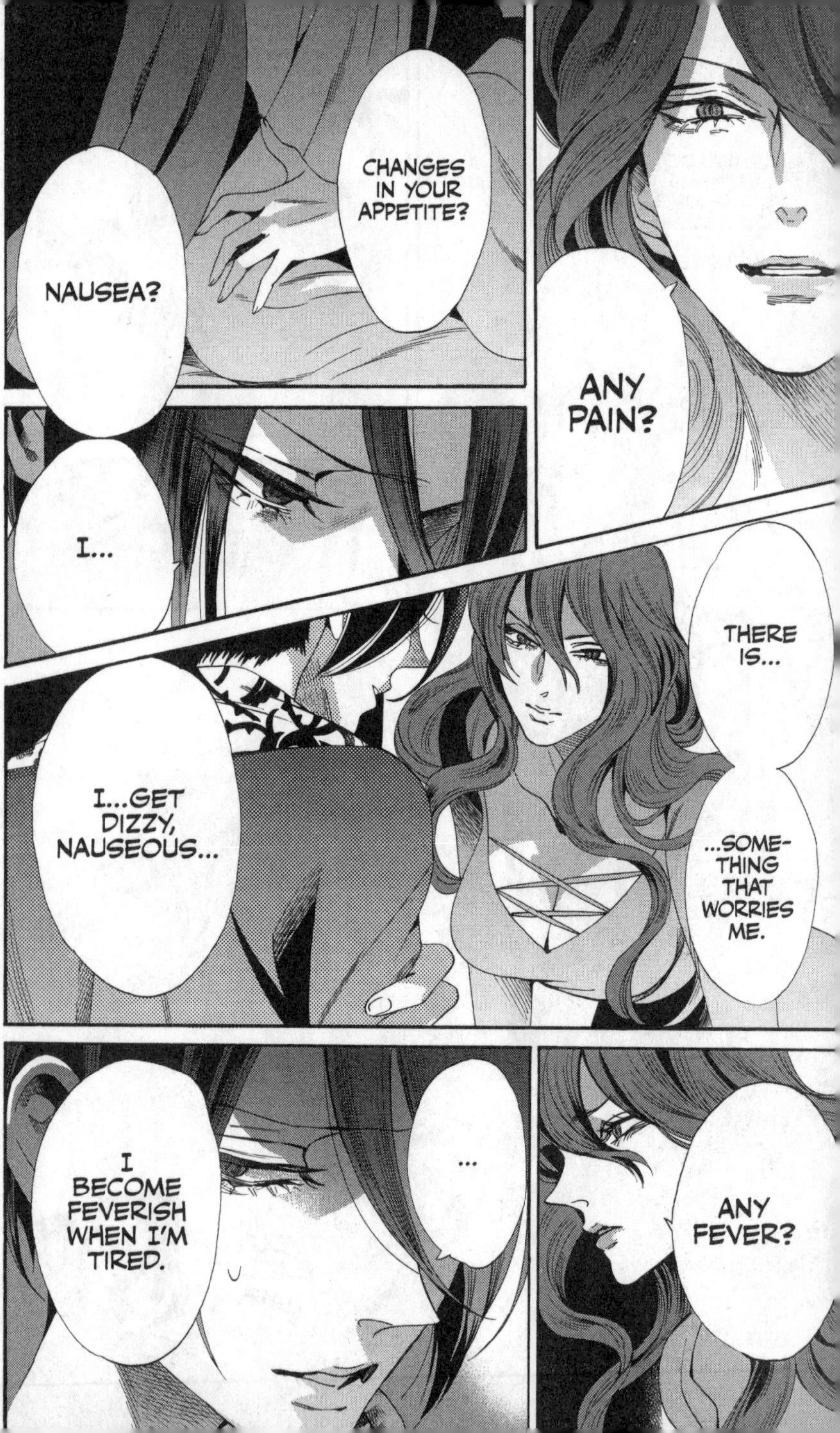
ANY PAIN?
CHANGES IN YOUR APPETITE?
NAUSEA?
I...
THERE IS...
...SOME-THING THAT WORRIES ME.
I...GET DIZZY, NAUSEOUS...
ANY FEVER?
...
I BECOME FEVERISH WHEN I'M TIRED.

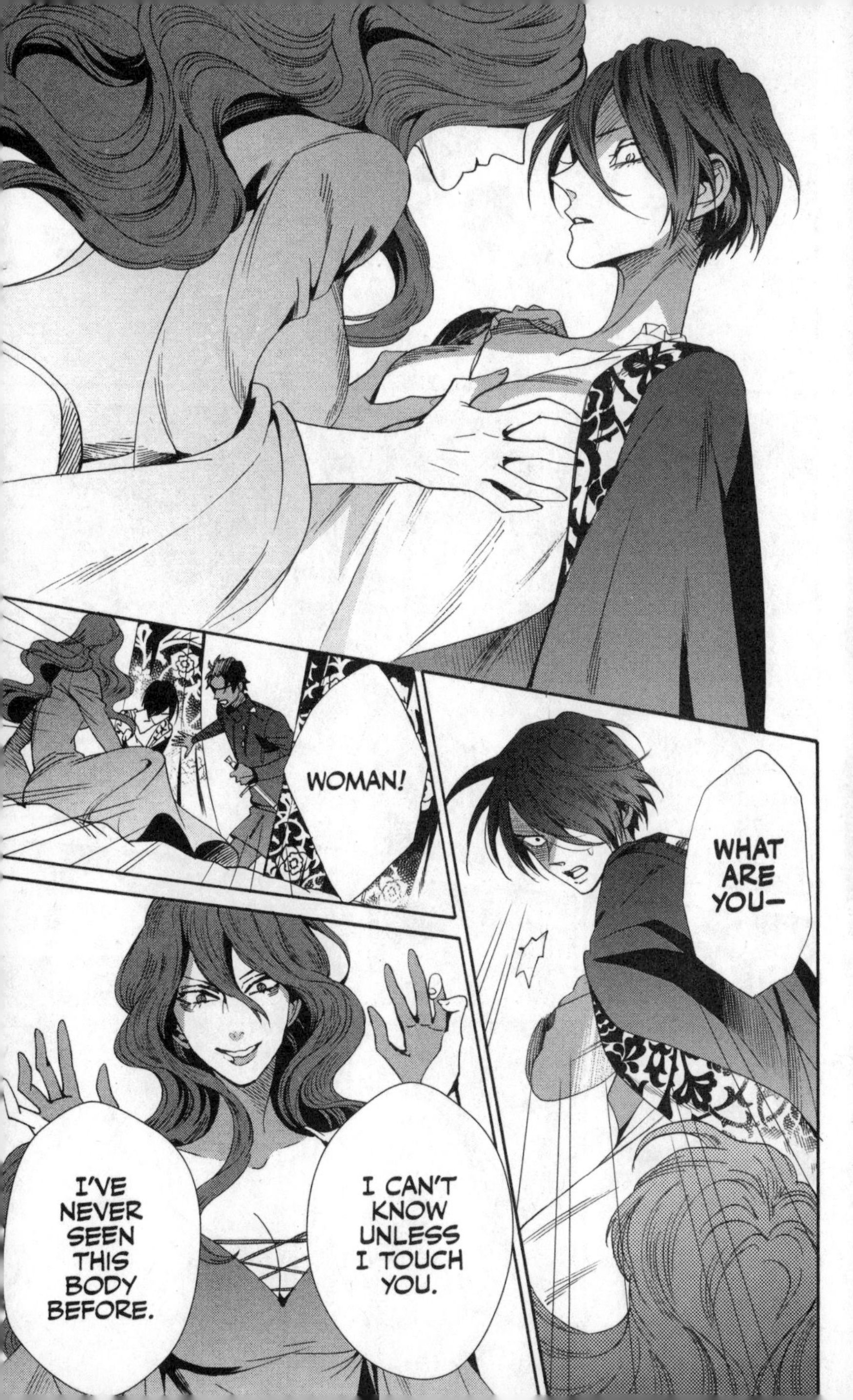
WHAT ARE YOU—
WOMAN!
I CAN'T KNOW UNLESS I TOUCH YOU.
I'VE NEVER SEEN THIS BODY BEFORE.

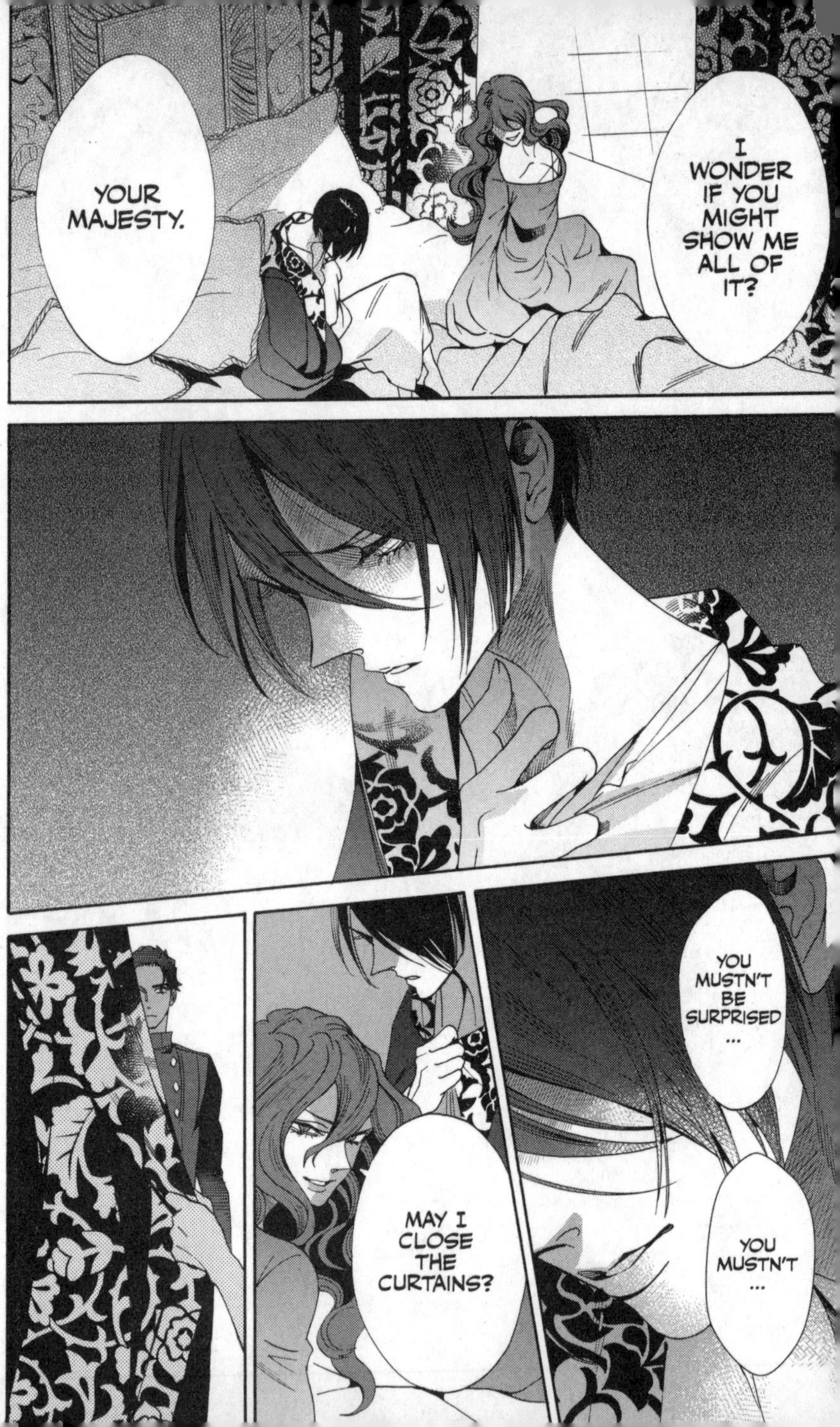
I WONDER IF YOU MIGHT SHOW ME ALL OF IT?
YOUR MAJESTY.
YOU MUSTN'T BE SURPRISED...
YOU MUSTN'T...
MAY I CLOSE THE CURTAINS?

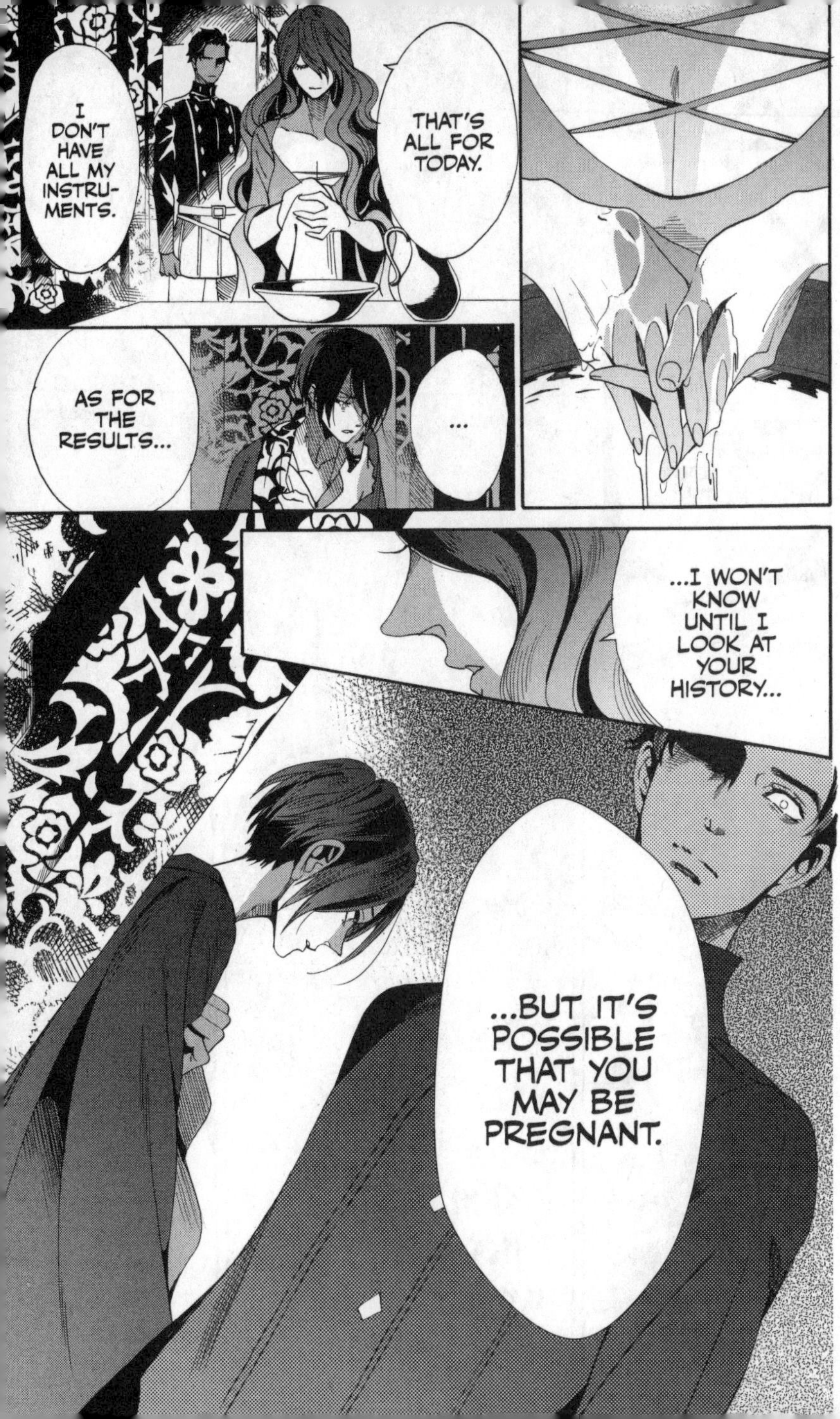
THAT'S ALL FOR TODAY.
I DON'T HAVE ALL MY INSTRU-MENTS.
...
AS FOR THE RESULTS...
...I WON'T KNOW UNTIL I LOOK AT YOUR HISTORY...
...BUT IT'S POSSIBLE THAT YOU MAY BE PREGNANT.

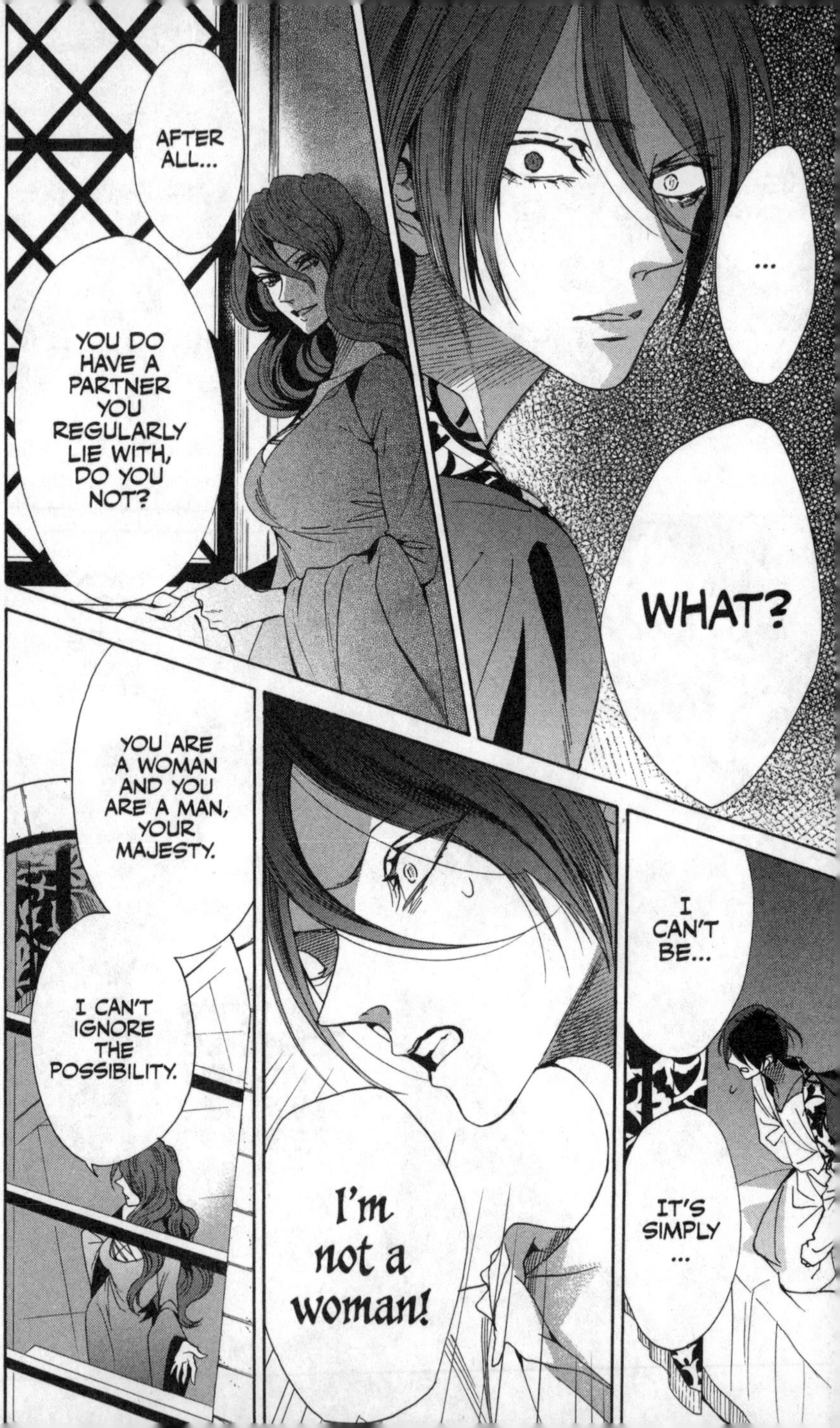
...
WHAT?
AFTER ALL...
YOU DO HAVE A PARTNER YOU REGULARLY LIE WITH, DO YOU NOT?
I CAN'T BE...
IT'S SIMPLY ...
I'm not a woman!
YOU ARE A WOMAN AND YOU ARE A MAN, YOUR MAJESTY.
I CAN'T IGNORE THE POSSIBILITY.

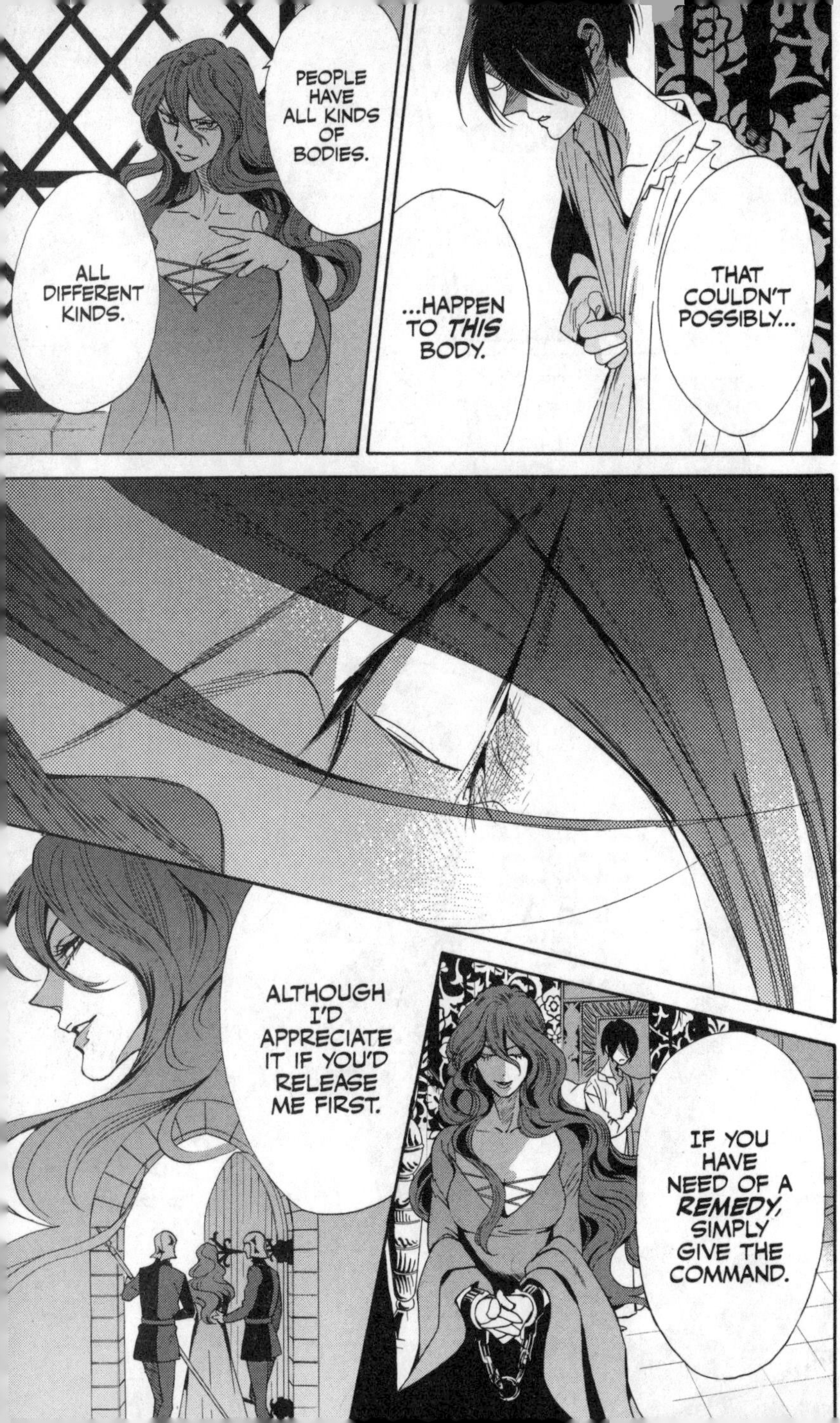
THAT COULDN'T POSSIBLY...
...HAPPEN TO *THIS* BODY.
PEOPLE HAVE ALL KINDS OF BODIES.
ALL DIFFERENT KINDS.
IF YOU HAVE NEED OF A *REMEDY,* SIMPLY GIVE THE COMMAND.
ALTHOUGH I'D APPRECIATE IT IF YOU'D RELEASE ME FIRST.

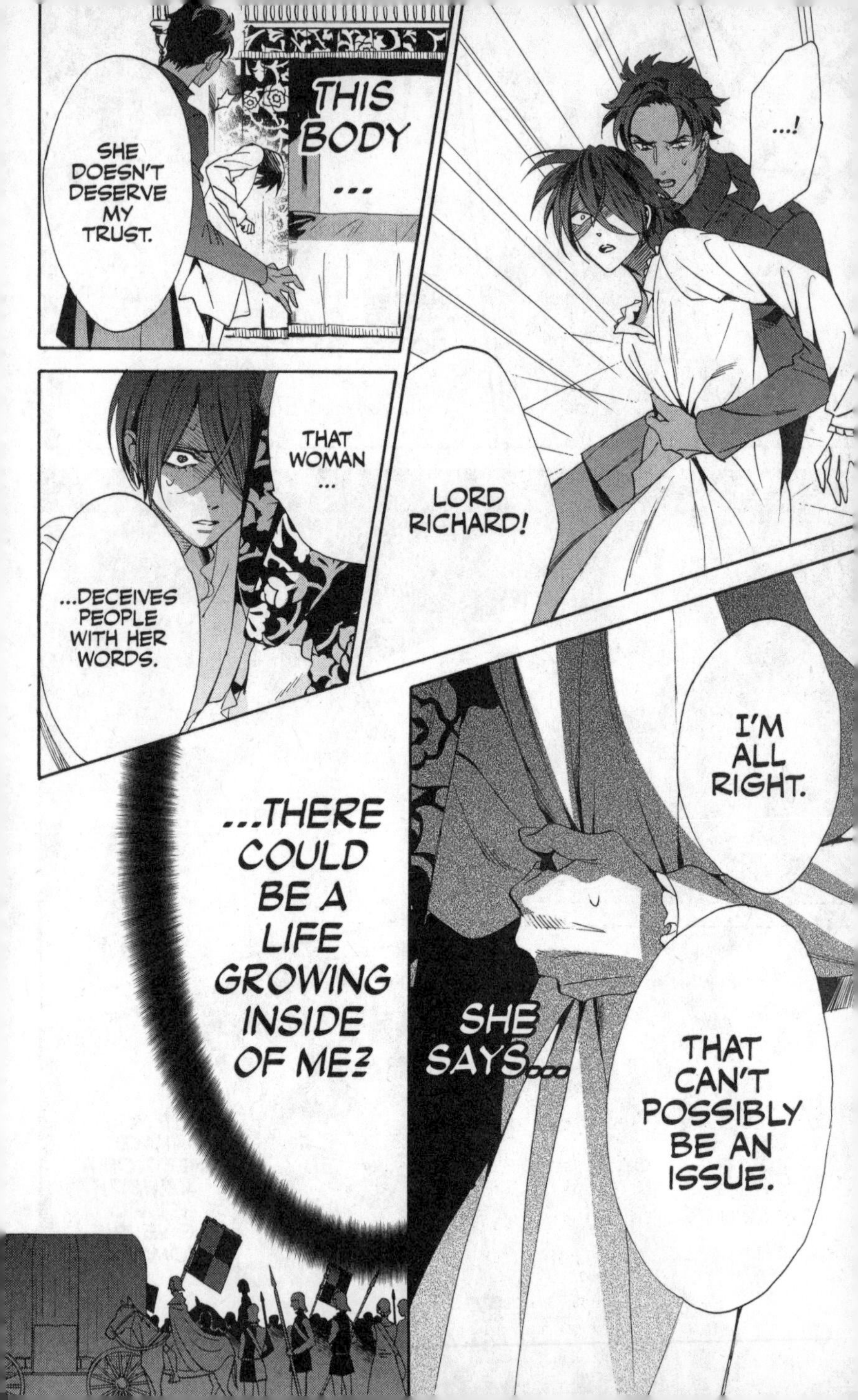
...!
LORD RICHARD!
THIS BODY ...
SHE DOESN'T DESERVE MY TRUST.
THAT WOMAN ...
...DECEIVES PEOPLE WITH HER WORDS.
I'M ALL RIGHT.
THAT CAN'T POSSIBLY BE AN ISSUE.
SHE SAYS...
...THERE COULD BE A LIFE GROWING INSIDE OF ME?

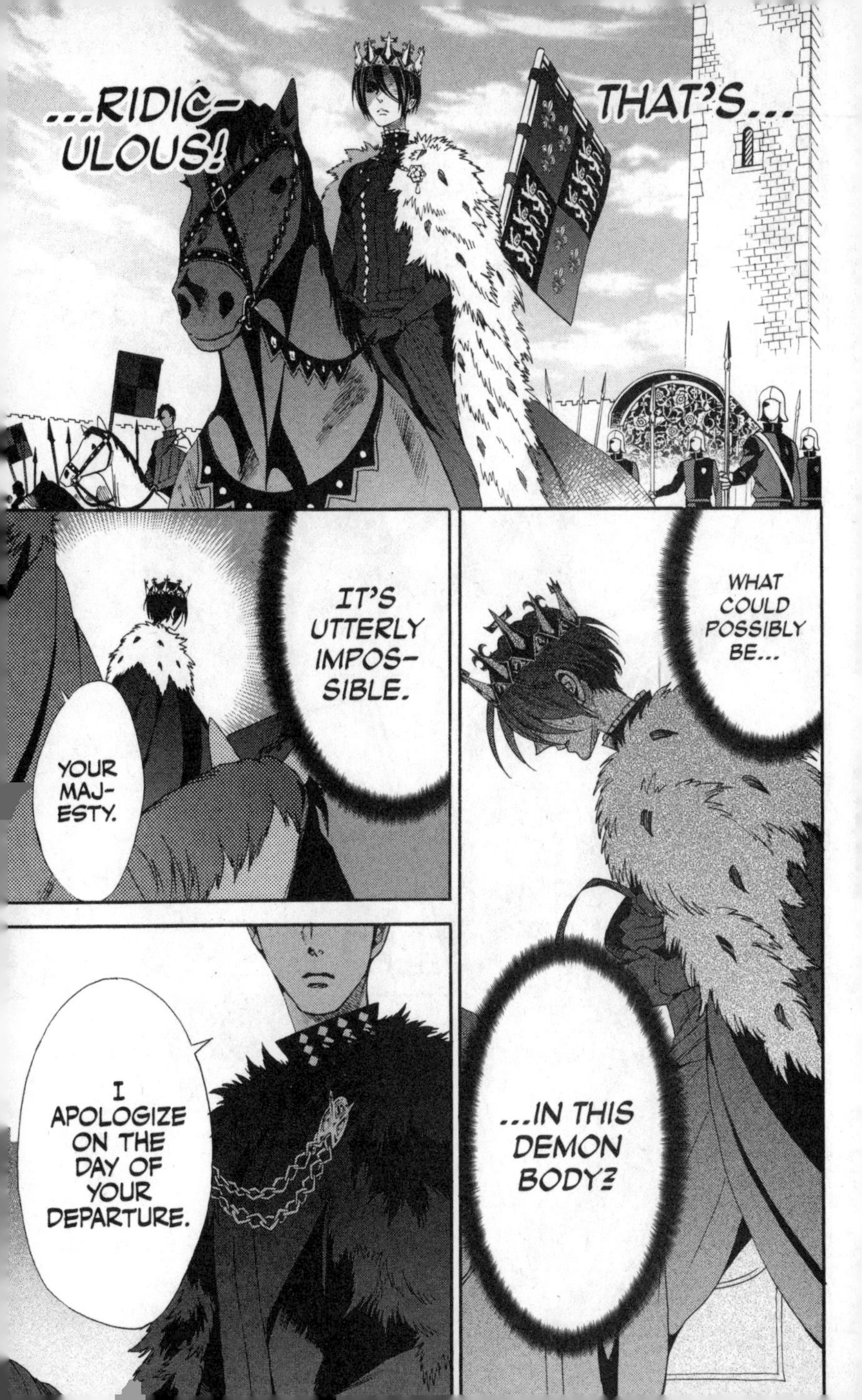
THAT'S...
...RIDIC-ULOUS!
WHAT COULD POSSIBLY BE...
...IN THIS DEMON BODY?
IT'S UTTERLY IMPOS-SIBLE.
YOUR MAJ-ESTY.
I APOLOGIZE ON THE DAY OF YOUR DEPARTURE.

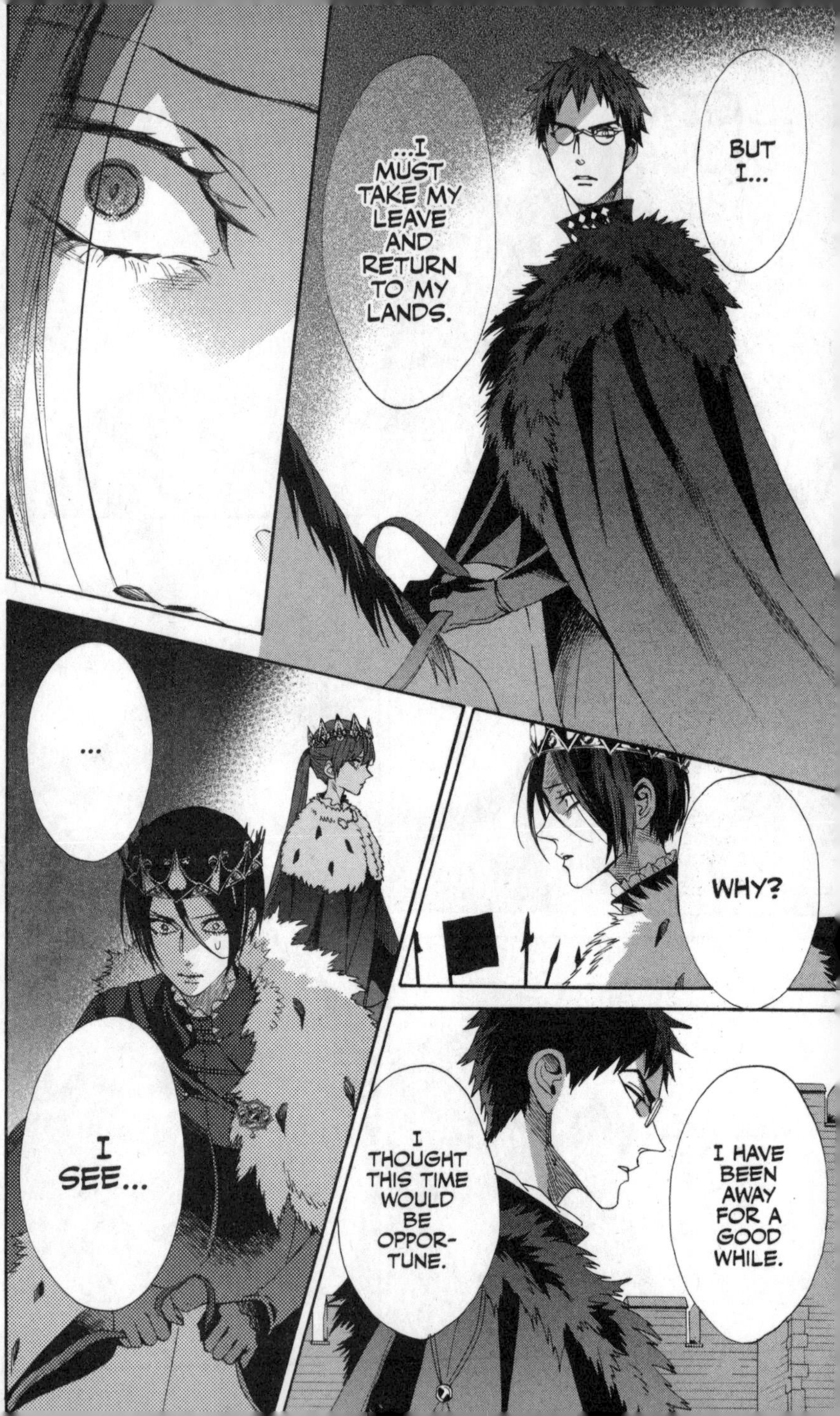
BUT I...
...I MUST TAKE MY LEAVE AND RETURN TO MY LANDS.
WHY?
I HAVE BEEN AWAY FOR A GOOD WHILE.
I THOUGHT THIS TIME WOULD BE OPPORTUNE.
...
I SEE...

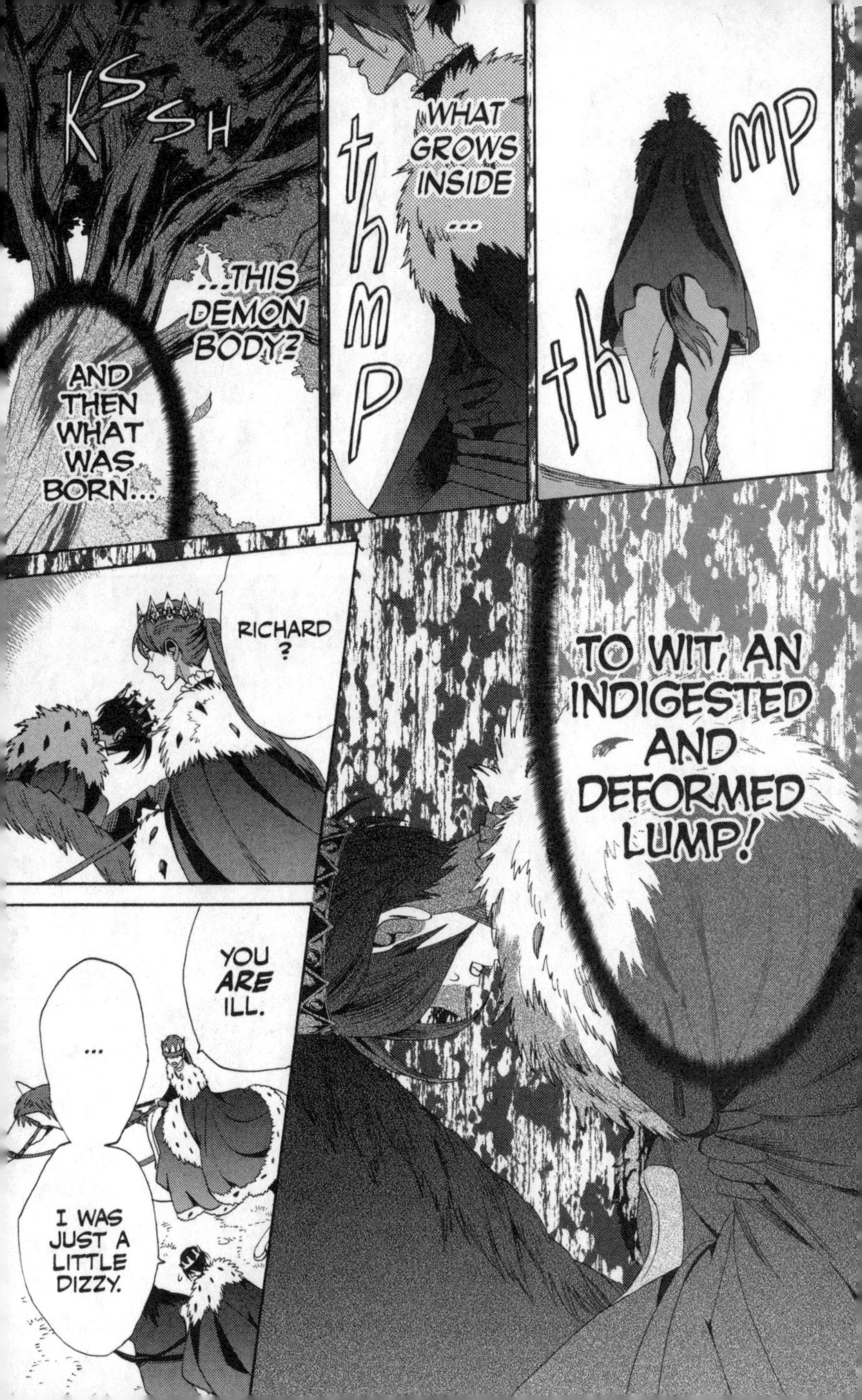
thmp
WHAT GROWS INSIDE ...
thmp
KSSH
...THIS DEMON BODY?
AND THEN WHAT WAS BORN...
TO WIT, AN INDIGESTED AND DEFORMED LUMP!
RICHARD?
YOU ARE ILL.
...
I WAS JUST A LITTLE DIZZY.

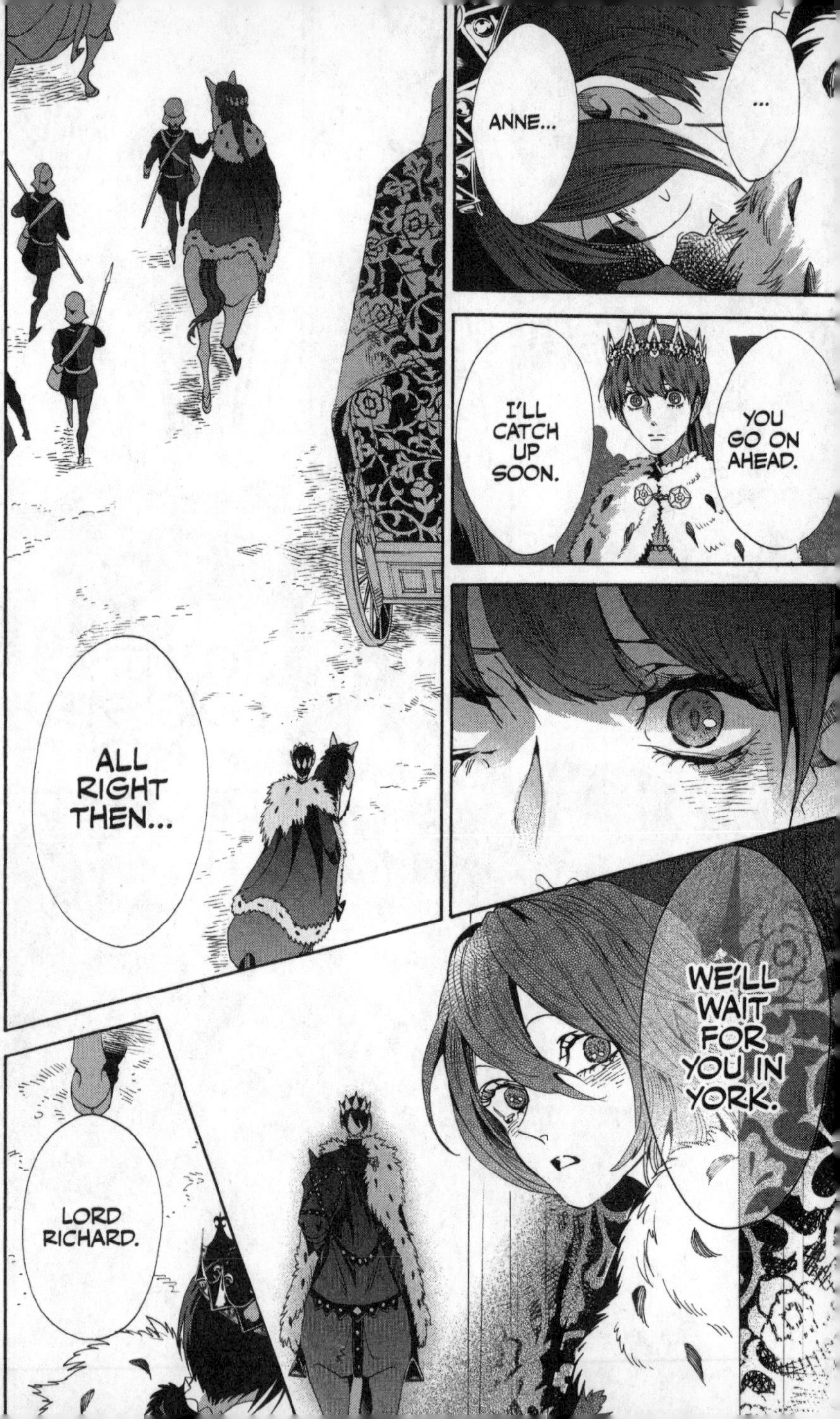
...
ANNE...
YOU GO ON AHEAD.
I'LL CATCH UP SOON.
WE'LL WAIT FOR YOU IN YORK.
ALL RIGHT THEN...
LORD RICHARD.

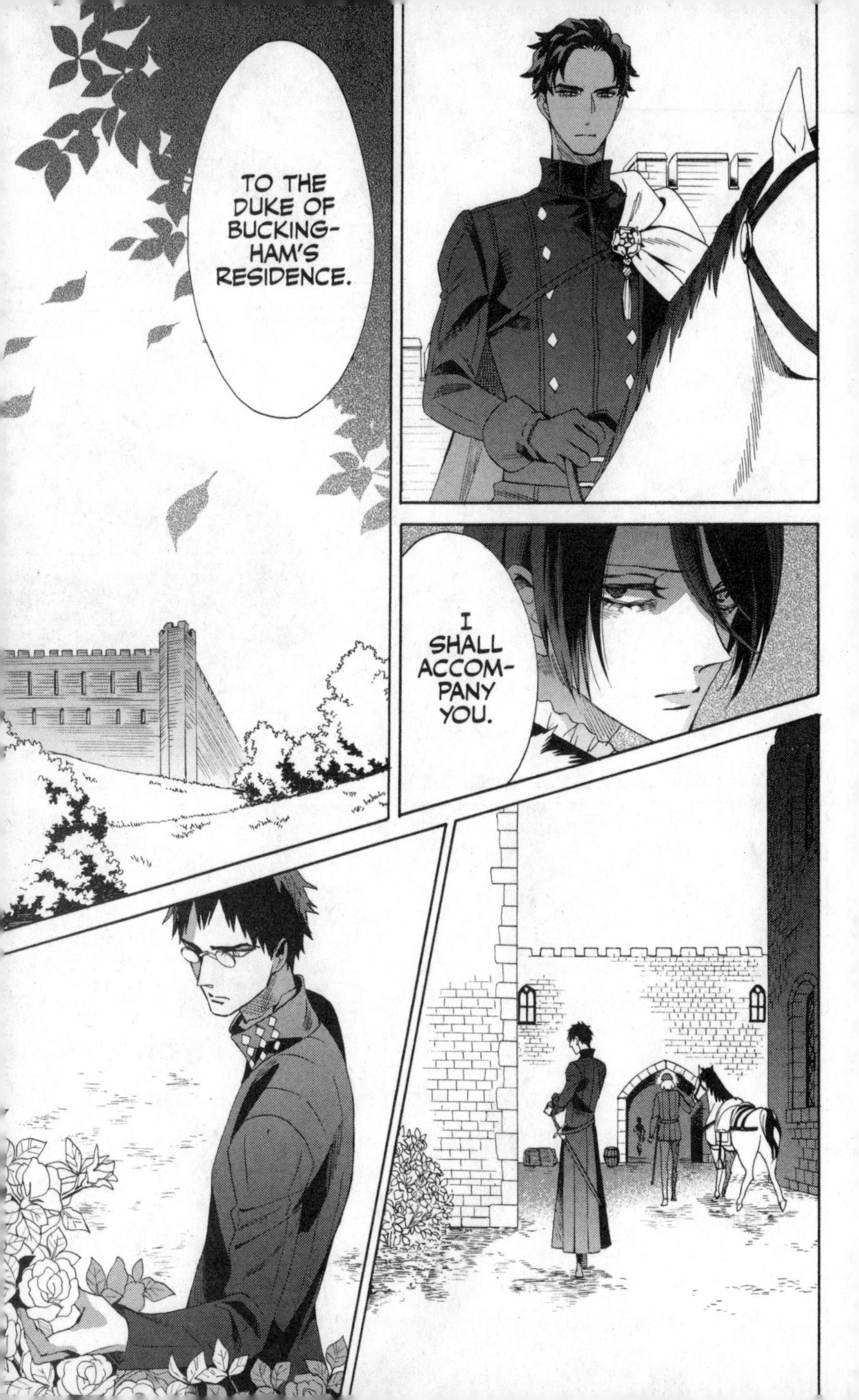
I SHALL ACCOMPANY YOU.
TO THE DUKE OF BUCKINGHAM'S RESIDENCE.

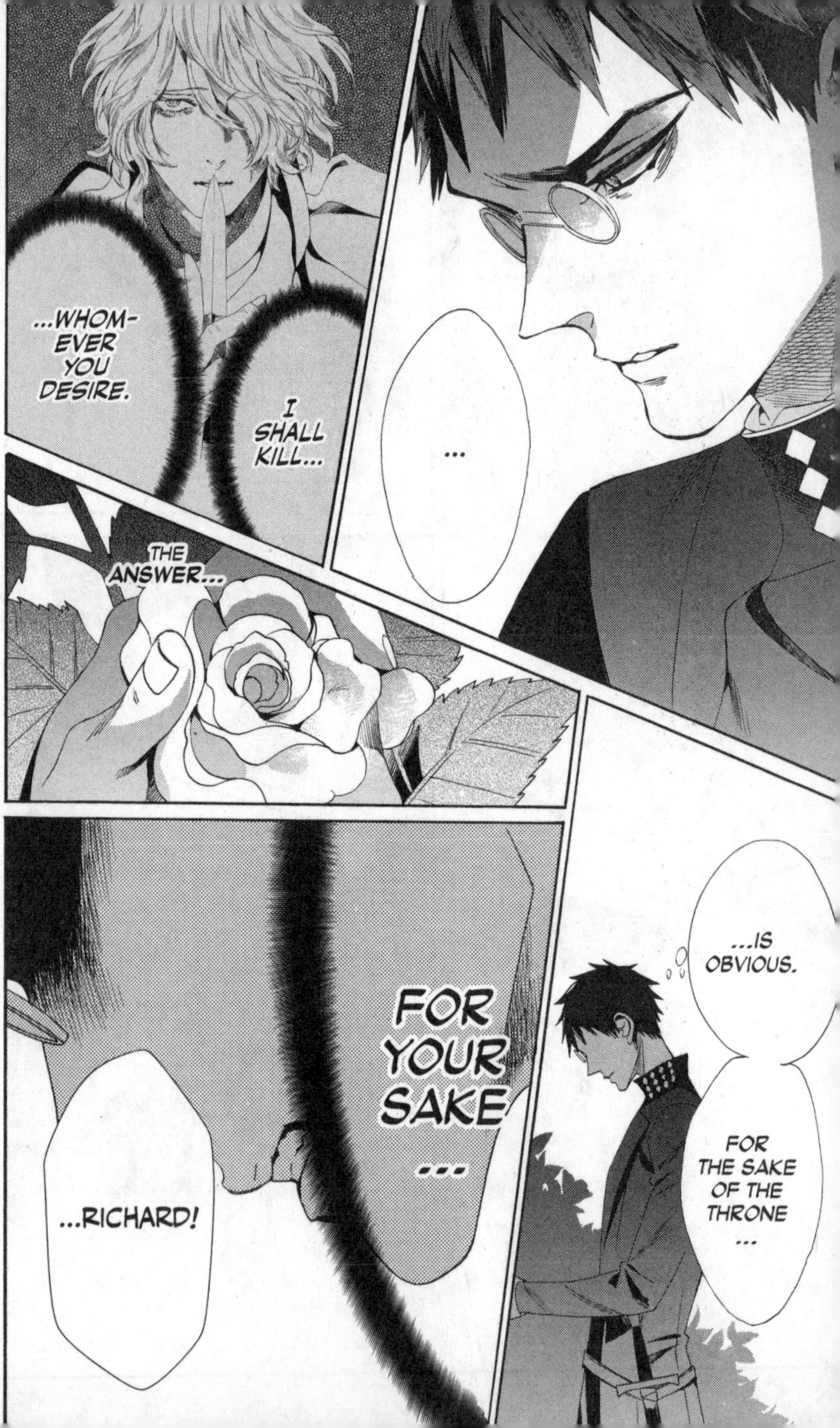
...
I SHALL KILL...
...WHOM-EVER YOU DESIRE.
THE ANSWER...
...IS OBVIOUS.
FOR THE SAKE OF THE THRONE ...
FOR YOUR SAKE ...
...RICHARD!

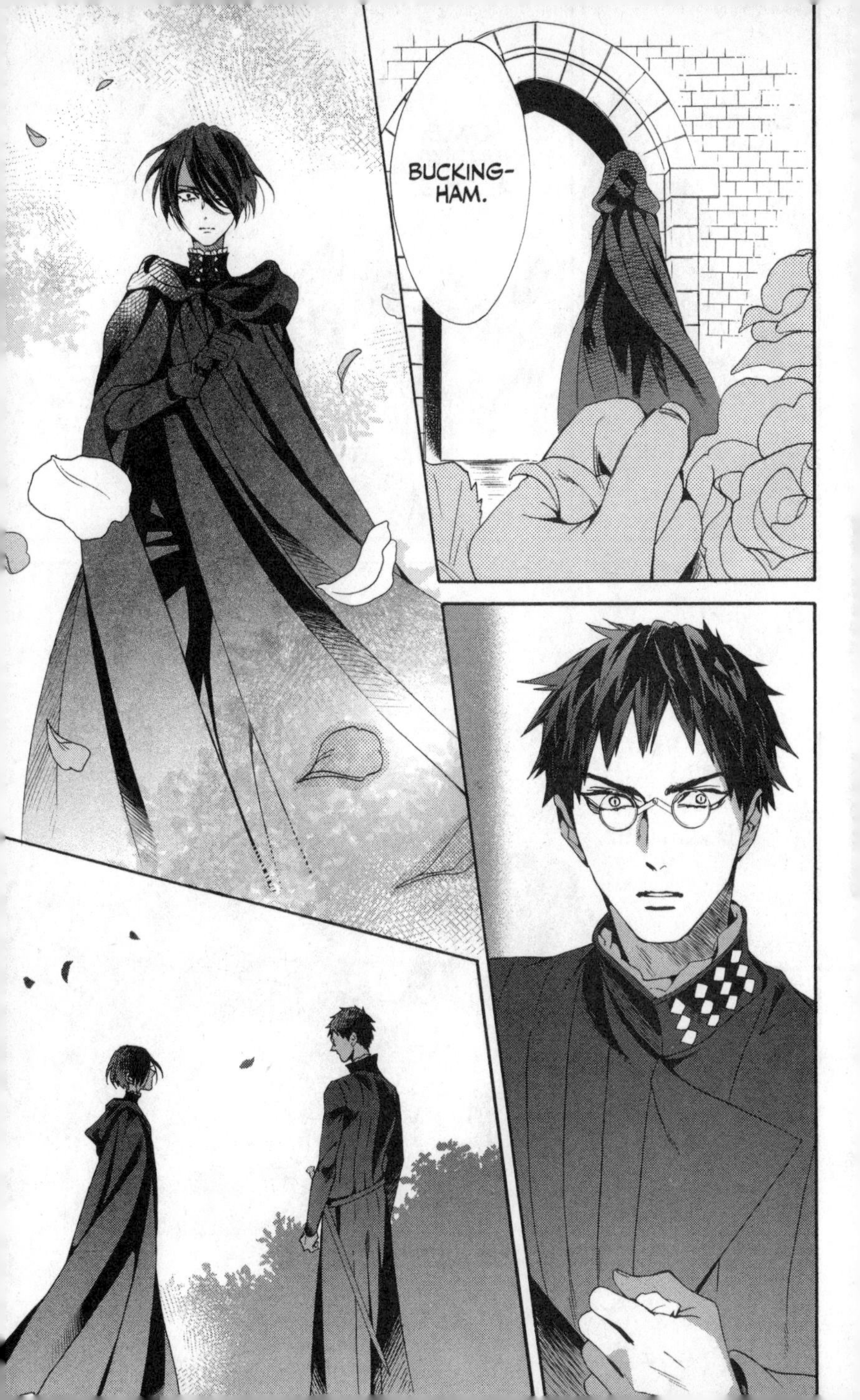
BUCKING-
HAM.

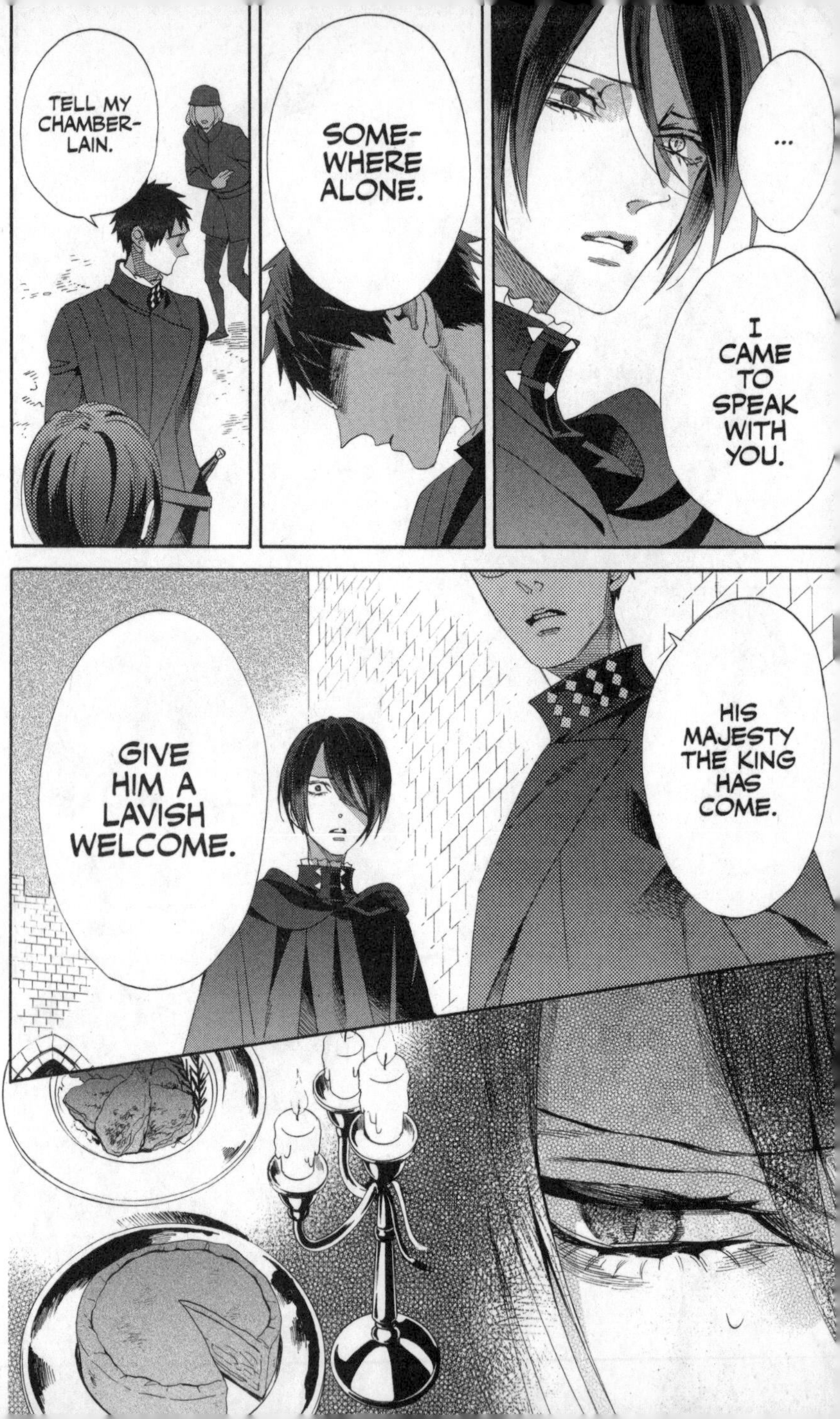
...
I CAME TO SPEAK WITH YOU.
SOME-WHERE ALONE.
TELL MY CHAMBER-LAIN.
HIS MAJESTY THE KING HAS COME.
GIVE HIM A LAVISH WELCOME.

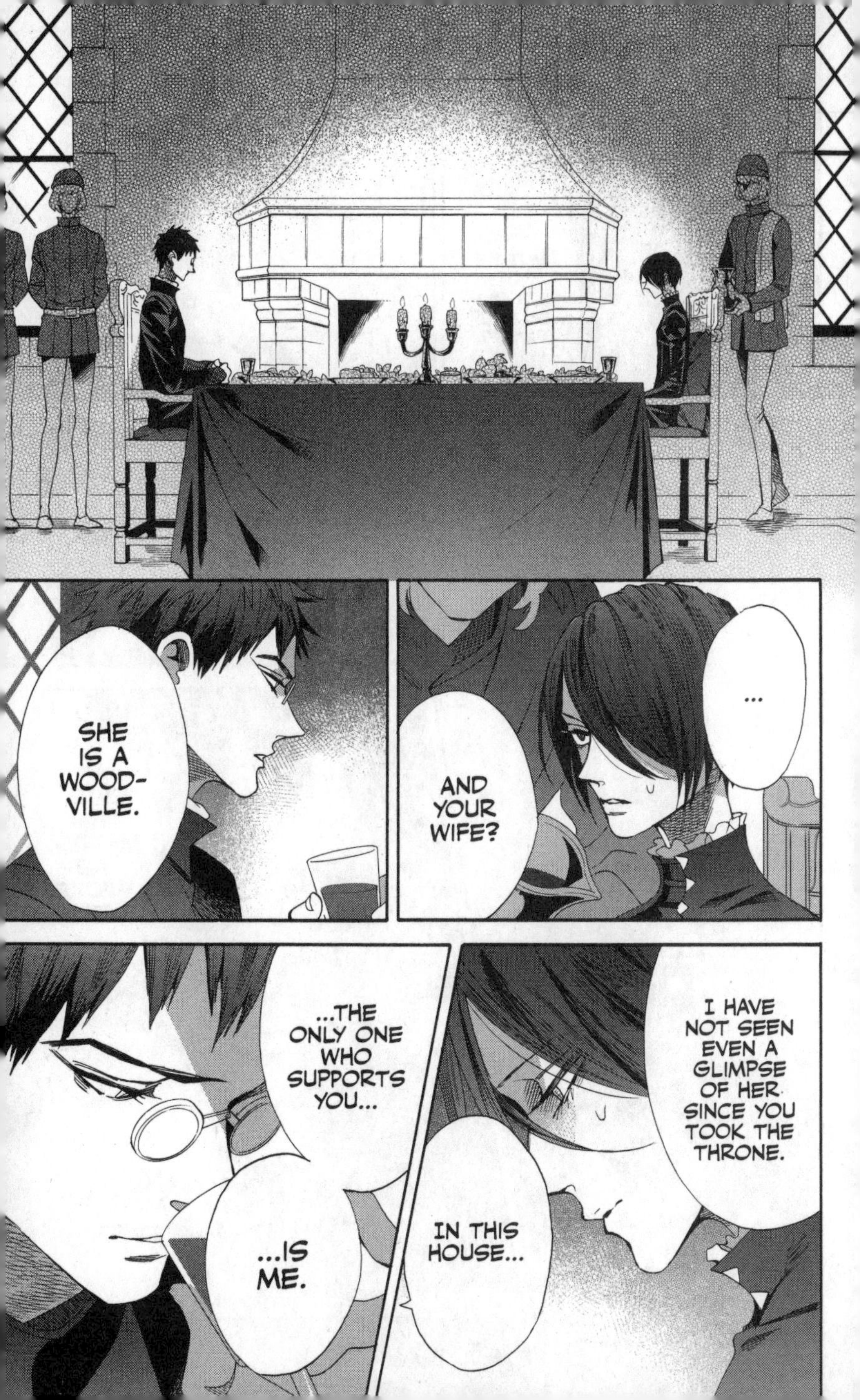
...
AND YOUR WIFE?
SHE IS A WOOD-VILLE.
I HAVE NOT SEEN EVEN A GLIMPSE OF HER SINCE YOU TOOK THE THRONE.
IN THIS HOUSE...
...THE ONLY ONE WHO SUPPORTS YOU...
...IS ME.

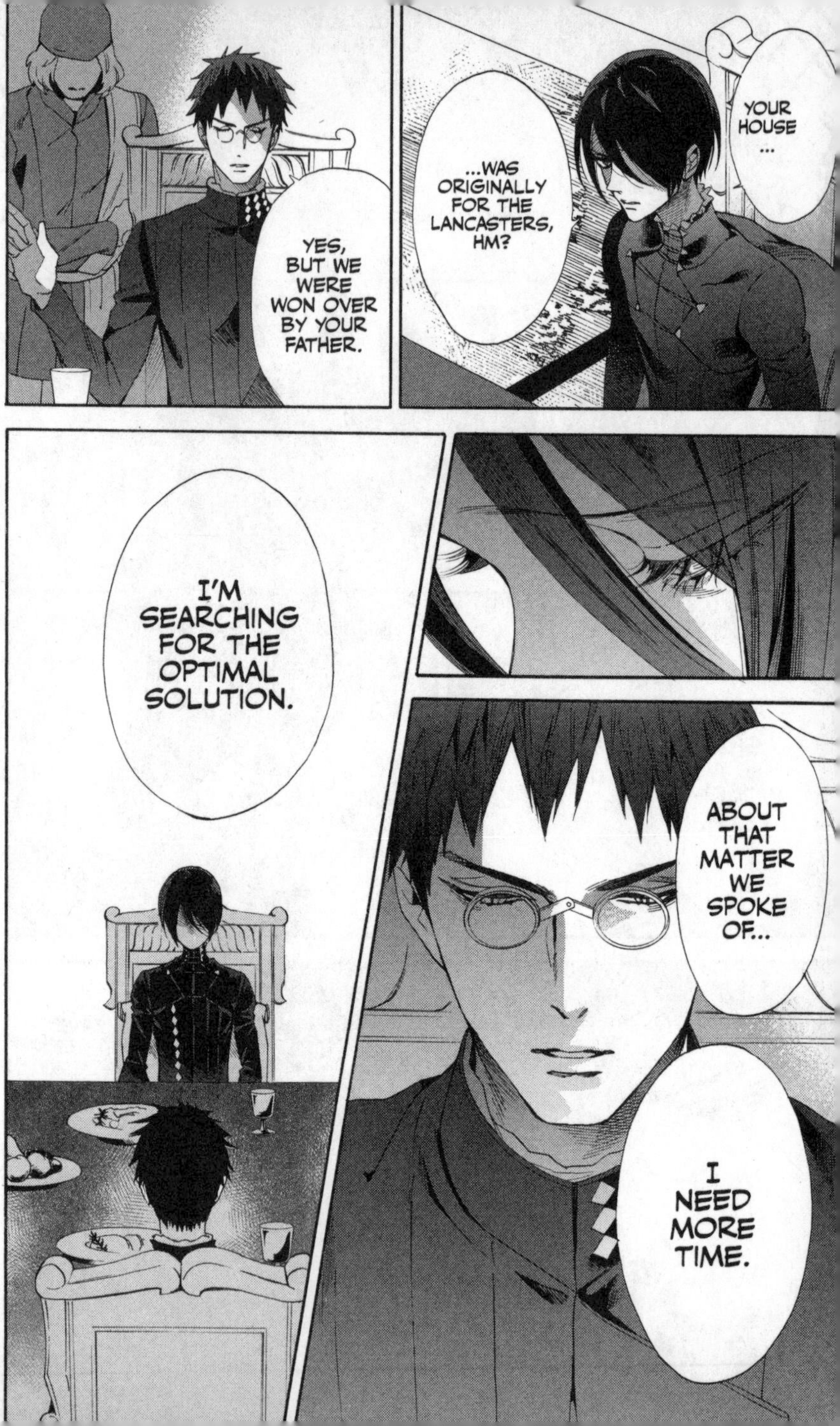
YOUR HOUSE ...
...WAS ORIGINALLY FOR THE LANCASTERS, HM?
YES, BUT WE WERE WON OVER BY YOUR FATHER.
ABOUT THAT MATTER WE SPOKE OF...
I NEED MORE TIME.
I'M SEARCHING FOR THE OPTIMAL SOLUTION.

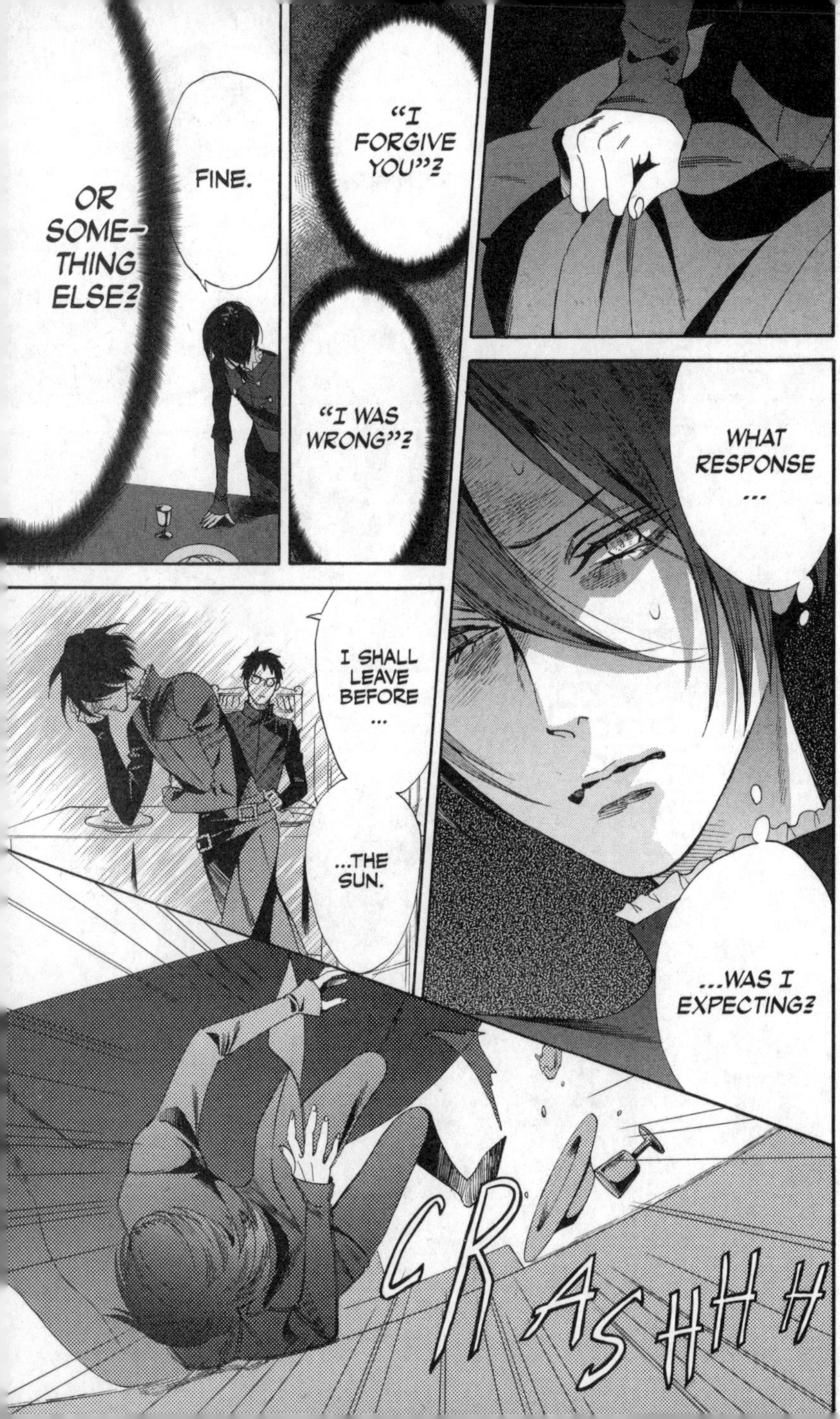
"I FORGIVE YOU"?
"I WAS WRONG"?
FINE.
OR SOME-THING ELSE?
WHAT RESPONSE...
...WAS I EXPECTING?
I SHALL LEAVE BEFORE...
...THE SUN.
CRASHHH

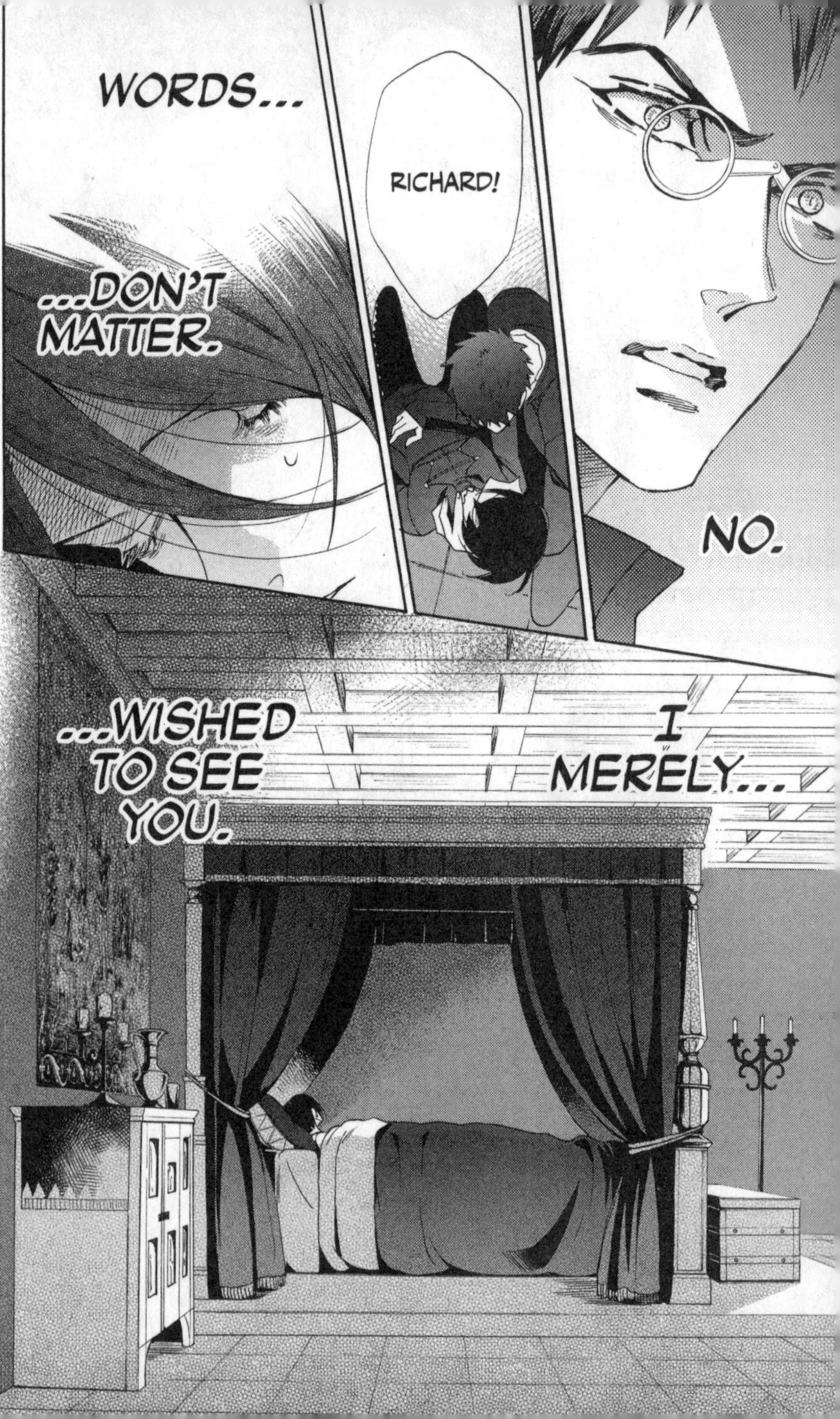
NO.
RICHARD!
WORDS...
...DON'T MATTER.
I MERELY...
...WISHED TO SEE YOU.

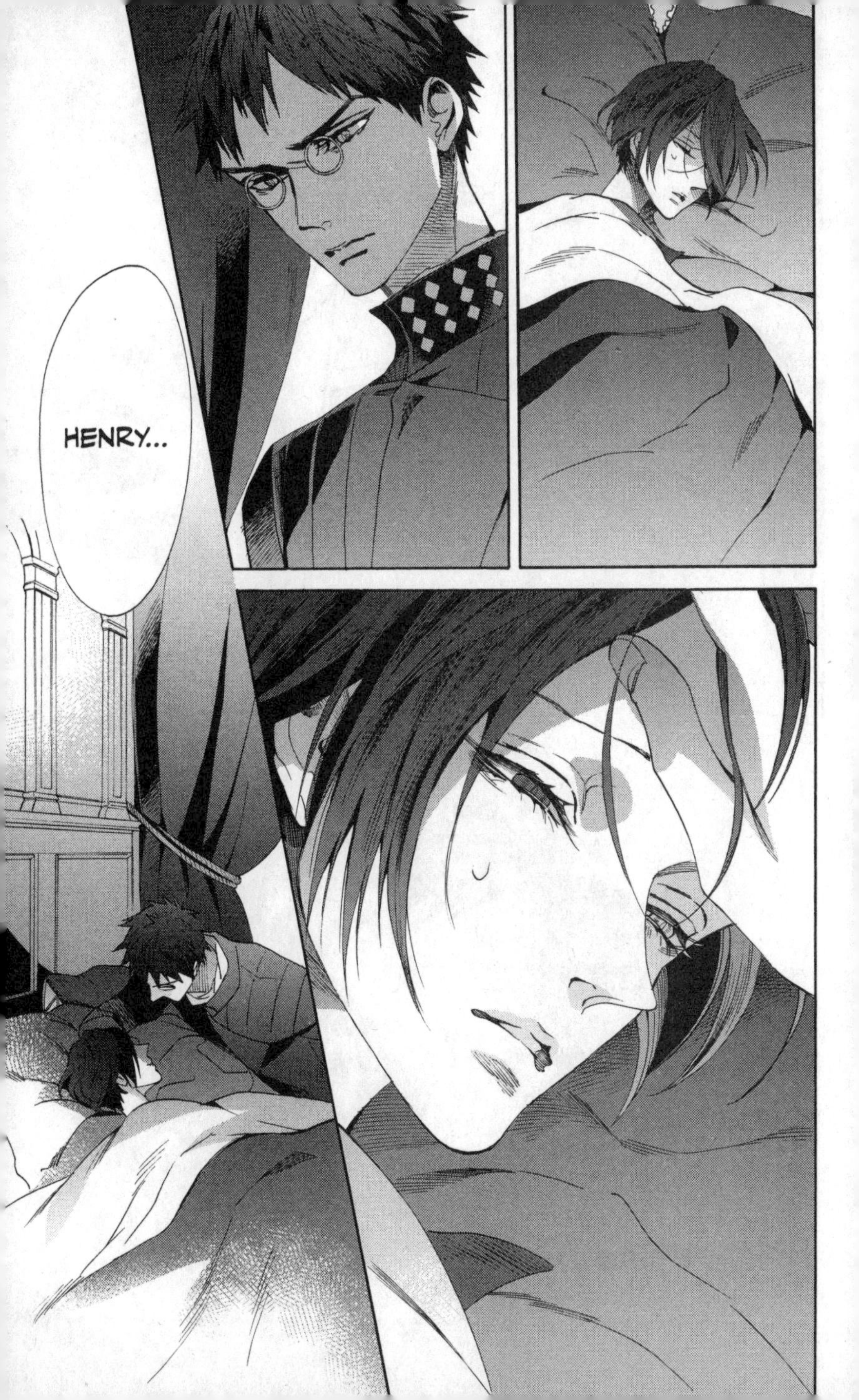
HENRY...

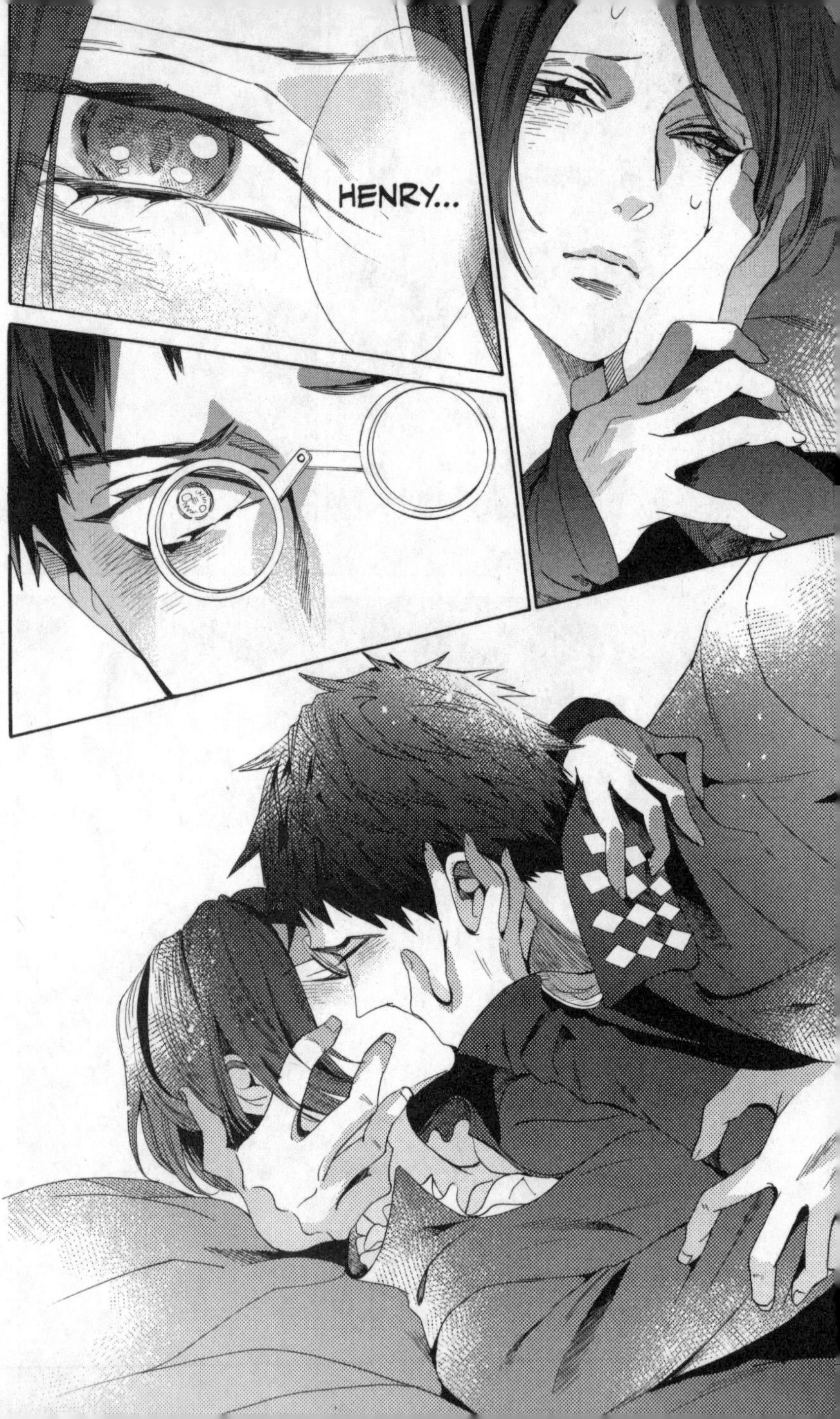
HENRY...

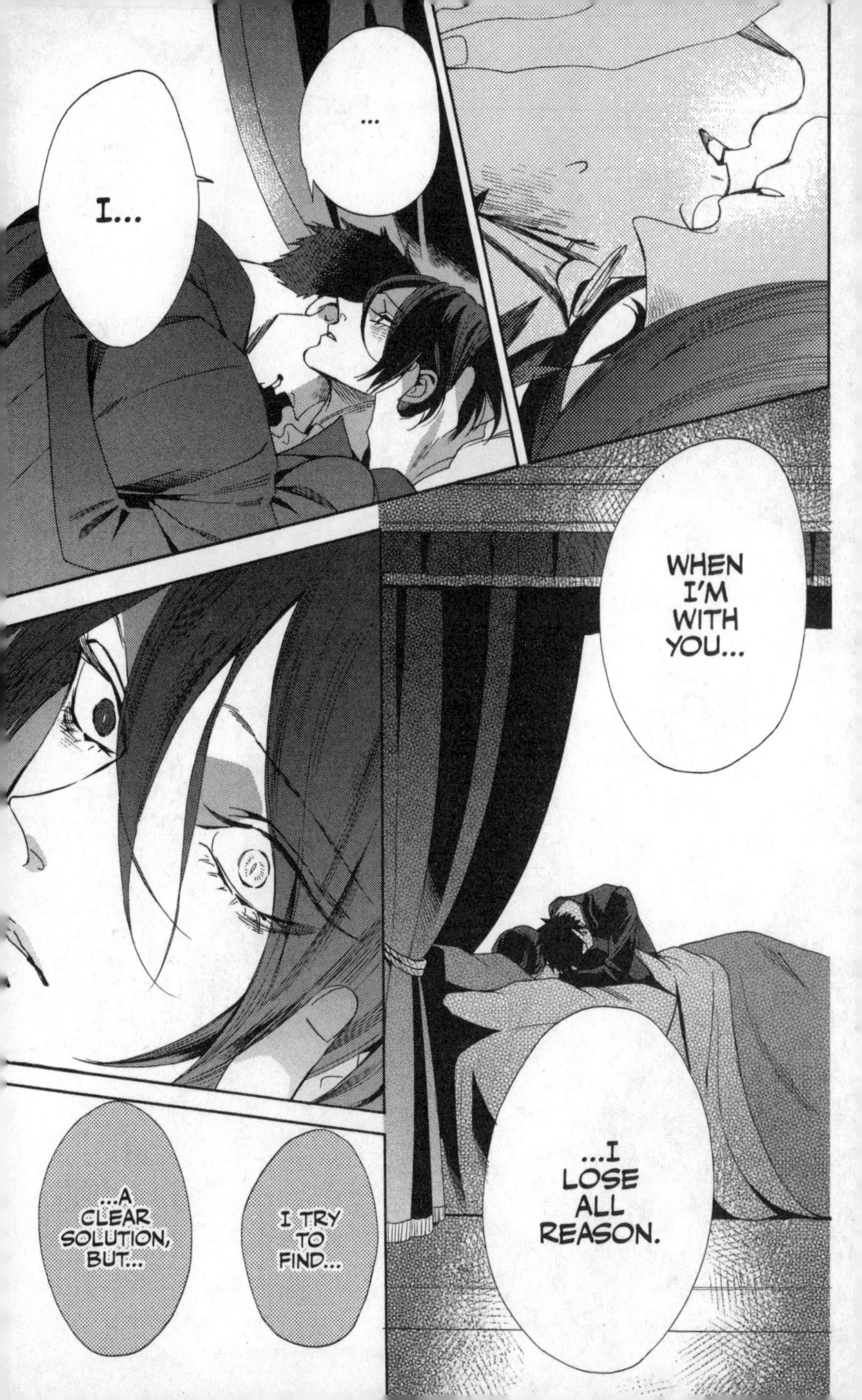
...
I...
WHEN I'M WITH YOU...
...I LOSE ALL REASON.
I TRY TO FIND...
...A CLEAR SOLUTION, BUT...

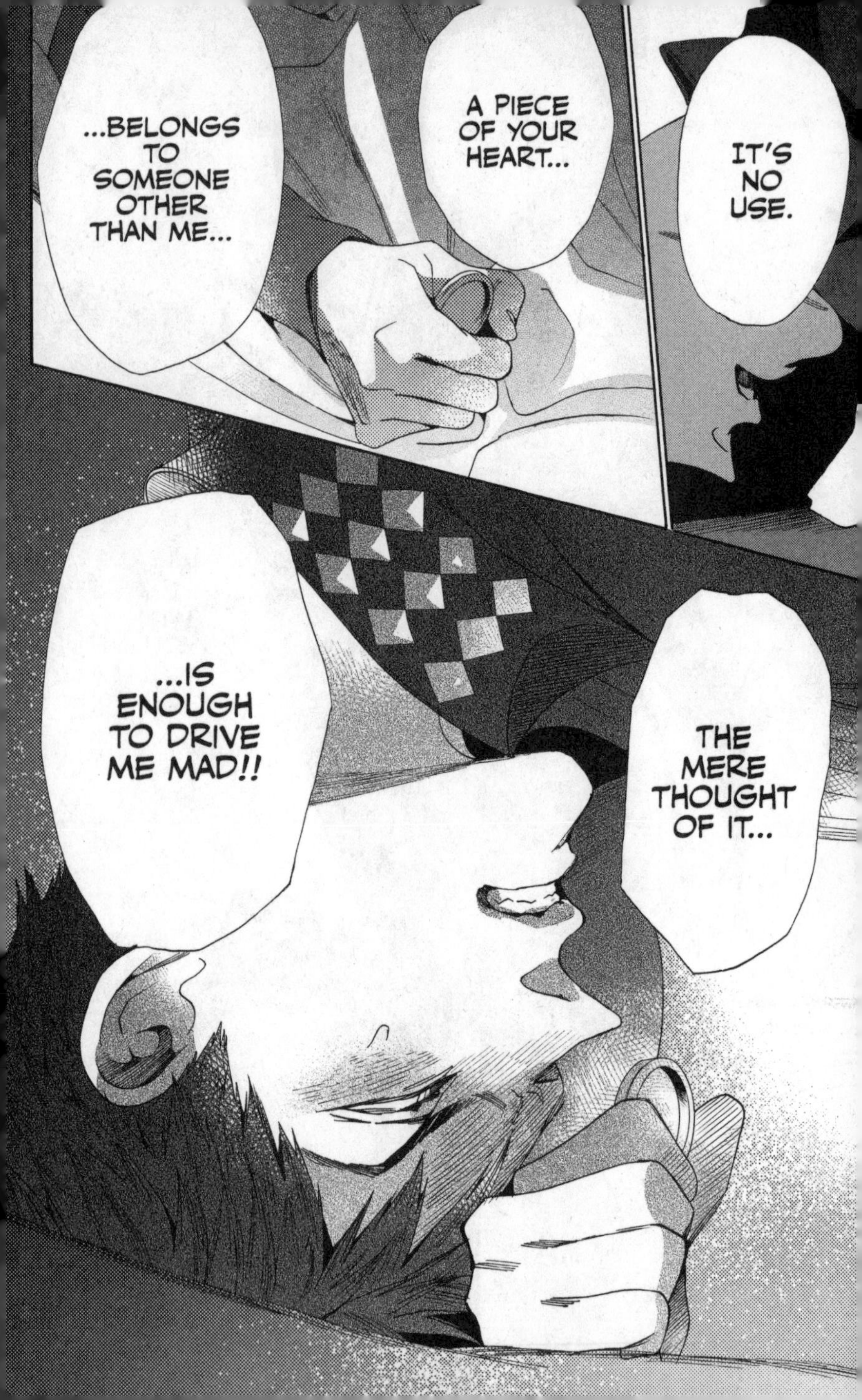
IT'S NO USE.
A PIECE OF YOUR HEART...
...BELONGS TO SOMEONE OTHER THAN ME...
THE MERE THOUGHT OF IT...
...IS ENOUGH TO DRIVE ME MAD!!

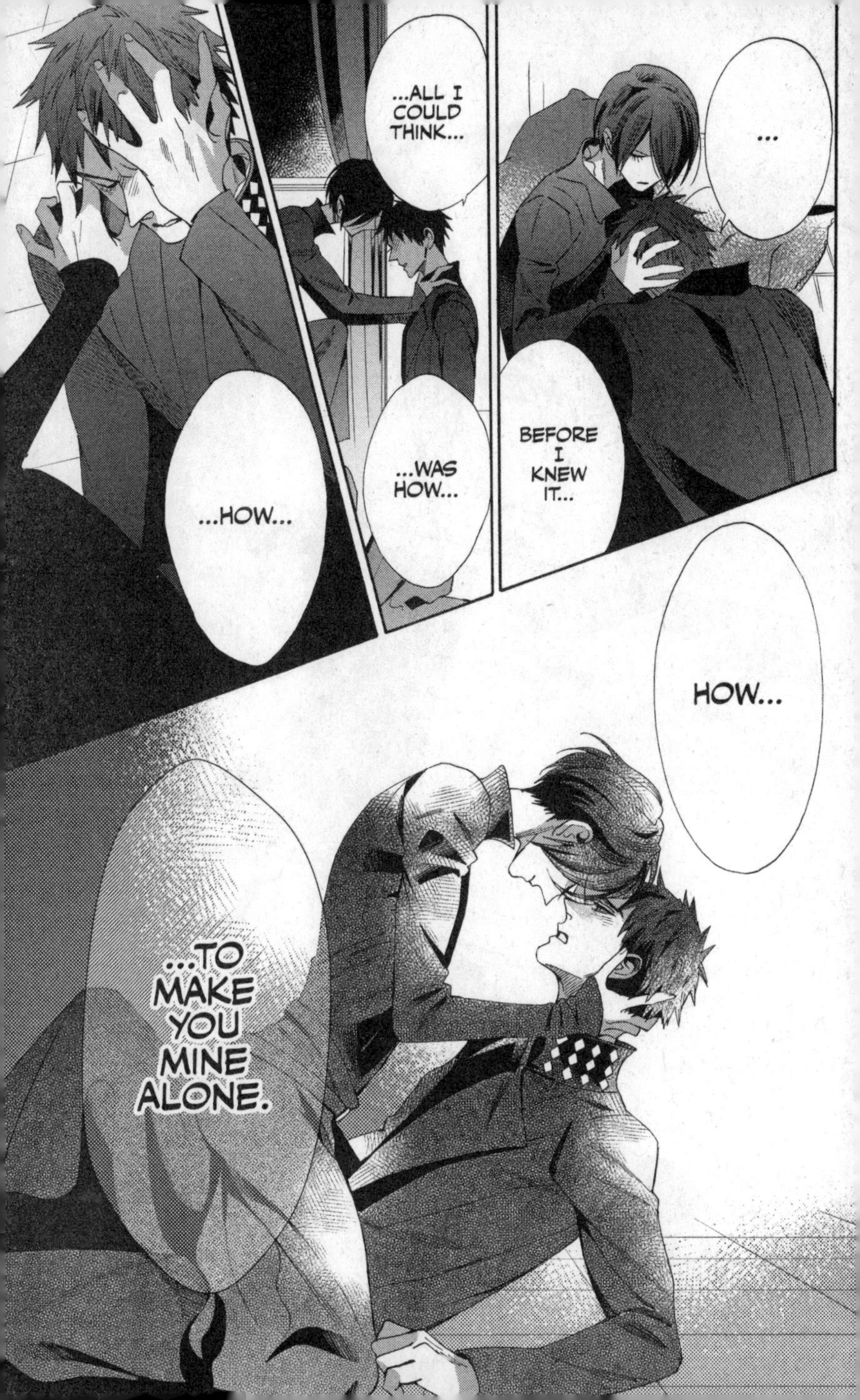
...
BEFORE I KNEW IT...
...ALL I COULD THINK...
...WAS HOW...
...HOW...
HOW...
...TO MAKE YOU MINE ALONE.

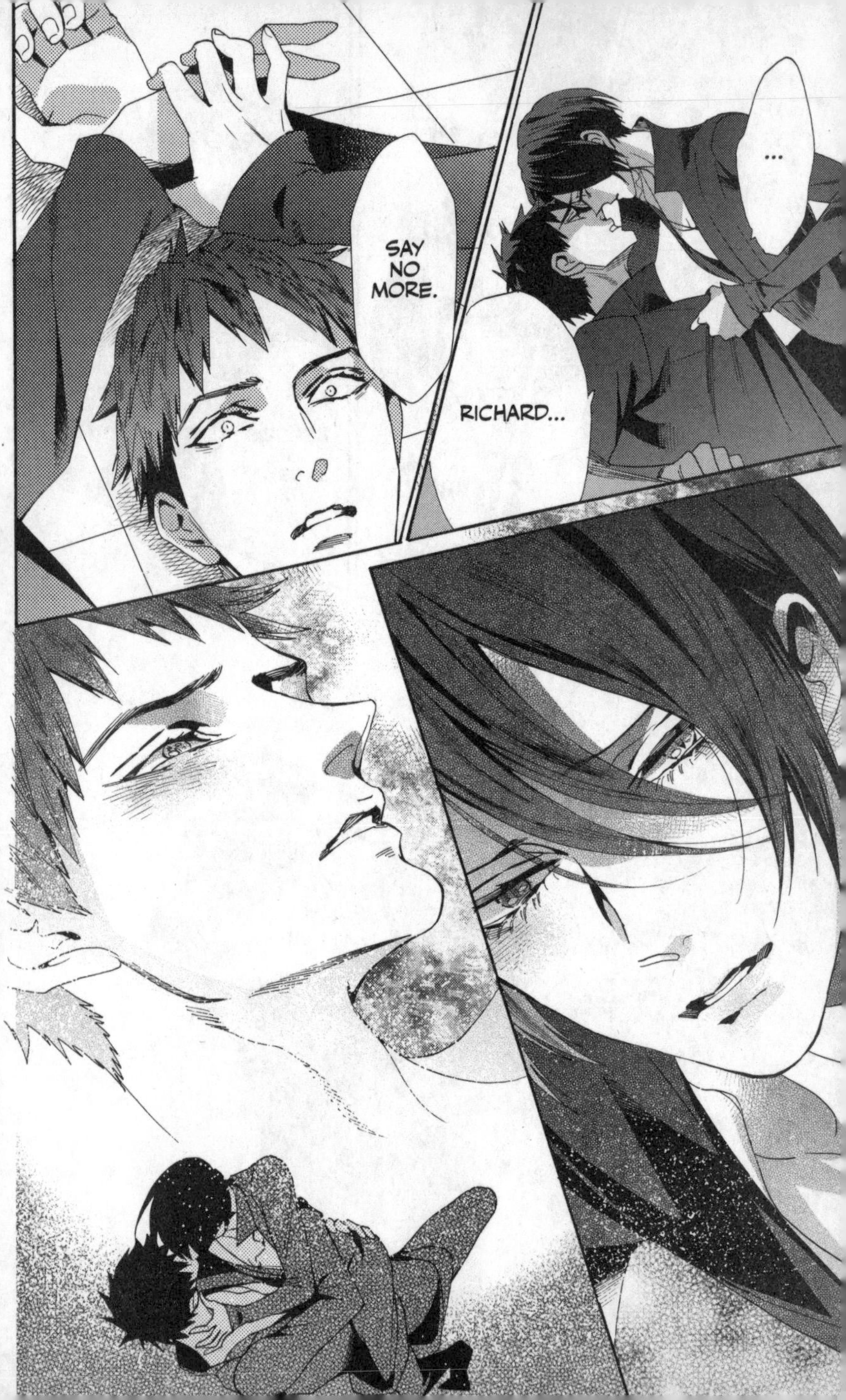
...
RICHARD...
SAY NO MORE.

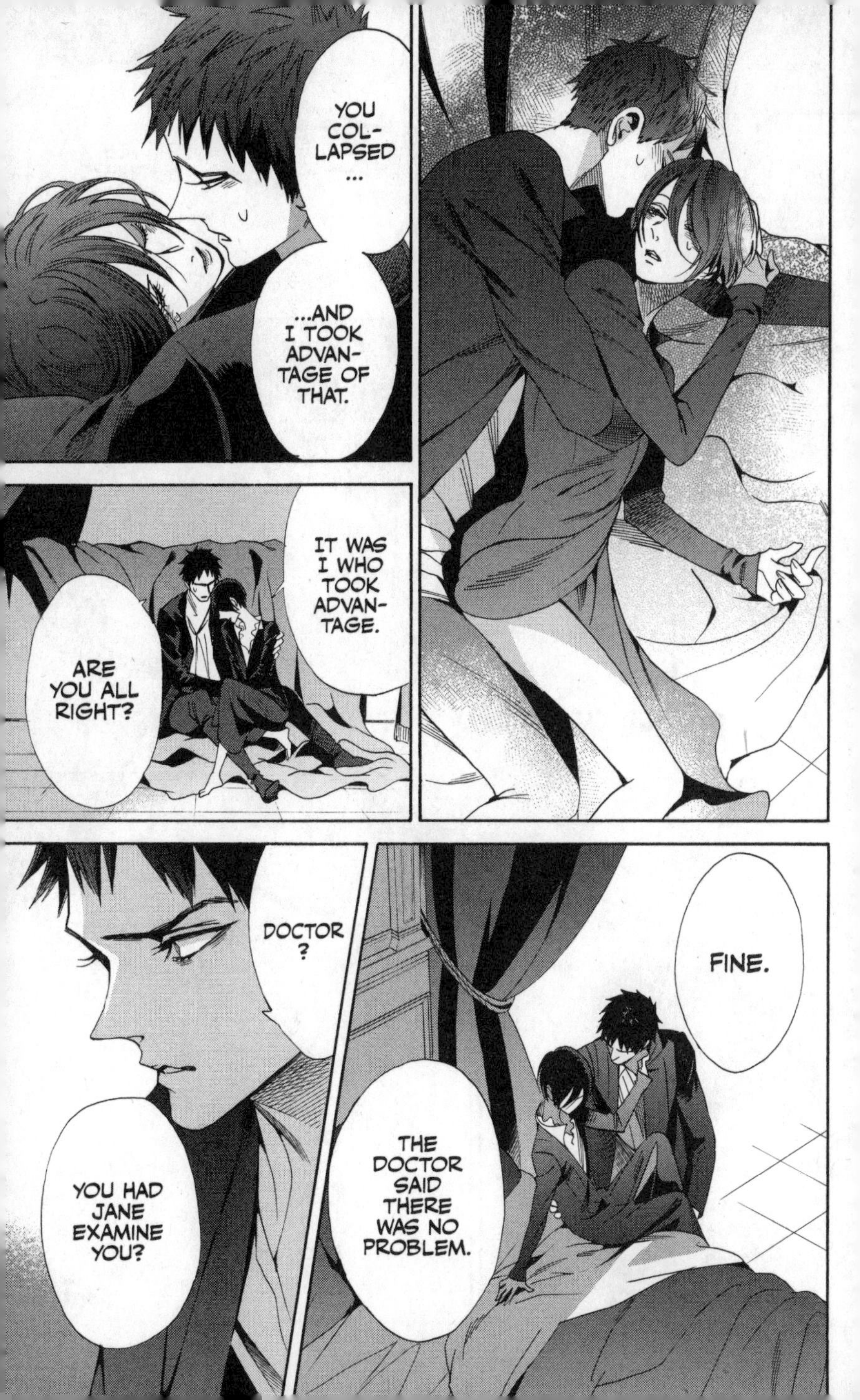
YOU COL-LAPSED ...
...AND I TOOK ADVAN-TAGE OF THAT.
IT WAS I WHO TOOK ADVAN-TAGE.
ARE YOU ALL RIGHT?
FINE.
THE DOCTOR SAID THERE WAS NO PROBLEM.
DOCTOR ?
YOU HAD JANE EXAMINE YOU?

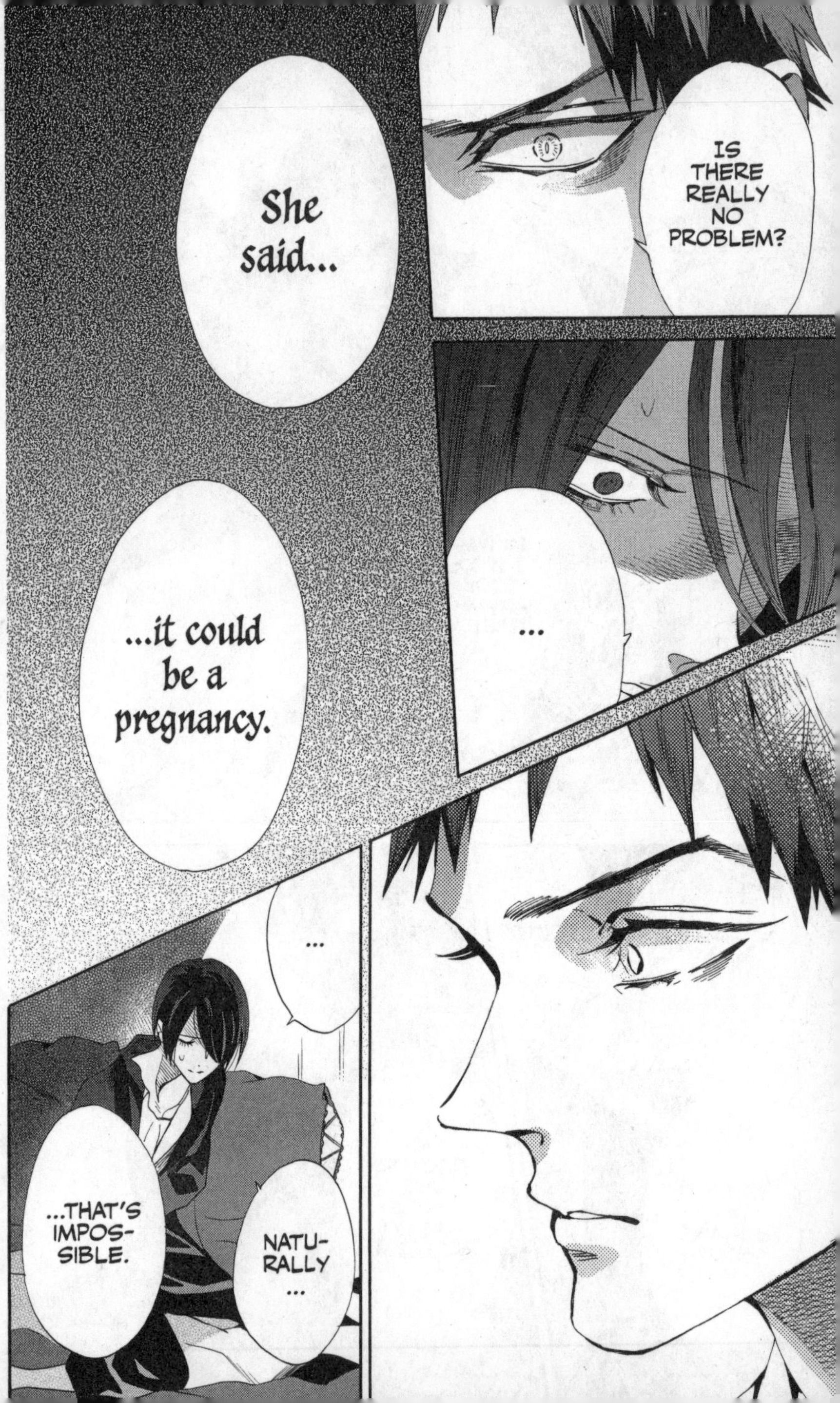
IS THERE REALLY NO PROBLEM?
...
She said...
...it could be a pregnancy.
...
NATU-RALLY ...
...THAT'S IMPOS-SIBLE.

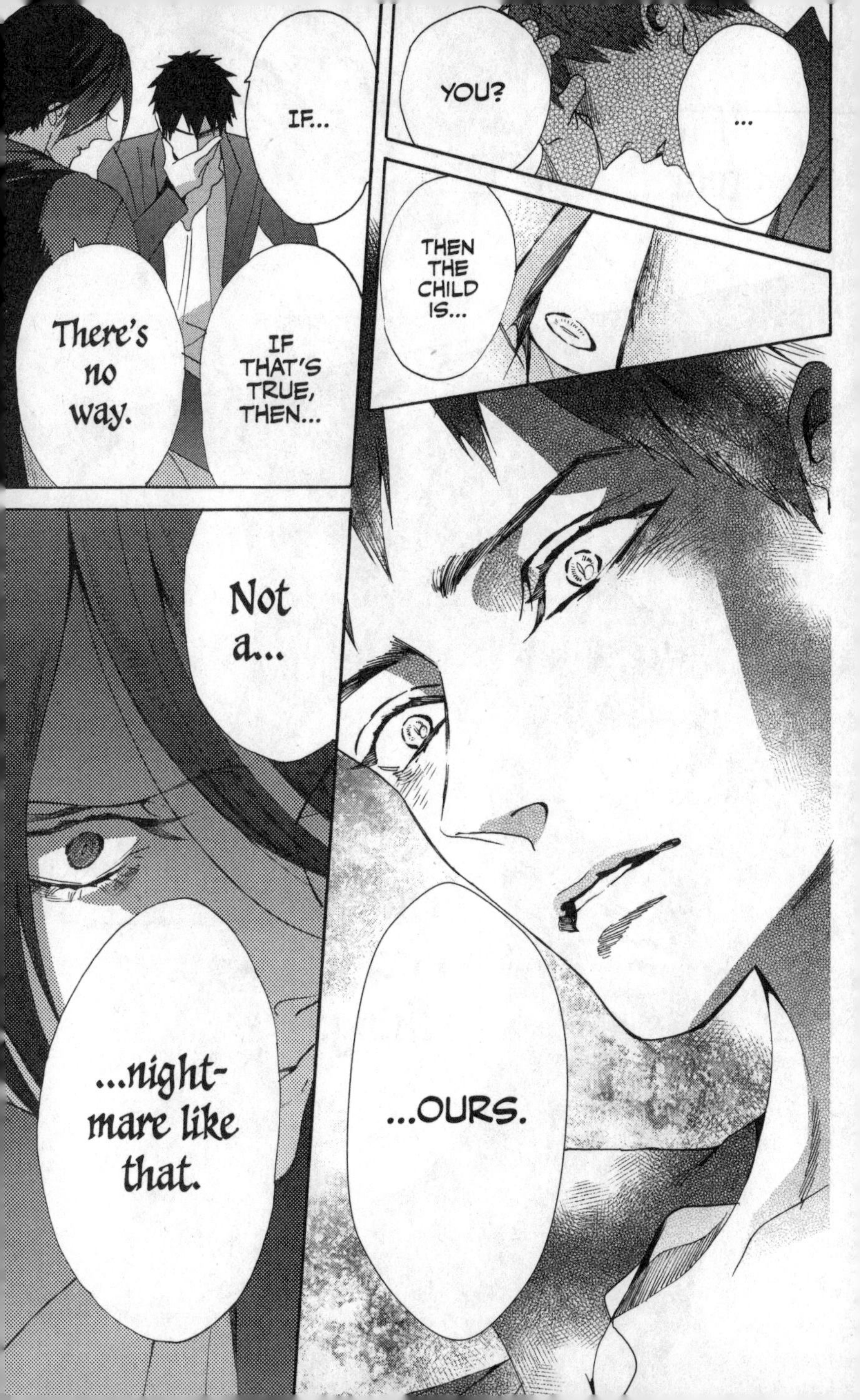
...
YOU?
THEN THE CHILD IS...
...OURS.
IF...
IF THAT'S TRUE, THEN...
There's no way.
Not a...
...night-mare like that.

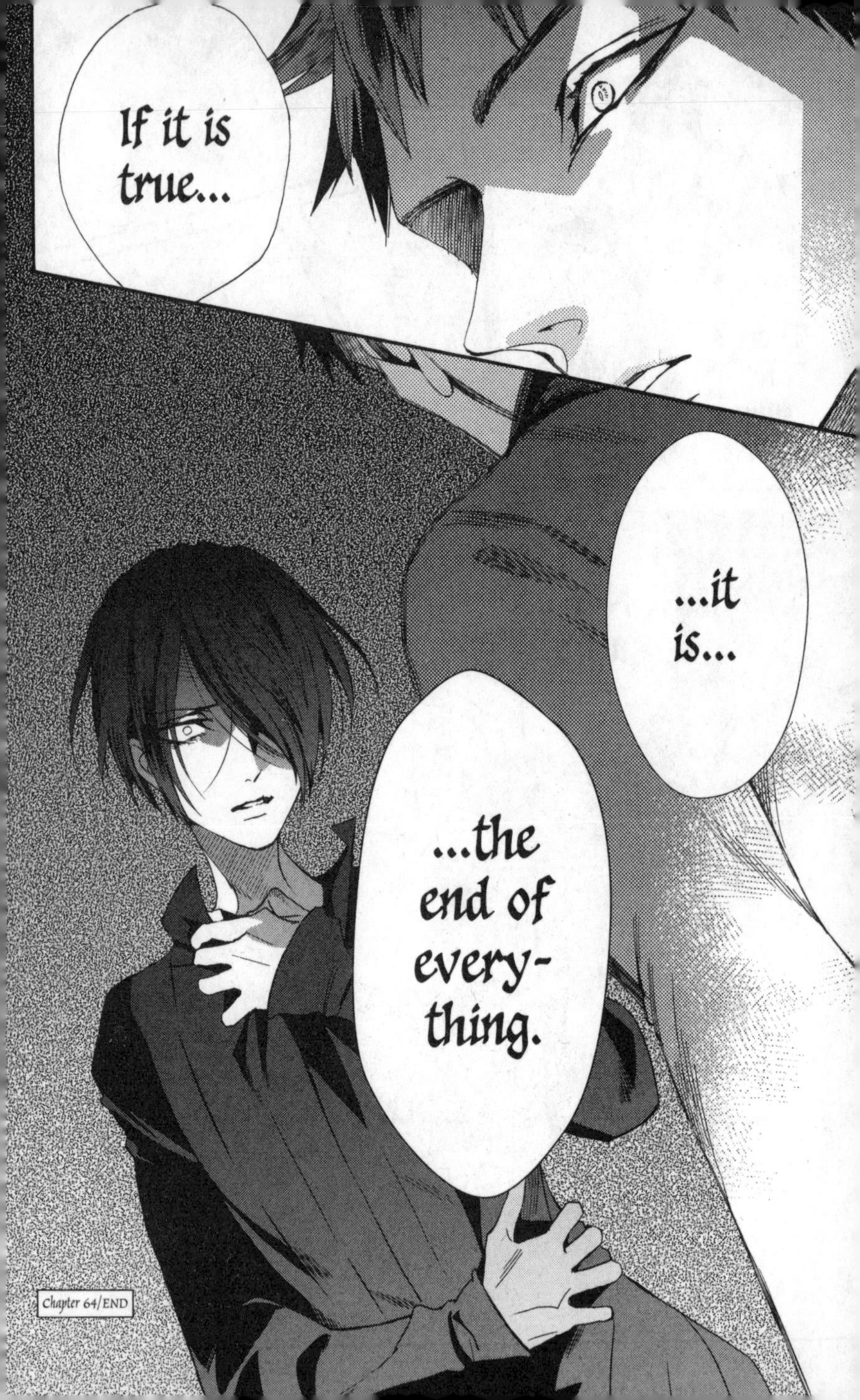
If it is true...
...it is...
...the end of every-thing.
Chapter 64/END

Chapter 65

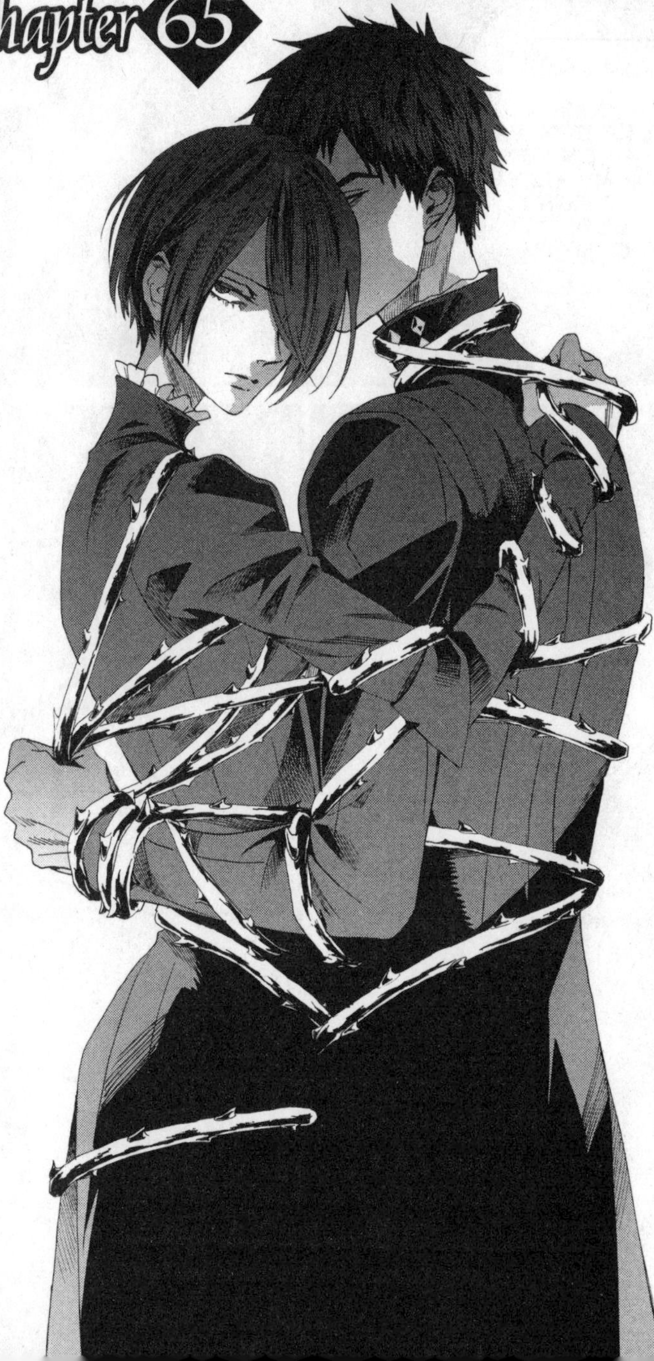

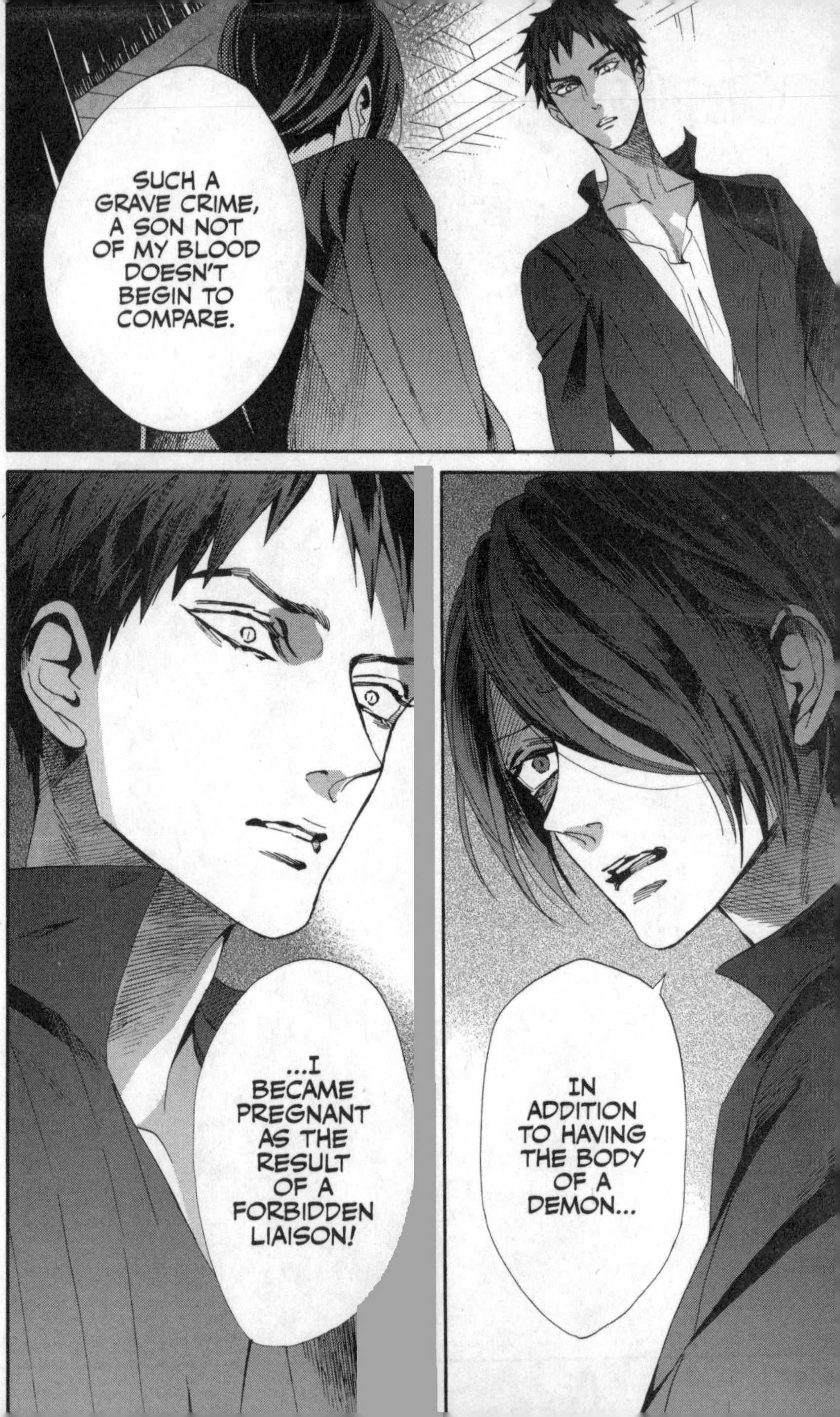
SUCH A GRAVE CRIME, A SON NOT OF MY BLOOD DOESN'T BEGIN TO COMPARE.
IN ADDITION TO HAVING THE BODY OF A DEMON...
...I BECAME PREGNANT AS THE RESULT OF A FORBIDDEN LIAISON!

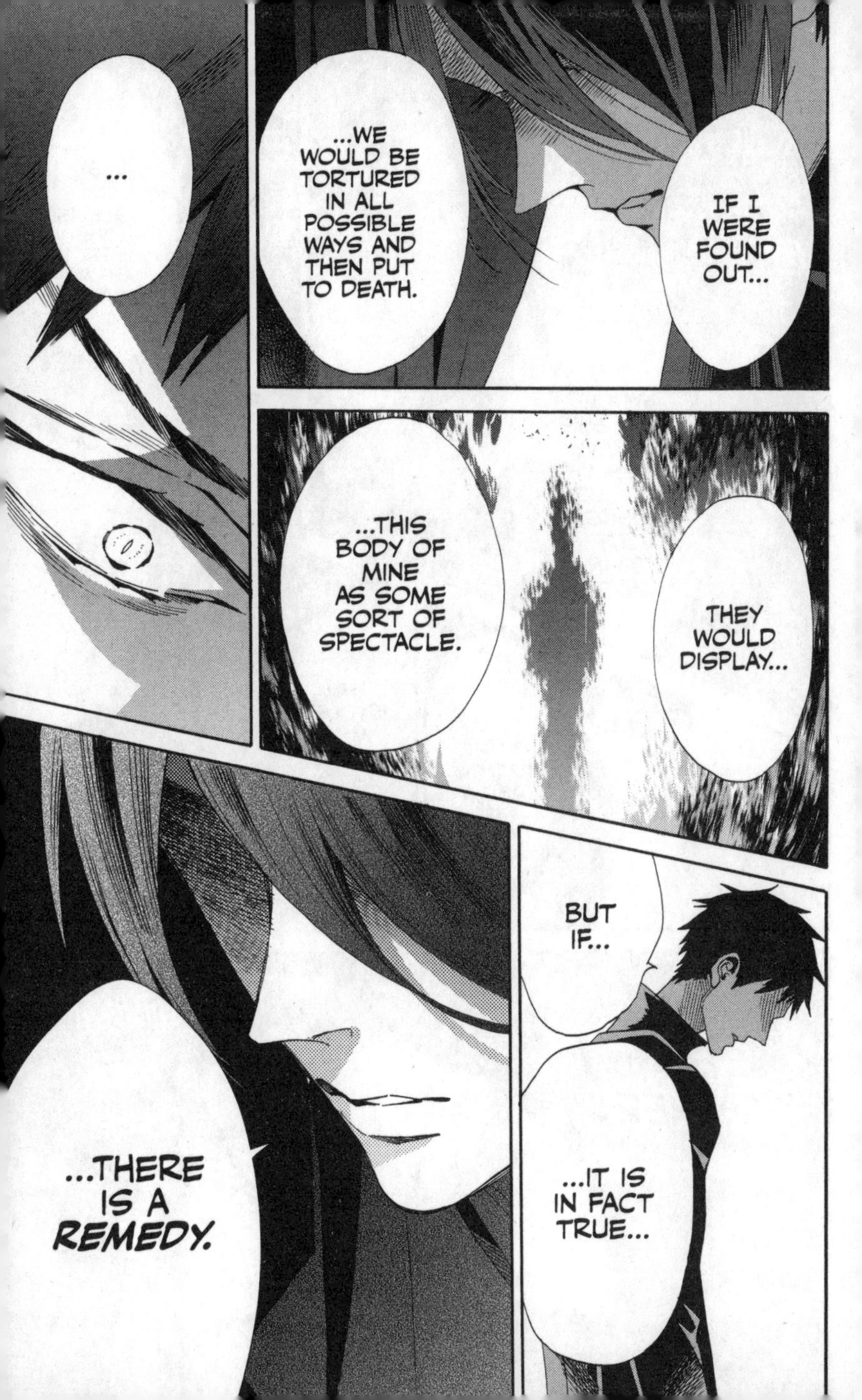
IF I WERE FOUND OUT...
...WE WOULD BE TORTURED IN ALL POSSIBLE WAYS AND THEN PUT TO DEATH.
THEY WOULD DISPLAY...
...THIS BODY OF MINE AS SOME SORT OF SPECTACLE.
...
BUT IF...
...IT IS IN FACT TRUE...
...THERE IS A *REMEDY.*

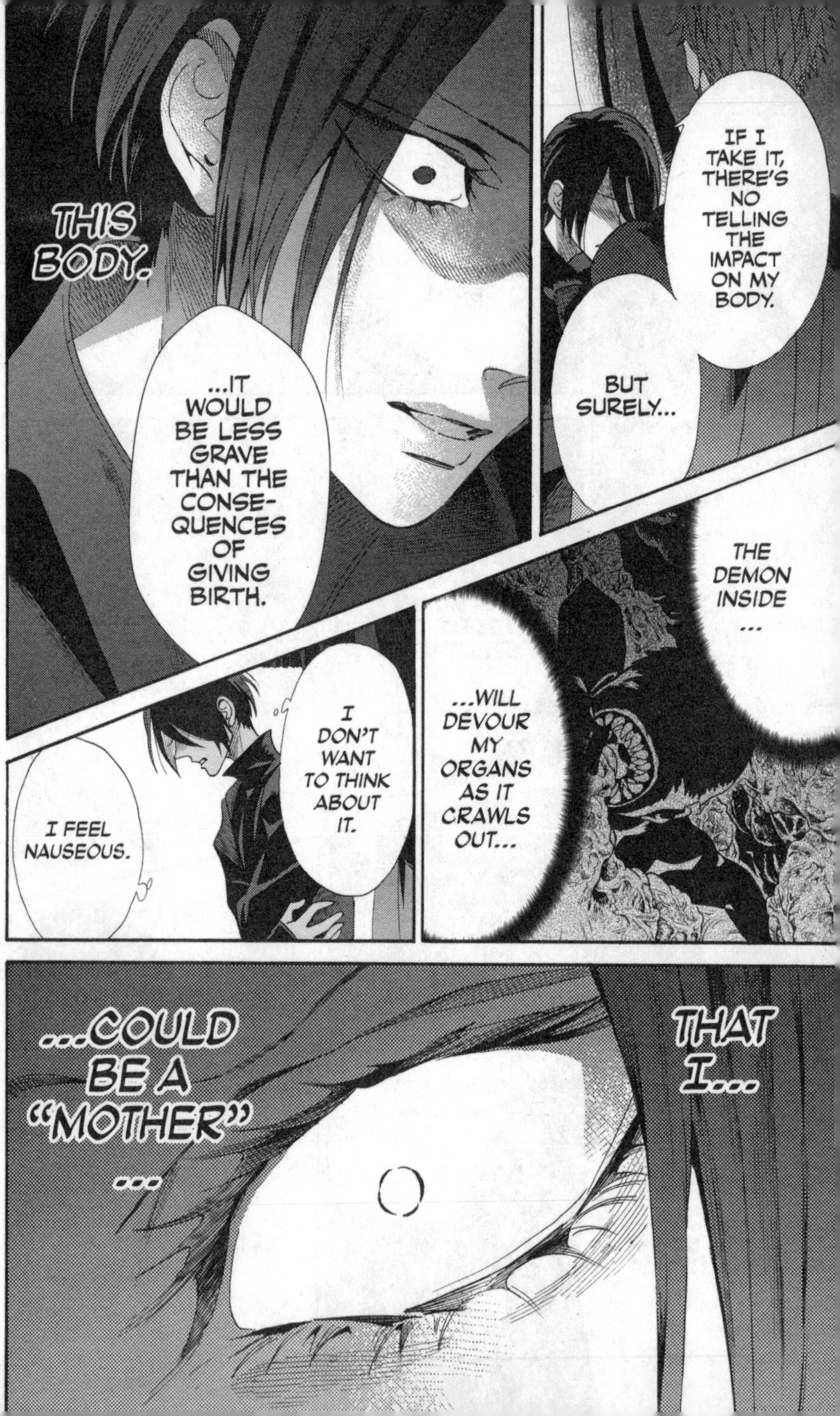
IF I TAKE IT, THERE'S NO TELLING THE IMPACT ON MY BODY.
BUT SURELY...
THIS BODY.
...IT WOULD BE LESS GRAVE THAN THE CONSE-QUENCES OF GIVING BIRTH.
THE DEMON INSIDE...
...WILL DEVOUR MY ORGANS AS IT CRAWLS OUT...
I DON'T WANT TO THINK ABOUT IT.
I FEEL NAUSEOUS.
THAT I...
...COULD BE A “MOTHER”...

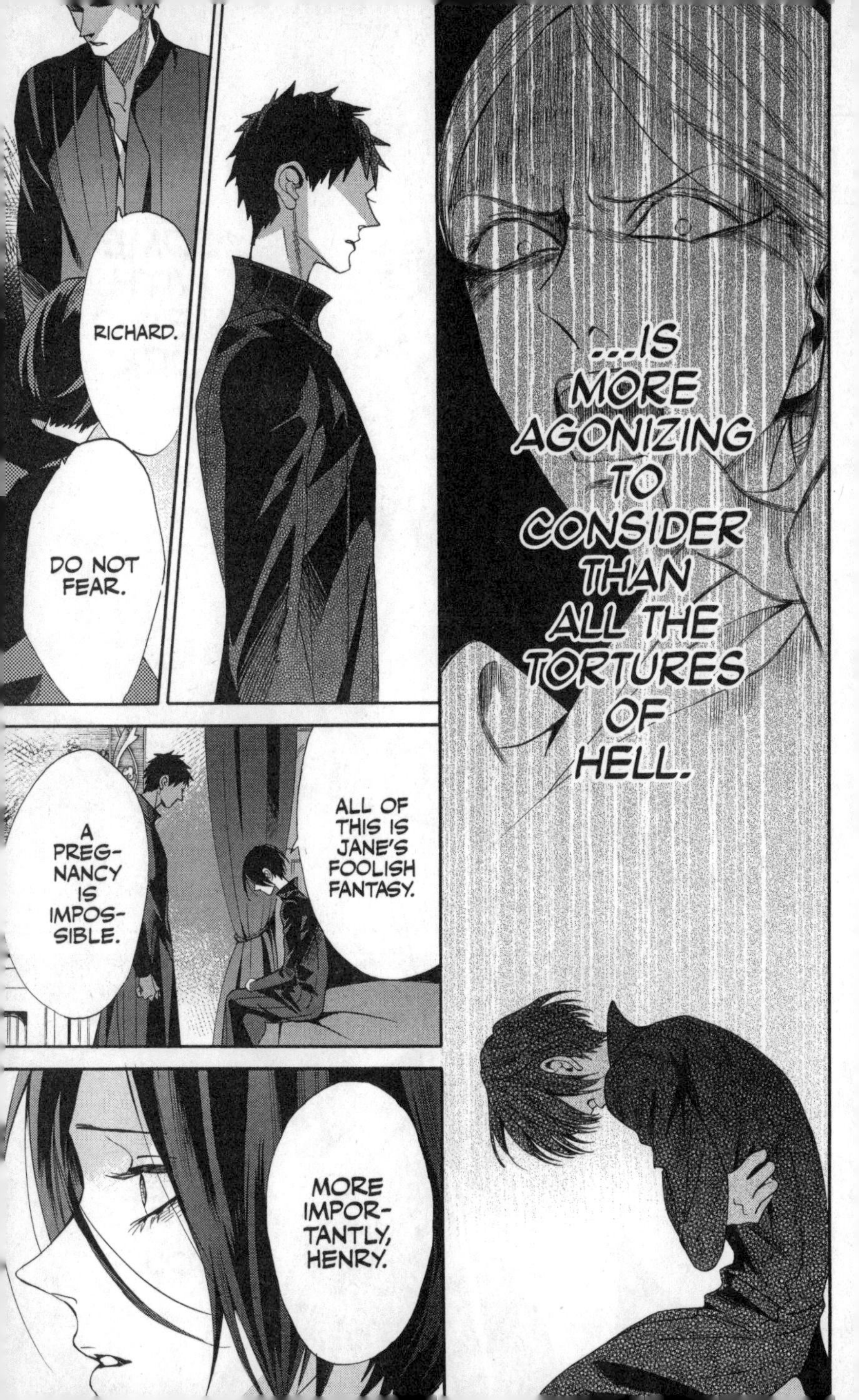
...IS MORE AGONIZING TO CONSIDER THAN ALL THE TORTURES OF HELL.
RICHARD.
DO NOT FEAR.
ALL OF THIS IS JANE'S FOOLISH FANTASY.
A PREGNANCY IS IMPOSSIBLE.
MORE IMPORTANTLY, HENRY.

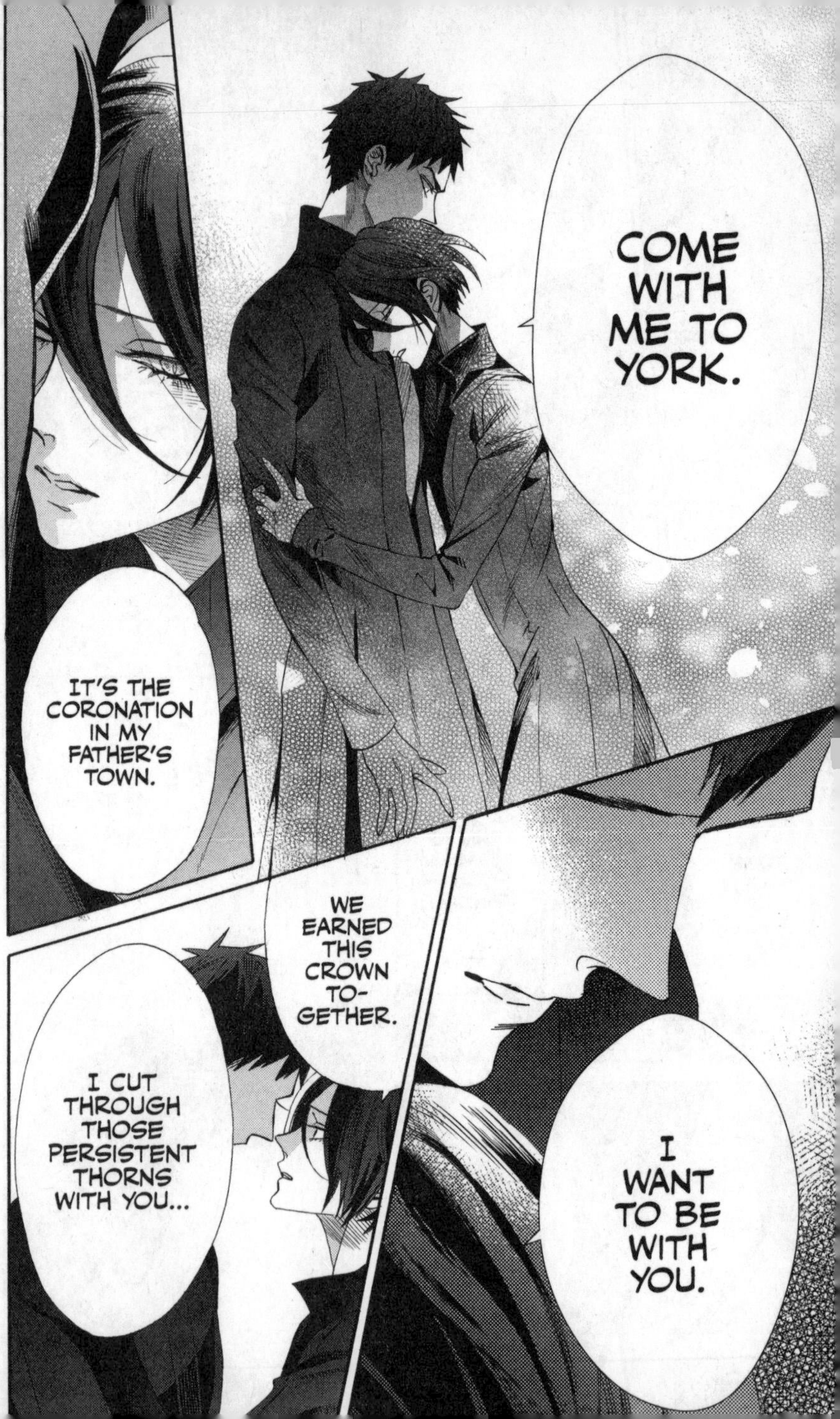
COME WITH ME TO YORK.
IT'S THE CORONATION IN MY FATHER'S TOWN.
I WANT TO BE WITH YOU.
WE EARNED THIS CROWN TO-GETHER.
I CUT THROUGH THOSE PERSISTENT THORNS WITH YOU...

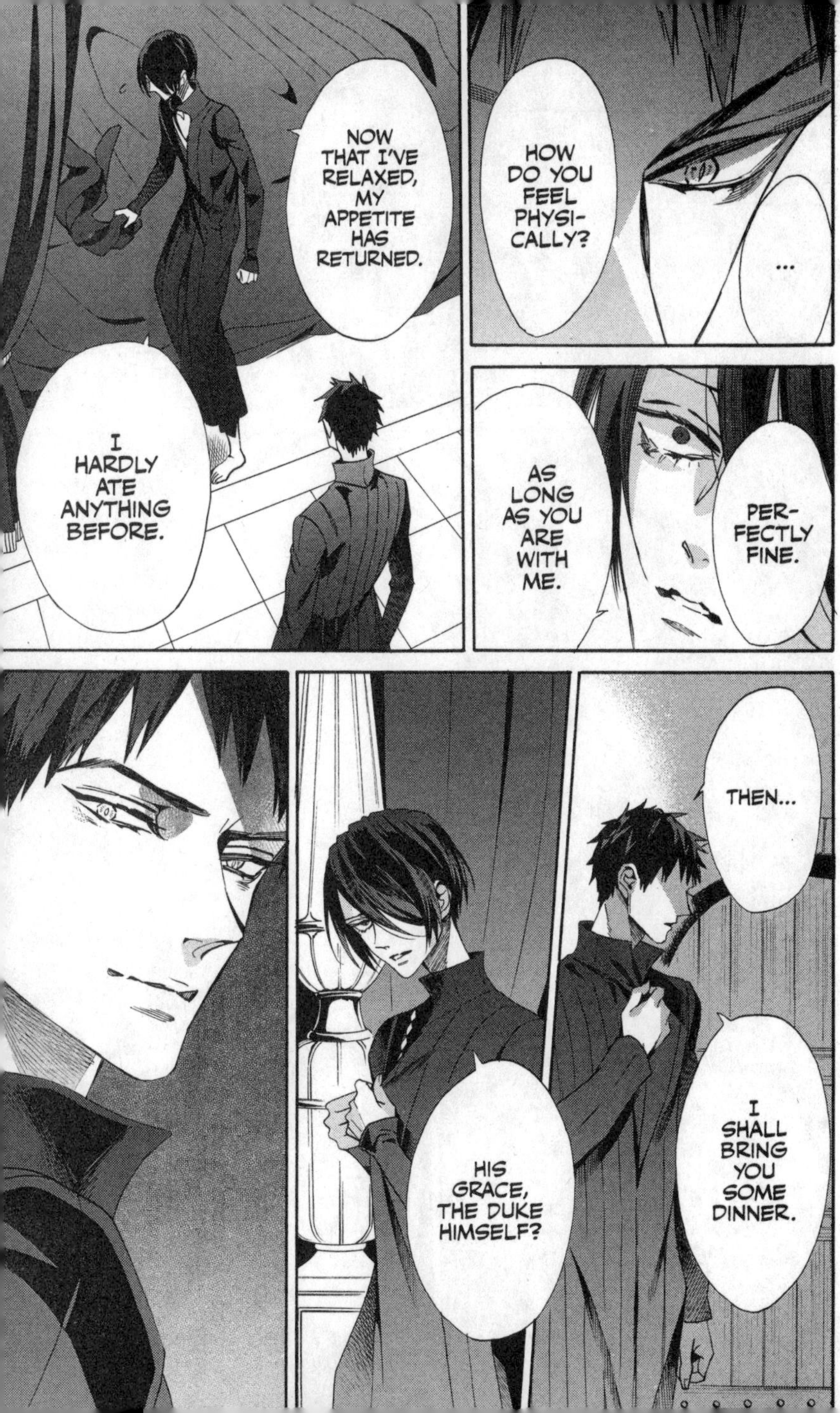
HOW DO YOU FEEL PHYSICALLY?
...
PERFECTLY FINE.
AS LONG AS YOU ARE WITH ME.
NOW THAT I'VE RELAXED, MY APPETITE HAS RETURNED.
I HARDLY ATE ANYTHING BEFORE.
THEN...
I SHALL BRING YOU SOME DINNER.
HIS GRACE, THE DUKE HIMSELF?

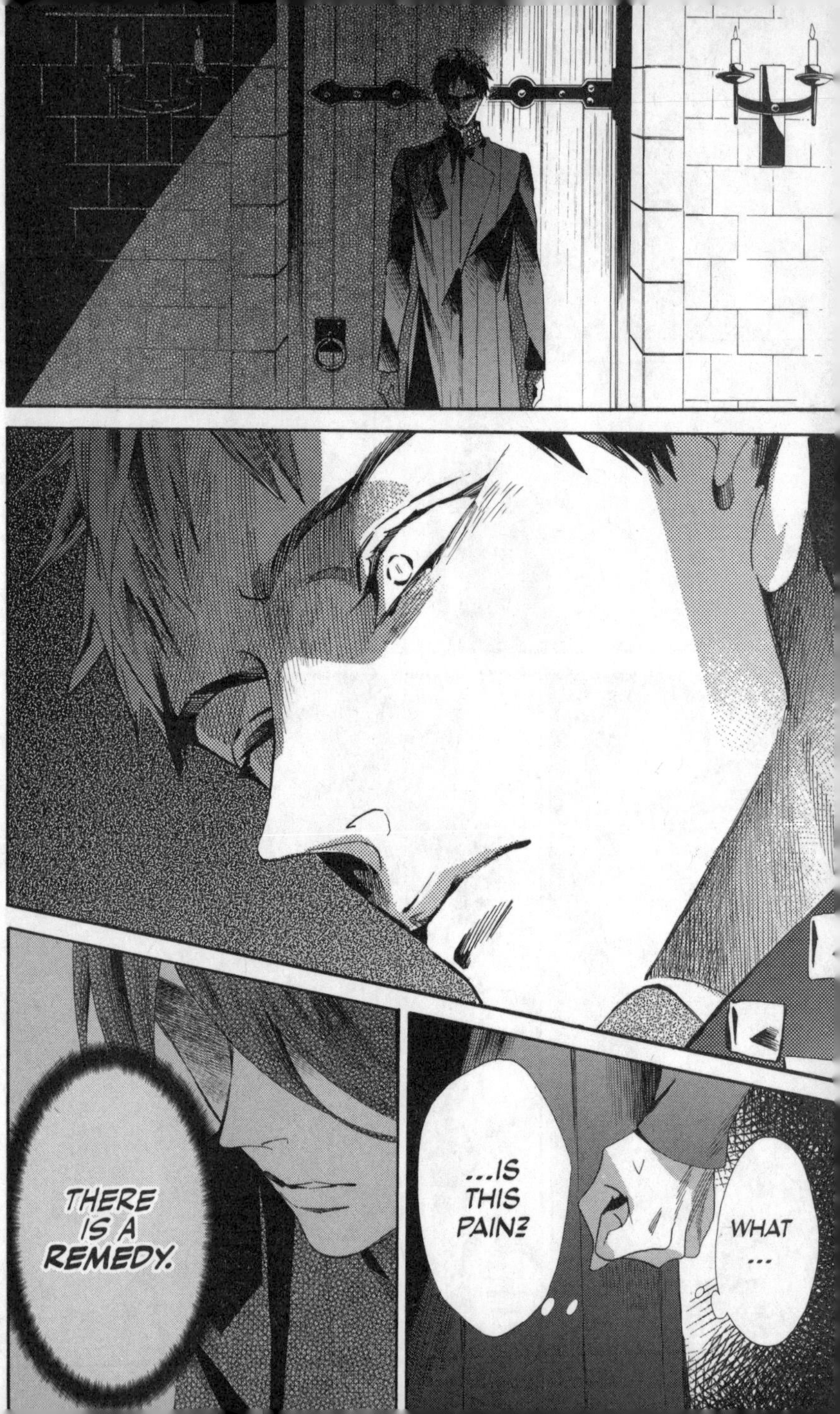
WHAT...
...IS THIS PAIN?
THERE IS A REMEDY.

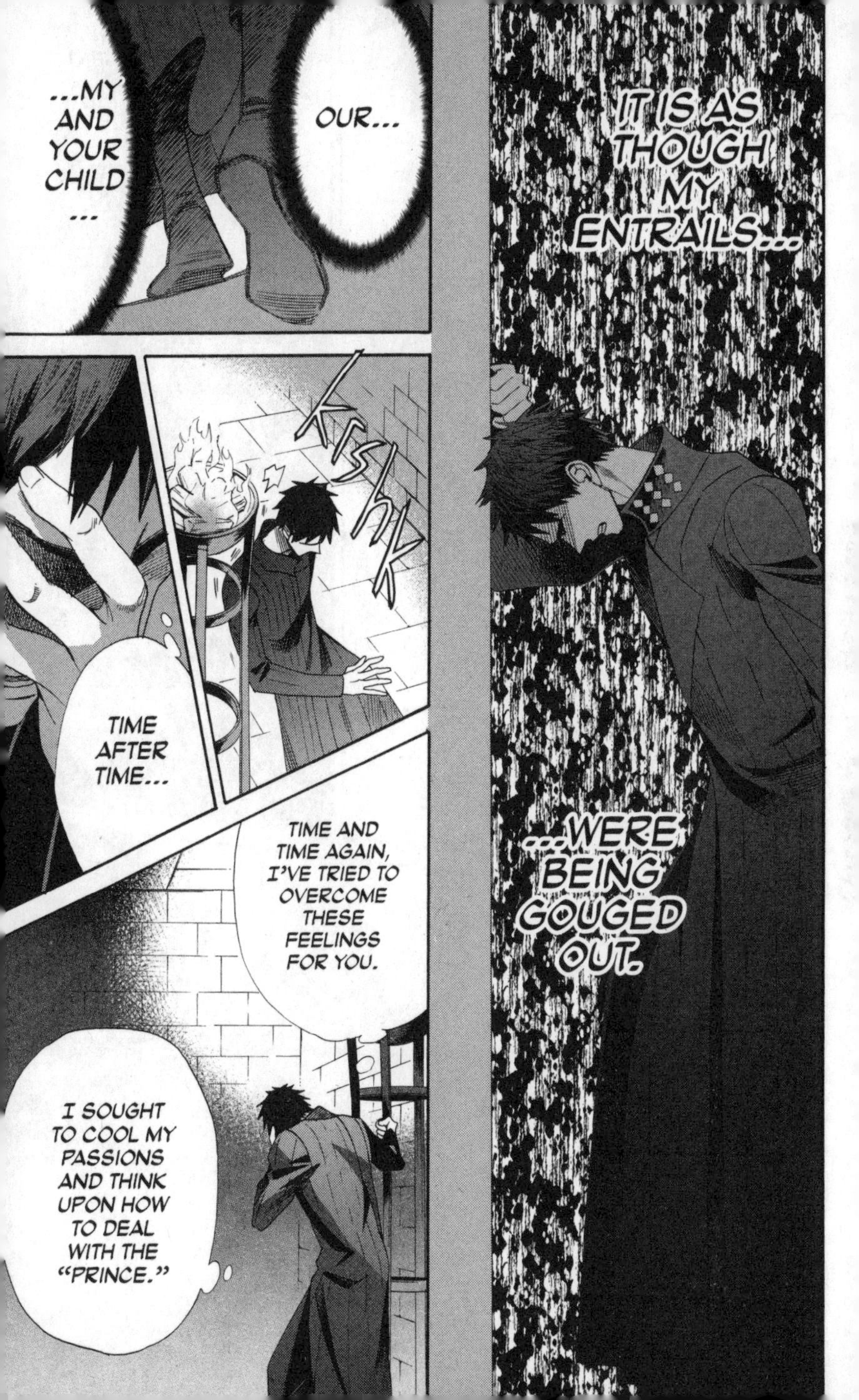
IT IS AS THOUGH MY ENTRAILS...
...WERE BEING GOUGED OUT.
OUR...
...MY AND YOUR CHILD ...
KRSHK
TIME AFTER TIME...
TIME AND TIME AGAIN, I'VE TRIED TO OVERCOME THESE FEELINGS FOR YOU.
I SOUGHT TO COOL MY PASSIONS AND THINK UPON HOW TO DEAL WITH THE "PRINCE."

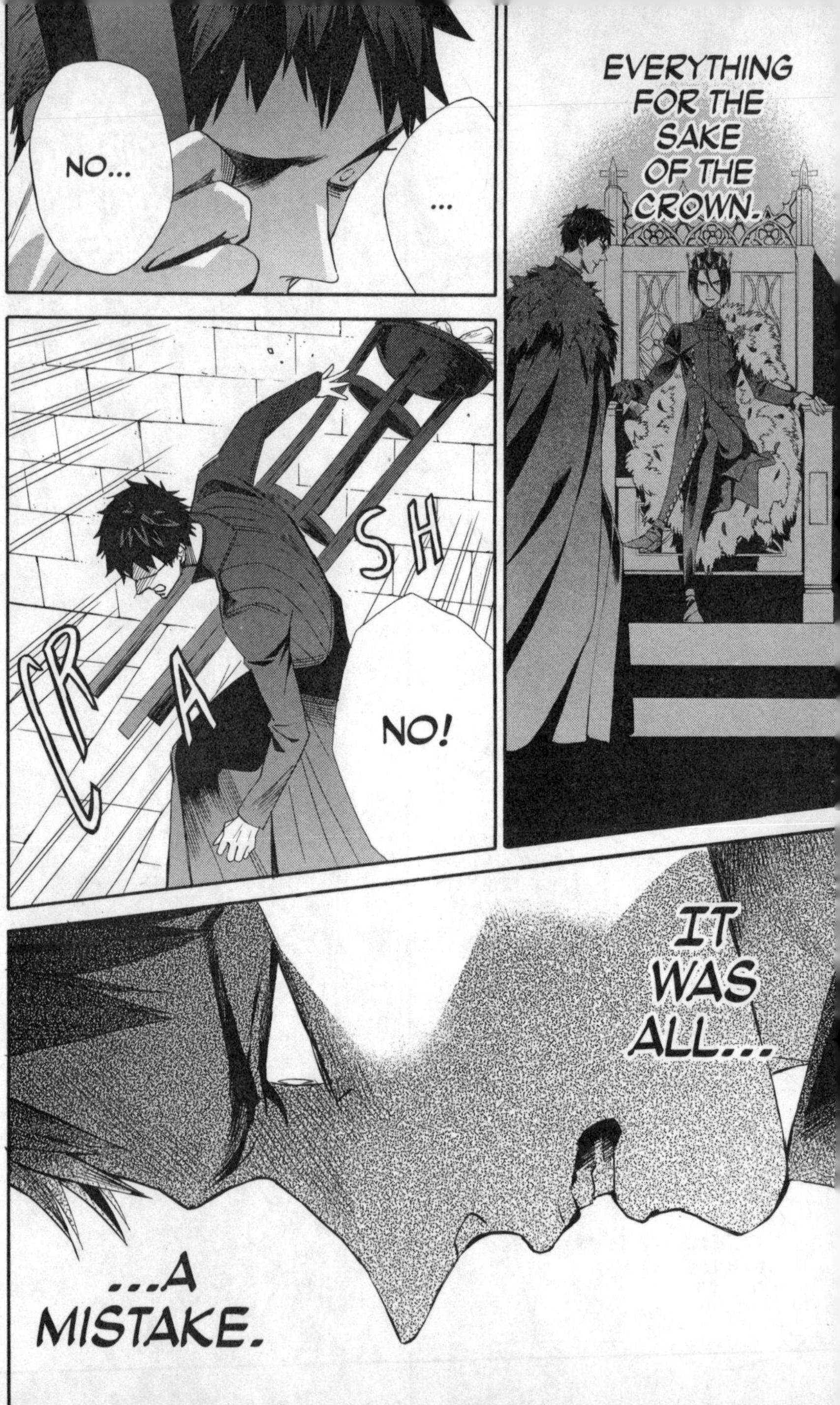
EVERYTHING FOR THE SAKE OF THE CROWN.
...
NO...
CRASH
NO!
IT WAS ALL...
...A MISTAKE.

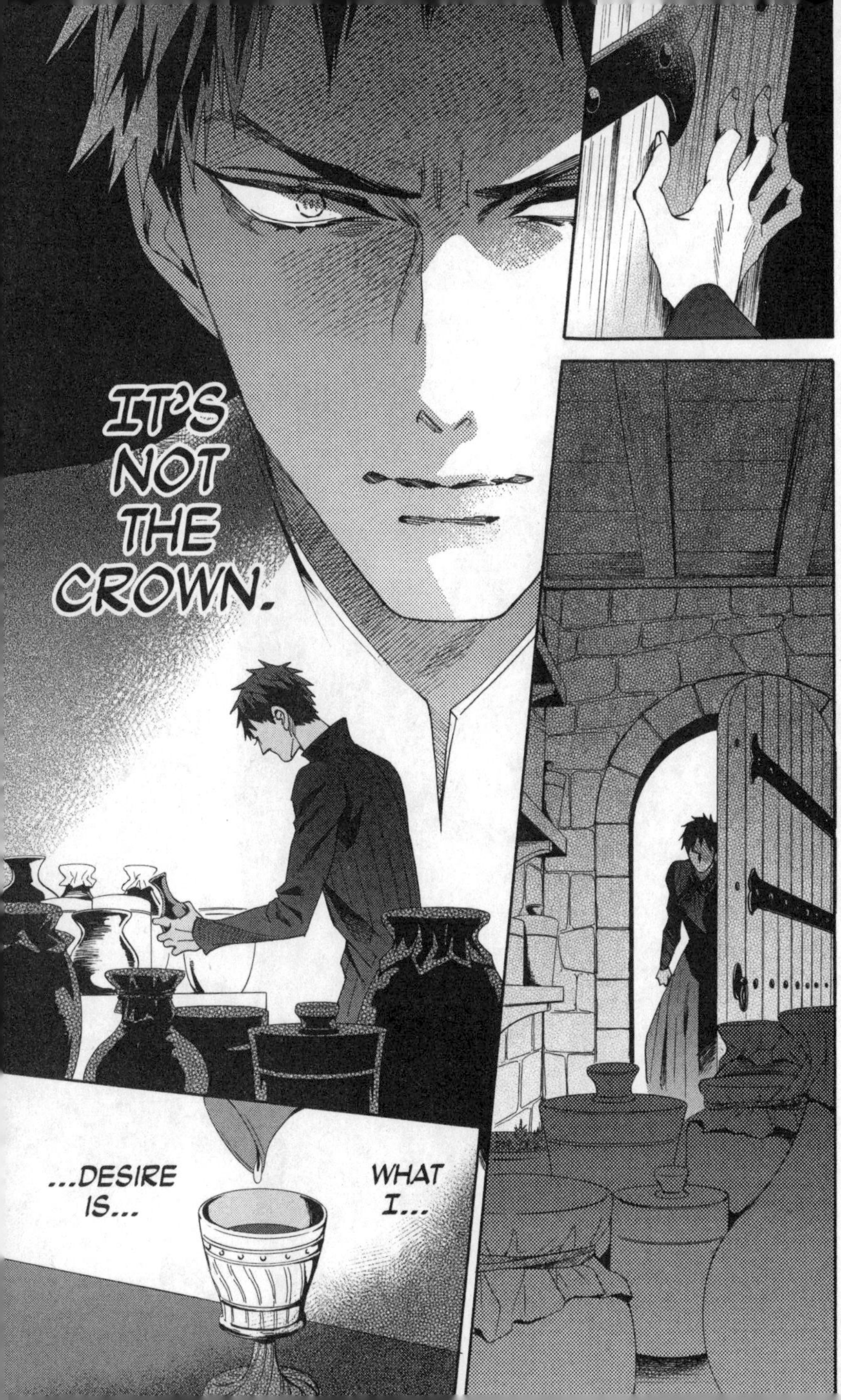
IT'S NOT THE CROWN.
WHAT I...
...DESIRE IS...

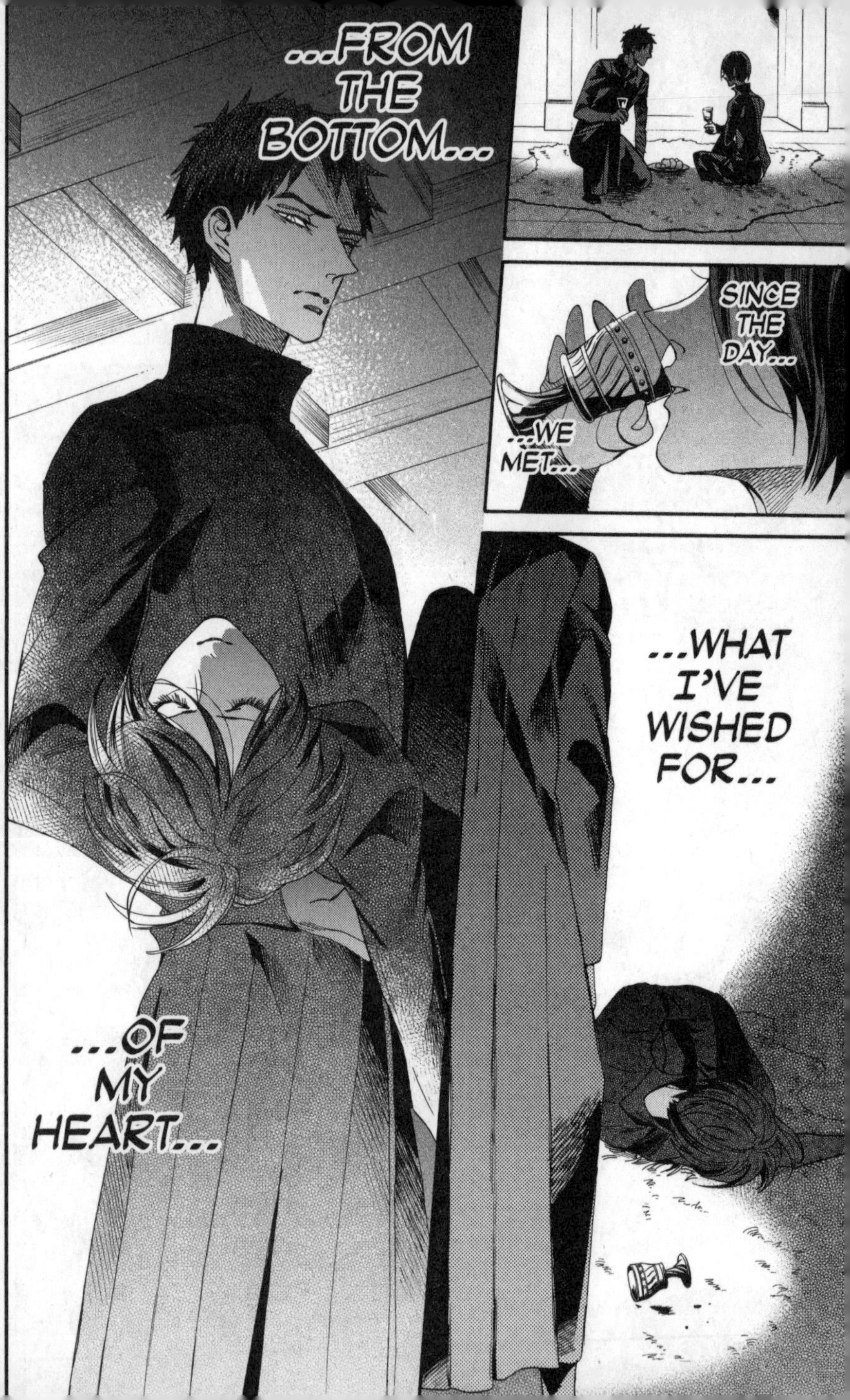
SINCE THE DAY...
...WE MET...
...WHAT I'VE WISHED FOR...
...FROM THE BOTTOM...
...OF MY HEART...

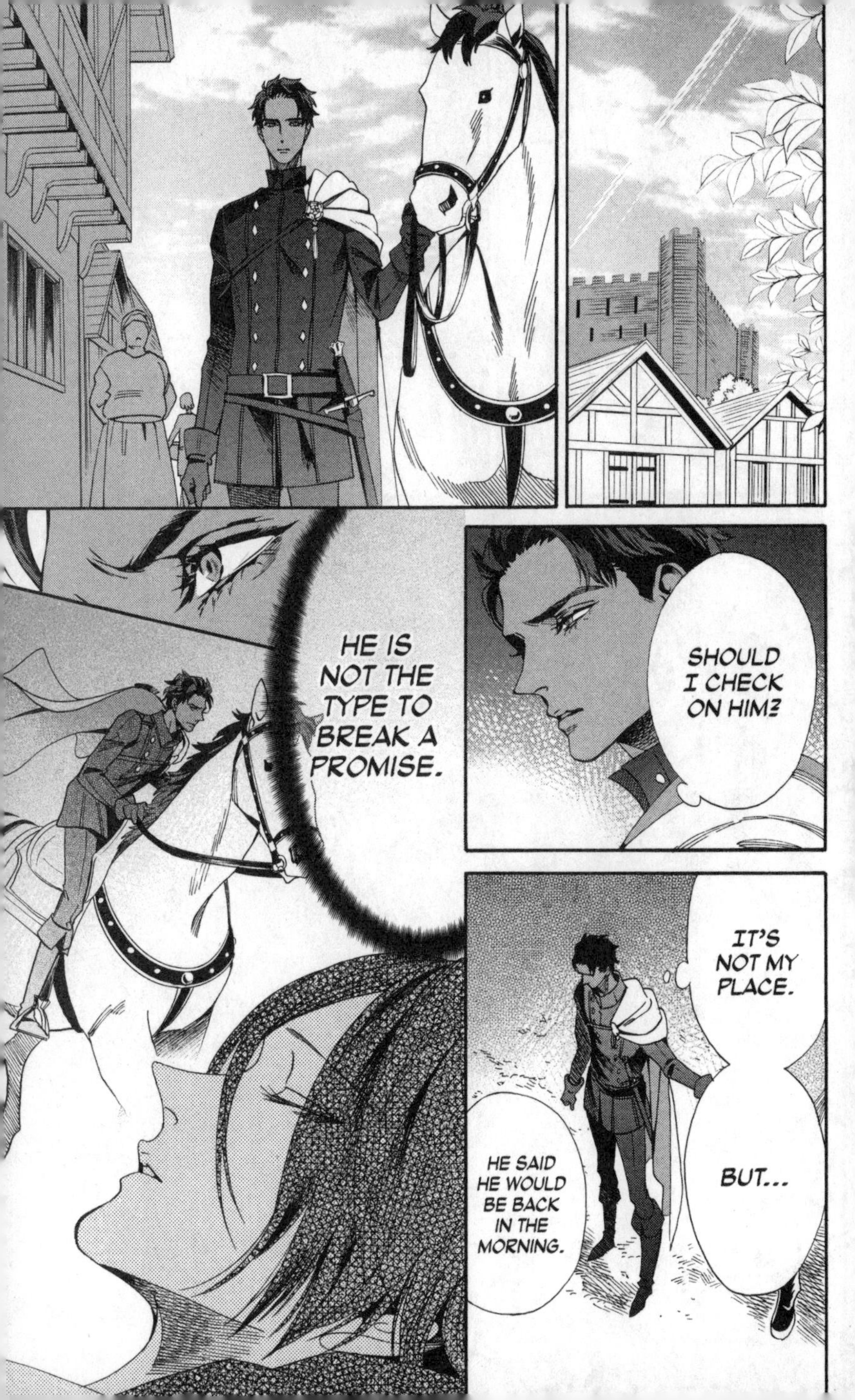
SHOULD I CHECK ON HIM?
IT'S NOT MY PLACE.
BUT...
HE SAID HE WOULD BE BACK IN THE MORNING.
HE IS NOT THE TYPE TO BREAK A PROMISE.

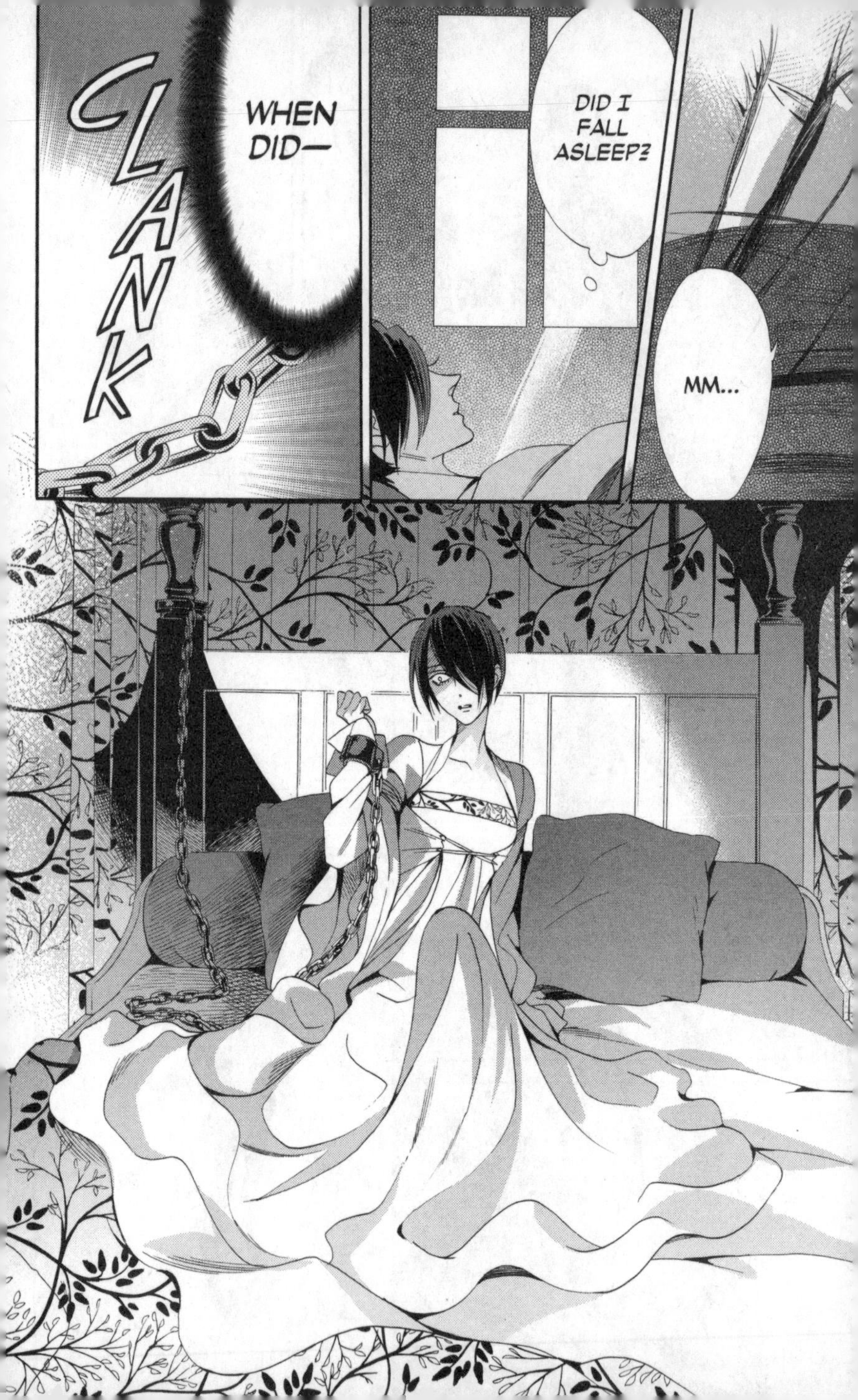
MM...
DID I FALL ASLEEP?
WHEN DID—
CLANK

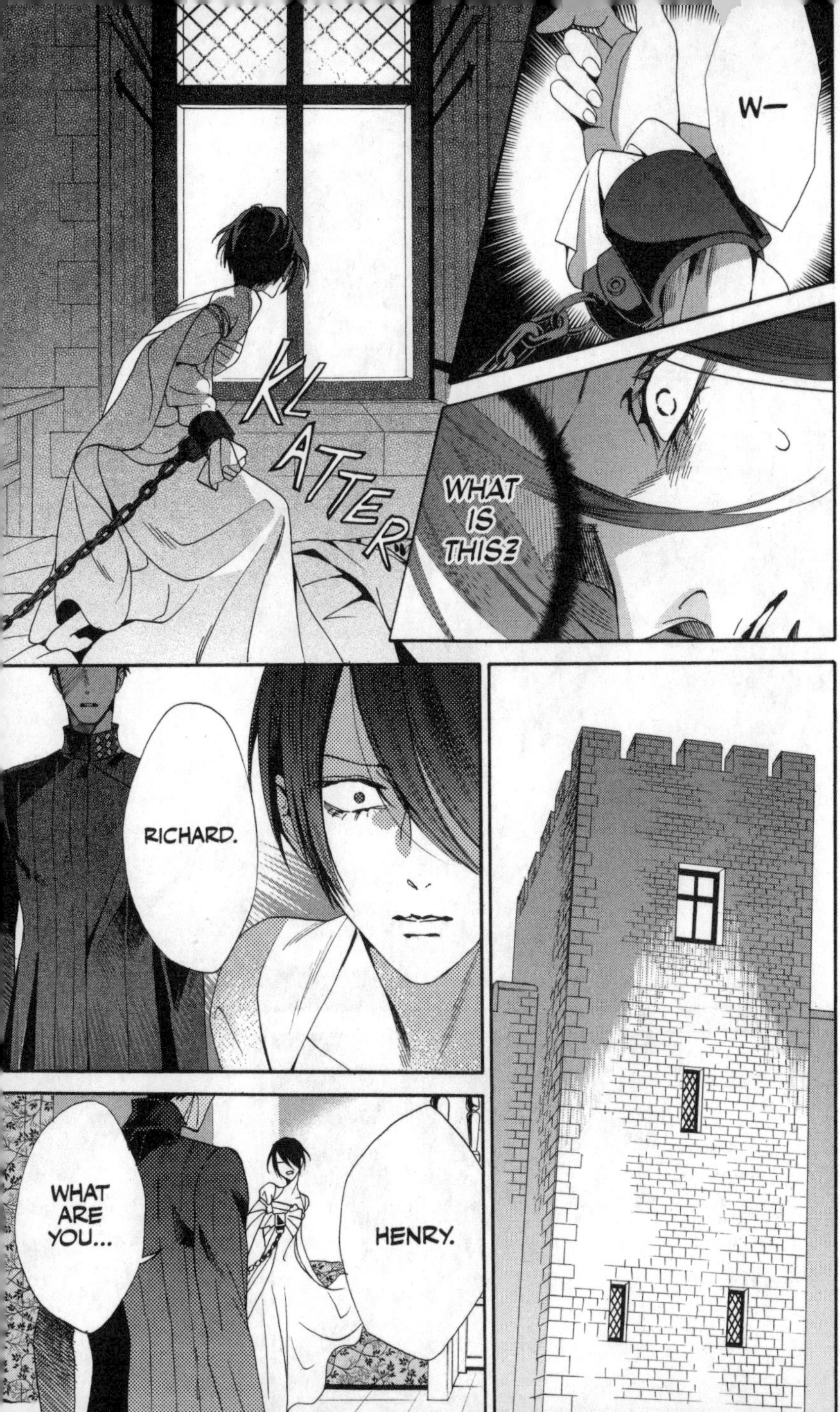
W—
WHAT IS THIS?
KLATTER
RICHARD.
HENRY.
WHAT ARE YOU...

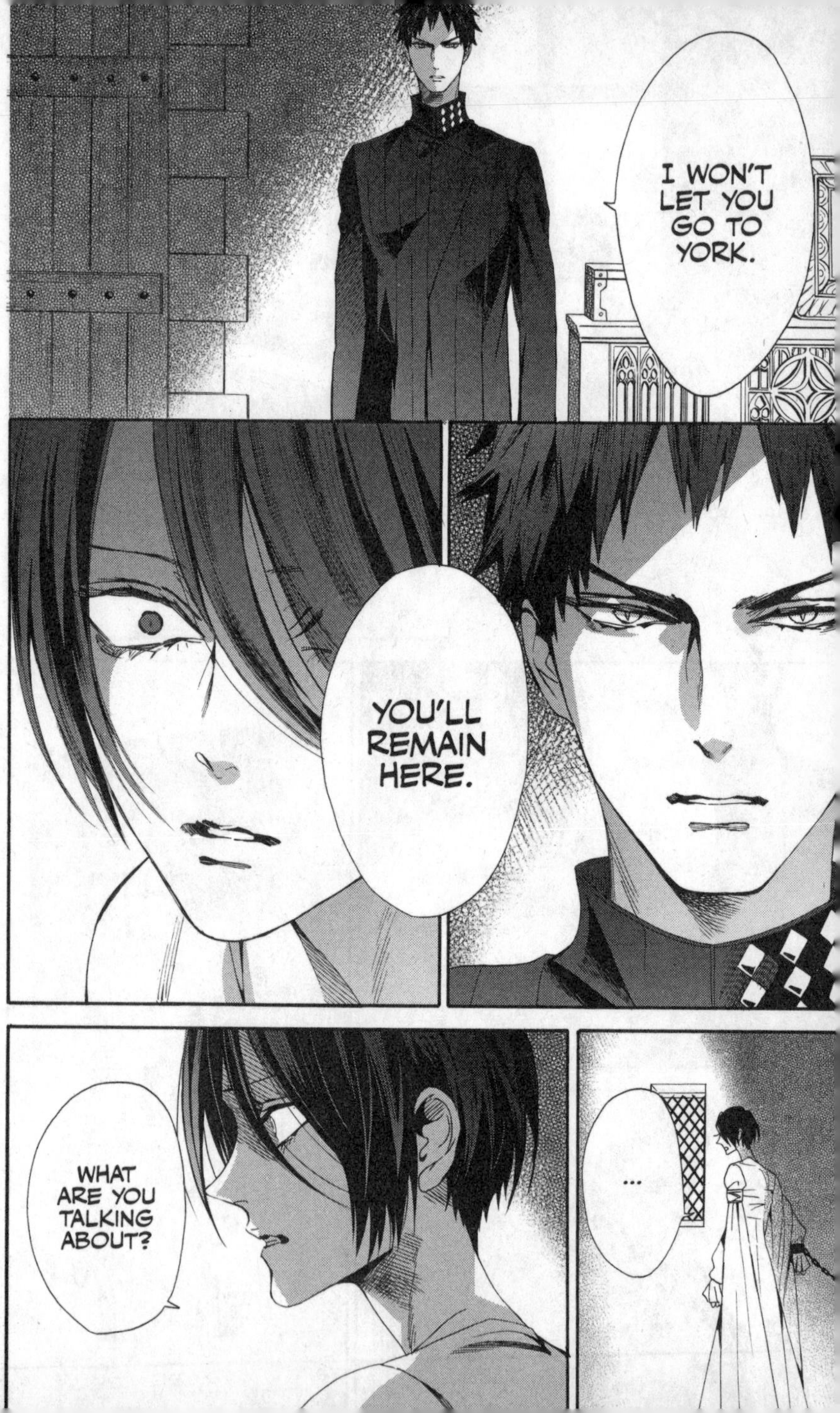
I WON'T LET YOU GO TO YORK.
YOU'LL REMAIN HERE.
...
WHAT ARE YOU TALKING ABOUT?

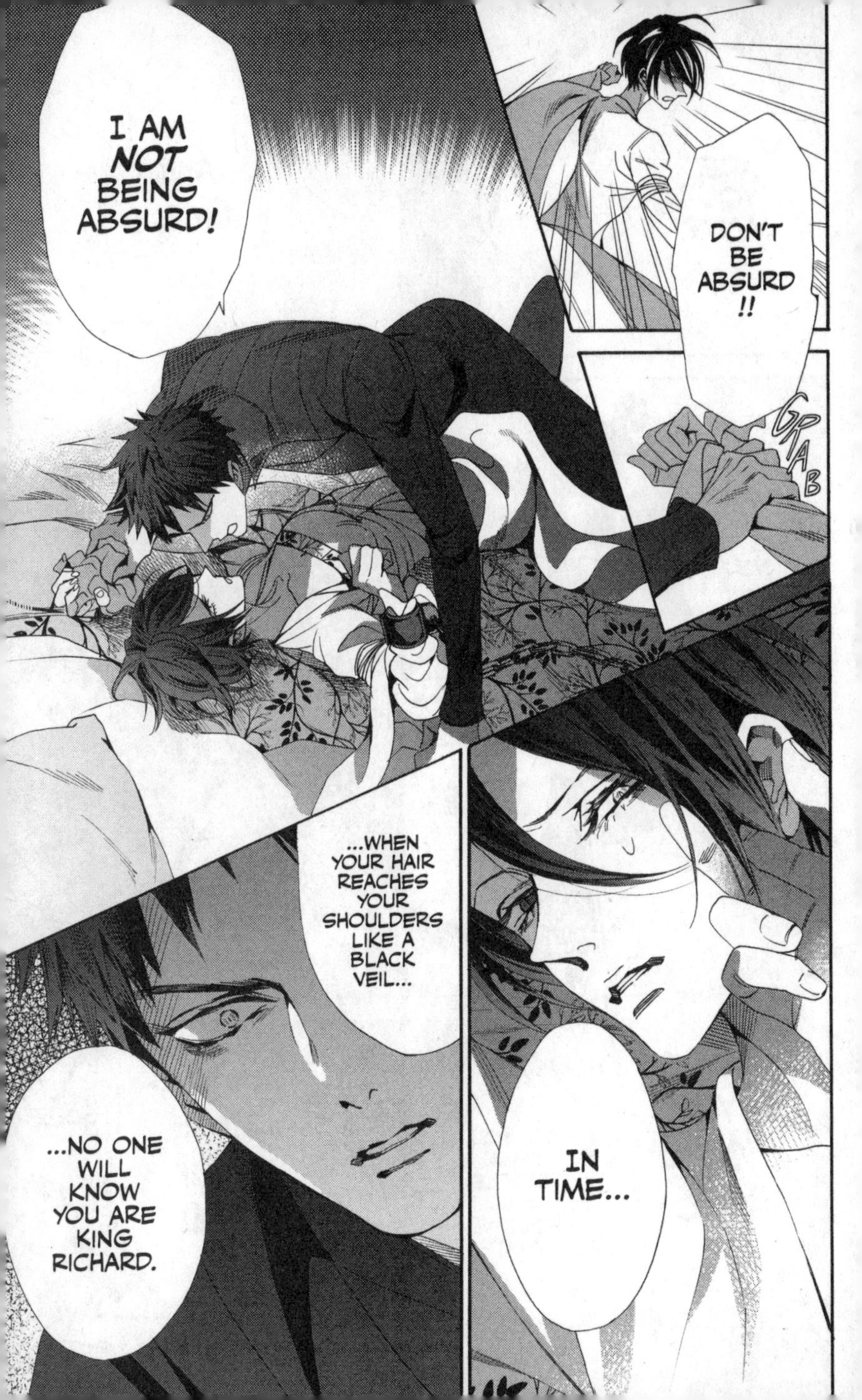
DON'T BE ABSURD!!
GRAB
I AM *NOT* BEING ABSURD!
IN TIME...
...WHEN YOUR HAIR REACHES YOUR SHOULDERS LIKE A BLACK VEIL...
...NO ONE WILL KNOW YOU ARE KING RICHARD.

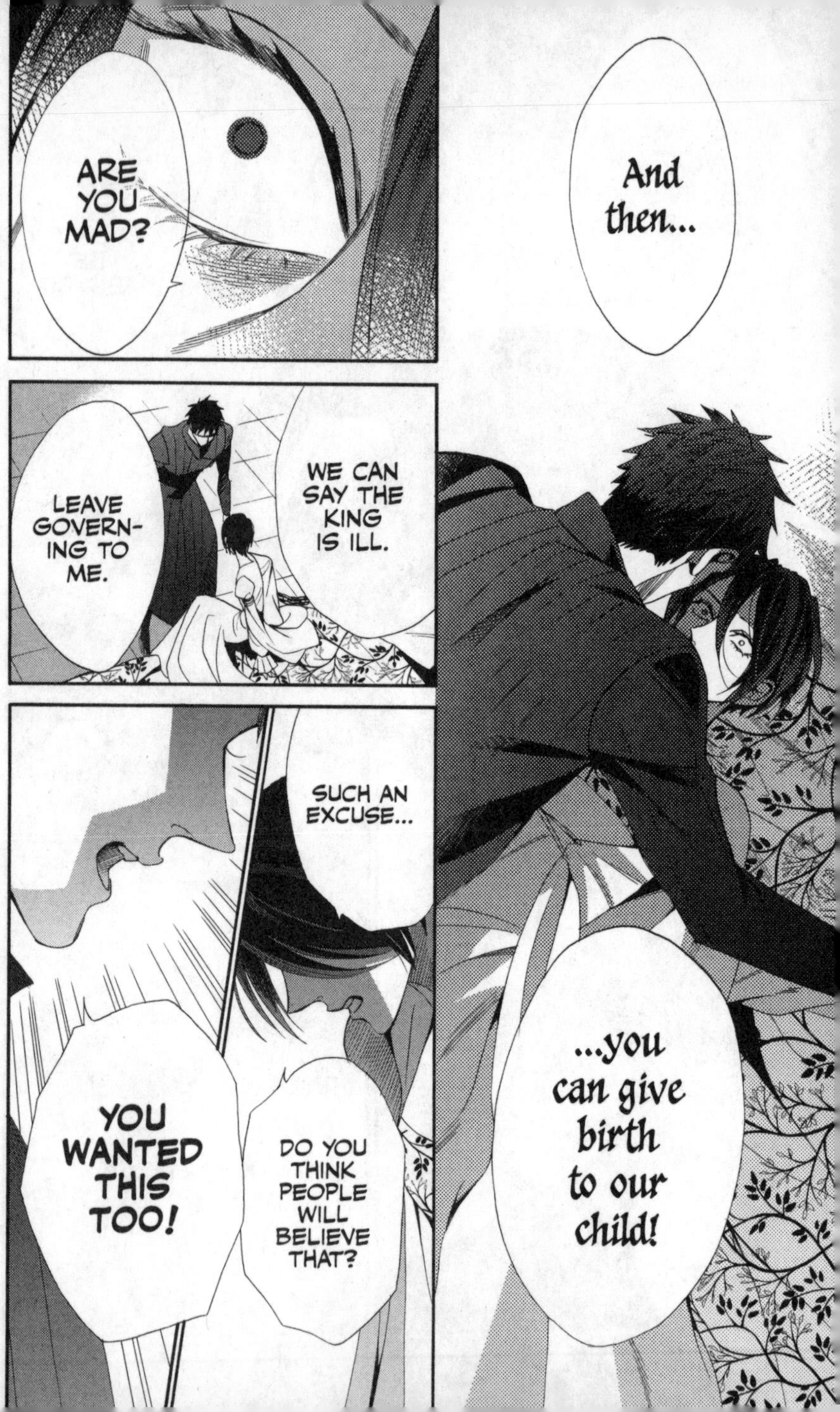
And then...
...you can give birth to our child!
ARE YOU MAD?
WE CAN SAY THE KING IS ILL.
LEAVE GOVERNING TO ME.
SUCH AN EXCUSE...
DO YOU THINK PEOPLE WILL BELIEVE THAT?
YOU WANTED THIS TOO!

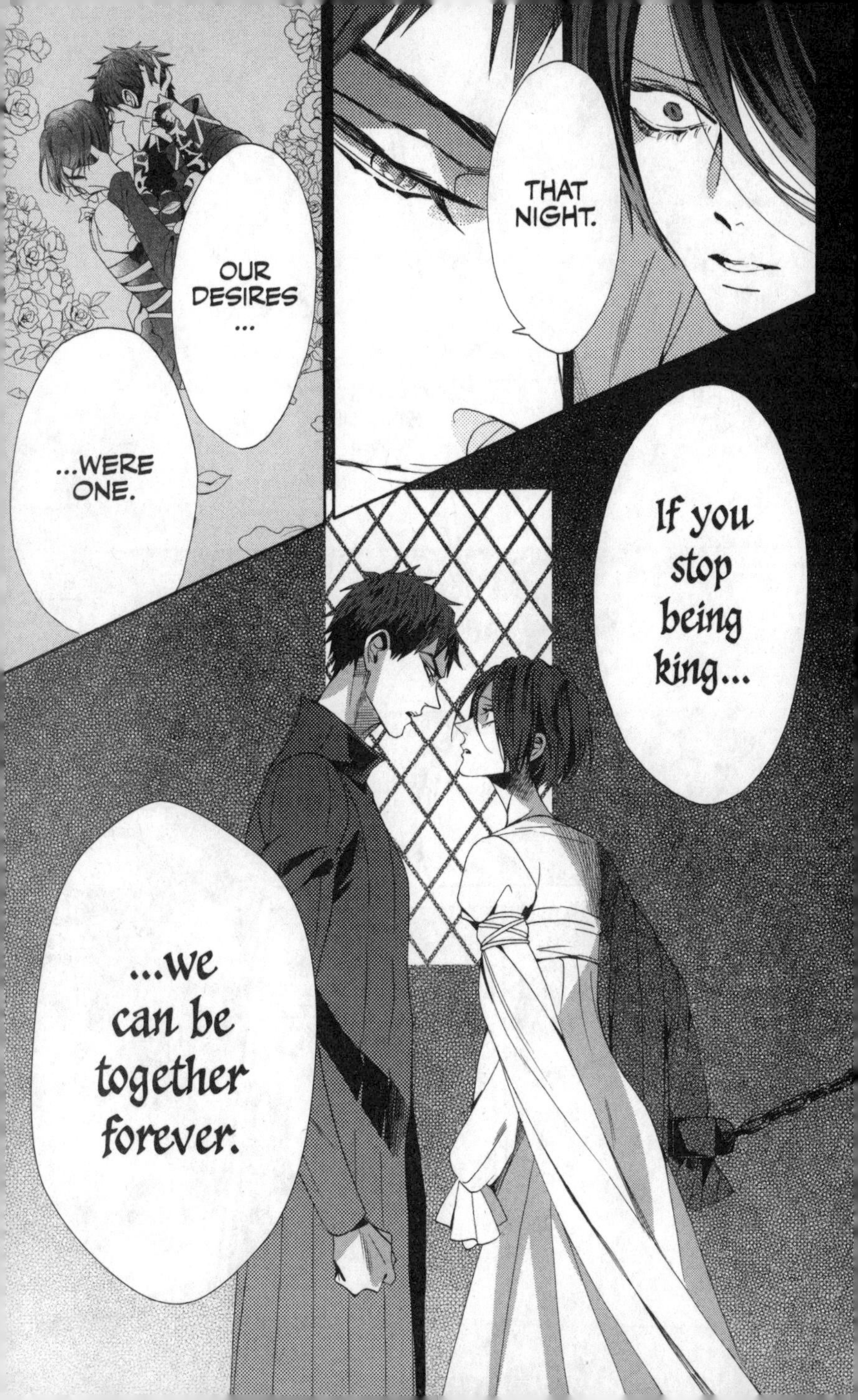
THAT NIGHT.
OUR DESIRES ...
...WERE ONE.
If you stop being king...
...we can be together forever.

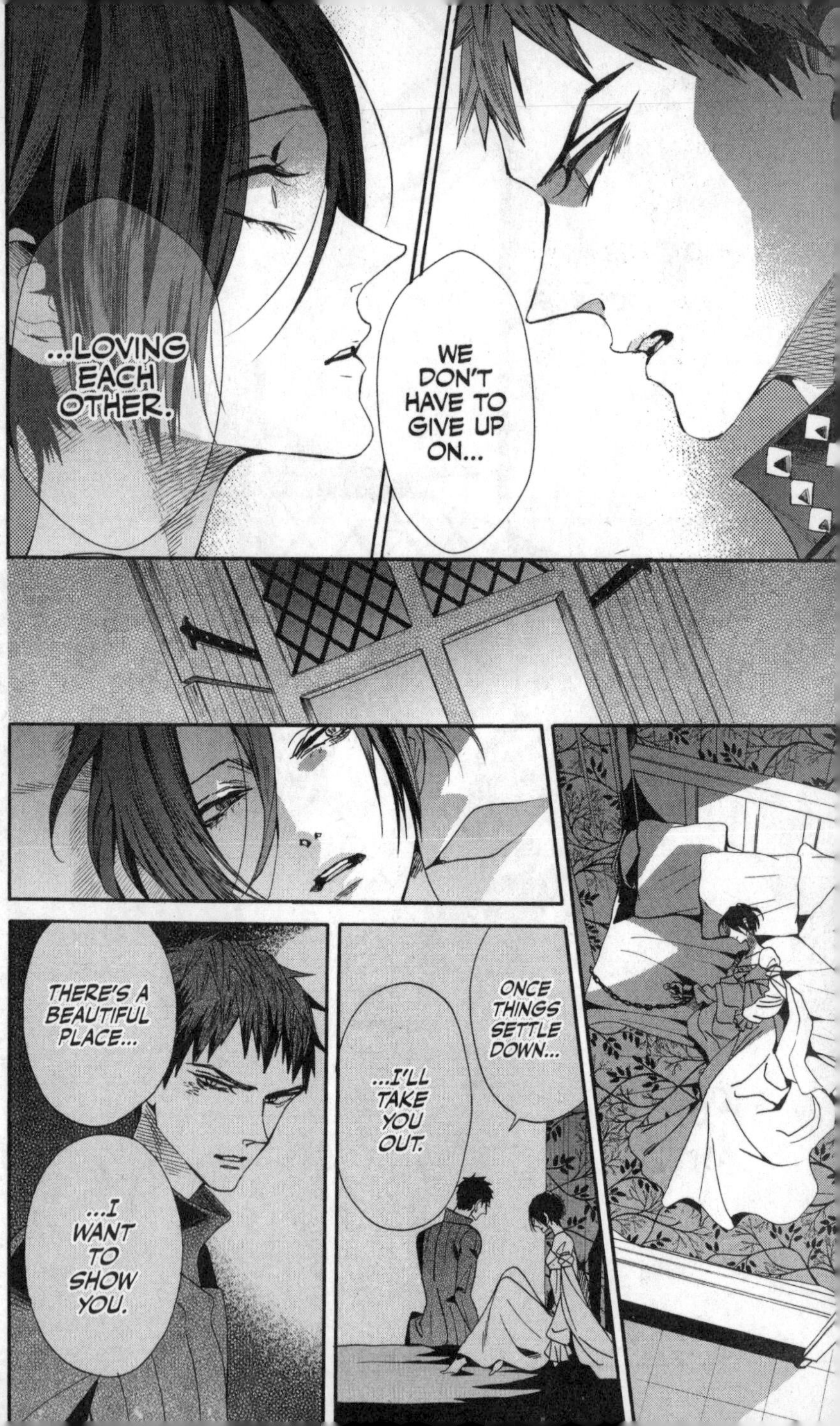
WE DON'T HAVE TO GIVE UP ON...
...LOVING EACH OTHER.
ONCE THINGS SETTLE DOWN...
...I'LL TAKE YOU OUT.
THERE'S A BEAUTIFUL PLACE...
...I WANT TO SHOW YOU.

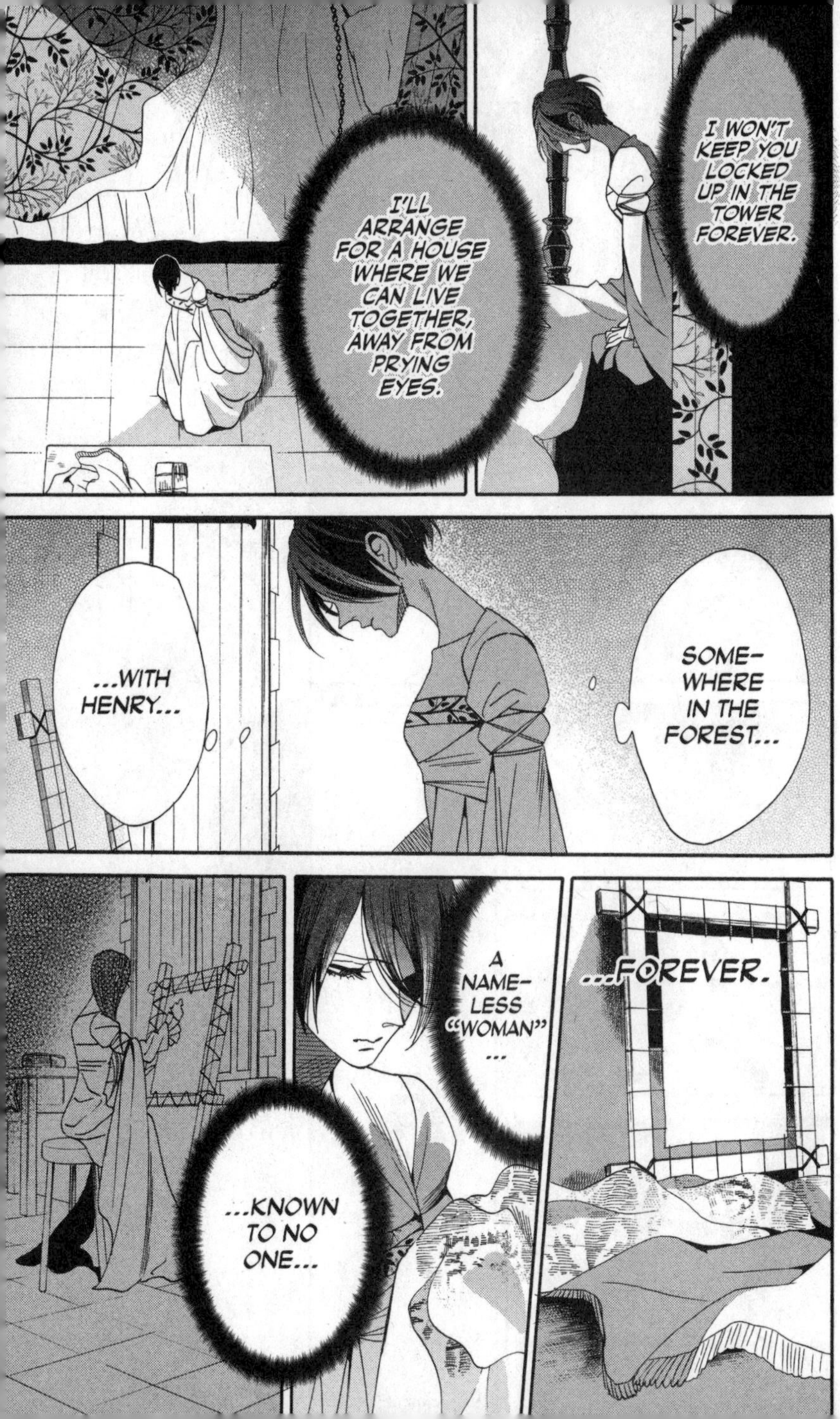
I WON'T KEEP YOU LOCKED UP IN THE TOWER FOREVER.
I'LL ARRANGE FOR A HOUSE WHERE WE CAN LIVE TOGETHER, AWAY FROM PRYING EYES.
SOME-WHERE IN THE FOREST...
...WITH HENRY...
...FOREVER.
A NAME-LESS "WOMAN" ...
...KNOWN TO NO ONE...

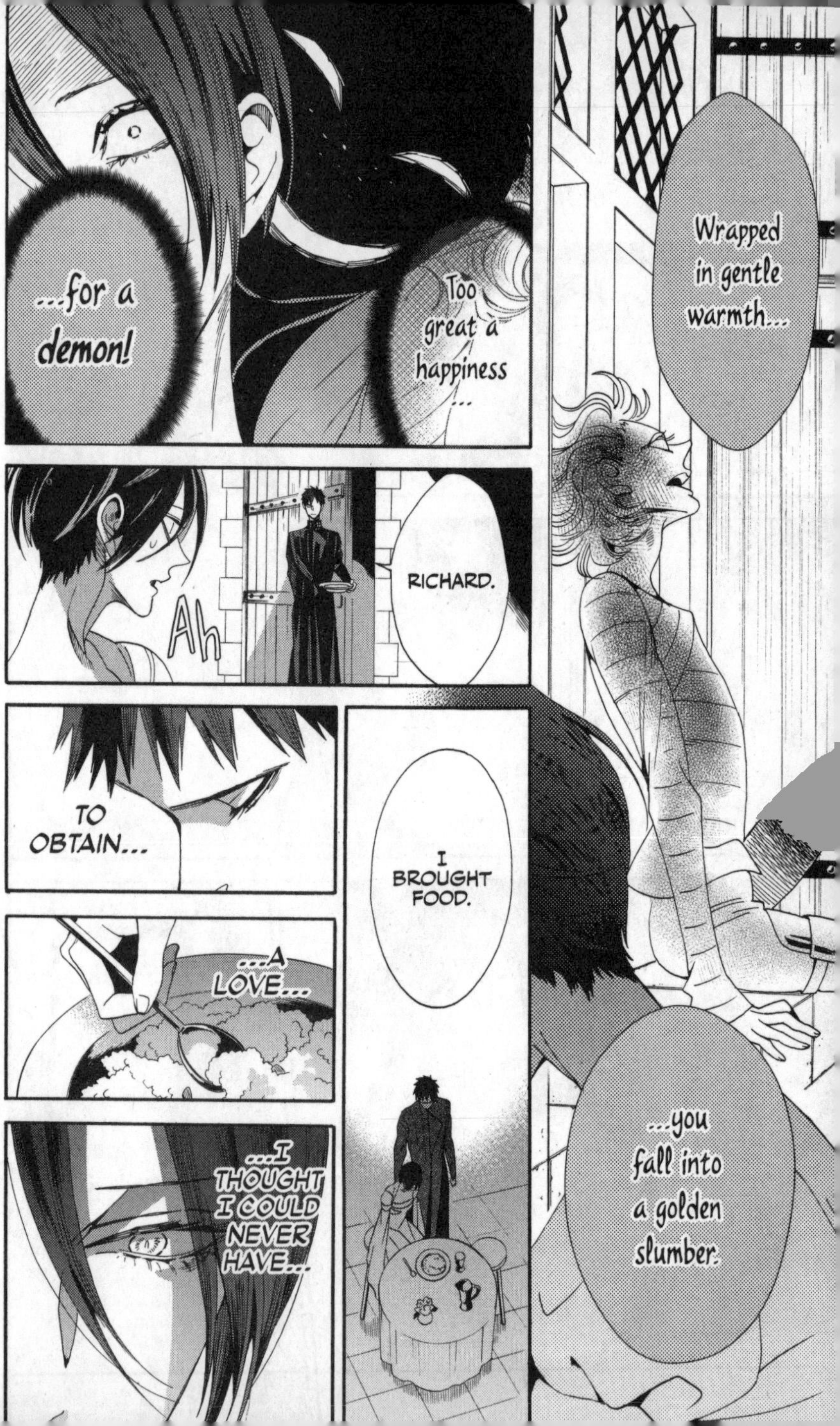

Wrapped in gentle warmth...
...you fall into a golden slumber.
Too great a happiness...
...for a demon!
RICHARD.
Ah
I BROUGHT FOOD.
TO OBTAIN...
...A LOVE...
...I THOUGHT I COULD NEVER HAVE...

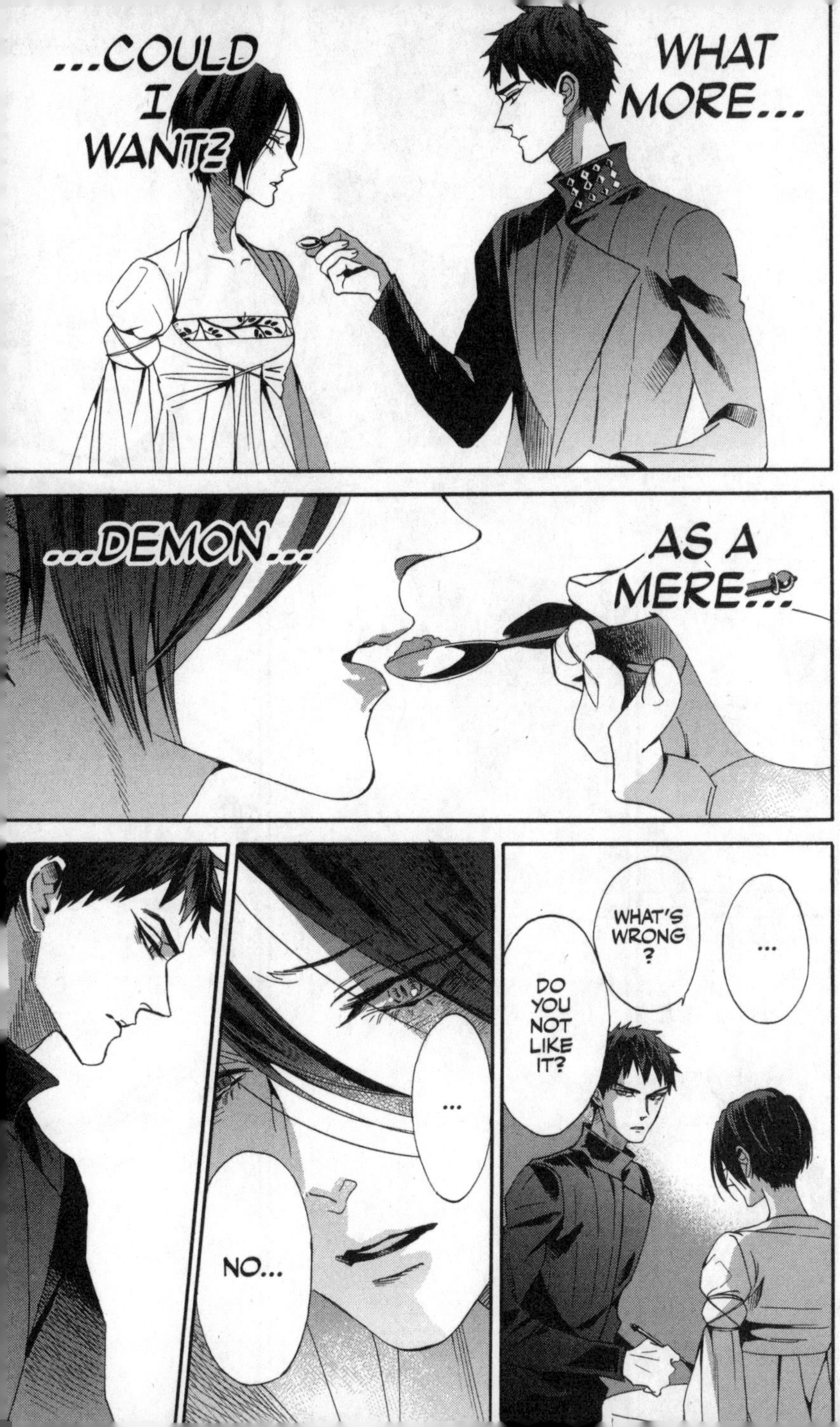
WHAT MORE...
...COULD I WANT?
AS A MERE...
...DEMON...
...
WHAT'S WRONG?
DO YOU NOT LIKE IT?
...
NO...

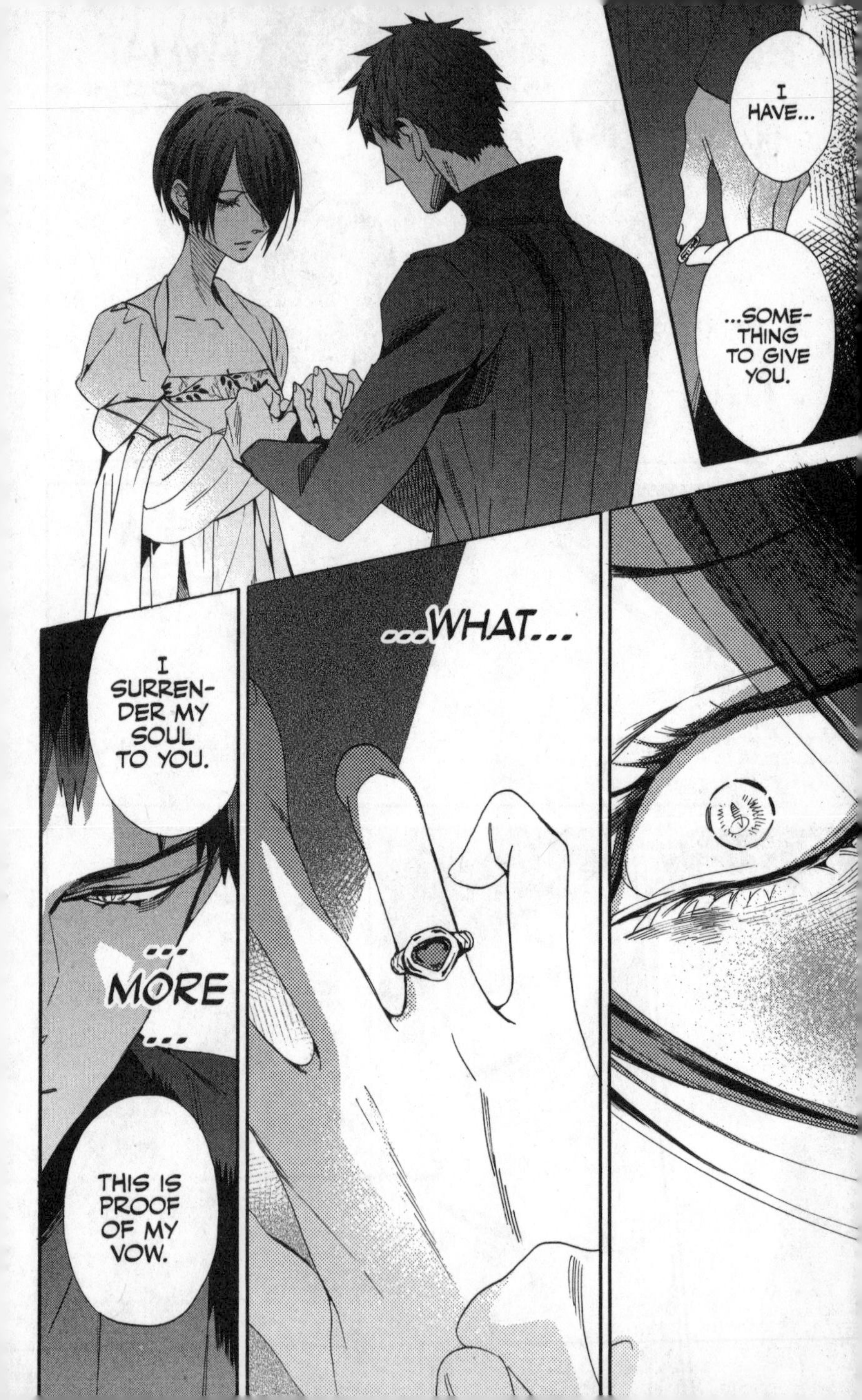
I HAVE...
...SOME-THING TO GIVE YOU.
...WHAT...
I SURREN-DER MY SOUL TO YOU.
...MORE...
THIS IS PROOF OF MY VOW.

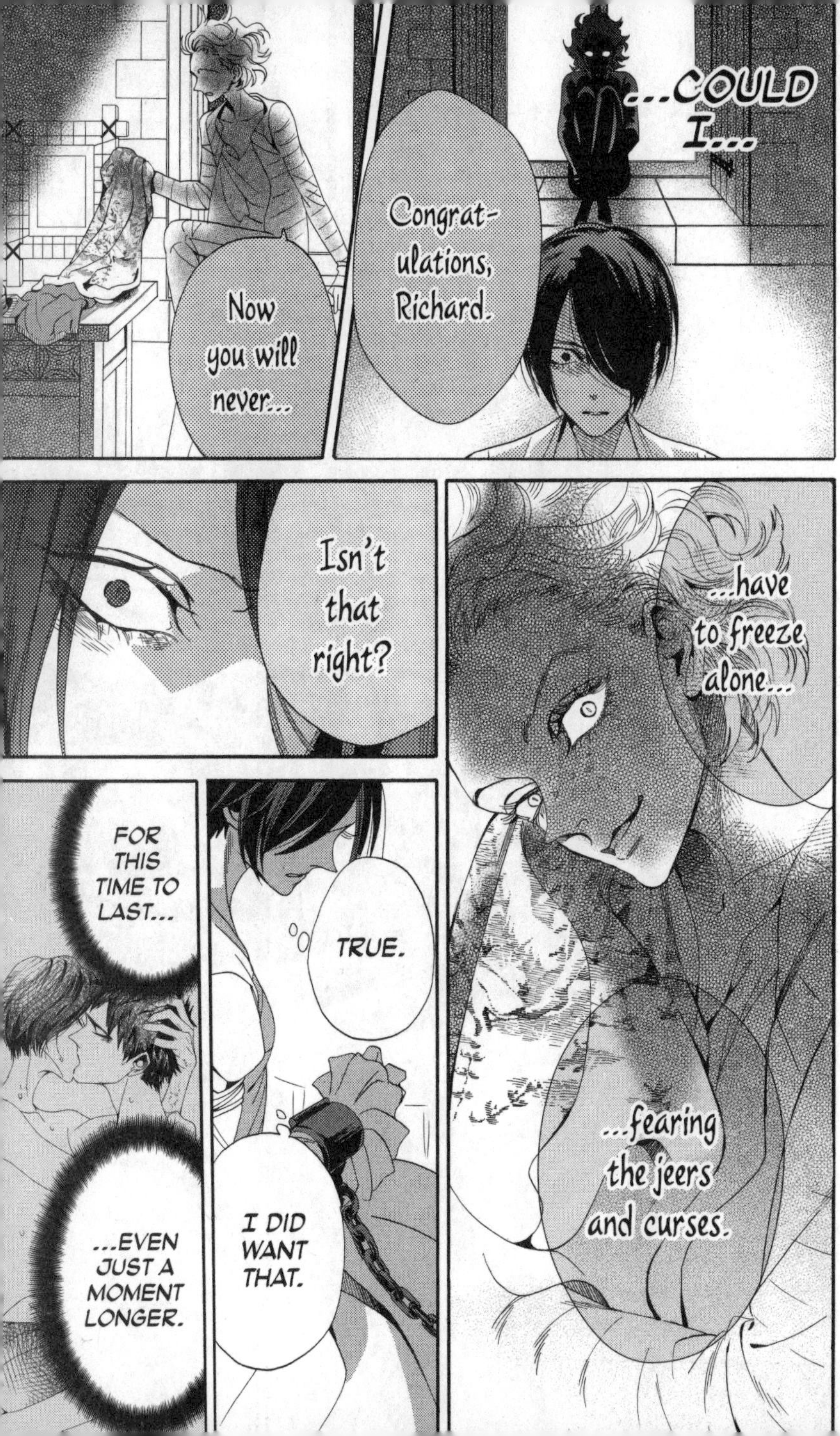
...COULD I...
Congrat-ulations, Richard.
Now you will never...
...have to freeze alone...
...fearing the jeers and curses.
Isn't that right?
TRUE.
I DID WANT THAT.
FOR THIS TIME TO LAST...
...EVEN JUST A MOMENT LONGER.

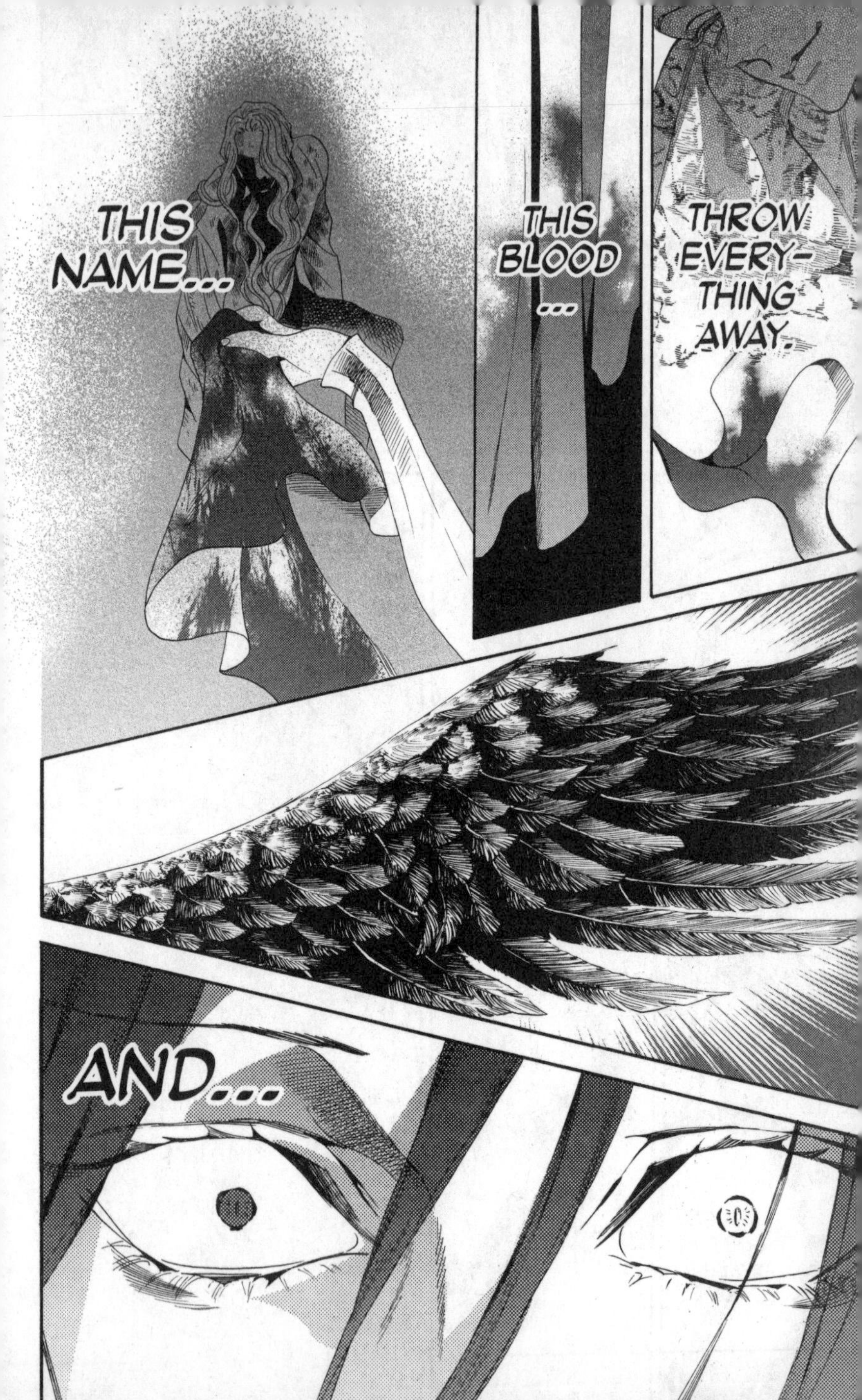
THROW EVERY-THING AWAY.
THIS BLOOD ...
THIS NAME...
AND...

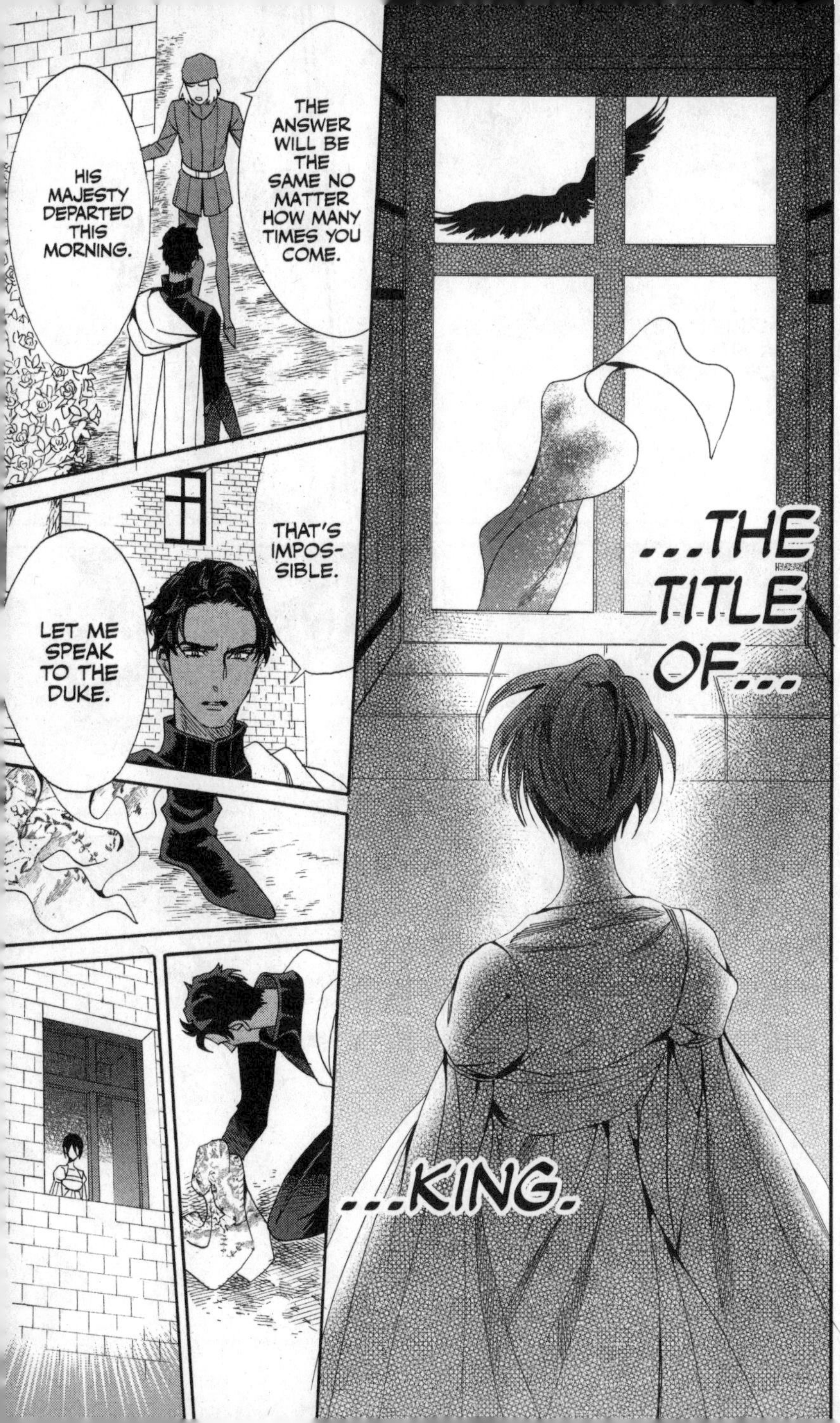
...THE TITLE OF...
...KING.
THE ANSWER WILL BE THE SAME NO MATTER HOW MANY TIMES YOU COME.
HIS MAJESTY DEPARTED THIS MORNING.
THAT'S IMPOSSIBLE.
LET ME SPEAK TO THE DUKE.

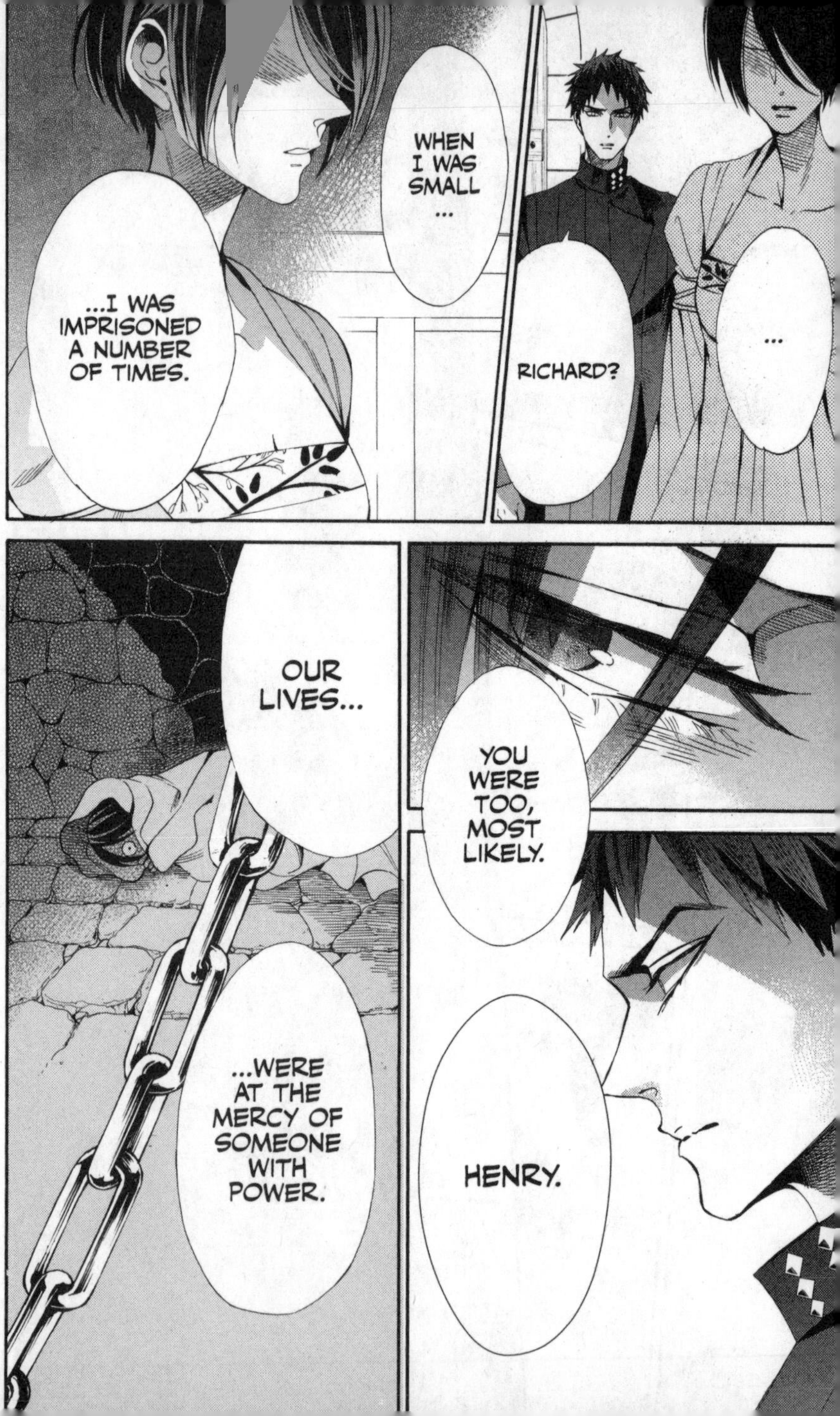
...
RICHARD?
WHEN I WAS SMALL...
...I WAS IMPRISONED A NUMBER OF TIMES.
OUR LIVES...
...WERE AT THE MERCY OF SOMEONE WITH POWER.
YOU WERE TOO, MOST LIKELY.
HENRY.

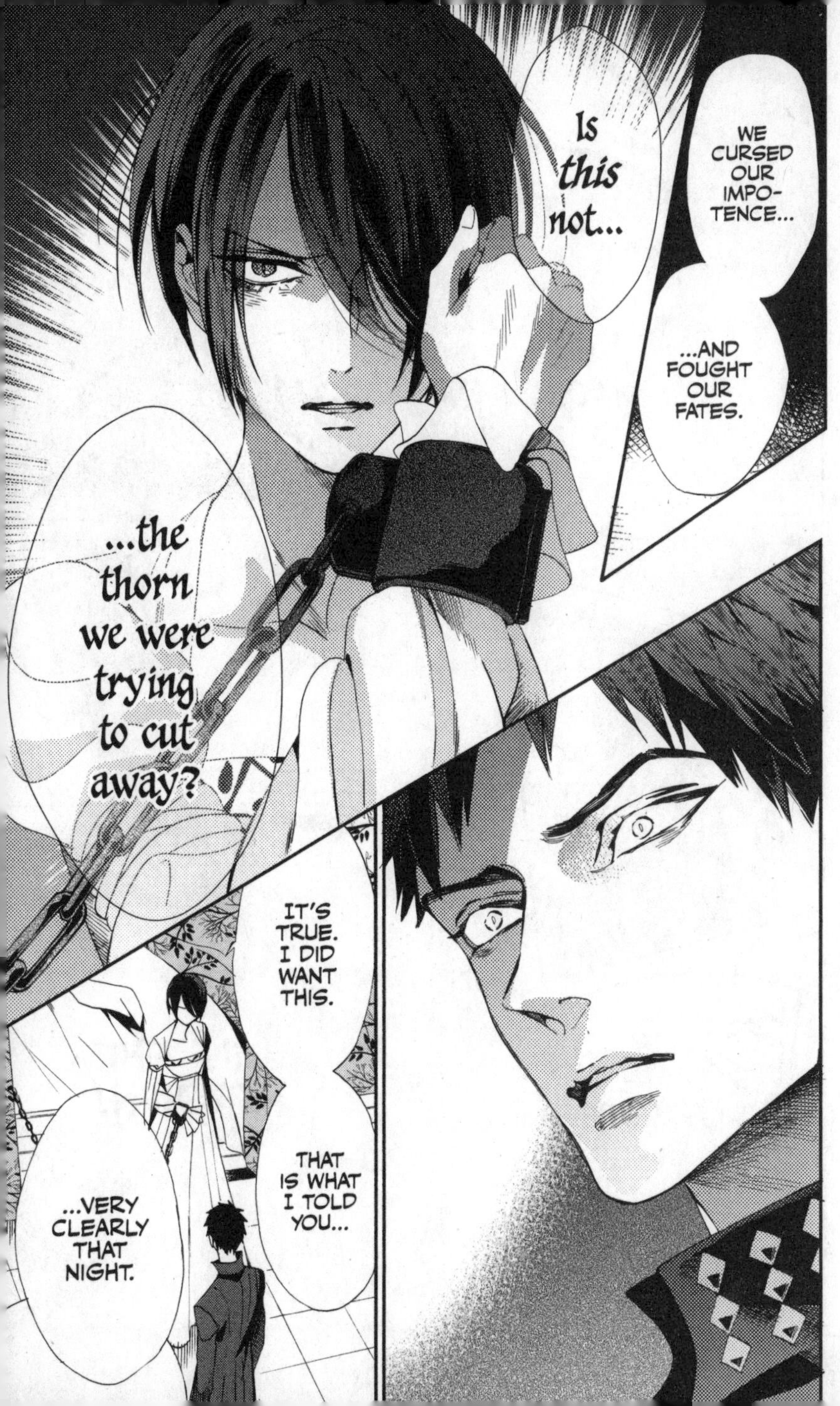
WE CURSED OUR IMPOTENCE...
...AND FOUGHT OUR FATES.
Is *this* not...
...the thorn we were trying to cut away?
IT'S TRUE. I DID WANT THIS.
THAT IS WHAT I TOLD YOU...
...VERY CLEARLY THAT NIGHT.

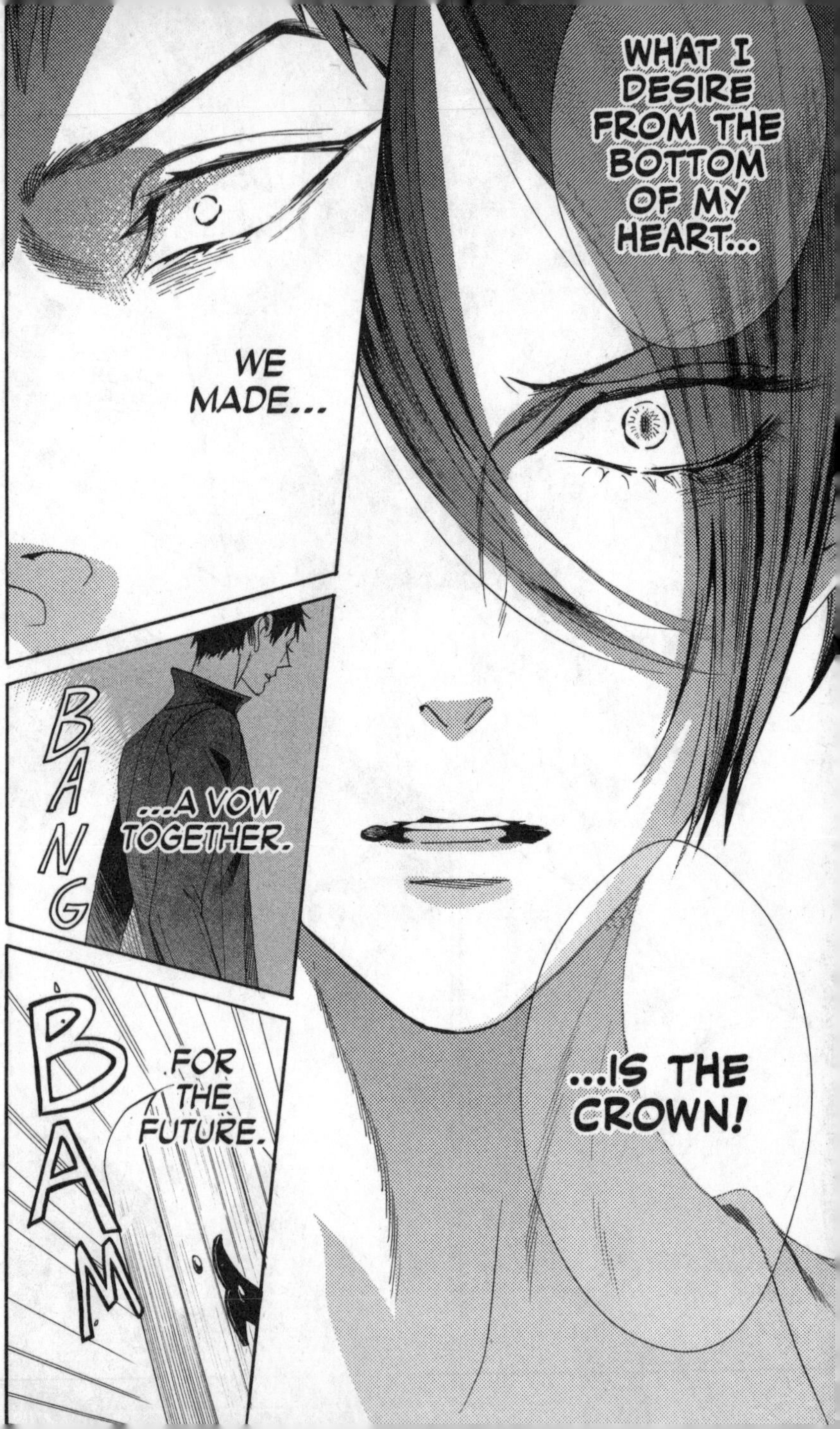
WHAT I DESIRE FROM THE BOTTOM OF MY HEART...
...IS THE CROWN!
WE MADE...
...A VOW TOGETHER.
BANG
FOR THE FUTURE.
BAM

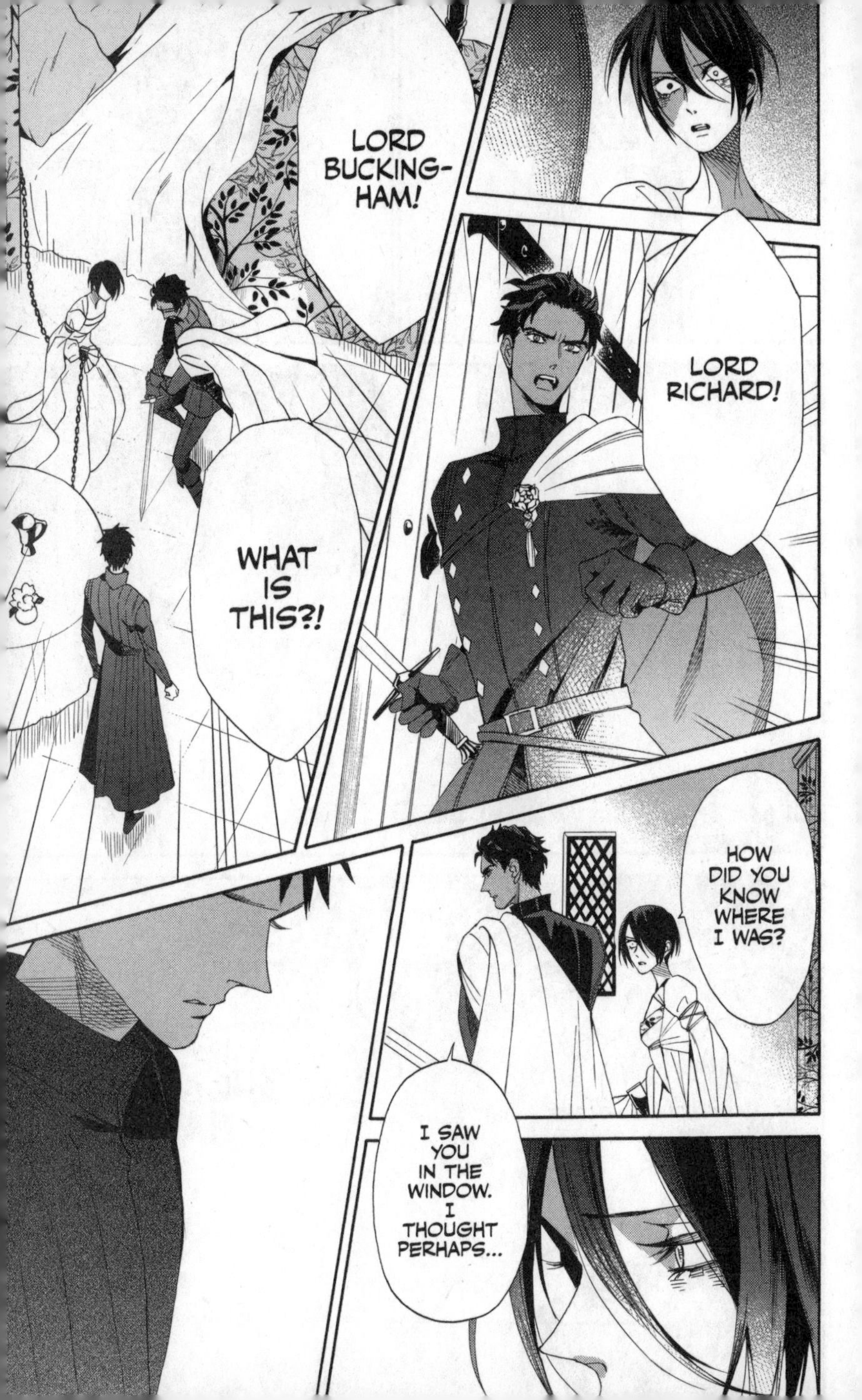
LORD RICHARD!
LORD BUCKINGHAM!
WHAT IS THIS?!
HOW DID YOU KNOW WHERE I WAS?
I SAW YOU IN THE WINDOW. I THOUGHT PERHAPS...

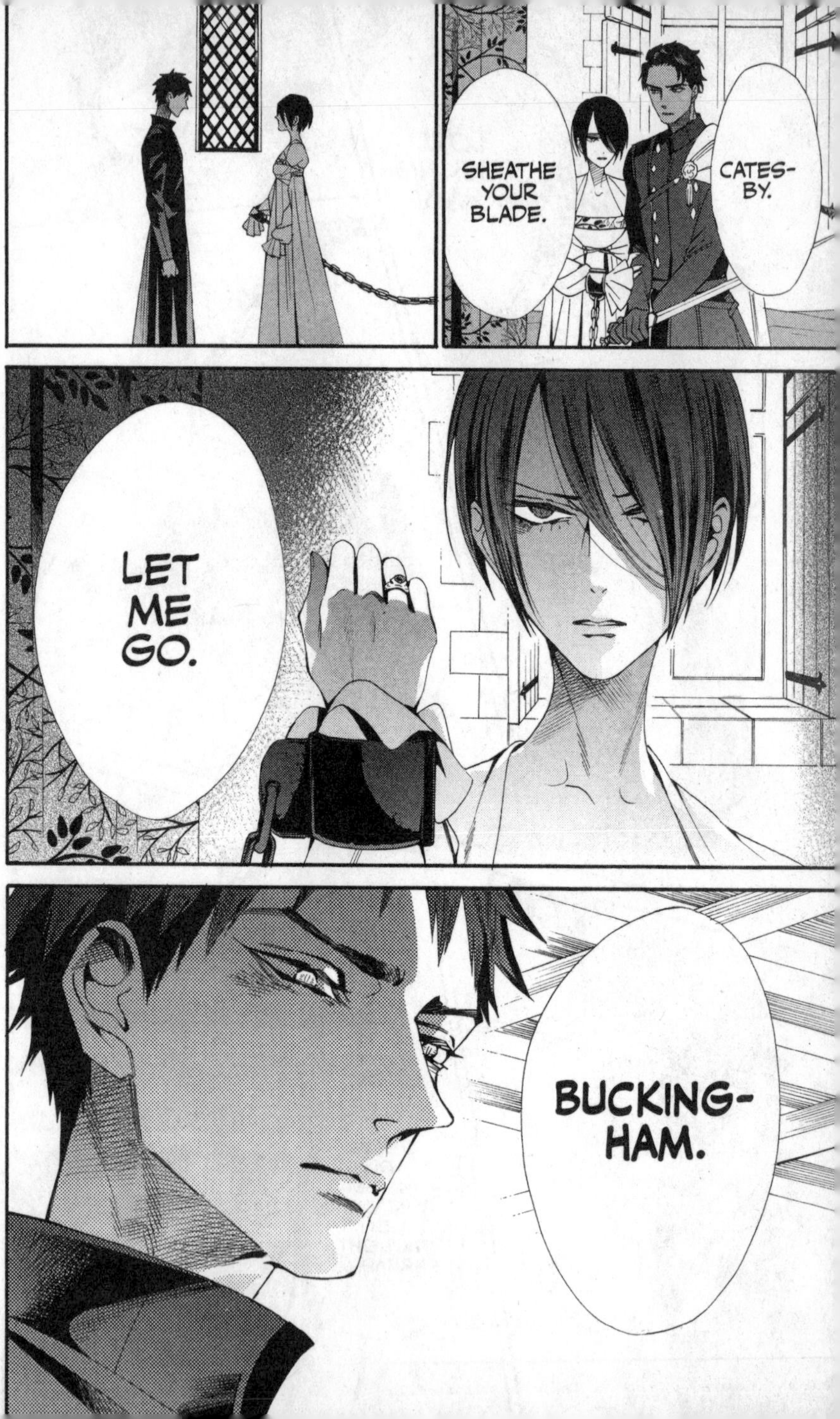
CATES-BY.
SHEATHE YOUR BLADE.
LET ME GO.
BUCKING-HAM.

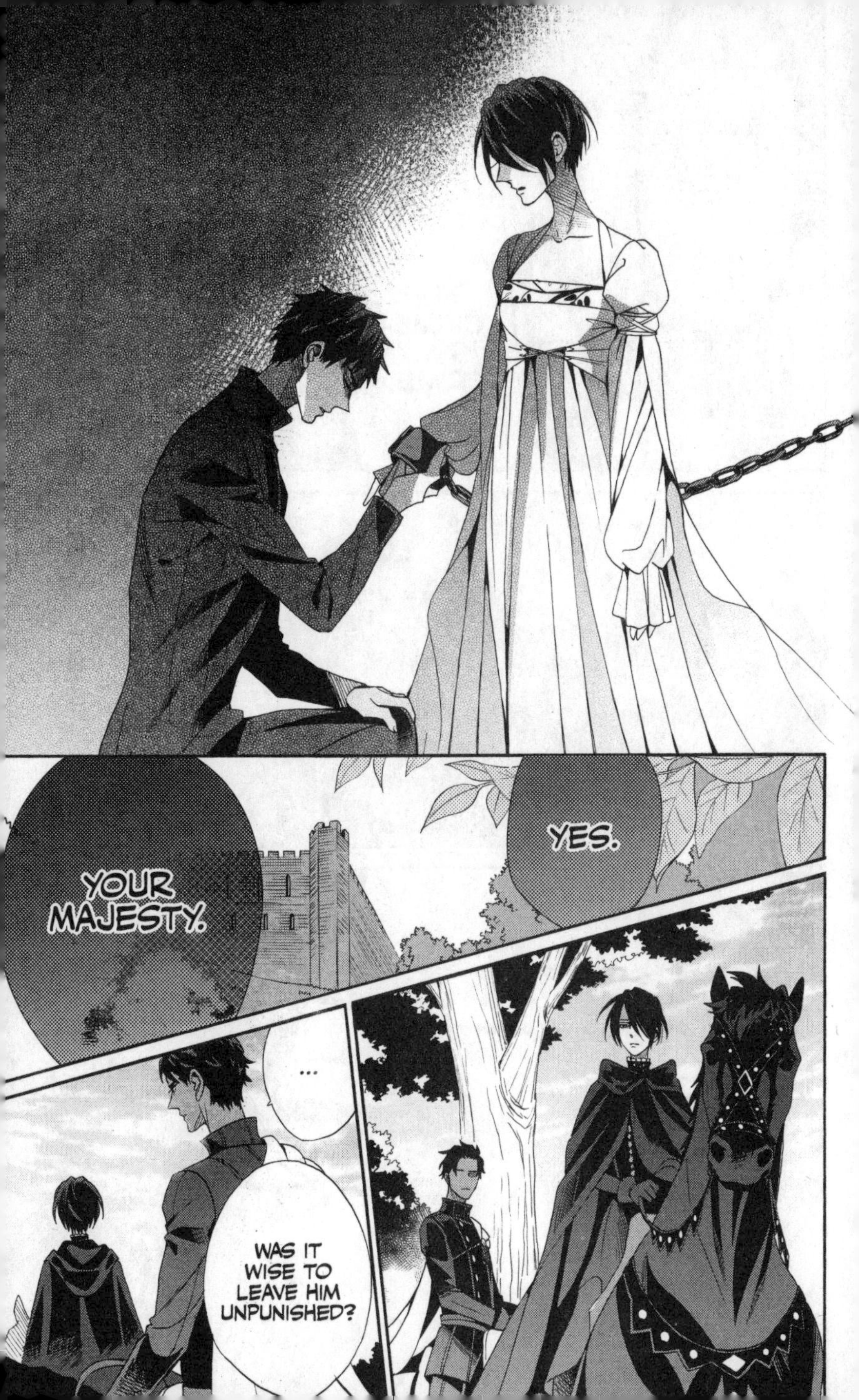
YES.
YOUR MAJESTY.
...
WAS IT WISE TO LEAVE HIM UNPUNISHED?

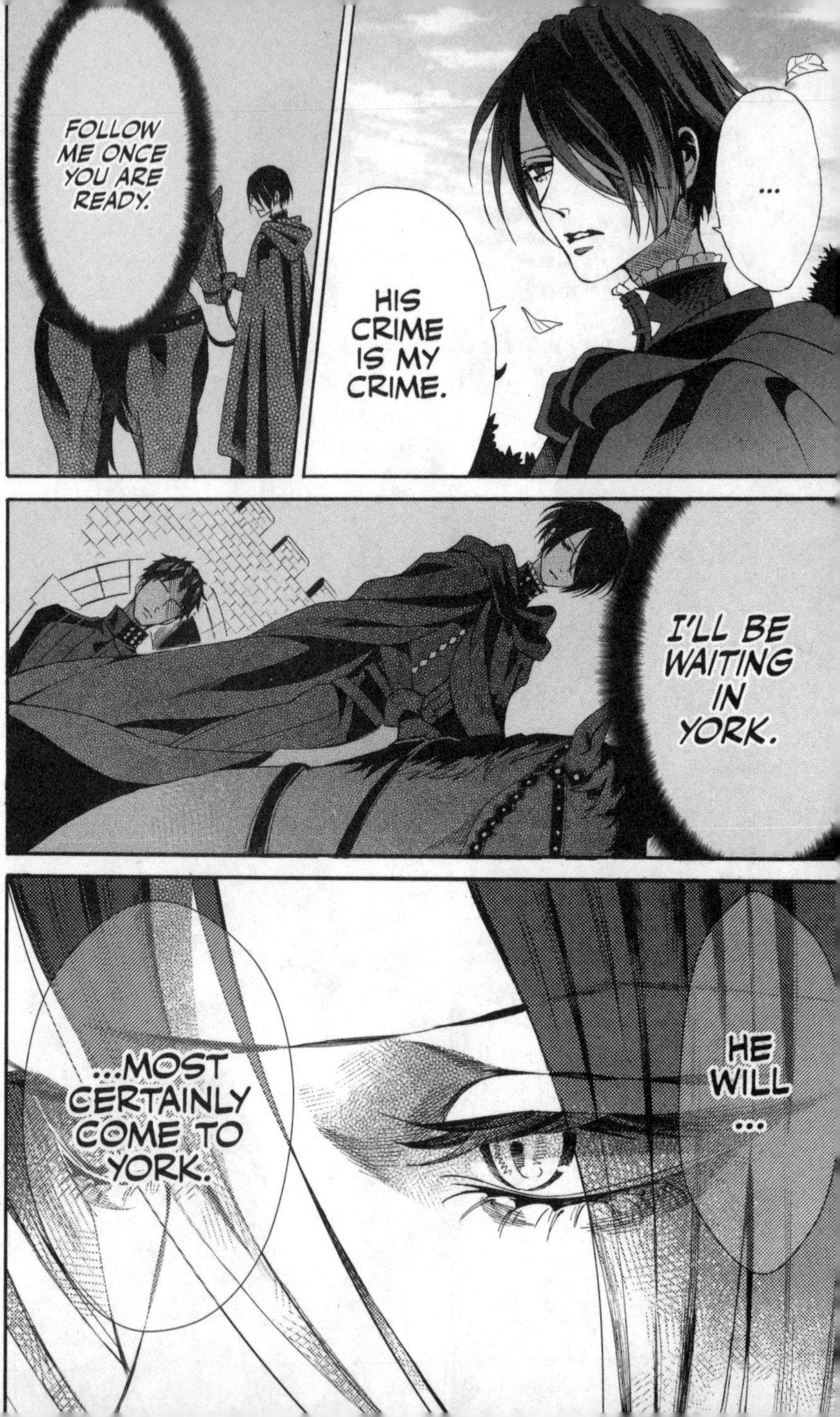
...
HIS CRIME IS MY CRIME.
FOLLOW ME ONCE YOU ARE READY.
I'LL BE WAITING IN YORK.
HE WILL...
...MOST CERTAINLY COME TO YORK.

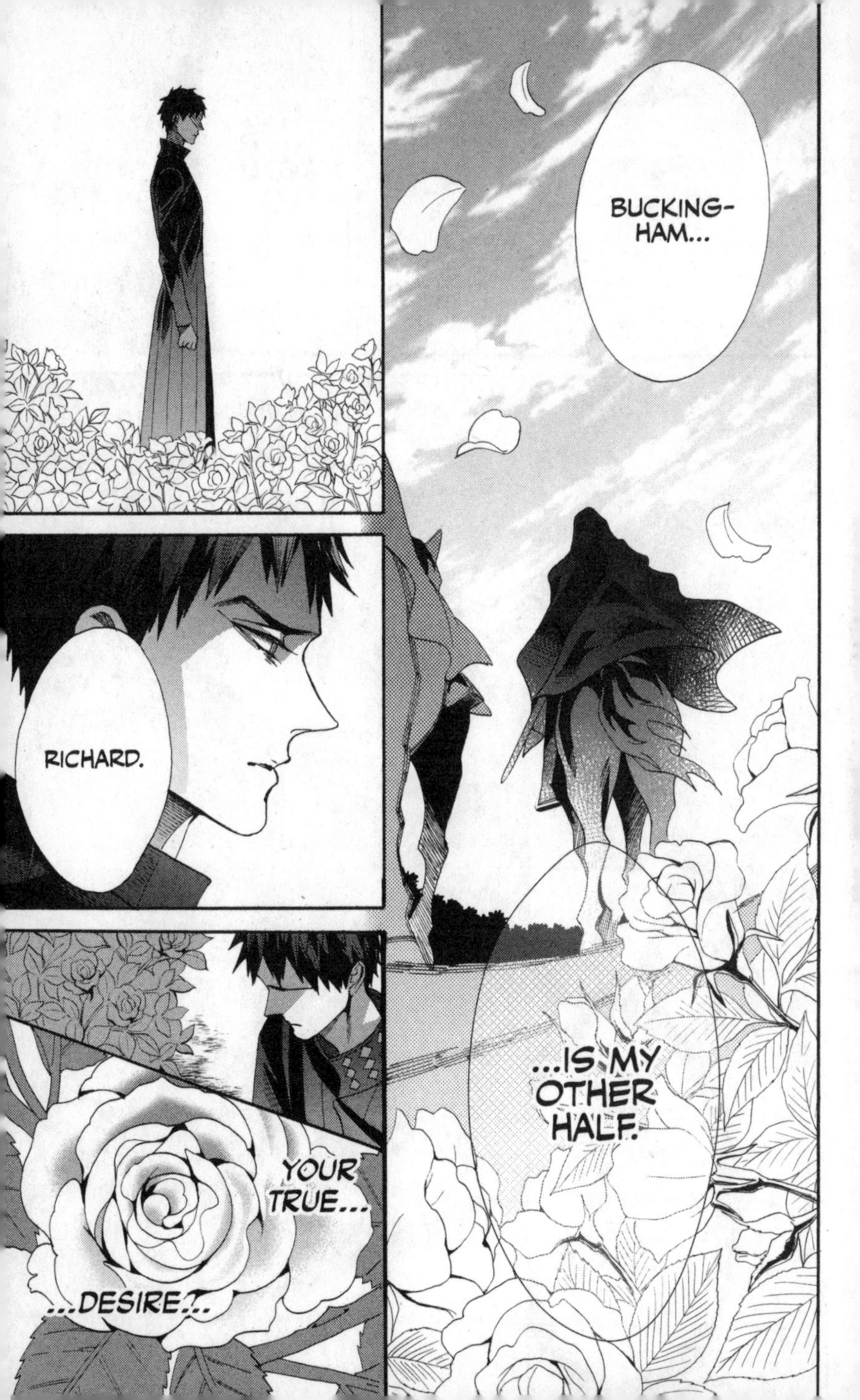
BUCKING-HAM...
...IS MY OTHER HALF.
RICHARD.
YOUR TRUE...
...DESIRE...

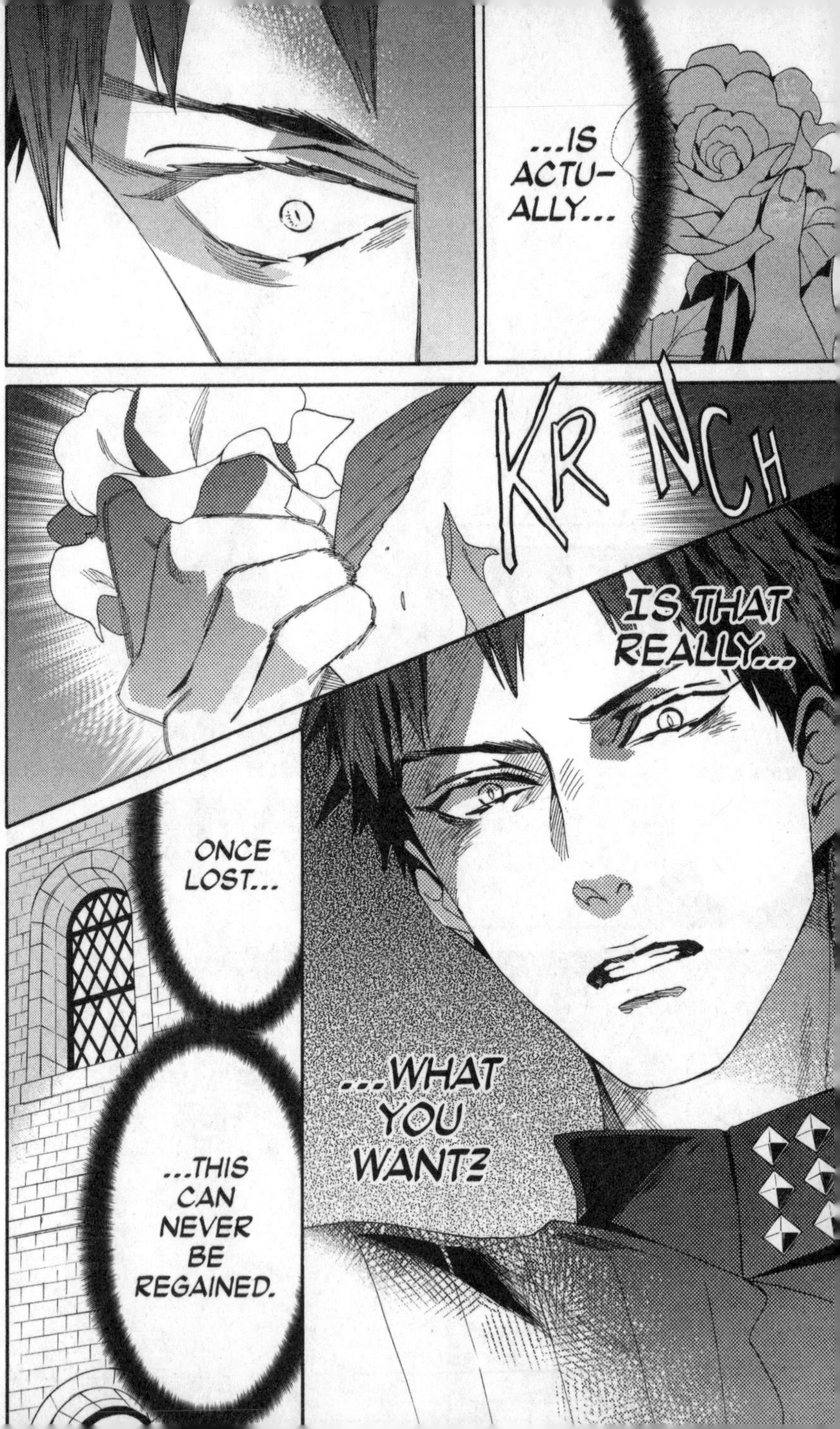
...IS ACTU- ALLY...
KR NCH
IS THAT REALLY...
...WHAT YOU WANT?
ONCE LOST...
...THIS CAN NEVER BE REGAINED.

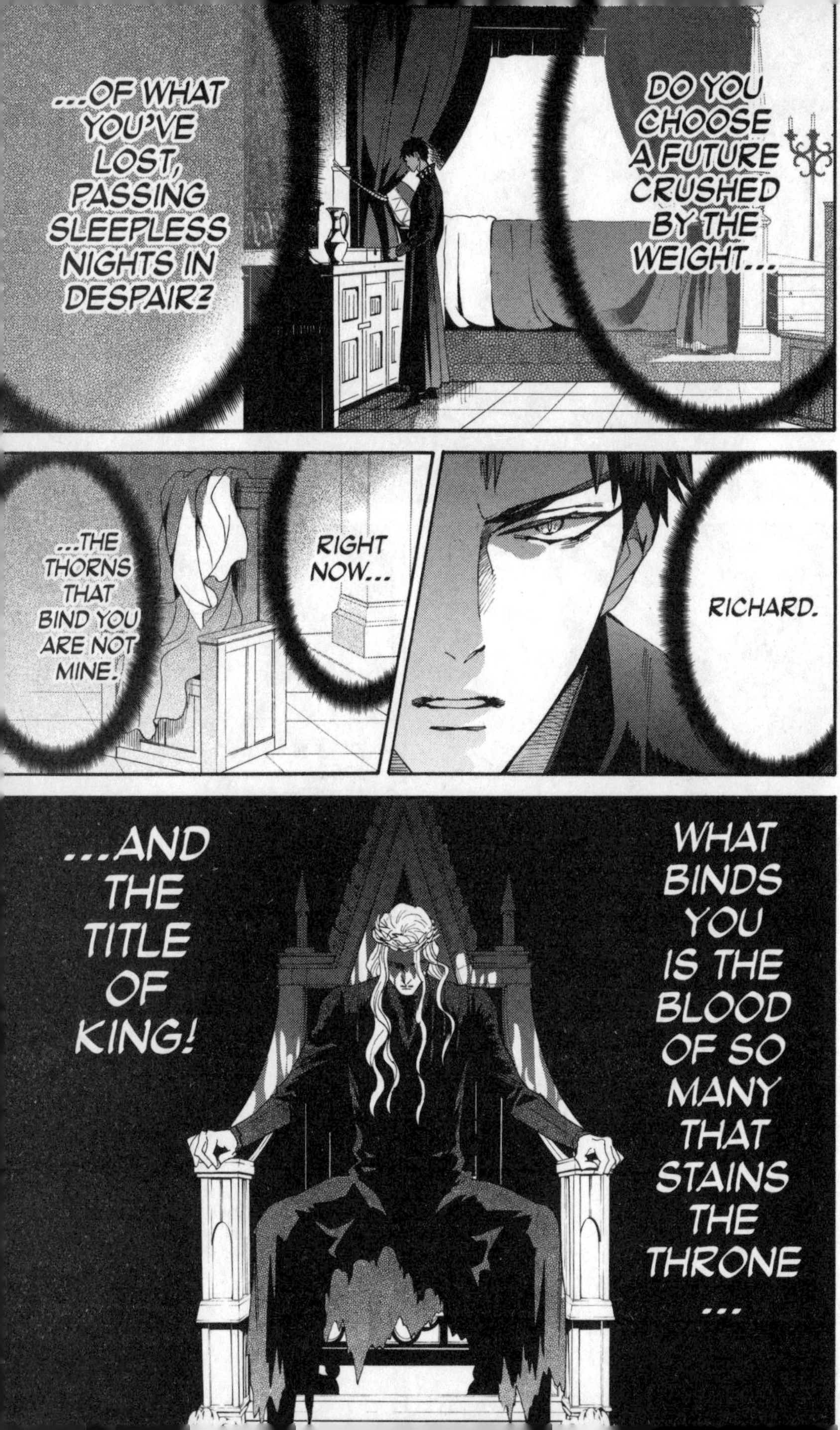
DO YOU CHOOSE A FUTURE CRUSHED BY THE WEIGHT...
...OF WHAT YOU'VE LOST, PASSING SLEEPLESS NIGHTS IN DESPAIR?
RICHARD.
RIGHT NOW...
...THE THORNS THAT BIND YOU ARE NOT MINE.
WHAT BINDS YOU IS THE BLOOD OF SO MANY THAT STAINS THE THRONE...
...AND THE TITLE OF KING!

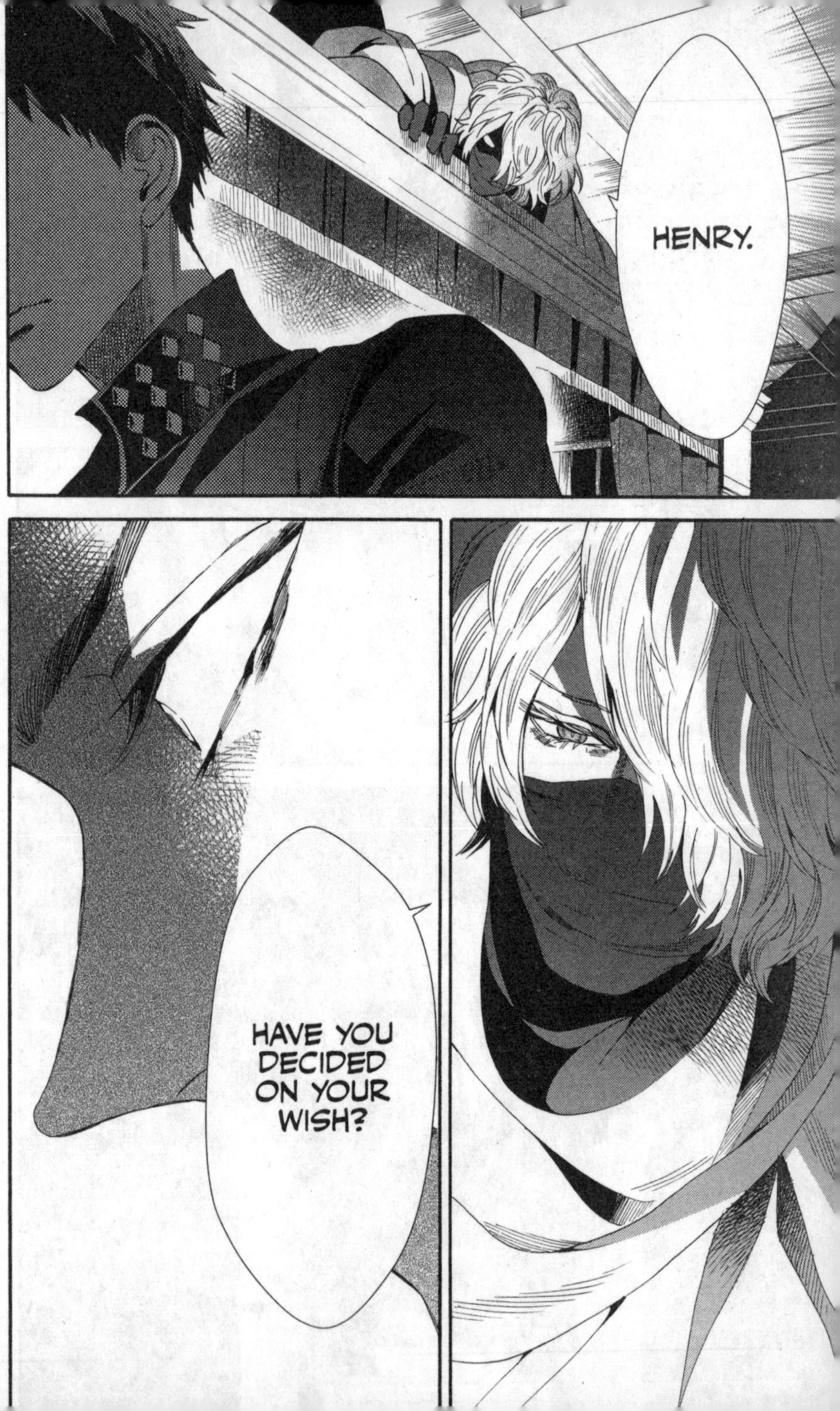
HENRY.
HAVE YOU DECIDED ON YOUR WISH?

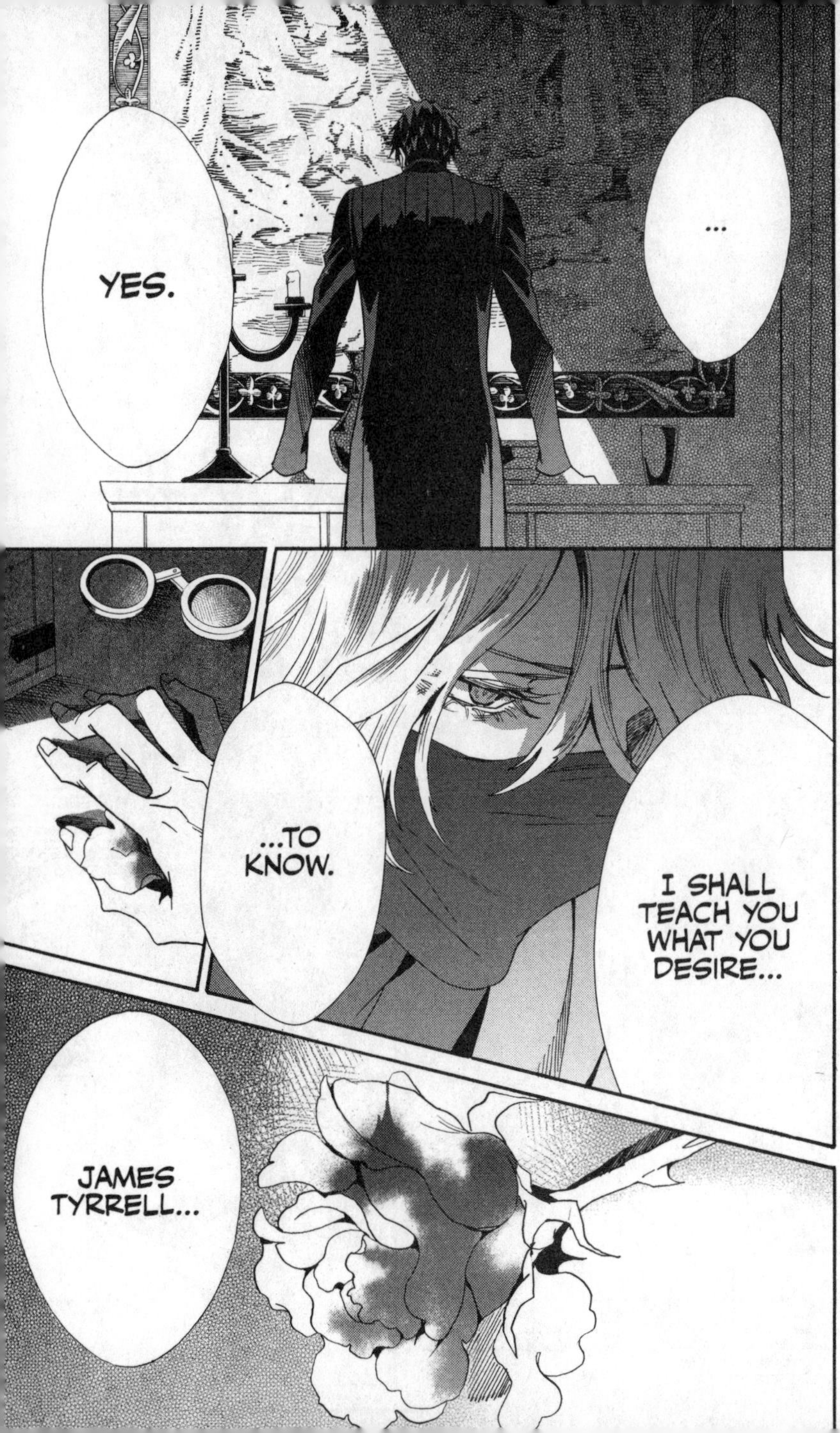
...
YES.
I SHALL TEACH YOU WHAT YOU DESIRE...
...TO KNOW.
JAMES TYRRELL...

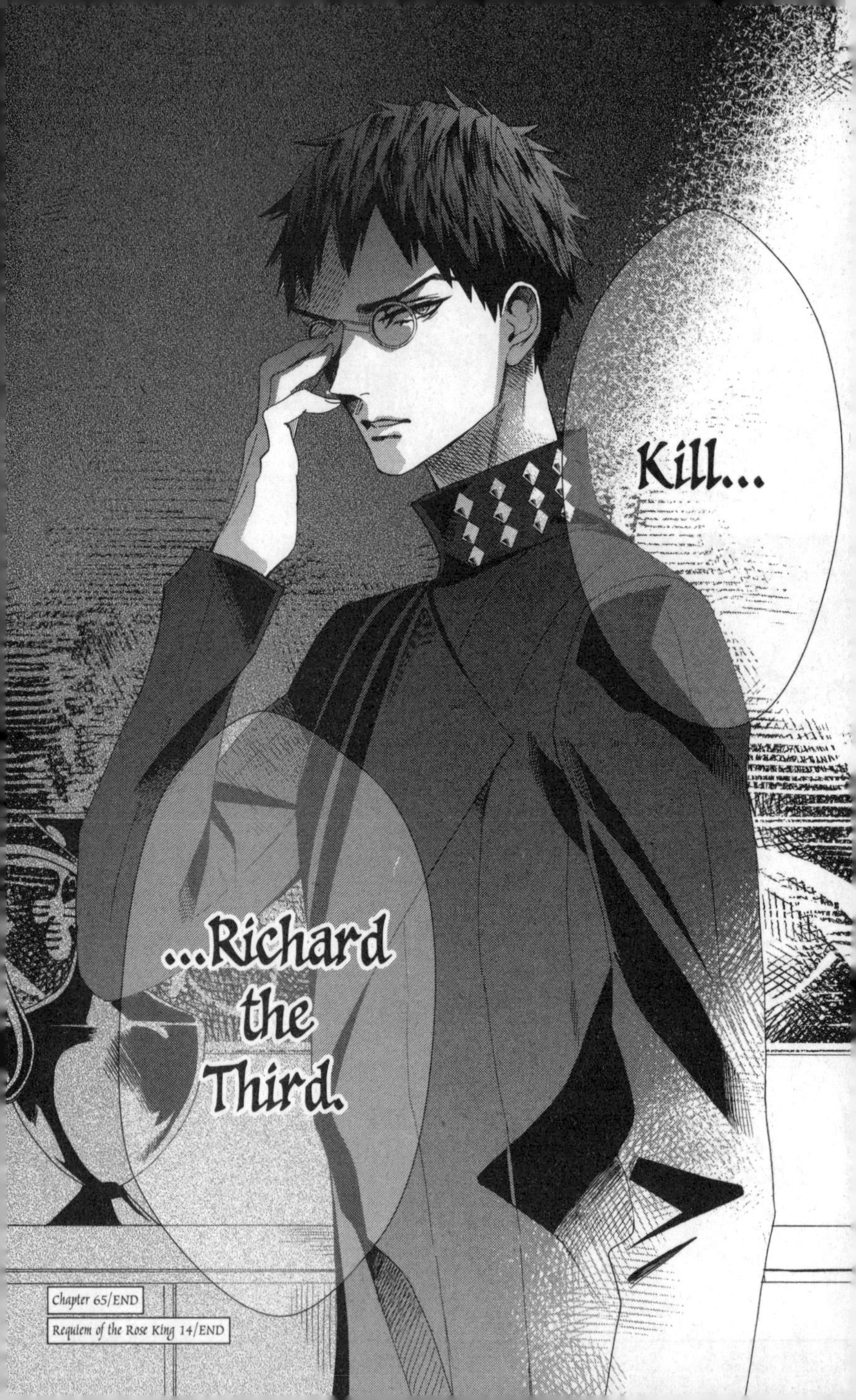
Kill...
...Richard the Third.
Chapter 65/END
Requiem of the Rose King 14/END